ANTHOLOGY OF
Ancient Greek
Popular
Literature

EDITED BY
WILLIAM HANSEN

Indiana
University
Press

BLOOMINGTON AND INDIANAPOLIS

This book is a publication of

Indiana University Press
601 North Morton Street
Bloomington, IN 47404-3797 USA

http://iupress.indiana.edu

Telephone orders 800-842-6796
Fax orders 812-855-7931
Orders by e-mail iuporder@indiana.edu

The paper used in this publication meets the minimum requirements
of American National Standard for Information Sciences—Permanence
of Paper for Printed Library Materials, ANSI Z39.48-1984.

Manufactured in the United States of America

Library of Congress Cataloging-in-Publication Data

Anthology of ancient Greek popular literature / edited by William Hansen.
    p. cm.
    Includes bibliographical references.
    ISBN 0-253-33366-0 (alk. paper).—ISBN 0-253-21157-3 (pbk. : alk. paper)
    1. Greek literature—Translations into English. 2. Popular literature—Greece.
3. Greece—Literary collections. I. Hansen, William F., date
PA3621.A58   1998
880.8'001—dc21   97-28207

3 4 5 6 07 06

ANTHOLOGY OF
Ancient Greek
Popular
Literature

CONTENTS

Part Two: Popular Compilations

Part Three: A Popular Handbook

Part Four: Popular Literature in Public Places

PREFACE

The argument of the present book is that the roots of Western popular literature lie in ancient Greece and that the first flowering of popular literature in the Western world took place during the first three or four centuries of our era.

It will certainly surprise many persons that among the ancient Greeks there were readers who enjoyed light reading. But such basic forms as the novel, the short story, the fable book, the jokebook, and simple handbooks of divination trace their lineage to the ancient Mediterranean, where we find many genres of now-familiar literature in their earliest known forms. Indeed, some compositions of this kind were so successful that they remained in circulation for centuries, even into the Middle Ages, and were translated into many other languages. Although on the whole they are less polished pieces of literary art than are the more familiar classics of ancient literature, these lively works remain enjoyable reading today and are at the same time fascinating social documents that reveal much about the daily lives, fantasies, humor, loves, anxieties, values, and ideology of ordinary men and women, free and slave, pagan and Christian.

I am happy to express my gratitude for their generous help in the present undertaking to Barry Baldwin, Thomas Drew-Bear, Kathleen Adair Foster, Henry Glassie, Mary Beth Hannah-Hansen, Eleanor Winsor Leach, John McDowell, Jeanne Peterson, Warren Roberts, Gregory Schrempp, Randy Stewart, and the graduate students in Folklore and in Classical Studies at Indiana University who in fall 1995 participated in my seminar on Ancient Greek Popular Literature: Robert Chavez, Esther Clinton, Lynn Gelfand, Danusha Goska, Elizabeth Locke, Fernando Orejuela, Andrea Salgado, David Sklar, Jennifer Smith, and Carolyn Starkweather. To these wonderful students I dedicate this book. Finally, I am grateful to Indiana University for the award of a fellowship that permitted me to develop the course that in turn suggested the idea for this book.

ACKNOWLEDGMENTS

The frontispiece, showing Aesop among the animals of his fables, is found in *Fabulae Aesopi, Graecè & Latinè . . . Cum elegantissimis in utroque libello figuris* (Amstelodami: Apud Judocum Pluymer, 1660). Lilly Library, Indiana University, Bloomington.

An Ephesian Tale. From THREE GREEK ROMANCES by Moses Hadas. Copyright 1953 by Moses Hadas. Used by permission of Doubleday, a division of Bantam Doubleday Dell Publishing Group, Inc.

The Acts of Paul and Thecla. From NEW TESTAMENT APOCRYPHA (Volumes I and II), edited by Edgar Hennecke and Wilhelm Schneemelcher. Used by permission of Westminster John Knox Press and James Clarke & Co., Ltd, The Lutterworth Press.

Secundus the Silent Philosopher, translated by Ben E. Perry. Printed with permission of the American Philological Association.

We are grateful to the Calder Educational Trust, London, for permission to publish Paul Turner's translation of Lucian's *Lucian: True History and Lucius or the Ass*.

Aesop Romance. From AESOP WITHOUT MORALS, translated and edited by Lloyd W. Daly. New York and London: Thomas Yoseloff, 1961.

Pseudo-Callisthenes, "Alexander Romance," translated by Ken Dowden, from COLLECTED ANCIENT GREEK NOVELS, ed. B. P. Reardon. University of California Press, Copyright © 1989 The Regents of the University of California.

PHLEGON OF TRALLES' BOOK OF MARVELS, translated with introduction and commentary by William Hansen. Exeter: University of Exeter Press, 1996.

INTRODUCTION

It may seem surprising to speak of ancient *Greek* popular literature, for although we are likely to associate Greek literature with many things, light reading is probably not among them. It may moreover seem inappropriate to speak of *ancient* popular literature at all, and indeed of any popular literature before the invention of the printing press in the fifteenth century, which permitted books and other reading matter to be produced cheaply, or even before the advent of mass literacy, which for the first time enabled large numbers of persons in some parts of the world to read the literature that now could be printed inexpensively.

What Is Popular Literature?

When we speak of popular literature, what exactly do we, or should we, mean? It may seem appealing to define popular literature by the kinds of writers who create it, but in fact it is difficult to do so, for the supposition that popular literature is produced by the same kinds of persons as those who consume it, on the analogy that learned books are written by learned persons for other learned persons, is often untrue.[1] For example, few of the newspapers and magazines that are read by working-class persons are written by other working-class persons, and although most romance novels, whose readership is almost exclusively female, are written by women, many are actually penned by men who publish their works under female pseudonyms.[2] What is known about authors of popular works as a group does not reveal significant ways in which they are alike, apart from the obvious fact of their literary enterprise.

Many literary scholars define popular literature in terms of its consumers. Victor Neuberg, in his history of popular literature in England, characterizes popular literature as that which unsophisticated readers choose for pleasure. He characterizes such readers as being mostly the poor, although he acknowledges that they may belong to any social class.[3] It is certainly possible to demarcate the reading matter of working-class persons or of less-educated persons or of any other group as a sociological category in order to identify it for the purpose of study, but a significant difficulty in this approach, at least from a literary viewpoint, is that the literature consumed by a particular group is not likely to be a *kind* of literature. For example, in nineteenth-century England several publishers produced cheap editions of Milton, Shakespeare, and other literary greats for the working-class market.[4] It is instructive that working-class readers, taken as a group, consumed not only so-called penny dreadfuls and other ephemeral novels but also some classics of English literature; but if one defines popular literature as literature read by working-class persons, the classics and the penny dreadfuls must sit together in a single literary category. So heterogeneous a grouping may work as a sociological category, but it does not amount to a useful literary concept.

Nor can we easily characterize popular literature qualitatively, for there is no justification for equating popular literature with literature produced by talentless authors or simply with bad literature.[5] Inexperienced and naive artists produce immature and naive art, regardless of whether their aim is high art or low art. Since every level of art has its failures, it would be arrogant to declare that all elite literature is automatically good by virtue of its lofty goals and that all other literature is poor because its aspirations are more modest.

The most obvious way to define popular literature doubtless is quantitatively: if many persons read a particular kind of literature, it is popular. To answer the question whether the ancient Greek novel enjoyed a popular and widespread readership in antiquity, as some scholars suppose, Susan Stephens cleverly tallies the fragments of Greek literary papyri that have been excavated from the sands of Greco-Roman Egypt, the remains of discarded and worn-out books.[6] Her idea is that the frequency of occurrence of different authors and genres provides a measure, however crude and approximate it may be, of their relative popularity, at least in the Greco-Egyptian communities in which they have been found. Her sample consists of fragments of books that were copied sometime between the first and sixth centuries A.D., approximately the heyday of the ancient Greek novel. The statistics that she derives do not support a picture of a small number of readers of high cultural works and a large number of patrons of low culture; rather, the collective remains of ancient novels are numerically modest (42 fragments in all), quantitatively about the same as the fragments of philosophic prose (43), and far less common than fragments of, say, the rather difficult historian Thucydides (75). As it turns out, the best-attested authors are the epic poet Homer (600) and the orator Demosthenes (120), although the high incidence of finds of Homer is probably due in part, as Stephens suggests, to the use of Homer's *Iliad* as a school text, and the same may be true of Demosthenes. She concludes that the ancient Greek novel was not a popular genre.

The reading matter of the majority or at least of relatively large groups within a society, like the reading matter of working-class persons, is certainly defensible as a category to investigate and interpret. If in the present case we accept Stephens's papyrological data as an accurate reflection of the reading preferences of Greek townspeople in ancient Egypt, and if we classify as specimens of popular literature the highest scorers (those authors and genres represented by, say, over a hundred fragments), our list will include Homer's *Iliad* (600), the Old and New Testaments (172), Greek lyric poetry (161), Greek tragedy (131), and Demosthenes (120).[7] The difficulty with this list is the same as that with other classifications by consumer preference, namely, that it is a sociological, not a literary, artifact. The works brought together, which include literature that we generally associate with high culture, are too heterogeneous to constitute a *kind* of writing in any real sense.[8]

Another problem with determining popular literature arithmetically, aside from the important fact that we normally do not know how many copies of particular publications were sold and read,[9] is the possibility of a dissonance between the genre itself and specimens of the genre. In the United States romance novels sell in the millions, but some romances must certainly be commercial failures. Does a romance that few persons read fail to qualify as popular literature? Is it possible to be popular on the generic level and not on the individual level?

For many investigators popular literature is not just the literature of the many; it is specifically mass-market literature. During most of Western history the publication of a book has been literally one of manufacture, that is, copyists reproducing manuscripts by hand. In the course of the fifteenth century the price of books dropped significantly after Johann Gutenberg of Mainz, Germany, devised a printing press with movable type, after which books could be produced more cheaply. Popular reception of the invention was so rapid and enthusiastic that within fifty years printers were at work in nearly every European capital, and of course the production of titles and copies soared. The printing press brought an end to the era of the manuscript book and introduced the reign of the printed book. Presently, moreover, publishers found additional ways to economize. For one thing, printing became mechanized, relieving the printer of having to press each sheet of paper by hand. For another thing, publishers substituted cheaper materials for more expensive ones: leather-covered wooden book covers yielded to cloth or paper covers, and rag paper gave way to pulp paper. Books became more affordable and even ephemeral, in some cases so cheap that they could be discarded after a single reading. At the same time the number of educated and literate persons in the Western world increased dramatically, both as an absolute number and as a proportion of the total population, a change that, as it happened, disproportionately affected the poor, since literacy rates among them had been especially low.[10]

These two complementary factors—cheaper costs and more readers—have resulted in the production of a vast amount of written material that for the most part is intended for and consumed by ordinary persons, and this literature, or some portion of it, has often been called popular literature. According to Russel Nye, the popular arts first arose during the eighteenth and nineteenth centuries in step with the emergence of the middle class as a majority of the population. Although the folk arts and the elite arts continued to answer the needs of small portions of the population, the new middle-class audience developed its own taste, and there arose to satisfy it an entertainment industry that was aided by modern technology, allowing low-cost production in large quantities and facilitating widespread distribution. For Nye, popular literature specifically is literature created by a commercial entertainment industry for the reading pleasure of a mass public.[11]

Although no one denies the development of a mass culture in modern times, it is nevertheless arbitrary to restrict the label of popular literature to modern mass-market literature, inasmuch as, so far as concerns literary character, the same sort of literature is also found in earlier times.[12] Mass-market literature is not so much a new form of literature as it is a commercial development of previously existing kinds of literature.

Instead of defining popular writing in terms of producers or consumers or in terms of quality or quantity, we should approach it as a kind of literature. The important question is: what attribute or attributes do works that we readily identify as popular literature share such that we feel they belong together?

A central trait, I suggest, is straightforwardness, the contrary of subtlety and indirection. Popular narratives such as popular fiction, popular journalism, and popular history entertain and are content to do little or nothing more than to entertain. Popular literature of a pragmatic sort, such as a dictionary of dream interpretation, informs and is content simply to offer information. The basic aim of popular literature is to provide readers with easy, immediate, and unbroken engagement while demanding little of them. To put it negatively, it does not attempt to provide either an "aesthetic experience," as Nye calls it,[13] or an intellectual challenge, features that threaten a reader's close and continued involvement.

What these traits amount to is an *aesthetic*. In the formulation of Pierre Bourdieu, the essence of the popular aesthetic is the primacy of content over form, and conversely the essence of the high (or elite or learned) aesthetic is the primacy of form over content.[14] That is, the essential difference between low art and high art lies in the relative importance each accords to substance as opposed to presentation, just as in the realm of cuisine, for example, popular taste inclines toward economical and filling foods whereas elite taste emphasizes presentation and style.

Using data collected in France, Bourdieu argues that artistic taste tends to correlate with educational level and social origin. The popular aesthetic is characteristic of persons of lower educational level and lower social origin, whereas the elite aesthetic correlates with the opposite variables. In Bourdieu's view the basis of the two aesthetics is economic. The popular aesthetic reflects a taste developed in a context of necessity, a taste that never loses sight of substance or of the function of things, whereas the elite aesthetic reflects a taste developed in an environment of ease in which attention shifts to manner, developing stylized forms that deemphasize function.

The popular aesthetic, argues Bourdieu, is based upon an unconscious view of a continuity between life and art: like everything else in a practical world, art should perform a function. A popular audience wants to enter into the game, to identify with the joys and sufferings of the characters, to enjoy itself; accordingly, it likes characters and situations that are simply drawn as opposed to characters that are ambiguous or enigmatic. It likes plots that make their way logically and chronologically toward a happy ending. Not caring for the intellectual's disinterested stance, it rejects formal experiments in literature and drama that discourage an audience from identifying with the characters and seeks instead entertainment that invites engagement from an audience and offers immediate satisfaction. But in the high-cultural tradition, Bourdieu argues, the mode of representation is more important than the object of representation. Here the artistic tradition is relatively more autonomous and self-referential. The aesthete adopts an attitude of detachment, displacing interest in, for example, the characters and plot for an interest in artistic effect and for the place of the artwork in the larger artistic tradition.

Bourdieu's formulation about the primacy of content or form is attractive in its simplicity and usefully separates popular from nonpopular expression for the most part, provided that in the case of literature the relative importance of content and form be understood to apply to a piece of literature taken not by itself but relative to a tradition; for the point must be how readers assess the importance of these features in a particular work relative to other works, not whether content or form has absolute primacy in a particular work. However, Bourdieu's criterion does not usefully distinguish works whose content is intellectually demanding from works that are undemanding, perhaps because he has formulated it more with the visual and performing arts than with literature in mind.

So let us say that a piece of literature is more popular in presentation to the extent that, in the estimation of readers, it accords more importance to nonintellectual content, as opposed to form, than a comparable work does. Popular literature reflects an aesthetic that values easy and continued engagement, minimizing features that encourage detachment.

A definition of popular literature by aesthetic escapes certain difficulties that other approaches entail. For one thing, we are not required to know about the education or class or gender of the authors, information that is not always available to us, for what is relevant is only whether the literature expresses a certain aesthetic. Of course, we are free to consider such biographical data as we may possess, and since the essence of a popular work does not lie in its being produced by a particular kind of author, it is possible for unsophisticated authors as well as sophisticated writers to produce works of popular literature. But a work must inevitably reflect its author's literary understanding. For example, an unsophisticated author may mix ordinary diction with affected phrases, reflecting a notion of how proper authors write.[15] Thus the anonymous author of the Latin work known as the *Bellum Hispanicum,* or *The Spanish War,* composed probably by one of Caesar's officers, mixes banal prose with elevated quotations from the poet Ennius. Such instances are not intrinsic features of popular literature, since popular literature can also be authored by sophisticated writers. Similarly, it is not of the essence of popular literature that it reflect the biases of a particular group of readers, only that it reflect the popular aesthetic. Works of popular literature that are aimed at groups of readers such as less-educated or less-affluent persons may contain themes such as anti-intellectualism and fantasies such as the acquisition of great personal power that are intended to appeal particularly to these groups, but these features are accidental, not necessary, qualities of popular writing.

A literary approach also escapes difficulties that arise in definitions according to consumer. As we have seen, groups of persons who read literature of some sort can read literature of more than one sort, and the mix can include literature commonly regarded as popular together with literature associated with high culture. Many readers have the capacity and desire occasionally to switch aesthetic frames—the ordinary reader who works through a challenging book, the professor who reads a thriller at bedtime—although sophisticated readers probably amuse themselves with something light more often than unsophisticated readers try something heavy; that is, the situation tends to asymmetry.[16] But unlike the hodgepodge of reading matter that a particular category of persons reads, the present concept of popular literature is unified in its literary aesthetic.

Popular literature thus defined resolves the classificatory dilemma of the romance novel that, failing to sell well, seems at once to be and not to be an instance of popular writing. For the status of the work is determined by its aesthetic, not by its sales. Nor need we identify the readers of a particular work or discover how many copies were sold, since readership and numbers are not defining criteria. The definition does not create rigid binary categories of high and low but an infinite series of steps in a continuum.

A definition by aesthetic also avoids the arbitrariness of a definition of popular literature as mass-market literature. Any work that expresses the popular aesthetic is popular literature.[17] Since literature informed by a popular aesthetic predates the Industrial Revolution and mass-market literature, it follows that the entertainment industry and the mass public did not invent literature of this sort but only facilitated its production, distribution, and consumption. We avoid the usual narrowness of assuming that popular literature is the offspring of the printing press, the advent of which is often the starting place for histories of popular literature.[18] The printing press and the advent of widespread literacy did not bring popular literature into being but only allowed it to flourish on an unprecedented scale, the printing press by allowing it to be produced more cheaply, newly enfranchised groups of ordinary readers by creating a large market for undemanding reading.

The popular aesthetic, as expressed in literature, manifests itself typically as writing that is easy to read, quickly and continually engaging, and replete with action and sensation. Its opposite is literature that is aesthetically or intellectually demanding, inviting the reader to savor its texture or ponder its implications. Naturally the extent to which a piece of literature should be regarded as demanding is relative to culture and time. Translated to another place or time, literature may rest higher on the cultural scale than it originally stood because of the greater demands it makes upon an audience for whom its conventions and context are less familiar; consequently, it is read by persons who find such challenges appealing, persons who are likely to rank among the more educated. The changed cultural context renders this literature intellectually and aesthetically more difficult, an incidental feature that mimics a deliberate feature of elite literature.

Ancient Greek Popular Literature

It is difficult to gain a clear understanding of publishing and literacy among the ancient Greeks because the evidence available to us is scanty. Literacy is a particularly complex topic and must be subdivided into several aspects: levels of literacy; the extent of literacy at different periods and in different regions; differences in education among males and females, among free persons and slaves, among wealthier classes and poorer classes, and among urban dwellers and rural dwellers. Moreover, literacy changed over time. In general, education and hence literacy were more common among males than among females, among the upper classes than among the lower classes and slaves, and among urbanites than among villagers and country folk; that is, one had the best chance of being able to read if one was a free adult male born of affluent parents and raised in a city. But literate persons were found in all sociological categories, including females, slaves, and country persons. It is impossible now to ascertain the percentage of readers in any group at any period; however, despite the strong value placed by Greeks on education and literacy, mass literacy did not prevail at any time.[19]

Publishing houses in the modern sense did not exist.[20] Professional scribes copied out books by hand, sometimes illustrators illustrated them, and we hear of bookstalls where books might be purchased. Since there was no copyright for authors, there was no legal protection for the integrity of written works, and profits from their sales accrued to those who sold them, not to those who authored them.[21] Although books were relatively costly inasmuch as they were handmade, they need not have been items of luxury. As in other things, the affordability of reading matter depended ultimately upon the personal resources of individual purchasers. Then as now, there were other ways to acquire a book than to buy it, for books could be inherited or simply borrowed for a while.[22] Some wealthy persons enjoyed being read to by literate slaves, and it is likely that persons of modest means or little education who could not afford books or could not read them sometimes heard a work read aloud by another person.

If evidence concerning literacy and publishing is meager, we are relatively well informed about ancient books as physical objects. Greek and Roman books had two forms, the bookroll and the codex.[23] The bookroll was the older. A bookroll was a continuous sheet of papyrus about nine to ten inches in height and, when it was unrolled, about thirty-five feet in length. When rolled up, it was an inch or two thick. Usually only one side of the sheet was written on because only one side of papyrus is smooth. The writing itself was done in vertical columns two to three inches wide. The reader unrolled the book from the right as he or she read, rolling it up again on the left in order not to have to handle an unwieldy length of papyrus. Since a bookroll could hold the equivalent of only a chapter or two of a modern book, most ancient works required more than one bookroll, and in reference to this the individual divisions of ancient works were called "books."

The younger form of the book was the codex. Essentially the type of the modern book, a codex consisted of so many sheets, usually of parchment (that is, specially treated animal skin), that were bound together at one end. Unlike papyrus, parchment could be folded and took writing on both sides. The codex not only held much more text than the bookroll but also was more compact. In the period covered by the present anthology, the two forms were both in use in the Greco-Roman world, but in the fifth century the codex superseded the bookroll, a feat that was repeated in modern times when the chapbook overtook the broadsheet.

Important developments in Greek literature took place in the centuries following the death of Alexander the Great in 323 B.C. The opening up of the East to Greeks brought about a fertile mixing of Greek and Eastern peoples. Greek authors extended their geographic range eastward, while Hellenized Syrians, Egyptians, Jews, Babylonians, and others composed literature in Greek. New literary themes and emphases appeared following the disappearance of the free and independent Greek city-state. "The Homeric hero is pre-civic, the Hellenistic or romantic postcivic," Ben Perry observed.[24] Greek authors of the Hellenistic and Imperial periods showed an interest in the plight of the individual as a being in a large and unpredictable cosmos with distant rulers rather than as a denizen of a small and cohesive Greek polis. To some extent this literature is one of questing and salvation, for protagonists frequently seek fulfillment in one or another kind of commitment: love (as in *An Ephesian Tale*), religion (as in *The Acts of Paul and Thecla*), the philosophic life (as in *Secundus the Silent Philosopher*), adventure and conquest (as in *The Alexander Romance*). The many practical works on divination and the considerable literature of magic similarly attest to a human yearning for more certainty and control.

In the Hellenistic and Roman periods, Greek literature was produced in greater quantity than ever before, responding to the development of reading as a private pastime. It also became more specialized and compartmentalized, like today's profusion of television channels, each dedicated to a particular theme. New forms arose, old ones were handled in different ways, and the extremes became more extreme. At one end authors turned toward the learned and recherché, writing for well-educated palates, while at the other end other writers produced simpler fare for simpler tastes. Or sometimes they were the same writers, for the poet and scholar Callimachus of Cyrene not only composed refined poems but also compiled a prose anthology of marvelous information. It is in the fourth and third centuries B.C. that the categories *popular* and *learned* first become useful to the historian of Greek literature; by the first century A.D. they are necessary.

The present anthology contains a selection of popular fare written in Greek during the first four centuries of our era, the period during which the extant Greek and Roman novels were written, the *floruit* of ancient prose fiction. Since the precise dates of individual works are usually uncertain, I do not arrange the selections chronologically. The aim of the collection in any case is to illustrate kinds of popular literature, not changes or directions in popular literature.

In these selections the emphasis of the authors is upon content. The texts generally reveal only modest concern for artistic presentation, none of it showing much refinement or subtlety; instead, the compositions are straightforward and aim to be quickly engaging. Most of the works fall into two broad classes—fictional literature and practical literature. The former recount their story in a lively manner and in simple prose, entertaining the reader while demanding little literary expertise. To put it negatively, they do not offer polished and referential narratives for the delectation of a select group of discriminating readers. Fantasies of wish fulfillment are little disguised—the courageous are admired, the clever exercise their wit, the adventurous experience the exotic, the lonely find companionship, the deserving are recognized, the pompous are discomfited. The observation made about chapbooks by a nineteenth-century English publisher—"they appealed to the love of the heroic, the marvellous, the pathetic, and the humorous"—would describe these works nicely.[25] The literature presumably offered readers then, as popular literature may be thought to do at the present day, a pleasant escape from the complexities and perceived inadequacies of life, a diversion that was relaxing because it was safe and fairly predictable and refreshing because it was undemanding.

The works that are pragmatic in nature also give primacy to content. Such books present practical information in ordinary language and in an intellectually undemanding way, avoiding controversy and theory except in a superficial and perfunctory manner in order to give the impression of authority. A handbook of divination does not seek out the complex truth of reality, signs, and causation but reassures its users by offering simple and certain correlations.

Although the authors of these works probably had the ordinary reader in mind, at least some of these writings were known also to more discerning readers, as we know because they sometimes allude to them, usually critically, as when Tertullian comments dismissively upon the content of *The Acts of Paul and Thecla*.[26] More sympathetically, other ancient authors recognized that among literate persons some readers were more sophisticated and some less so and that certain forms of literature were apt for each type of reader. Origen, referring to works composed in the form of questions and answers, observes that religious literature of this kind, although it does not move intelligent persons, can be quite effective for the more numerous, simpler sorts of readers.[27]

Several traits are characteristic of ancient Greek popular literature. One is *unknown authorship*. The proportion of this literature that is anonymous (or falsely attributed to prominent persons) is much higher than in ancient Greek literature generally. Thus of the six selections of fiction in the present volume, five are of unknown authorship: *The Acts of Paul and Thecla, Lucius or the Ass, Secundus the Silent Philosopher, The Aesop Romance,* and *The Alexander Romance.* Only the author of *An Ephesian Tale* is known to us, Xenophon of Ephesus, though even here we know little about him, and some scholars suspect that his very name is merely a pseudonymn chosen to call to mind his classical predecessor, Xenophon of Athens. Of the four compilations and handbooks included here, the authorship of two is unknown: the compiler of the fable collection known as the *Collectio Augustana* and the composer of the book of fate entitled *The Oracles of Astrampsychus*. The title of the latter parades the name of the well-known magician Astrampsychus in order to claim for the work something of his prestige and authority.

A second common trait of Greek popular literature is *textual fluidity*. In general the texts of popular literature were treated with some freedom by copyists.[28] The integrity of anonymous and pragmatic literature was not respected as much as that of an epic, play, history, speech, or essay by a known author, for the former types were felt in some sense to lie in the public domain, not only legally (since they were unprotected by copyright, *all* published works were in the public domain) but also morally. An anonymous piece of fiction was anyone's work, and the value of a practical composition such as a compilation or a handbook lay in its usefulness, not in its identity as a literary work. Accordingly these writings were often reworked in whole or in part. The diction might be modernized. Tales might be added or dropped in a fable collection, or the morals modified. In novels such as *The Aesop Romance* and *The Alexander Romance* whole episodes might be inserted or excised or expanded or abbreviated. An entire work might be abridged, as happened in the case of the comic novel *Lucius or the Ass* (the original is now lost, and we possess only the abridgment) and as some scholars believe happened in the case of *An Ephesian Tale*. Favorite parts of larger compositions might become detached and circulate independently, enjoying literary lives of their own. Religious authors sometimes modified works in a Christian or Jewish direction. Thus in an edition of *The Oracles of Astrampsychus* the oracular question "Will I be reconciled with my girlfriend?" was changed to "Will I become a bishop?"

Sometimes changes were so drastic that they led to the creation of multiple recensions of a composition, as we find in the anonymous fable collections, *The Aesop Romance,* and, most remarkably, in *The Alexander Romance*. Literature of this sort stands midway between conventional literature, in which texts ideally possess a single, unvarying form, and oral narrative such as myth, legend, and folktale, in which certain kinds of variation, including the development of ecotypes, or local recensions, are the norm.[29]

Multiplicity raises difficult problems of identity, for works of art that are found in multiple forms exist simultaneously on two levels, that of the individual text, expressing as it may a particular branch of a tradition, and that of the collectivity, the tradition as a whole. Literary scholars respond to this situation variously, just as folk-narrative scholars do to multiple oral texts. One way is to attempt a reconstruction of the archetype from the extant texts that have developed from it. In this case the original work is by implication the truly valid text. Thus in their translation of *The Oracles of Astrampsychus* Randall Stewart and Kenneth Morrell omit certain Christian accretions to the text, returning the work to a form approximating its pre-Christian state.

A different approach is to treat the tradition itself as the primary reality and the individual texts as imperfect manifestations, as in the well-known dictum of Claude Lévi-Strauss that a myth consists of all its variants. This philosophy underlies Lloyd Daly's translation of *The Aesop Romance* and Ken Dowden's rendering of *The Alexander Romance,* each translator producing a composite work made up of one recension supplemented by material found elsewhere.

A third approach is to treat the extant texts as valid in their own right, accretions and deficiencies and all. A modern reader may then read the same text as that which an ancient or medieval reader actually read at a particular time in the past, and the modifications can be viewed as expressions of the continuing vitality of a living work rather than as signs of degeneration.

Anonymous authorship, textual fluidity, and continued popularity over a long period are typical of the *folkbook,* or *chapbook.* These terms refer primarily to a kind of publication that flourished in Europe from around the fifteenth to the seventeenth centuries and continued in many cases into the following centuries, but they have also been used in connection with books in other places and times, and in particular the term *folkbook* has been employed occasionally to refer to certain ancient books of a popular nature.[30] European folkbooks are usually local versions of international works whose original author and date are obscure (for example, a Danish folkbook of the sixteenth century may be an abridged retelling of a medieval French verse romance). They are found in a number of languages and have appeared in one edition after another for as long as several centuries. Their primary consumers since the eighteenth century have been ordinary persons of little education, although previously these works had also been read by the upper classes. The concept is certainly apt for describing much of the literature included in the present volume.

A third trait that is typical of Greek popular literature is *nonorganic composition.* A work of prose fiction may consist of a plot frame filled with episodes having a loose relationship to one another and to the whole, a compositional structure that I shall call a *conglomerate.*[31] In such a work a problem may occur (lovers are separated or a man is transformed into an animal), and in the end the difficulty is resolved happily (the lovers are reunited, the man regains his original form). In between these correlative events there occurs a sequence of episodes illustrating obstacles and successes experienced by the protagonist as he or she works toward a solution. It is not characteristic of this literature that each episode fits tightly into a whole, contributing crucially to the atmosphere or characterization or development of the plot; instead, within certain bounds the arrangement of the adventures seems to be more or less arbitrary, for often we might imagine a different sequence with apparently no great effect upon the story. Since the overall composition is relatively casual, the point at which the resolution of the plot takes place can be abrupt, as if the author simply decides to finish his story. For example, in *An Ephesian Tale* the loving couple Anthia and Habrocomes are forcibly separated, whereupon they seem endlessly to enter in and out of danger, experiencing exciting close calls in episode after episode as individually they come into the power of one greedy or lustful person after another, until finally (and for no better reason perhaps than everyone's exhaustion) they chance to discover each other again and happily return home together. The tale is to be enjoyed one part at a time as it unfolds rather than for the orchestration of the whole.

The Selections

The selections are grouped into four categories: popular fiction, popular compilations, a popular handbook, and popular literature in public places.

The Greek novel—in the sense of works of extended prose fiction—arose in the late Hellenistic period and flourished during the first four centuries of our era. Unfortunately the proto-novels have not survived so that we cannot trace the early development of the genre. Despite this fact or because of it, much scholarly energy has been devoted to the question of the novel's origins as well as to the question of who actually read novels, but no clear answers have emerged.[32] The earliest complete specimens date from about the first century A.D., among them the charming and unsophisticated romantic novel by Xenophon of Ephesus, *An Ephesian Tale,* with which the present anthology begins.[33]

Greek popular fiction was not limited to the romantic novel. Christians wrote works of interest for fellow Christians, among them novelizations of the adventures of the apostles as they traveled through the world spreading the gospel. The apocryphal Acts of the Apostles, illustrated here by *The Acts of Paul and Thecla,* an account of the trials of a remarkable woman after her conversion to Christianity by the apostle Paul, resemble in many ways the Greek romantic novels.

Biography was also cultivated at this time among pagan and Christian authors alike, and two fictionalized biographies of famous persons are included here, *The Aesop Romance* and *The Alexander Romance,* one comic, the other heroic. *Lucius or the Ass,* another comic novel, is an account of the strange and ribald adventures of a man who has been magically transformed into a donkey. Although this narrative is among the more sophisticated of the popular novels, its uncertain authorship as well as the fact of its surviving only in an abridged and popularized form suggests that it was on its way to becoming a folkbook. A final work of fiction, *Secundus the Silent Philosopher,* is a piece of wisdom literature composed for the nonlearned reader.

Written collections of just about everything collectible—inscriptions, decrees, proverbs, mythology, epigrams, fables, anecdotes, jokes, marvels, and so on—began appearing in the fourth and third centuries B.C.[34] The format could accommodate both sophisticated and unsophisticated aims. Since compilations lend themselves to sampling, I present here three compilations in excerpt rather than one in full. The first is the *Book of Marvels,* a collection of amazing facts and events made by a Greek freedman of the Emperor Hadrian, Phlegon of Tralles. Paradoxography, or writing about marvels, arose as an independent genre in the Hellenistic period and remained a popular genre for many centuries, but inasmuch as very little of it has been translated it is virtually unknown to modern readers. The second excerpt is a selection from an ancient fable book known to scholars as the *Collectio Augustana,* and the third is from an ancient Greek jokebook, *The Laughter-Lover.*

Practical handbooks were another form suitable for both sophisticated and unsophisticated literature, as they are in our day as well. Produced in considerable variety from the fourth century B.C. onward, they included didactic works as well as compositions structured as lists of information of one kind or another. Didactic handbooks offered practical instruction in topics ranging from letter writing to pseudosciences such as physiognomics, palmistry, and the making of amulets, while others concerned themselves with domestic matters such as cooking and sexual technique. Some of these works were clearly popular in nature, such as the ancient sex manuals (which unfortunately are not extant) and instructions for the making of magic amulets (which happily are).[35]

Many such books were probably little more than codifications of folk belief, and this must have been particularly true of handbooks in the form of lists. Thus dream dictionaries—a literary type for which there are Egyptian and Mesopotamian antecedents—reflect the lore of ordinary persons as well as of professional dream interpreters about the meanings of different dreams.[36] Just as, for example, a tingling in one's ears signifies in Anglo-American popular divination even today that one is being talked about, and just as a witch in Shakespeare's *Macbeth* can divine from a sensation in her fingers ("By the pricking of my thumbs, / Something wicked this way comes"), so also in antiquity the significance of bodily sensations was explained in detail in divinatory dictionaries of twitching, throbbing, and the like. Here is an entry from a handbook of divinatory twitching compiled by Melampus, an author of the third century B.C.:[37]

> *Right ear.* A twitching or tingling means joy at something. For a slave it means good cheer; for a maiden, further acquisition; for a widow, good.

Another kind of popular divinatory work was the oracle book, from which the consulter learned his or her fortune by means of sortition.

Elaborate oracle books contained lists of questions from which the consulter might choose, lists of possible responses, and a device for discovering the correct response to the question asked on a particular occasion.
The finest example of this genre to survive from antiquity is *The Oracles
of Astrampsychus,* a complex oracle book featuring 92 questions and
1,030 responses. I include it here, translated into English for the first
time, as representative of ancient Greek divinatory handbooks.

In addition to works inked onto perishable materials for private use,
there existed compositions carved into stone and displayed in the open
for the literate public to read. Thus when the Greek traveler Pausanias
visited the healing sanctuary of Asclepius at Epidaurus in the second century A.D., he saw among the noteworthy sights a number of stone tablets
upon which were inscribed the accounts of men and women who had
been miraculously healed by the god. Six tablets remained in his day,
although in the past there had been more. Of those read by Pausanias,
fragments of four survive, containing around seventy stories of miraculous healing recounted in simple prose in the Doric dialect.[38] For example, the fourth story on the first tablet reads as follows.

> Ambrosia from Athens, blind in one eye. She came as a suppliant to the god.
> As she walked around the sanctuary she ridiculed some of the cures as being
> incredible and impossible, that the lame and the blind became well from
> merely seeing a dream. But while she slept she saw a vision. It seemed to her
> that the god stood there and said that he would make her well but she would
> have to pay a fee, the offering of a silver pig to the sanctuary as a memorial
> of her ignorance. After saying this he opened up her sick eye and poured
> some medicine in it. In the morning she left well.

Ambrosia is represented as having made a preliminary tour of the sanctuary and reading the abundant testimonials of miraculous healing that we
know were recounted and pictured there on painted wooden or terra
cotta plaques. Although a suppliant herself who must have nurtured
some hopes of being healed, she scoffed at the miracle narratives. During
her incubation the kindly god did nevertheless heal her but also fined her
for her unenlightened behavior; and in the end her own experience joined
the public records that she originally mocked for their apparent simple-
minded credulity. Or so claims the tablet.

The most common form of popular literature on stone was found in
cemeteries, for the epitaphs that the bereaved had inscribed on grave
markers often took the form of poetic memorials of the dead.[39] Thousands of epitaphs are known, ranging over many centuries. Most com-
memorated ordinary persons and presumably were composed by other
ordinary persons. Poetically some of the poems are more original than
others, some are more formular, some are more successful, but few beg
to be classified as elite literature. I conclude the anthology with a selec-

tion of Greek gravestone verses that are contemporary with the larger works of literature anthologized here, approximately the first to the fourth centuries A.D., as representative of a nearly ubiquitous form of popular literary expression in public places.

It requires an act of the imagination to put ourselves back into the literary world of ancient Greece and Rome. Think away the printing press and the rest of the modern technology of publishing, think away newspapers and magazines, think away paperbound books that are so cheap you can discard them after you read them. Then think away not only mass literacy but probably even literacy as a common attainment.[40] But don't think away books and readers.

NOTES

1. Escarpit 1964:6. (For full bibliographical details, see Works Cited at the end of the book.) In the same spirit, popular *culture* is defined sometimes as that culture which originates among the people; see Storey 1993:12. So Peter Burke describes popular culture as "unofficial culture, the culture of the non-elite" (1994:xi, and further xvi–xxiv).

2. See Mike Hinkemeyer (a.k.a. Vanessa Royall), "Can a Man Write Romance Novels?" in Falk 1990:323–328. Hinkemeyer lists female pseudonyms used by male writers. On the readership of romance novels, see Modleski 1982 and Radway 1987.

3. Neuburg 1977:12. As popular literature Neuburg includes also practical literature that is read for instruction more than for pleasure, such as almanacs, and literature that is chosen for, rather than by, unsophisticated readers, such as religious tracts.

4. Neuburg 1977:12–13, 174–184, 190–191, 206–212, 214.

5. Similarly, popular culture is sometimes defined as substandard culture, as what is left over when one subtracts high culture; see Storey 1993:7–10. Judgments on the quality of the popular arts vary, some scholars of popular culture condemning it and others defending it; Russel Nye probably speaks for many other scholars when he says that there is both good and bad popular art but that aesthetically the overall quality of the popular arts is less than that of the elite arts (1971:4–7).

6. Stephens 1994. Cf. Harris 1989:227–28 and his comment: "There was no such thing as 'popular literature' in the Roman Empire, if that means literature which became known to tens or hundreds of thousands of people by means of personal reading."

7. On the basis of her data Stephens draws the negative conclusion that the ancient novel was not a popular genre, but she does not draw the positive conclusion to which her study equally leads, that if the only criterion of popular literature is statistical frequency, then Homer and Demosthenes are the clearest instances of ancient Greek popular literature.

8. Similarly, everything that intellectuals read could be labelled collectively "elite literature," but it would not thereby denote a kind of literature, since it would include newspapers, magazines, light reading, and so on, in addition to

more demanding literature. The concept of popular culture as the culture in which many persons participate is open to the same objection, since it results in a mix of cultural features, some of them usually regarded as belonging to low culture, others to high culture; see Storey 1993:7.

9. Just as we usually do not know how many readers read, or how many buyers bought, particular works of literature in the past, frequently we do not know who read certain publications, even though we may commonly assume that a certain kind of literature must have appealed to a certain kind of person. Thus it seems natural to suppose that in sixteenth-century France, almanacs should have interested the peasants. But did country folk actually read them? Not much, apparently. See Natalie Zemon Davis, "Printing and the People," in Davis 1975:189–226.

10. See Wroth 1938, Steinberg 1961, Chappell 1970.

11. Nye 1971:1–3. On popular culture as mass culture, see also Bell 1989 and Storey 1993:10–12. This concept emphasizes not producers or consumers but rather the relationship of the two.

12. Some scholars, however, distinguish popular culture from mass culture, the latter presupposing a culture industry; so, for example, Ginzburg 1980:130–131.

13. Nye 1971:6.

14. Bourdieu 1984, especially 4–5, 32–34, 41–44. The antithesis of the popular aesthetic is called by Bourdieu the *pure aesthetic.*

15. For a discussion of "preciousness" in popular fiction, see Bayer 1971:27–33.

16. Cf. Burke 1994:28.

17. For the respective natures of fine art, folk art, popular art, and primitive art in the visual arts, see Glassie 1989.

18. See for example Nyerup 1816, Nisard 1864, and Neuburg 1977.

19. The difficult subject of literacy at different periods in ancient Greece and Rome has been much discussed; see, for example, Harris 1989, especially 273–284, for the period upon which the present anthology focuses. Since the number of readers of ancient popular literature is neither knowable nor directly related to the concept of popular literature set forth in the present work, I do not enter into the debate.

20. For a brief treatment of Greek books during the Hellenistic and Imperial periods, see P. E. Easterling, "Books and Readers in the Greek World: The Hellenistic and Imperial Periods," in Easterling and Knox 1985:16–41.

21. Literature reflecting a popular aesthetic was produced even when there was little or no commercial incentive for authors to produce it, indicating that the wish of authors to express themselves in the popular mode, together with the presence of readers who are receptive to this mode of communication, is a sufficient explanation for the making of popular literature.

22. It is suggestive to compare the case of the thoughtful sixteenth-century Italian miller Menocchio, a literate man of modest means whose reading and thought are the subject of a study by Carlo Ginzburg. So far as one can tell, Menocchio's library consisted of eleven books, and Ginzburg poses the question of how Menocchio got hold of them (1980:28–31). It is known that he purchased one of them; concerning three others we have no information. The remaining six (more than half of his collection, as Ginzburg points out) were loans.

23. On ancient books, see Schubart 1921, Kenyon 1951, Knox and Easterling 1985, Stephens 1988, and Blanck 1992.

24. Perry 1967:59.

25. William Chambers, *Memoir of Robert Chambers,* 6th ed. (1871), quoted by Neuburg 1977:204–205.

26. See introduction to selection 2, *The Acts of Paul and Thecla.*

27. Origen *Contra Celsum* 4.52, cited by Lloyd W. Daly in Daly and Suchier 1939:16. Daly comments further: "Now no one would raise any objection to calling many examples of our question-and-answer form popular, but I can imagine that some one might find difficulty in calling some of the religious pieces popular, especially a few of those written by various Church Fathers. . . . The point of calling them popular at all, is that, by whatever author, whether known or unknown, they were written essentially for popular consumption. I say essentially, because, although in the Middle Ages the circle of readers would be comparatively small, confined to those who had education enough to be at least literate, it was essentially unlearned."

28. Since we usually do not know exactly who is responsible for the changes, let us call them simply the "copyists."

29. For an example see Thompson 1953. For the concept of ecotypes in folk narrative, see Bødker 1965:220.

30. On folkbooks see Paulli 1936, Schenda 1970:299–305, and Classen 1995. M. L. West (1984:122) observes: "What is meant by a *Volksbuch?* A book, I suppose, whose author has been forgotten, and which continues to circulate because of the interest of its subject matter, and of which the text is subject to progressive change. The Byzantine Alexander Romance would be an example." On chapbooks see, e.g., Ashton 1882, Preston and Preston 1995. Chapbooks are named for the itinerant "chapmen" (cf. German *Kaufmann*), that is, merchants, who peddled them.

31. Bayer (1971:52–57) speaks of the interchangeability of episodes in popular fiction, in which episodes exist more for themselves than for their organic contribution to the whole. The term *conglomerate* I borrow from folklorist Carl W. von Sydow (1948:72), for whom a conglomerate is a folktale with a stable frame within which a varying number of illustrative episodes can appear in different combinations. An example is the international oral tale known as the *Anger Bargain;* see Aarne and Thompson 1961: Types 1000–1029 (Type 1000 is the frame, and Types 1001–1029 are episodes that may appear between the introduction and conclusion).

32. Recent surveys of ancient prose fiction include Hägg 1983, Morgan and Stoneman 1994, Holzberg 1995, and Schmeling 1996. For whole novels in English translation, see Reardon 1989. For the fragments of lost novels, see Stephens and Winkler 1995. On the question of who read the ancient novels, see Bowie 1996.

33. For a discussion of the unsophisticated element in the Greek novel, see Anderson 1996.

34. Perry 1940:406.

35. For a translation of a treatise on the manufacture of amulets, see Waegeman 1987; on ancient Greek sex manuals, see Parker 1992; for ancient handbooks of letter writing including model letters, see Malherbe 1988. Except for one small fragment, no ancient sex manuals have survived. But from what can be learned of them, they were popular in spirit, quite unlike the polished and subtle parody of such manuals by the Roman poet Ovid, the *Ars Amatoria,* or *Art of Love.*

36. For a translation of a Greek dream book in dictionary format, see Artemidorus 1975; however, unlike most other compilers of dream dictionaries, Artemidorus includes serious theoretical discussion of the principles of dream

interpretation. For the Egyptian dream book, see Gardner 1935:7–27; for the Mesopotamian dream book, see Oppenheim 1956.

37. See the study of Diels 1907–1908. The translated entry is Melampus A:45 (Diels 1:24).

38. See LiDonnici 1995. The Epidaurian miracle narratives were inscribed in the fourth century B.C. during the monumentalization of the sanctuary. Internal evidence indicates that some were copies of older testimonia. For another, slightly younger kind of miracle narrative on stone, see the inscription of the third century B.C. recounting an epiphany of the Muses to the future poet Archilochus of Paros, in Müller 1985, 1992.

39. See, e.g., Lattimore 1942. For other public verse, inscribed in stone in connection with ancient dice oracles, see the introduction to selection 10. A more modest but virtually ubiquitous kind of popular writing was graffiti, casual inscriptions scratched onto cups, potsherds, walls, and so on, that in many cases have lasted till our own day. There was also a considerable magical literature of curses, prophylactic spells, etc., written on lead, papyrus, and other materials and intended to be read by the god or other being(s) to whom they were addressed; see Preisendanz 1973, Betz 1992, Gager 1992.

40. I borrow the phraseology from Burke (1994:xiii), who speaks of the leap of imagination that is necessary in order to enter into the minds of the peasants and craftsmen of early modern Europe.

PART ONE

Popular Fiction

I

ROMANTIC NOVEL

An Ephesian Tale is a short novel of action and emotion featuring stereo-typed characters, short and suspenseful scenes of eroticism and danger, an equal number of narrow escapes, and a happy ending—all of it re-counted straightforwardly in simple prose and with no serious reflection. In short, it is pure entertainment.

About its author we know next to nothing. The single manuscript in which the novel is found gives his name as Xenophon, and according to a Byzantine lexicon he was from Ephesus.[1]

> Xenophon, Ephesian, a historical narrator. *An Ephesian Tale,* which is a love story in ten books about Habrocomes and Anthia. Also *On the City of the Ephesians* and other works.

Other ancient writers ignore him and his novel, just as they make almost no mention of other novelists and their works. Indeed, the Greeks were so far from recognizing the novel as a genre of literature that they had no regular term for novel or novelist, and Xenophon is described here as a "historical narrator" or "historian" *(historikos)*.

An Ephesian Tale is possibly the earliest surviving European novel. Since Xenophon is generally assigned to the second century of our era but may have lived as early as the first, it is uncertain whether he wrote before or after Chariton, whose novel *Callirhoe* is often regarded as the first surviving novel. In any case neither *An Ephesian Tale* nor *Callirhoe* was the first Greek novel to be written, but of their predecessors we possess only fragments.

The language of Xenophon's work is extremely plain and unadorned, a typical sentence being declarative and paratactic. His diction moreover is repetitive to the point of being formulaic. For example, when he wishes to introduce a prominent man into his narrative, he usually describes him as "a man who was one of the most important persons" in the area, using the same group of words each time:

> There was in Ephesus *a man who was one of the most important persons in* the region, Lycomedes by name.

> He was the person in charge of peace in Cilicia, Perilaos by name, *a man who was one of the most important persons in* Cilicia.

> And a certain person came from Byzantium (Byzantium was close to Perinthos), *a man who was one of the most important persons in* the region, proud because of his wealth and power; he was called Aristomachus.[2]

Xenophon writes the same way throughout his novel, expressing recurrent dictional and narrative ideas in similar or identical ways. It may be that this formulaic quality of Xenophon's novel is ultimately a reflection of the oral storyteller, for some oral styles are characterized by verbal and structural repetition, the effect of which is generally more enjoyable for a listener than it is for a reader.[3] But it could also reflect the author's own aesthetic, his limited range, and the speed and lack of care with which he composed his work.

Five ancient Greek novels of love survive in their entirety.[4] They are all difficult to date. Listed in the sequence in which most scholars currently believe they were written, they are Chariton's *Callirhoe,* Xenophon's *An Ephesian Tale,* Longus's *Daphnis and Chloe,* Achilles Tatius's *Leucippe and Clitophon,* and Heliodorus's *An Ethiopian Tale.* The novels of Chariton and Xenophon, plainer in language and simpler in conception than those of the three later authors, are commonly classified as "nonsophistic" novels in order to distinguish them from the more refined, "sophistic" novels of Longus, Achilles Tatius, and Heliodorus. But on an abstract level the plots of all five are more or less the same: two lovers of aristocratic family wish to consummate their love or actually get married and do so, but obstacles arise and keep them apart for a long time until finally they succeed in being united. The outer frame accounts for little of the actual narrative, since the novels dwell on the central complications that prevent the protagonists' union and happiness. In Xenophon's story the handsome Habrocomes and the beautiful Anthia fall in love, get married, fall presently into the hands of pirates, become separated, then individually experience many sensational adventures and trials before they are united again for good.

After the protagonists are separated, Xenophon switches back and forth between them, bringing each episode to a conclusion before turning to the other protagonist. The obstacles to their happiness sometimes take the form of greedy persons who wish to profit financially from the protagonists, but more often it is lustful persons who wish to enjoy them sexually. Since the lovers are extraordinarily good-looking and have sworn to be faithful to each other, they pass much of their time warding off would-be lovers, Habrocomes while seeking his beloved, Anthia while hoping to be found. Anthia, for example, is captured by pirates, one of whom falls in love with her; she escapes this close call when the leader of the pirates selects her for himself with the aim of selling her; but sometime later she is forced to wed a certain lowly goatherd, whom however she is able to persuade to honor her chastity; after a time her goatherd husband is ordered to kill her but out of compassion arranges for her escape; not long afterwards she is about to be sacrificed by a priest in a strange religious ritual among brigands when she is saved by the sudden appearance of a local sheriff; but presently the lawman in turn falls in love with her; and so on. Structurally this central portion of the novel is a conglomerate, a loose assemblage of episodes in which the protagonists work or drift toward a solution to their problems. The number and arrangement of the central episodes is virtually arbitrary, and the point at which they come to a close appears to be almost a matter of chance. Their presence simply answers to the reader's desire for material, as in much other popular literature, and when Xenophon deems his reader has had enough, he allows the protagonists to be reunited.[5]

Once Habrocomes and Anthia are separated, the reader may be concerned whether they will ever be reunited, although in fact Apollo's oracle at the beginning of the tale has informed everybody that in time all will be well. Similarly, whenever the freedom, chastity, or life of the lovers is threatened, the reader may worry, but not for long, since Xenophon does not really protract the suspense. The author achieves a kind of light suspense, introducing some tension into his novel but not a great deal, as though he were afraid of frightening the reader overmuch. (In a similar spirit, perhaps, one of the anonymous redactors of selection 10, *The Oracles of Astrampsychus,* adds brief reassurances to the oracular responses here and there in order to calm the fears of anxious questioners: "You have not been poisoned. *Don't be distressed.*") But it is hard to decide whether the degree of suspense present in Xenophon's novel is the result of a conscious choice on his part or has to do with his limited talents and experience as a writer of sentimental fiction, for it is possible that he may not have known how to make his story more suspenseful.[6]

The characters are essentially unchanging types, usually representing one extreme or another. The two protagonists are incredibly good-looking persons who love each other passionately and would rather die than be unfaithful. Most of the other characters are either facilitators or complicators. In the former category we find faithful slaves, adopters (persons who adopt other persons, name them as heirs, and die), rescuers, and other kindly persons of various sorts. The latter category includes mostly lustful types (seducers and rapists) and profiteers (pirates, brigands, slavers, pimps). Except for the fact that a character may change from one extreme type to another, as when a rescuer turns lustful, the characters change little or not at all throughout the story, neither growing nor learning from their experiences.[7]

The novel exhibits a small number of narrative routines, which it recycles throughout the story, the narrative counterpart of the stereotyped diction. Episodes sometimes exhibit considerable independence, as episodes in oral stories characteristically do, resulting in occasional inconsistencies between episodes, as when Habrocomes abruptly makes or changes a plan for no apparent reason or when the characters cease knowing something that they knew (all the characters forget the reassuring portion of the initial oracle, causing them to despair needlessly). As in oral story, action is primary, and since character is a function of action, the basic nature of a character may shift in the course of the novel according to the needs of the plot.[8] Taken together, the author's episodic composition and sometimes unskillful storytelling occasionally make for confusion in the mind of the reader.

As in ancient New Comedy and modern romantic novels, the protagonists see love as their salvation. It is love that really makes life worth living, not family or community or honor or wealth or piety, although these too have their importance. In Xenophon's story, the characters fall in love at first sight, overwhelmed by physical beauty. Love is instantaneous, irresistible, and sometimes violently emotional. Unlike modern mass-market romances, however, Xenophon's novel recounts not so much the quest of a would-be lover for love as it does the quest of committed lovers for reunion, since Anthia and Habrocomes fall in love at the beginning of the novel. In all the Greek novels love is a mutual and symmetrical bond between social equals that results in marriage. Generally both parties fall in love with the other at the same time, both are equally faithful, and for that matter both are equally passive, so that neither is dominant and, although the males are more mobile than the females, neither really rescues the other.[9] Furthermore, although the principal interest lies in the heterosexual love of the protagonists, *An Ephesian Tale* includes both heterosexual and homosexual relationships. There is no double standard for males and females or for heterosexuals and homosexuals in the novel.

About Xenophon's ancient readers we can only speculate, since we have little evidence for the consumership of the ancient novels.[10] Presumably *An Ephesian Tale* appealed to unsophisticated readers as well as to some sophisticated readers who enjoyed losing themselves in exciting literature that made little demand upon them.

This translation of Xenophon's novel by Moses Hadas captures the charm and earnestness of the work but not its plain diction, which Hadas makes to be more sophisticated than Xenophon's original.

NOTES

1. *Suda*, s.v. Xenophon.

2. *Ephesiaca* 1.1.1; 2.13.3; 3.2.5 (translations are mine); the phrase occurs about six times in the novel. O'Sullivan (1995:179–187) lists Xenophon's formulaic expressions.

3. O'Sullivan (1995:69–98) makes the case for an oral background, suggesting that *An Ephesian Tale* may be a transitional text, a narrative deriving from oral tradition but composed with literary features. But dictional and structural formulism is commonly found in popular literature of all kinds.

4. For recent translations of the Greek novels, see Reardon 1989; for the fragments of the lost novels, see Stephens and Winkler 1993. On the ancient Greek novel generally, see Hägg 1983, Holzberg 1995, and Schmeling 1996.

5. See Bayer 1971:52–57, Schmeling 1980:84. For the term *conglomerate*, see Introduction.

6. On the lack of tension in Xenophon, see Schmeling 1980:80–93; on the lack of real tension in modern romantic fiction, see Bayer 1971:58–59.

7. Schmeling 1980:83.

8. See O'Sullivan 1995:38, 49, 86–92, who calls such unmotivated changes in character "thematic shifts." On episodic composition in oral story and orally inspired literature, see further Hansen 1983, especially 48–52.

9. See Schmeling 1980:103, 144 and Konstan 1994. For a comparison of ancient and modern romantic novels, see Scobie 1983 and Montague 1994.

10. The readership of the ancient novels has been much discussed; see Schmeling 1980:131–138, Stephens 1994, and Bowie 1996.

LITERATURE

Hägg 1971. Kytzler 1996. O'Sullivan 1995. Ruiz-Montero 1994. Schmeling 1980. (For full bibliographical details, see Works Cited.)

XENOPHON OF EPHESUS

An Ephesian Tale

translated by Moses Hadas

1 At Ephesus lived a man named Lycomedes, a principal figure in that city. He had to wife Themiste, who was also a native Ephesian, and their son was Habrocomes, a prodigy of beauty unrivaled in Ionia or elsewhere. This Habrocomes grew handsomer day by day, and the qualities

of his soul kept equal pace with the beauty of his person. He was diligent in every form of culture, and practiced the various arts; his training included the chase and horsemanship and fencing. By all the Ephesians was he cherished, and likewise by the inhabitants of other parts of Asia; all expected that he would one day bring great distinction to his city. They honored the lad as he were a god, and indeed some there were who bowed down when they saw him and offered him prayer. Now the youth conceived a high opinion of himself; he vaunted himself upon the merits of his spirit, but much more upon the beauty of his person. Whatever the world counted beautiful he despised as inferior and indeed negligible in comparison with himself. Nothing that the world had to show or tell did Habrocomes deem worthy of himself. And if any spoke of some lad as handsome or some maid as comely he laughed at their ignorance; the only true beauty, of course, was himself. He even denied that Eros was a god; nay, he dismissed him as a cipher and banished him utterly. He declared that no one at all had ever been mastered by love or become subject to that "god" unless he wished to be. And if ever he saw a sanctuary or statue of Eros he ridiculed it and boasted that he was handsomer than any Eros. Actually that seemed the case, for wherever Habrocomes came into view no statue seemed beautiful, no image was admired.

At this Eros waxed wroth; jealous is that divinity, and to the proud inexorable. He sought for some device to snare that lad, for even to the god he seemed hard to overreach. He accoutered himself, therefore, cap-a-pie, armed himself with his powerful love philters, and marched against Habrocomes. The local festival of Artemis was in progress, and the procession moved from the city to the shrine; the distance was seven furlongs. Usage required that all the maidens of the region, richly attired, and all the lads of Habrocomes' age join in the procession. Habrocomes was now sixteen years of age and already classed a cadet, and he played the principal role in the cortege. A great concourse had assembled for the spectacle; there were many Ephesians and many visitors, for it was customary for bridegrooms to be found for maidens at that festival, and wives for the cadets. And so the procession moved past. In the van were the sacred objects, the torches, the baskets, and the incense. Following these were horses and dogs and hunting gear; there was some display of military equipment, but more of the arts of peace.

The girls in the procession were all decked out as if to meet lovers. Of the band of maidens the leader was Anthia, daughter of the Ephesians Megamedes and Evippe. Anthia was a prodigy of loveliness and far surpassed the other maidens. Her age was fourteen, and she had bloomed into mature shapeliness. Her grooming enhanced her charm. Her hair was yellow, for the most part loose, but with some tresses braided, and it stirred at the movement of the breeze. Her eyes were lively, shining sometimes like a girl's, sometimes severe, as of a chaste goddess. Her dress was a frock of purple, fitted down to the knee and hanging loose over the arms. Her wrap was a fawn skin, and a quiver hung from her shoulder. She carried bow and javelins, and dogs followed at her heels. Time and again when the Ephesians saw her in the sacred precinct they bowed down as to Artemis. And now too when Anthia came into view the entire multitude cried out in astonishment; some of the spectators asserted that she was the very goddess, others declared she was a replica fashioned by the goddess. But all did obeisance to her and bowed down and called her parents blessed. From all the spectators there arose cheers for Anthia the beautiful, and of all the maidens in the procession only Anthia was spoken of. But however beautiful the spectacle of the maidens had been, they were forgotten completely when Habrocomes appeared with the cadets. The people gazed at him, were smitten by the sight, and cried out, "Habrocomes is beautiful!" "None is so fair!" "He is the image of a beautiful god!" There were some too who now added, "What a marriage that of Habrocomes and Anthia would be!" This was the first stage in Eros' campaign. Each of the young people soon heard reports of the other. Anthia was eager to see Habrocomes, and Habrocomes, who had been insensible to love, now wished to see Anthia.

When the procession was finished the entire multitude approached the shrine to offer sacrifice, and the order of the march was broken up. Now there was no distinction of sexes; cadets and maidens mingled, and could eye one another. Anthia was captivated by Habrocomes, and Habrocomes was laid low by Eros. His stare was fixed on the girl, and though he would withdraw his eyes he could not; the god pressed him hard and held him fast. Anthia for her part was no less smitten. With her whole being she caught the beauty of Habrocomes, which flowed into her wide open eyes. And now she disregarded maidenly modesty; she murmured words for Habrocomes to overhear and uncovered as much of her person as she could for Habrocomes to see. And Habrocomes gave himself wholly to the sight; the god's bound prisoner was he. When the sacrifice was finished they parted from one another, sadly and with regret at the brevity of the encounter. Wishing mightily to look upon one another, ever and again they turned about, and halted, and discovered many pretexts for delay. But it was when each arrived home that they realized the depth of their distress. Each was overwhelmed by the impression the other had left, in each was love's flame kindled. During the remainder of the day their agitation grew, and when they retired to sleep they found themselves in deep anguish. Upon each love pressed irresistibly.

Habrocomes pulled his hair and ripped his clothes. "Ah me for my troubles!" he said. "What, unlucky that I am, has happened to me? Till now I was that stalwart Habrocomes, the champion who despised Eros, the man who reviled the god, and now I am taken prisoner and vanquished and forced into slavery to a girl; now another seems fairer to me than myself, and I acknowledge that Eros is a god. Ah, but I am a spine-less coward! Shall I not now resist, shall I not show courage and endure? Shall I not be handsomer than Eros? Now must I overcome that god who is only a cipher! Fair is the maiden, granted; but what then? To your eyes, Habrocomes, Anthia is comely; but if you are so determined, not to *yourself*. This then must be my doctrine; Eros must never be my master." So he said, but the god pressed him the more vehemently, and dragged him, though he resisted, and tormented him, though he was otherwise minded. And when he could withstand no longer he flung himself down upon the ground, and said, "Thou hast conquered, Eros; great is thy trophy for victory over chaste Habrocomes. Thou seest him suppliant before thy feet. Preserve him who seeks asylum of thee, who art master of all creatures. Do not abandon me, nor too strictly punish my foolhardiness. Out of ignorance, Eros, I behaved arrogantly in thy domain. But now give me Anthia! Show thyself a god not only severe to the recalcitrant but also benevolent to the vanquished." So he said, but Eros continued angry and planned how he might make Habrocomes render full payment for his insults.

Anthia too was in deep distress, and when she could bear it no longer she roused herself in an effort to conceal her state. "Unhappy that I am," said she, "what has come over me? I am a maid, and love beyond what suits my age; I am tormented by pains that are strange and unbecoming to a girl. I am mad with love for Habrocomes, who is handsome indeed, but exceedingly proud. What will be the limit of this passion, what the end of this woe? Formidable is the man I love, and I am a maid, kept under ward. Whom shall I find to be my help? To whom can I confide my distress? Where shall I see Habrocomes?" Thus did each of the two lament the whole night through. Their mutual likenesses they kept before their eyes, and each stamped upon his own soul the molded image of the other.

When day broke Habrocomes went to his usual exercises, and the maid went, as her custom was, to minister to the goddess. Their sufferings through the night had left their bodies wearied, their eyes listless, their complexions wan. This state continued long, and they obtained no solace. During this while they passed whole days in the temple of the goddess, gazing upon one another but constrained and afraid to reveal the truth to one another. Only so much: Habrocomes would groan and weep and would make his prayers most pitiful when the girl was within hearing. Anthia endured like suffering, but was afflicted with this greater distress: whenever she observed other maidens or women gazing upon the youth (and all her sex did gaze fondly upon Habrocomes) her suffering was plain to see, for she feared she would be outdone in his esteem. But their prayers to the goddess were common to both; without their being aware of it their petitions were identical.

As time went on the young man languished. His frame was emaciated and his spirit was so crushed that Lycomedes and Themiste fell into despair; what had befallen Habrocomes they knew not, but what they could see filled them with apprehension. In similar dread were Megamedes and Evippe for the fate of Anthia: they observed that her beauty was drooping, but the cause of the calamity was not apparent. At length they fetched soothsayers and holy men to Anthia, to find some solution for the trouble. These busily offered divers sacrifices and poured divers libations and pronounced certain unintelligible syllables in order to appease, as they said, certain demonic powers, and they feigned that the malady was a visitation of the gods of the nether world. For Habrocomes, too, did Lycomedes and his friends offer many sacrifices and prayers. But no solution for their malady was vouchsafed either; nay, the fire of love burned yet fiercer. They lay then there, the two of them sick, their disease now so critical that nothing less than speedy death was looked for, and they were yet unable to give utterance to their own calamity. Finally the fathers of both sent to consult the divine oracle for the cause of the disease and the means for its relief.

The shrine of Apollo in Colophon was but a short distance away; the crossing from Ephesus was a matter of only eighty furlongs. When the emissaries dispatched by the two parents arrived there they besought the god to render a true oracle; for this purpose had they come. And the god delivered a single oracle in common to both, in meter, in form as follows:

Why yearn ye to learn the end of disease or its beginning?
Both a single malady holds fast, and hence the solution issues.
Yet perceive I for these twain fearful suffering and toils protracted.
Both shall flee o'er the brine pursued by pirates,
They shall be laden with fetters by men who live by the sea.
For both a bridal chamber will serve as a tomb, and fire the destroyer;
And by the floods of the river Nile upon holy Isis
The savior goddess you will thereafter bestow rich gifts.
But after their woes their lot grants a fortune that is better.

When the oracle was brought to Ephesus the fathers forthwith fell into a quandary, being at a complete loss to know what the evil might be. To divine the dark sayings of the god they were not able, nor could they guess the meaning of the malady or the flight or the fetters or the tomb or the river or the help the goddess would vouchsafe. After long deliberation it seemed to them best to mitigate the oracle so far as in them lay and to join their children in marriage, for such seemed the will of the god in the oracle he had rendered. This they determined to do, and they resolved to send the young people away to sojourn abroad for a time after their marriage.

The city was now filled with feasting, everything was bedecked with garlands, and the intended marriage was widely bruited abroad. Felicitations were offered on all hands—to the young man for the excellent wife he would lead home, and to the young woman for the splendid spouse she would enjoy. When Habrocomes learned of the oracle and of the marriage, he was greatly rejoiced at coming into possession of Anthia; the predictions frightened him not at all, for his present happiness seemed to him to overweigh any evil. And after the same fashion Anthia rejoiced that she would possess Habrocomes; she cared little for the flight and other troubles, having in Habrocomes solace for any future tribulations. When the season for the marriage was come, vigils were celebrated the night through and numerous victims were sacrificed to the goddess. And when these rites were done and night was come (but Habrocomes and Anthia thought it very tardy), they conducted the girl to the bridal chamber with torches, chanting the hymeneal hymn, and they pronounced propitious blessings upon them, and introduced them to their bridal couch. The fashion of their bridal chamber was as follows: the couch of gold was spread with purple coverings, and over the couch was a canopy of Babylonian stuff richly embroidered: there were sportive Cupids, some ministering to Aphrodite (Aphrodite herself was represented in a figure), some riding mounted on sparrows, some were twining wreaths, and some were bearing flowers. These designs occupied one side of the canopy. On the other there was Ares, without his weapons, but finely dressed, as if to meet his beloved Aphrodite, wearing a wreath and draped in a cape. Eros was conducting him on his way, carrying a lighted torch. Under this canopy they caused Anthia to recline, after they brought her to Habrocomes, and then they closed the doors.

Their emotions were identical. They were able neither to address a word one to the other, nor to look upon each other's eyes; but they lay there languid with delight, modest, timid, breathing rapidly. Their bodies trembled, their souls were agitated. Finally Habrocomes collected himself, and embraced Anthia. She wept: 'twas her soul that sent forth those tears in token of her yearning. Then said Habrocomes, "O Night most fondly desired and at long last won, after the miseries of so many earlier nights! Darling, dearer to me than light, blissful beyond all utterance, you hold in your arms the man who loves you; with him may it be vouchsafed you to live and to die, a chaste wife." When he had so spoken he kissed her, and collected her tears, and to him those tears seemed more delicious than any nectar and a more potent anodyne than any drug. She in turn murmured some words to him, and said, "Am I truly fair in your sight, Habrocomes? Inferior as I am to your beauty, do I still please you? Timid and fearful lad, how long will you delay your love-making? How much time will you waste? From my own anguish I know what you must have suffered. But see, now, take these my tears, and let your pretty hair drink up this potion of love. Let us cleave to one another and commingle, let us drench these garlands in one another's tears, that they too may join in love with us." When she had said all this she fondled his face and drew all his hair to touch her eyes; and then she removed the wreaths, and applied her lips to his in a close kiss, and the thoughts that were in the mind of each they transmitted through their lips from the soul of one to the soul of the other. And when she kissed his eyes she said, "Ah, ye twain that have so often inflicted pain upon me, ye that first thrust the goad into my spirit, ye that were then cruel but now filled with love, well have ye served me, passing well have ye conveyed love of me into the soul of Habrocomes. Therefore do I love you passing well, and to you I will apply close these eyes of mine, now the handmaids of Habrocomes. Ever may ye see as ye see this day: show no other fair to Habrocomes, and let no other lad seem handsome in my sight. Now ye possess the souls which yourselves have set aflame: guard and preserve them in like fashion." Such things she spoke, and then, clinging one to the other, they went to their rest and plucked the first fruits of Aphrodite. The whole night they spent in eager rivalry with one another, contending which should appear the more ardent lover.

When day shone forth they arose happier and with better cheer, because they had attained mutual enjoyment of the bliss for which they had long yearned. All of life seemed to them a festival, all was filled with good cheer, so that the oracle slipped into forgetfulness. But fate slipped not into forgetfulness, nor was that god negligent who determined these things. When a little time had passed the fathers resolved to send the young people from the city, as they had previously decided. Their purpose was to explore another country and other cities and, so far as this was possible, to mitigate the oracle of the god by absenting themselves from Ephesus for a season. All things, then, were made ready against their departure; a stately ship and suitable seamen to sail it was got ready, and supplies were stowed aboard—a great abundance and variety of clothing, much silver and gold, and huge stocks of provisions. Before the voyage sacrifices were offered to Artemis; prayers were uttered by all the folk, and all shed tears, as if they were about to be separated from children that belonged to the whole people. It was for Egypt that the voyage had been prepared. When the day of departure was come, a crowd of menservants and maidservants [embarked with their young masters], and when the vessel was about to weigh anchor the whole multitude of the Ephesians attended to see them off, and there were many [strangers] also, with torches and sacrifices. Lycomedes and Themiste, in the meanwhile, when they recalled the whole series of events—the oracle, their son, his departure—collapsed to the ground in their despair. Megamedes and Evippe shared the same distress, indeed, but nevertheless took better heart when they reflected on the final issue of the oracle. And now the shouts of the sailors rang out, and the hawsers were loosed, and the skipper took his post, and the ship began to move. There was a great outcry, in which were mingled voices from the shore and those on the ship. These cried out, "Dearest children, shall we who begat you ever see you again?" And those, "Dear parents, shall we ever find you again?" There were tears and lamentations, and each called upon his own kindred by name, leaving the name as it were a memorial for one another. Now Megamedes took a chalice in hand, and as he poured libation he prayed so that he might be heard by those on shipboard, saying, "Children, may you prosper greatly and avoid the hard sayings of the oracle; may the Ephesians receive you safe home again, and may you recover your own beloved country. If any different issue should befall, know that we shall not continue in life. The path upon which we send you is sad indeed, but inevitable." Even as he was speaking a burst of tears checked his utterance. The parents then returned to the city, the multitude encouraging them to be of good heart.

But Habrocomes and Anthia lay intertwined in one another's arms, brooding over many things in their minds. They pitied their parents, yearned for their homeland, dreaded the oracle, were apprehensive of the voyage; but for all these things their sufficient solace was that they voyaged together. That day they had the advantage of a tail wind, and with good sailing they made Samos, the sacred island of Hera. There they offered sacrifice and took their dinner and said many prayers, and when night came on they continued their journey. Again sailing was favorable, and they had much conversation with one another. "Will it be vouchsafed us to live our lives out with one another?" Then indeed did Habrocomes fetch a deep sigh when he recalled what fate awaited him, and he said, "Anthia, dearer far to me than life, may it indeed be our lot to be blessed and preserved together. But if it be fated for us to undergo affliction and somehow be separated one from the other, let us swear an oath to one another, dearly beloved, you that you will abide chaste unto me and never tolerate another man, and I that I shall never consort with another woman." When Anthia heard this she exclaimed, "Why this, Habrocomes? Can you believe that if I am separated from you I can take thought for a man and for marriage when I cannot even live at all without you? I solemnly invoke to witness our great ancestral goddess, great Diana of the Ephesians, and this sea upon which we sail, and that divinity who has so well implanted in us passionate love for one another, that if I am separated from you even for any short shrift of time, I shall not live, shall not longer look upon the sun." So spoke Anthia, and Habrocomes too swore, and the circumstances and occasion lent solemnity to their oaths. Meanwhile their ship skirted Cos and Cnidos, and then the large and fair island of Rhodes hove into view. There they must needs disembark, for the sailors declared they must draw water and themselves take rest in preparation for the long voyage that faced them.

And so the ship made land at Rhodes and the sailors disembarked. Habrocomes, too, went ashore, holding Anthia by the hand. Astonished at the beauty of these two the Rhodians gathered in a crowd, and none who saw them passed in silence. Some said that these were divinities come to sojourn on the island; others bowed down to them and sought their favor. Quickly through the entire city the names of Habrocomes and Anthia were spread abroad. Public prayers were addressed to them and many victims were sacrificed, and their arrival was celebrated as a festive day. They for their part toured the whole city; in the shrine of the Sun they deposited a golden panoply as a votive offering, and inscribed upon it this memorial of their dedication:

> These golden gifts to thee have strangers dedicated—
> Anthia and Habrocomes, townsmen of sacred Ephesus.

When they had made this offering and had sojourned in the island for some days, at the insistence of the crew they embarked again; the ship was provisioned, and the entire multitude of the Rhodians escorted them to their sailing.

At first they were borne along with a prospering wind, and they took great pleasure in the voyage. That day and the night following they traversed the sea called Egyptian, but on the next day the wind dropped into a dead calm. The sailors were idle and took to drink; then came drunkenness and the beginning of the oracle's fulfillment. Habrocomes had a vision of a woman standing over him, fearful to behold, of stature larger than human, and clothed in a scarlet robe. She seemed to him to set the ship afire; the others, it seemed, perished, while he and Anthia swam free. As soon as he saw this vision Habrocomes was deeply disturbed; he foresaw that his dream would have some dreadful issue, and dreadful indeed were the events that transpired.

It happened that pirates, who were Phoenicians by race, had had their large galley moored near them at Rhodes. They were numerous and rugged, and pretended that they carried merchandise. These men learned that the Ephesian vessel was laden with gold and silver and many valuable slaves, and so they determined to attack it, put to death those who should offer resistance, and carry the others and the rest of the valuables off to Phoenicia for sale. The Ephesians they despised as incapable of strenuous resistance. The leader of the pirates was called Corymbos; he was a young man of large frame and fierce aspect, and his hair was rough and unkempt. When the pirates had laid their plans, at first they sailed quietly near Habrocomes' ship; but then, when it was about noon, and the crew was lying about sluggish with drink and idleness, some asleep and some helpless, Corymbos and his men urged their galley ahead with great speed. When they drew alongside they leapt upon the vessel fully armed and brandishing naked swords. Thereupon some flung themselves into the sea, surprised out of their wits, and perished; others who showed resistance were massacred. But Habrocomes and Anthia ran to the pirate Corymbos and said, "Keep the property and ourselves as slaves, master, but spare our lives and do not murder those who willingly submit to you. Do not so, we beseech you, by the sea itself, by your right hand. Take us whithersoever you will, sell us who are your slaves; only take pity and dispose of us to the same master."

When Corymbos heard this he issued orders immediately for the slaughter to cease, and when he had transshipped the more valuable freight, including Habrocomes and Anthia and a few selected slaves, he set fire to the vessel, and all the others were consumed in flames. To carry them all Corymbos was not able, and he saw that it was not safe. Pitiful indeed was the spectacle, some being carried off in the galley, others consumed in the burning ship, stretching their hands out and wailing. Some cried out, "Whither, masters, are you bound? What shores will receive you and in what city do you dwell?" Others said, "Blessed are those who will happily die before they have tasted chains, before they have looked upon bondage to robbers." Amid such cries some were haled off, some devoured by the flames. Meanwhile the tutor of Habrocomes, now an old man of venerable aspect and pitiful because of his age, when he could not endure to see Habrocomes carried off, flung himself into the sea and swam to overtake the galley, crying as he went, "Where will you leave me, my child, the old man, your tutor? Where are you off to, Habrocomes? Kill me yourself, wretch that I am, and bury me. How can I live without you?" Thus he said, and at length, despairing of seeing Habrocomes any longer, he gave himself up to the waves and died. To Habrocomes this was the most harrowing thing of all. He stretched his hands out to the old man and besought the pirates to take him up, but they paid no attention and sailed on. In three days they made land at Tyre, the Phoenician city where the pirates had their dwellings. Their booty they took not to the city itself but to a nearby retreat that belonged to the chief of the band, Apsyrtos by name. Him Corymbos served as lieutenant for wages and a share of what was taken.

In the course of the voyage Corymbos had seen Habrocomes daily and had fallen violently in love with him, and his familiar association with the young man had added fuel to his passion. During the voyage itself he judged that it was impossible to sway Habrocomes, for he saw that he was woefully disheartened in spirit, and saw too that he was in love with Anthia. He realized, furthermore, that it was inadvisable to employ force, for he feared that Habrocomes might do himself some hurt. But when they landed at Tyre he could no longer refrain himself. At first he showed Habrocomes every attention, and urged him to be of good heart, and provided him with every care. Habrocomes thought that it was because Corymbos pitied him that he was so solicitous. But then Corymbos confided his love to one of his fellow pirates, Euxinos by name; him he besought to be his aid, and to counsel him how he might persuade the lad. Euxinos was highly pleased to hear Corymbos' story, for he himself was in wretched state because of Anthia, with whom he had fallen fearfully in love. His own story, therefore, he confided to Corymbos; and advised him to suffer torment no longer, but to set at once to work. "For," said he, "an ignoble thing it were if when we have undergone peril and exposed our lives we should have no secure enjoyment of what our labors have won. We shall be able," he added, "to obtain these select items from Apsyrtos as a gift." These words easily persuaded that lover. Accordingly they agreed each to speak on the other's behalf; Euxinos would persuade Habrocomes, and Corymbos Anthia.

In the meanwhile those two were depressed in spirit; they anticipated many difficulties and spoke of them one to the other, and ever and again they swore to observe their pledges to one another. Then came to them Corymbos and Euxinos and said they wished to speak to them privately, and the one led Anthia apart, and the other Habrocomes. The hearts of these two were deeply troubled, and they expected that no good would come of it. Then Euxinos spoke to Habrocomes on Corymbos' behalf. "My lad, likely enough you feel depressed, finding yourself a slave instead of free, poor instead of rich. But you ought to charge everything up to fortune, to accommodate yourself to the lot which rules you, and to love those that have become your masters. You must know that it is possible for you to recover your wealth and your freedom if you are willing to yield to your master Corymbos. He is passionately in love with you and is ready to make you master of everything he possesses. You will undergo nothing disagreeable, but render your master more benevolent toward you. Consider the situation in which you find yourself. There is no one to help you. The country itself is alien, your masters are robbers, and there is no refuge whatever from punishment if you disdain Corymbos. What need have you now for a wife and a household? What need have you of a sweetheart at your time of life? Throw it all overboard; it is only to your master that you need to look, and to hearken to his bidding." When Habrocomes heard this he was straightway struck dumb, stupefied, and could find no answer to make; he could only weep and groan at the thought of his plight. But then he did speak to Euxinos: "Allow me, master, to deliberate a little," he said, "and I shall give you a full reply." Euxinos departed. But Corymbos spoke to Anthia of Euxinos' love, mentioning her straits and the necessity of yielding to her masters. He also made many promises if she should be persuaded— lawful matrimony, money, and abundance of all things. She too made a similar reply, requesting a short time for deliberation. Together Euxinos and Corymbos waited for the decisions, having little doubt that they could sway Habrocomes and Anthia.

2   Habrocomes and Anthia met at their humble lodging, and each gave the other his news. They flung themselves down and wept and wailed. "Father!" they cried. "Mother!" "Dear home!" "Family!" "Kinfolk!" Finally Habrocomes collected himself and said, "Miserable wretches that we are, what tribulations shall we undergo in this barbarous country, delivered to the brutality of pirates? The woes prophesied now begin. Now is the god exacting vengeance of me for my overweening pride. Corymbos is in love with me, Euxinos with you. Ah for our unseasonable beauty! It is for this, forsooth, that I have preserved my chastity until now, that I might submit to the filthy passion of a robber in love. What manner of life will be left for me when I have become a harlot instead of a man and have been deprived of my dear Anthia? No, by that chastity which has been my companion from childhood until now, I will not submit myself to Corymbos. Sooner shall I die, and as a corpse shall be proven chaste." So he said, and shed many tears. And Anthia, "Alas for our woes!" said she. "All too soon shall we be compelled to take thought of our oaths. Soon we shall know what slavery means. A man desires me and expects to sway me and to come to my bed after Habrocomes and to lie with me and satisfy his passion. But may I never show myself so abjectly in love with life nor survive, being thus outraged, to look upon the sun. So let our determination be fixed. Let us die, Habrocomes; we shall possess one another after death and none shall trouble us."

Thus they two resolved. But in the meantime Apsyrtos, the chief of the robber band, when he learned that the party was Corymbos had returned and that the valuables they had brought were plentiful and marvelous, came to that country retreat. He observed Habrocomes and Anthia and was struck by their beauty, and, thinking he would derive large profit from them, he asked for them at once. The rest of what they had taken—money, valuables, girls—he distributed to Corymbos and his party. Euxinos and Corymbos were loath to yield Habrocomes and Anthia to Apsyrtos; yield them, however, they did. And so these two departed; but Apsyrtos took Habrocomes and Anthia, and two slaves, Leucon and Rhode, and brought them to Tyre. Their procession attracted much attention. Everyone admired their beauty, and the barbarian folk who had never before seen such comeliness thought the persons they saw were gods and felicitated Apsyrtos on the quality of the slaves he had acquired. Apsyrtos brought them to his house and turned them over to a trusted slave, whom he bade have particular care of them, for he expected large profits if he could sell them at a just price.

Such was the situation of Habrocomes and Anthia. After a few days had passed Apsyrtos departed to Syria on other business, and his daughter Manto fell in love with Habrocomes. She was pretty, and ripe for marriage, but she fell far short of Anthia's beauty. Proximity had aroused Manto's passions; she could not contain herself, and knew not what to do. To speak to Habrocomes she dared not, for she knew that he had a wife and could not hope to persuade him; nor could she speak to anyone of her people for fear of her father. Hence she burned the more ardently, and was in a wretched state. And when she could endure it no longer she determined to speak of her love to Rhode, who was Anthia's companion, her age-fellow and a girl. In her alone she hoped to find one who would assist her in her passion. Seizing then on a suitable opportunity, she took the girl to the ancestral chapel in her house and implored her not to betray her and exacted an oath, and then told of her love for Habrocomes and besought her to take her part and made large promises if she would. Said she, "Know you that you are my slave, know too that you will feel my fury, a barbarian's fury, if you do me hurt." When she had said so much she dismissed Rhode, who now found herself at an impasse. To speak to Habrocomes she abhorred, for she loved Anthia; but she dreaded the fury of the barbarian. And so she decided to tell Leucon what she had heard from Manto. Between Rhode and Leucon there was a lovers' understanding; they had been intimate even in Ephesus. Finding him alone, then, Rhode said, "We are utterly lost, Leucon; no longer shall we have our companions. The daughter of our master Apsyrtos has conceived an ardent love for Habrocomes and threatens to do us grievous hurt if she does not obtain her desire. See, then, what we have to do. To refuse a barbarian woman is a dangerous thing, to separate Habrocomes from Anthia an impossible one." When Leucon heard this he burst into tears, foreseeing great evils to come. But then he collected himself and said, "Silence, Rhode! I shall manage the whole matter."

When he had so said he went to Habrocomes. Habrocomes had no other concern than to love Anthia and to be loved by her, to talk with her and to hear her talk. Leucon approached them and said, "What are we to do, comrades? How shall we plan, fellow slaves? One of our masters, Habrocomes, finds you beautiful. The daughter of Apsyrtos is in a desperate state about you, and it is a hard thing to reject a barbarian girl in love. Be advised then as seems to you best, but save us all and do not look idly on when we are about to succumb to the fury of our masters." When Habrocomes heard this he was incensed. He glared at Leucon and said, "You scoundrel, more barbarous than the Phoenicians here, have you dared to utter such words to Habrocomes, to mention another girl when Anthia is present? A slave I am, indeed, but I know how to keep engagements. They may have power over my body, but my soul I keep free. Let Manto now threaten swords, if she will, and nooses and fire and all the tortures that can force the body of a slave: never shall I be persuaded willingly to deal unfairly with Anthia." This is what Habrocomes said, but Anthia was stupefied by the disaster and could not utter a word. Finally and with difficulty she roused herself, and she said, "I possess your heart, and I believe that I am most singularly loved by you. But I beg of you, who are master of my soul, do not betray yourself nor deliver yourself to a barbarian's fury; submit to the passion of your mistress. I shall go off somewhere and kill myself. So much I ask of you: bury me yourself, and kiss me when I have fallen, and remember Anthia." All of this plunged Habrocomes into even greater distress; he knew not what to expect. Such then was the situation in which they found themselves.

Manto, when Rhode delayed in returning, could no longer master herself, but wrote a letter to Habrocomes, in words as follows:

> *To Habrocomes the fair: thy mistress salutes thee.*
>
> Manto loves thee, and can no longer endure. Unseemly perhaps my conduct is for a maiden, but, for one who loves, necessary. I implore thee, do not scorn me, and do not affront one who has thy interests at heart. If thou hearken to me, I will persuade my father Apsyrtos to marry me to thee; we shall get rid of thy present wife, and thou wilt be rich and blessed. But if thou refuse, consider what pains thou wilt suffer when she that is affronted wreaks her vengeance, and what pains await thine associates who have proven themselves counselors to thine arrogance.

This letter she took and sealed, and gave it to one of her own servants, a barbarian woman, and bade her deliver it to Habrocomes. He received it and read it, and was sore troubled by all it said, but chiefly he was distressed by the threat to Anthia. That tablet he retained, and he wrote another and gave it to the handmaiden, of which the words were the following:

> Mistress, do what thou wilt, use my body as a slave's. If thy wish is to slay me, I am ready; if to torture me, torture as thou wilt. To thy bed I shall not come, nor should I obey in such matters even if thou command me.

When Manto received this letter she fell into fury unrestrained, compounded of all passions—envy and jealousy and pain and fear; and she planned dire punishment for the man who disdained her.

At this conjuncture Apsyrtos returned from Syria, bringing with him a young man named Moeris as a groom for his daughter. When he arrived Manto straightway staged her plot against Habrocomes. She pulled her hair apart, tore her robe in tatters, went to meet her father, fell at his knees, and cried, "Take pity, Father, upon your daughter who has been outrageously entreated by a slave. That virtuous Habrocomes has made an attempt upon my maidenhood and so has betrayed you too, saying that he was in love with me. Punish him as his infamous boldness deserves. But if you do consent to give your own daughter to slaves, I will prevent you by killing myself."

When Apsyrtos heard this he thought she spoke truth and took no thought to inquire into the matter. He summoned Habrocomes and said to him, "Creature vile and accursed, have you dared to outrage your own masters and have you sought to corrupt a maiden, yourself a slave? But you will take no pleasure from your conduct. I will punish you, I will make your horrible suffering an example for other slaves." He spoke, and, impatient and unwilling to listen, he ordered his slaves to rip Habrocomes' garments off, to bring fire and whips, and to scourge the lad. Pitiful indeed was the spectacle. The torments disfigured that whole body, which was unused to slave punishments, the blood flowed down, and his beauty faded away. They brought fearful chains and applied fire and used excruciating torments upon him—to demonstrate to his daughter's bridegroom that he would marry a virtuous maiden. In the meanwhile Anthia fell at Apsyrtos' knees and implored him on Habrocomes' behalf. But he said, "Nay, rather shall he be more cruelly tortured for your sake, for you too had he injured, loving another though he had you to wife." Then he bade them bind him in chains and incarcerate him in a dark dungeon.

Now was Habrocomes fettered and cast into prison; dark despair seized upon him, and especially when he saw no Anthia. He tried many methods of inducing death, but could find none, for those who guarded him were many. But Apsyrtos celebrated the marriage of his daughter and kept festival for many days. Anthia for her part was a mass of grief. Whenever she was able to cajole the jailers she entered in to Habrocomes secretly and lamented their catastrophe. And when the bridal company were now preparing to depart to Syria, Apsyrtos escorted his daughter with many gifts, and he presented her with Babylonian fabrics and boundless silver and gold. To his daughter Manto he presented also Anthia and Rhode and Leucon. When Anthia learned of this and knew that she would be carried to Syria with Manto, she contrived to enter the prison, and embraced Habrocomes, and said to him, "My lord, I am being taken to Syria, given as a gift to Manto; I am delivered into the hands of that jealous woman. You will remain in the prison and die pitifully, and you will have no one to care for your body. But I swear to you by the power that controls us both that I will remain yours, whether I live or whether I needs must die." So saying, she kissed him and embraced him and caressed his chains and writhed at his feet.

At length she departed out of the prison. But he, just as he was, flung himself upon the ground and wept, saying, "O my dearest Father, O Themiste my Mother! Where now is that happiness that once distinguished us in Ephesus? Where are the brilliant and famous Anthia and Habrocomes, those admired beauties? She has gone to the far ends of the earth as a captive, and I now am deprived of my sole solace and shall wretchedly die in prison and alone." When he said this sleep overtook him and there appeared to him a dream. He thought he saw his own father, Lycomedes, clothed in black, wandering over every land and sea, and finally arriving at the prison, freeing him and releasing him from the dungeon. Himself he saw then transformed to a horse and galloping over much territory in pursuit of another who was a mare; finally he found the mare and recovered his human shape. After he saw this dream he rose up, and was somewhat more hopeful.

But Habrocomes remained immured in the prison, and Anthia was taken to Syria, along with Leucon and Rhode. When those in Manto's party reached Antioch (which was Moeris' country), she dealt maliciously with Rhode, and hated Anthia bitterly. She gave orders at once that Rhode and Leucon should be loaded on a ship and sold in some place remote from the Syrian country. Anthia she planned to join to a slave, and at that to the vilest sort, a rustic goathered; this she thought a suitable vengeance. And so she summoned the goatherd, whose name was Lampo, and delivered Anthia to his hands and bade him take her to wife, and she ordered him to use force if Anthia should be unwilling. Anthia was carried off to the country to cohabit with the goatherd. But when she arrived where Lampo kept his goats she fell at his knees and begged him to pity her and preserve her chastity. She explained who she was, and told of her high birth, her husband, her captivity. When Lampo heard these things he took pity upon the girl and swore that he would verily keep her chaste and bade her take heart.

And so Anthia lived at the goatherd's in the country, lamenting Habrocomes all the while. Apsyrtos, rummaging through the cubicle where Habrocomes had lived before his punishment, came upon Manto's letter to Habrocomes. He recognized the writing, and realized that Habrocomes had been unjustly punished. He ordered that he be loosed forthwith and brought into his presence. Though he had been so disgracefully and cruelly treated, Habrocomes fell at his knees; but Apsyrtos raised him up and said, "Take heart, my boy; unjustly did I condemn you, being persuaded by my daughter's words. But now I will make you a free man instead of a slave. I will put you in charge of the management of my house, and I will procure the daughter of one of my fellow citizens to be your wife. Do not cherish evil thoughts for what has happened; it was not of my own will that I did you injury." These were the words of Apsyrtos, but Habrocomes said, "I thank you, master, for learning the truth and for recompensing my virtue." Everyone in the whole household was delighted for Habrocomes' sake, and they thanked the master on his behalf. But he himself was in deep distress because of Anthia, and frequently did he reflect to himself: "What good is freedom to me? What good is wealth and the management of Apsyrtos' affairs? That is not the sort of man I want to be. It is that girl that I would wish to find, whether

she be alive or dead." Such, then, was Habrocomes' situation. He managed Apsyrtos' affairs, indeed, but he kept thinking when and where he
might find Anthia. Now Leucon and Rhode had been carried to Xanthos,
a city in Lycia, not far from the sea, and there they were sold to a certain
old man who treated them with great consideration; he regarded them as
his own children, for he was himself childless. They passed their time in
ease and plenty, but were grieved because they no longer saw Anthia and
Habrocomes.

Now Anthia lived for some time at the goatherd's; but Moeris, Manto's husband, who visited that country place frequently, conceived a passion for Anthia. At first he tried to dissemble his love, but finally he spoke
to the goatherd and made him lavish promises if he would lend him his
efforts. For his part the goatherd agreed to Moeris' proposal, but he
feared Manto, and so went to her and informed her of Moeris' love. She
then fell into a rage and said, "Most unfortunate of all women am I. My
own rival I carry with me; through her at first in Phoenicia I was deprived
of my love, and now I risk losing my husband to her. But Anthia will
find no pleasure in having attracted Moeris too by her beauty. Here my
vengeance shall be harsher than in Tyre." For the time being Manto kept
her peace, but when Moeris was away on a journey she summoned the
goatherd and ordered him to seize Anthia, carry her into the thickest part
of the forest, and there kill her; for this service she promised to pay him
well.

The goatherd took pity on the girl, indeed, but dreaded Manto; so he
came to Anthia and told her all that had been decreed against her. She
cried out and lamented, saying, "Alas, everywhere that fatal beauty
proves a snare for both of us. Because of that beauty Habrocomes has
died in Tyre, and I die here. But I pray you, dear goatherd Lampo, deal
piously with me as you have done heretofore. If you kill me give me
burial, however humble, in the earth nearby, and place your hands over
my eyes, and as you bury me call the name of Habrocomes repeatedly.
Such a burial would be for me the happiest." So she spoke, and the goatherd took pity upon her. He reflected that he would be perpetrating an
infamous crime in killing a girl who was guilty of no wrong, and one so
fair. Though he laid hold of the girl, he could not endure to kill her.
Instead he said to her, "Anthia, you know that my mistress, Manto, has
ordered me to seize and murder you. But I fear the gods and have pity
for your beauty, and so I choose rather to sell you far away from this
country, so that Manto may not learn that you have not died and so will
not hurt me." At this Anthia wept and clasped his feet and said, "May
the gods and our ancestral deity, Artemis, render the goatherd due re-
quital for his benefactions!" She urged him then to sell her. And so the
goatherd took Anthia and went to the harbor. There he found Cilician
merchants, to whom he sold the girl, and when he had received her price

he returned to his fields. The merchants took Anthia and embarked her upon a boat, and as night came on they sailed for Cilicia. But they were caught by contrary winds, and upon the ship breaking up only few were able to reach shore by clinging to planks; these had Anthia with them. Where they landed was a dense forest, in which they wandered through the night; later they were taken captive by the brigand Hippothoos and his band.

In the meanwhile there arrived from Syria a slave bringing a letter from Manto to her father, Apsyrtos, in the words following:

> You gave me to a husband in a foreign land. Anthia, whom you presented to me along with other slaves, worked much evil against me, and I ordered her to live in a rural district. My handsome Moeris, who saw her constantly in that country place, fell in love with her. When I could no longer tolerate this situation I summoned the goatherd and bade him sell the girl again in some city of Syria.

When Habrocomes learned of this he could no longer find the heart to stay; eluding Apsyrtos and all the rest of the household, he went forth in search of Anthia. Presently he reached the countryside where Anthia had passed her days with the goatherd. He encountered that same goatherd, Lampo, to whom Manto had given Anthia to wife, and begged him to tell whether he had any knowledge of a girl from Tyre. The goatherd told him of a Tyrian girl, named Anthia, and recounted the rest—the marriage, his pious conduct toward her, the love of Moeris, the decree against her, and the journey to Cilicia. He said, too, that the girl was always speaking of one Habrocomes. Habrocomes himself did not reveal his identity, but he rose early in the morning and took horse for Cilicia, hoping to find Anthia there.

That first night, in the meanwhile, Hippothoos and his robber band spent in feasting, and on the following day they busied themselves with sacrifice. Everything was got ready—the image of Ares, wood, and garlands—and the sacrifice was due to take place in the customary fashion. Whatever victim they were going to sacrifice, whether it were human or animal, they would hang from a tree and then take position at a distance and aim their javelins at it; when they hit the mark they thought the sacrifice was acceptable to the god, and when they missed it they would renew their offerings to gain Ares' favor. For this service of sacrifice Anthia was the chosen victim. When everything was now ready and they were about to hang the girl, a crashing was heard in the forest and the beat of marching men. This was the chief of law and order in Cilicia, Perilaos by name, one of the principal personages in Cilicia. This Perilaos attacked the brigands with a large force, and dispatched them all, taking a few alive as captives. Only Hippothoos was able to escape and take his weapons with him. Anthia came into the hands of Perilaos, and when he learned of the ordeal she had been about to undergo he took pity upon her. But that pity was the beginning of great woe for Anthia. Her and those robbers whom he had made prisoner he took to Tarsus in Cilicia. Proximity and the frequent sight of the girl led him on the path of love, and little by little Perilaos was wholly captivated by Anthia. When they arrived at Tarsus, the brigands he delivered to imprisonment, but to Anthia he paid steady court. Neither wife nor children had Perilaos, and the sum of his possessions was by no means inconsiderable; and so he urged upon Anthia that she would be all in all to him—wife and chatelaine and children. At first Anthia refused, but since she had no means of rejecting his vehemence and his great persistence, and feared lest he might grow so bold as to use violence, she finally agreed, indeed, to the marriage, but pleaded with him to wait for a short period, as much as thirty days, and to keep her untouched in the interval, alleging some pretext or other for her request. Perilaos agreed and swore he would preserve her untouched until the stated period should elapse.

And so Anthia remained in Tarsus with Perilaos, awaiting the season of her marriage. Now Habrocomes proceeded on his road to Cilicia. Not far from the cave of the brigands (he had wandered from the straight road) he encountered Hippothoos, who was fully armed. When the latter saw him he ran to meet him and greeted him in friendly wise and invited him to share the road with him. "Whoever you may be, my boy," said he, "I see that you are handsome to look at and have a manly bearing. Your wandering about indicates that you have somehow been wronged. Let us leave Cilicia behind, then, and go to Cappadocia and to Pontus; those that live there, they say, are happy." Habrocomes said nothing of his search for Anthia, but he agreed to the proposal of Hippothoos, who was insistent, and they swore to render one another co-operation and assistance. It was Habrocomes' hope that in the course of much wandering he might find Anthia. For that day, then, they returned to the cave, to spend as much of it as was left in refreshing themselves and their horses. For Hippothoos, too, had a horse, which he kept concealed in the forest.

3   On the next day they left Cilicia and made their way toward Mazacos, a large and beautiful city in Cappadocia. There Hippothoos had it in mind to recruit a body of rugged young men and to reconstitute his robber band. As they proceeded through large villages they found a great abundance of all necessaries. Hippothoos was familiar with the Cappadocian language, and everyone treated him like a native. After ten days of travel they arrived at Mazacos; there they found lodging near the city gates, and they resolved to spend some days in refreshing themselves from the laborious journey. It chanced as they were feasting that Hippo-

thoos fetched a deep sigh and began to weep. Habrocomes inquired what the cause of his tears might be. "Mine is a long history," said Hippothoos, "and one rich in tragedy." Habrocomes begged him to speak, and promised that he would recount his own history in turn. They happened to be alone, and so Hippothoos, beginning his tale at the beginning, related the following narrative of his life:

"By birth I belong to the city of Perinthos, which lies near Thrace, and my family is among the most distinguished in that place. You have surely heard tell how celebrated a city Perinthos is, and how happy its inhabitants are. In Perinthos, when I was still young, I fell in love with a lad; he was a native boy, and his name was Hyperanthes. My love first began when I saw him wrestling in the gymnasium, and I could not contain myself. When a local festival that included all-night vigils was being celebrated, I approached Hyperanthes and implored him to take pity on me; and when the lad heard all my story he promised to show me compassion. The first stages of love were kisses and fondlings and (on my part) abundant tears. Finally we seized an opportunity to be alone together; our equal age obviated suspicion.

"For a long time we were together and loved one another passionately, until some deity begrudged us. There came from Byzantium (Byzantium is near Perinthos) a certain man who held great influence there; he was proud and rich, and he was called Aristomachos. As soon as this man set foot in Perinthos—as if some deity had specifically sent him to my bane—he caught sight of Hyperanthes and was straightway smitten; he admired the lad's beauty—which was indeed enough to allure anyone. And, having fallen in love, he could not keep his passion within moderation, but immediately sent proposals to the boy. When this proved futile (for Hyperanthes would admit no one because of his affection for me) he persuaded the lad's father, who was a vile creature with a weakness for money. The father delivered Hyperanthes over to the man on the pretext of education, for he was an accomplished rhetorician. So the man took him, and at first kept him shut up fast, and afterwards went off to Byzantium with him. I abandoned all my own concerns and followed, and on every possible occasion I was in the lad's company; but the occasions were few indeed; a rare kiss fell to my lot, a snatch of difficult conversation—there were too many people to keep watch.

"Finally, when I could endure it no longer, I roused myself to action; I returned to Perinthos, sold everything I possessed, and with the moneys I collected I went to Byzantium. I took a dagger (this had been agreed to by Hyperanthes), entered Aristomachos' house at night, and found him lying beside the boy; filled with fury, I struck Aristomachos a fatal blow. It was quiet and everyone was asleep, and I departed as secretly as I had come, taking Hyperanthes with me. All that night we made our way to Perinthos, and at once, none being privy, we went aboard ship and sailed for Asia. Up to a point our voyage prospered well, but presently, when we were near Lesbos, a mighty gale struck us and overturned our vessel. I swam along with Hyperanthes, supporting him and making his swimming lighter; but when night came the boy could no longer sustain the effort and gave over swimming and so died. I did what I could to get the body safe to land and bury it. Much did I weep and groan, and I collected the remains; and when I succeeded in securing a suitable stone I set up a marker on the grave, and as a memorial of the unfortunate lad I inscribed upon it an epitaph which I composed on the spur of the moment:

This monument hath Hippothoos fashioned for famous Hyperanthes,
Not worthy of a sacred citizen deceased,
A famous flower, whom on a time from land to the deep a deity
Ravished in the sea, when a stiff gale blew.

"Thereafter I determined not to return to Perinthos, and directed my footsteps through Asia to great Phrygia and Pamphylia. There, for want of livelihood and in discouragement at my lot, I devoted myself to brigandage. At first I became an underling in a robber band, but eventually I myself set up such a band in Cilicia. I achieved a great reputation, until, shortly before I caught sight of you, the men of my company were taken prisoner. Such then is the narrative of my fortunes. And now do you, dear friend, tell me your story, for it is plainly by reason of some great compulsion that you lead a vagabond existence."

Habrocomes said that he was of Ephesus, that he fell in love with a girl and had married her, and then he told of the oracles, the voyage abroad, the pirates, Apsyrtos, Manto, the imprisonment, the escape, the goatherd, and the journey to Cilicia. While he was yet speaking Hippothoos joined in his lamentations, saying, "O my parents, O my country which I shall nevermore behold, O Hyperanthes dearer to me than all! You, Habrocomes, will see your beloved, and someday will recover her; but I can never see Hyperanthes again." As he spoke he showed a lock of his beloved's hair, and wept over it. Now when they had both had their fill of sorrow Hippothoos looked at Habrocomes and said, "One episode I omitted in my narrative. A little before the robber band was made prisoner, there arrived at our cave a beautiful girl who had lost her way. She was of the same age as yours, and mentioned your home city as her fatherland; I learned nothing more about her. We decided to sacrifice her to Ares, and all was in readiness when our pursuers launched their attack. I myself escaped; what became of her I do not know. She was very beautiful, Habrocomes; she was simply dressed, her hair was yellow, her eyes charming." While he was yet speaking Habrocomes cried out, "It is my Anthia that you have seen, Hippothoos! Whither can she have fled? What country holds her now? To Cilicia let us return, and there search for her; she cannot be far from the robbers' cave. Verily, by the soul of Hyperanthes, I implore you, do not willfully wrong me, but let us go where we shall be able to find Anthia!" Hippothoos promised to do all in his power, but declared that it was essential for them to enlist a few men for the sake of safety on the road.

This, then, was their situation, and they pondered how they might best make their way back to Cilicia. But for Anthia the thirty days had now passed, and preparations were on foot for her marriage to Perilaos. Sacrificial animals had been brought in from the country, and there was a great abundance of other things. All his relatives and friends had gathered together to share in the festivities and many of his fellow citizens joined in the celebration for Anthia's marriage.

At the time when Anthia was rescued from the robber band there came to Tarsus an elderly Ephesian, Eudoxos by name and a physician by profession; sailing toward Egypt, his ship had been wrecked near the Cilician shore. This Eudoxos went about soliciting all the gentry of Tarsus, asking some for clothing and others for money, and recounting his misfortunes to each. He approached Perilaos also, and told him that he was an Ephesian and a physician by profession. Perilaos took him up, and brought him to Anthia, thinking that she would be overjoyed to see a man from Ephesus. She gave Eudoxos a friendly welcome, and inquired whether he had any news to tell of her own people. He said that he had been long absent from Ephesus and so had no tidings; nonetheless Anthia took pleasure in his society, for it brought to her mind memories of people at home. And thus Eudoxos became a familiar of the household and frequently addressed himself to Anthia; he enjoyed all the resources of the house, but always besought her to have him sent back to Ephesus, for he had a wife and children in that city.

Now when all preparations had been completed for the marriage of Perilaos and the day was at hand, a sumptuous feast was prepared for them and Anthia was decked out in bridal array. But neither by night nor by day had she surcease of tears; always she had Habrocomes before her eyes. Many thoughts coursed through her mind—her love, her oaths, her country, her parents, her constraint, her marriage. And when she found herself alone she seized the occasion and tore her hair and said, "Ah, wholly unjust am I and wicked, for I do not requite Habrocomes' loyalty to me. To remain my husband, he endured fetters and torture, and now may somewhere lie dead; but I am oblivious to all these things, and am being married, wretch that I am, and someone will chant the hymeneal over me and I shall go to the bed of Perilaos. But ah, Habrocomes, dearest soul of all, do not afflict yourself over me; never willingly would I wrong you. I come to join you, and until death will remain your bride."

Thus she said, and when Eudoxos, the Ephesian physician, came to her, she led him aside to a certain vacant chamber, and fell at his knees and petitioned him not to reveal anything she would say to anyone, and exacted an oath by their ancestral deity, Artemis, that he would help her in whatever way she would request. Eudoxos raised her up as she wailed disconsolately, and bade her take heart, and promised upon oath that he would do everything. She told him then of her love for Habrocomes, of the oaths she had sworn to him, and of their engagements in regard to chastity. And then she said, "If it were possible for me, being alive, to recover Habrocomes alive, or else to flee from this place in secret, I should take counsel for such courses. But since Habrocomes is dead and it is impractical for me to escape and impossible to abide the approaching marriage—for I will neither transgress my pledges to Habrocomes nor will I despise an oath—do you then be my helper; find me somewhere a drug which will release wretched me from my tribulations. In return for this service you will receive much recompense from the gods, whom I shall ardently and frequently beseech on your behalf before my death, and I myself will give you money and arrange your return to Ephesus. Before anyone discovers anything that has transpired, you will be able to take ship and sail to Ephesus. And when you arrive there inquire for my parents, Megamedes and Evippe, and give them a report of my death and all that happened on my travels; say, too, that Habrocomes has perished."

When she had so spoken she writhed at his feet and implored him not to refuse to give her the poison. Then she produced twenty minae of silver and her necklaces (all things she had in abundance, for all Perilaos' property was at her disposal) and gave them to Eudoxos. He deliberated for a long while: he pitied the girl for her misfortunes, he yearned to return to Ephesus, he coveted the money and the jewels; and so he promised to give her the drug, and went off to fetch it. She, in the meantime, was sunk in grief. She lamented her youth and was anguished at the thought of her untimely death; and frequently she called upon Habrocomes as though he were present. After no long while Eudoxos arrived bringing a drug, not lethal, however, but only hypnotic, so that no real harm should come to the girl and he himself meanwhile make arrangements for travel and be on his way. Anthia received the potion, thanked him warmly, and dismissed him. He then took ship and sailed away, and Anthia awaited a suitable moment for imbibing the poison.

Now was night fallen, and the bridal chamber was made ready, and those charged with the duty came to lead Anthia forth. She did go forth, all unwilling and suffused with tears, and she held the drug hidden in her hand. When she drew near the bridal chamber the members of the household chanted the propitious hymeneal, but Anthia grieved and wept, saying, "Just so, upon a time, was I led to my bridegroom, Habrocomes, and the torches of love escorted us, and the hymeneal was sung for our propitious union. And now what will you do, Anthia? Will you wrong Habrocomes, your husband, who loves you, who has died because of you? Nay, I am not so cowardly nor have my misfortunes made me so fearful. It is resolved: I shall drink the drug. Habrocomes must be my only husband; him do I desire though he is dead." This she said, and she was conducted in to the bridal chamber.

And now she found herself alone, for Perilaos was still feasting with his friends. She pretended that the agitation had made her thirsty, and bade one of the servants to bring her water to drink. And when the cup was brought, she took it, when no one was by, and cast the drug into it, and she wept, saying, 'Ah, dearest soul, Habrocomes, lo, I discharge my promises to you, and I embark upon my journey to you, an unhappy journey but an inevitable one. Receive me gladly, and make my sojourn there with you a happy one." When she had so spoken she drank up the drug. Immediately sleep held her fast and she fell to the ground; the drug had accomplished its full task.

When Perilaos entered the chamber, as soon as he caught sight of Anthia lying unconscious, he was stunned and cried out. There was a great tumult among the whole household, and mingled emotions—lamentations and horror and stupefaction. Some were moved by pity for the girl seemingly dead, others sympathized with Perilaos' affliction, all bewailed what had happened. Perilaos rent his garments and threw himself upon the body, saying, "Ah, my dearest girl: before your marriage, alas, you have left your lover behind, his destined bride of but a few days. . . . Is it the tomb to which we shall bring you as a bridal chamber? Happy indeed that Habrocomes, whoever he was, truly blessed is he, receiving such a gift from his beloved." So he lamented, and he held all her body close, and caressed her hands and feet, saying, "My poor bride, my more unhappy wife." Then he adorned her, wrapping rich robes about her body and decking it with much gold. The sight of her was too much for his endurance, and when day dawned he placed Anthia (who lay unconscious) upon a bier and conveyed her to the cemetery near the city. There he deposited her in a funerary chamber, having immolated many victims and consumed many garments and other attire in flames.

When he had completed the customary rites Perilaos was conducted back to the city by his household. Anthia, who had been left in the tomb, recovered her consciousness, and when she realized that the potion had not been lethal she groaned and wept, saying, "Ah, drug that has deceived me, that has prevented me from pursuing my happy journey to Habrocomes. Wholly hapless as I am, I am balked even in my yearning for death. But it is yet possible for me to remain in this tomb and by starvation bring the work of the drug to accomplishment. From here none shall remove me, nor would I look upon the sun, nor shall I rise to the light of day." Thus saying she made her heart firm and awaited death with fortitude.

In the meanwhile certain robbers had learned that the girl had received a rich burial, that much female finery had been deposited with her,
and a large quantity of silver and gold; when night fell they approached
the tomb and broke through the doors of the vault and entered it. They
laid hands on the valuables, and beheld Anthia alive. They reckoned that
this too would be a great profit, so they raised the girl up and wished to
carry her off. But she humbled herself at their feet and petitioned them
earnestly, saying, "Sirs, whoever you may be, all this attire, as much as
there is, and the things buried with me here, take and carry off; but spare
my person. I am consecrated to two deities, Love and Death: leave me
free for my devotion to them. I pray you, in the name of your own ancestral gods, do not show to the light of day one whose misfortunes deserve
night and darkness." Thus she spoke, but could not persuade the robbers. They brought her out of the tomb and conducted her down to the
sea and placed her upon a boat, upon which they sailed for Alexandria.
On the vessel they tended her well and bade her take heart. But she reflected upon the evils into which she was again fallen, and lamented and
moaned, saying, "Again brigands and the sea, again am I a captive. But
now I am the more wretched, for I am not with Habrocomes. What country will now receive me? What manner of men shall I see? Never, I pray,
a Moeris, never Manto, never Perilaos, never Cilicia. But may I come
where I might at least see the tomb of Habrocomes!" Whenever she
thought upon these things she wept. She herself would take no drink and
no sustenance, but the robbers compelled her to do so. They prosecuted
their voyage, and after many days' sailing arrived at Alexandria. There
they disembarked Anthia, and resolved to sell her to certain merchants
forthwith.

Perilaos for his part learned that the tomb had been broken open and
the body spirited away, and suffered affliction great and intolerable. Now
Habrocomes pursued his search and busily inquired whether anyone had
any knowledge of a foreign girl who had been taken captive by robbers
and carried off. When he could discover nothing he was wearied and
returned where they lodged. Those with Hippothoos had prepared a
meal for them, and the others, too, dined with them. But Habrocomes
was low in spirits and threw himself upon the couch and wept; there he
lay, and would take no food. As those in Hippothoos' company proceeded with their drinking a certain old woman there present, named
Chrysion, began to tell a story. "Listen, friends," said she, "to a tale of a
thing that lately happened in the city. A man called Perilaos, one of the
important people here, was elected chief of law and order in Cilicia, and
went out to search for brigands. He did arrest some robbers and brought
them in, and with them was a beautiful girl; her he persuaded to marry
him. All the preparations for the wedding were completed, and the girl
entered the bridal chamber. Then, whether she had gone mad or because

she was in love with some other she drank poison she had somehow procured, and died. So the manner of her death was described."

When Hippothoos heard this he said, "That is the very girl for whom Habrocomes is searching." Habrocomes too had heard the tale, but had let it pass because he was so dispirited. But at the sound of Hippothoos' voice he finally, and with difficulty, aroused himself and said: "Now of a certainty is Anthia dead; but perhaps her grave is here and her body is safe." So saying, he besought the old woman, Chrysion, to conduct him to Anthia's tomb and show him the body. But she fetched a deep sigh and said, "Now comes the most unfortunate thing of all that has befallen that unhappy girl. For his part Perilaos buried her sumptuously and provided ornaments; but robbers who learned of the valuables buried with her broke open the tomb and carried off the ornaments and spirited the body away. Perilaos has instituted an intense investigation into the affair." When Habrocomes heard this he tore his tunic to tatters and wailed loudly for Anthia, who had so nobly and chastely died, but who had so unhappily perished after her death. "What robber," he cried, "is so passionate a lover as to lust even for your corpse and snatch your dead body away? Wretch that I am, I am deprived even of your remains, my only solace. Now am I altogether determined to die; but first I must endure until I find your body, and when I have embraced it I shall bury myself along with it." So he said in his grief; but Hippothoos and his company bade him take heart. Then they went to their rest for all that night.

But the mind of Habrocomes was invaded by many thoughts—of Anthia, of her death, of her burial, of her loss. And then, when he could no longer endure it, without attracting notice (drink had put Hippothoos and his friends into a deep sleep) he went out as if to satisfy some need, and made his way down to the sea. There he came upon a boat about to depart for Alexandria; upon this he embarked and sailed, hoping that he might overtake in Egypt the robbers who had plundered and ravaged all. In this course his guide was the hope of despair. And so Habrocomes sailed to Alexandria. In the morning Hippothoos and his friends were chagrined at his departure, but when they had taken a few days to refresh themselves they determined to proceed toward Syria and Phoenicia to engage in brigandage.

Now the robbers had sold Anthia to merchants in Alexandria and had received a high price for her. These merchants fed her lavishly and tended her person, being always on the lookout for a purchaser who would pay a just price. There had come to Alexandria from India a prince of that country for the purpose of seeing the sights of the city and of transacting business; his name was Psammis. This Psammis saw Anthia in the merchants' establishment and was much taken with the sight: he paid the merchants their high price, and took the girl to be his handmaid.

No sooner had that barbarian fellow bought her than he attempted to force her in order to satisfy his desires. Anthia was unwilling and at first refused; then she pretended to Psammis (your barbarian is superstitious by nature) that at her birth her father had consecrated her to Isis until the season of her marriage, and she declared that the period had still a year to run. "If you commit an outrage upon a maiden dedicated to the goddess," she added, "the goddess will grow angry and her punishment will be hard." Psammis was persuaded by the story; he prostrated himself to the goddess and abstained from Anthia.

And so Anthia was under watch in the house of Psammis, and supposed to be consecrated to Isis. But the ship which carried Habrocomes missed the course to Alexandria and was cast up near the mouth of the Nile called Paralion, by the shores of Phoenicia. As the crew came tumbling out of their ship they were overrun by shepherds of the region. These plundered their cargo and threw the men into chains, and then brought them by a long desert trail to Pelusium, a city of Egypt; there they sold one to one purchaser and another to another. Habrocomes was purchased by a veteran soldier who was retired, named Araxos. This Araxos had a wife who was ugly to look at but much worse to listen to; her intemperance passed imagination, and her name was Bitch. Bitch conceived a passion for Habrocomes as soon as he was brought into the house; nor could she at all refrain herself, but was terrible in her love and terrible in her desire to give play to her passion. Araxos for his part was fond of Habrocomes and treated him as a son; but Bitch spoke to him only of sex and begged him to consent and promised to take him for a husband and to kill Araxos. To Habrocomes this seemed monstrous, and at the same time he thought much of Anthia, of the oaths, and of the chastity which had already cost him much woe. But finally he assented to Bitch's insistence. When night came Bitch killed Araxos, with a view to having Habrocomes as her husband, and she told Habrocomes what she had done. But Habrocomes could not tolerate so uninhibited a woman, and so he departed from the house and left her behind, declaring that he could never lie beside so foul a murderess. But Bitch collected herself, and at daybreak went to where the populace of Pelusium congregated; there she bewailed her husband and said that a newly bought slave had murdered him. She lamented long and loud, and the multitude believed that she spoke the truth. Immediately they arrested Habrocomes, and then sent him in chains to the then governor of Egypt. And so Habrocomes was taken to Alexandria to pay the penalty for his alleged murder of his master, Araxos.

4   Now Hippothoos and his company moved from Tarsus and proceeded toward Syria, making themselves master of everything that came in their way. Villages they burned, and they massacred many people.

Sweeping on in this manner, they arrived at Laodicea in Syria, and there they sojourned, not, however, as robbers, but as if they had come to see the sights of the city. There Hippothoos particularly busied himself to see whether he could find Habrocomes, but his efforts were futile. And so the men refreshed themselves, and then turned to the road toward Phoenicia, and thence toward Egypt, for they had decided to overrun Egypt. When they had assembled a large band of robbers they marched toward Pelusium, then sailed the river Nile to Egyptian Hermopolis and Schedia. Then they entered the canal of the river constructed under Menelaos, and so by-passed Alexandria but reached Memphis, the sacred city of Isis, and then Mende. From the natives, too, they recruited men to share their robber life and to serve them as guides of the way. They passed through Taua and arrived at Leontopolis, and then passed not a few other villages, of which the greater number were undistinguished [*emended text:* "they extinguished"] and arrived at Coptos, which is near Ethiopia. There they decided to set up their practice of brigandage, for the route was much frequented by merchants who traveled regularly to Ethiopia or to India. Moreover their band now amounted to five hundred men; and so when they had seized the heights on the Ethiopian side and had put their caves in order, they resolved to plunder those that traveled past.

The people of Pelusium had sent to the ruler of Egypt an account of what had happened there—that Araxos had been murdered and that it was a slave who had dared perpetrate the deed. When Habrocomes came to him, therefore, he knew all the details, and, not troubling to make inquiries concerning what had in fact taken place, he ordered the men who had brought Habrocomes to fix him to a cross. His many troubles had made Habrocomes lethargic, and he consoled himself for his imminent death by the thought that Anthia too had died. Those to whom the task was assigned brought him to the banks of the Nile where a sheer cliff looked out upon the channel of the river. There they set up their cross and attached him to it, making his hands and feet fast with ropes; for such was the procedure in crucifixion among the people of that region. Then they left him and departed, for the man crucified was secure.

But Habrocomes turned his eyes to the sun, and then looked upon the stream of the Nile, and said, "O thou of gods most benevolent to man, who dost hold Egypt in thy sway and hast made earth and sea appear to all mankind: if Habrocomes has committed any wrong, may I perish miserably and undergo even crueller punishment than this, if such there be; but if I have been betrayed by a lewd woman, may the stream of Nile never be polluted by the body of a man unjustly done to death, and may you never look upon the spectacle of a man innocent of any wrong perishing here in thy land." So he prayed, and the god had compassion upon him. Suddenly a gust of wind arose and smote the cross and crumbled the earth of the cliff upon which the cross was fixed. Habrocomes fell into the stream and was borne along, and neither did the water injure him nor his bonds impede him nor wild beasts do him hurt; but the flood was his escort, and he was borne along until he reached the mouth of the Nile, where it empties into the sea. There those who were posted as guards seized him and brought him to the administrator of Egypt as a fugitive from punishment.

The governor was even more deeply incensed and thought this a consummate wickedness; he therefore ordered his men to erect a pyre, place Habrocomes upon it, and consume him in flames. And now all was made ready: the pyre was built at the mouth of the Nile, Habrocomes was placed upon it, the pyre was kindled. But just as the flame was on the point of enveloping his body, Habrocomes again prayed briefly, as best he was able, that he be saved from instant destruction. Then did the Nile rise in waves and its stream poured over the pyre and extinguished its flames. To those present the event seemed miraculous; they took Habrocomes and brought him to the ruler of Egypt and recounted the circumstances and explained the intercession of the Nile. When he heard what had happened the governor marveled, and he gave orders that Habrocomes should be under guard, indeed, in prison, but that every care should be shown him, ". . . until," he said, "we learn who this man is, and why it is that the gods are so concerned for him."

And so Habrocomes was kept in prison. But Psammis, who had purchased Anthia, resolved to depart to his own home, and made all things ready for the journey. His travels would take him to Upper Egypt and toward Ethiopia, where Hippothoos' robber band was located. Everything was in the best of order: there were many camels and asses and sumpter horses, there was an abundance of gold and also of silver, there were many garments, and Anthia too was carried along. She, when she had passed Alexandria and was now in Memphis, took position before the temple of Isis and prayed to her as follows: "O thou greatest of divinities, until now I have remained chaste, for I was believed to be thine, and I have preserved my marriage to Habrocomes unsullied. But now I am on my way to India, a far stretch of land from Ephesus, far from the remains of Habrocomes. Either, then, deliver me, the unfortunate, from this place and return me to Habrocomes in life, or, if it is inexorably fated that we die apart from one another, accomplish this: let me remain chaste to him that is dead." Thus she prayed, and they proceeded on their way. They had passed through Coptos and were ascending the hills of Ethiopia, when Hippothoos fell upon them. Psammis himself he killed, and many of those with him; and he took possession of the chattels and made Anthia prisoner. When he had gathered together all the booty that had been taken, he carried it to the cave which they had designated as the depository of their acquisitions. Thither went Anthia also; she did not recognize Hippothoos, nor did Hippothoos recognize Anthia. And when he inquired of her who she might be and whence, she did not speak the truth, but declared that she was a native Egyptian and that her name was Memphitis. And so Anthia abode in the robbers' den with Hippothoos.

In the meanwhile the ruler of Egypt summoned Habrocomes and made detailed inquiries of him and learned his story. He pitied his lot and gave him money and promised to bring him to Ephesus. Habrocomes thanked the governor warmly for his deliverance, and requested that he be permitted instead to continue his search for Anthia. And so he received rich gifts and embarked upon a vessel and sailed for Italy, with a view to making inquiries concerning Anthia in that region. The ruler of Egypt, having now learned how Araxos has met his death, had Bitch brought to him and crucified her.

While Anthia was in the den, one of the robbers who kept watch over her, Anchialos by name, fell in love with her. This Anchialos was one of those who had followed Hippothoos from Syria, being a Laodicean by birth; Hippothoos had high regard for him, for he was energetic and had great authority in the robber band. When Anchialos fell in love with Anthia he first addressed her with persuasive words, thinking to himself that he would so win her and ask Hippothoos for her as a gift. But she rejected every argument and allowed nothing to trouble her, neither the cave nor bonds nor a menacing brigand. She still kept herself pure for Habrocomes, even though she believed him dead, and frequently would she cry out, whenever she was able to escape notice, "Habrocomes' wife only do I wish to remain, even if I must die, even if I must suffer affliction worse than I have suffered." Her attitude reduced Anchialos to greater distress, and the daily sight of Anthia added fuel to his love. And when he could no longer endure it he resolved to use violence. Once upon a night when Hippothoos with the others was gone on a foray, he arose against Anthia and attempted to force her. Finding herself in an ineluctable extremity, she seized a sword that was lying by and struck Anchialos, and the blow proved fatal. For while he was about to embrace her and kiss her and was leaning his whole body over her, she brought the point of the sword against his chest and so smote him. And so Anchialos received condign punishment for his wicked passion.

But Anthia was overwhelmed by fear for what she had done, and turned many plans over in her mind: now that she would kill herself—but she still had a vestige of hope for Habrocomes; now that she would flee from the cave—but this was impractical, for there was no easy road or anyone to give her guidance. And so she resolved to remain in the cave and endure whatever her fate would decree. So, then, did she pass that night, getting no sleep, her mind occupied with many thoughts. But when day came, there arrived Hippothoos and his company, and they saw Anchialos done to death and Anthia near the body. They conjectured what had happened, and when they questioned Anthia they learned all. Filled with wrath at the deed, they determined to avenge their deceased friend and considered various modes of punishing Anthia. One urged that she be killed and buried with the body of Anchialos, another that she be crucified. Hippothoos, who was sorely grieved at his comrade's death, devised a punishment yet more cruel. He bade them dig a trench, wide and deep, and in it cast Anthia together with two mastiffs, that she might thus meet with retribution appropriate to the brazenness of her crime. His men did as they were ordered, and Anthia was taken to the trench, and with her the dogs; these were of Egyptian breed, large and vicious and of terrible aspect. Now when they had cast them all into the pit, they placed wooden beams over it and heaped earth over them—the place was but little distant from the Nile—and set one of the robbers, Amphinomos by name, to stand guard over it.

This Amphinomos had even before this been smitten by Anthia, and now he had greater compassion for her and pitied her unhappy lot; and so he bethought him how she might prolong her life and how the dogs might be prevented from harming her. Each day, then, he removed the beams that closed the pit, and threw into it loaves of bread and provided water, and therewith exhorted Anthia to be of good cheer. The dogs, being well fed, did her no hurt, but became gentle and docile. But Anthia, taking thought of herself and reflecting upon her plight, lamented: "Woe is me for my afflictions! What punishment is this that I endure—a pit, a prison, mastiffs shut in with me—who are yet gentler far than the brigands. Now are my sufferings, Habrocomes, like yours. You too endured similar affliction; you were imprisoned in Tyre when I left you. Yet if you are alive these woes are nothing: someday, perhaps, we shall yet possess one another. But if you are dead, then it is in vain that I endeavor to live, in vain does my benefactor, whoever he may be, take pity on my lot." Thus she said, and she lamented incessantly. And so Anthia was immured in the pit with the dogs, and Amphinomos consoled her daily, and by feeding the dogs made them tractable.

5 Now Habrocomes, pursing his voyage from Egypt, did not indeed reach Italy itself, for his ship was buffeted by a gale and strayed from its course, but was carried to Sicily and reached the large and handsome city of Syracuse. Arrived there, Habrocomes resolved to traverse the island and to make inquiries for Anthia; with luck he might obtain information. He took lodging near the sea in the house of an old man named Aigialeus, who was a fisherman by trade. Now this Aigialeus was a poor man and an alien, and scarcely able to keep himself by his trade; nevertheless he welcomed Habrocomes gladly, and regarded him as his own son, and showed him singular affection. Once on a time, as result of their great familiarity with one another, Habrocomes recounted the whole story of

his life to the old man, speaking of Anthia and his love and his wanderings; and then Aigialeus in turn began the narrative of his own life.

"Habrocomes, my child," said he, "I am neither Sicilian nor a native, but a Spartiate of Lacedaemonia, and among the most powerful and the wealthiest of the Spartans. When I was young I fell in love with a girl who was also Spartan, Thelxinoe by name, and Thelxinoe returned my love. When a festival vigil was being celebrated in the city, we came together one with the other, some deity guiding each of us on his way, and we took our joy of the object for which we had come together. For a space of time we consorted with one another, keeping our union secret, and we repeatedly swore to remain faithful to one another unto death. But some god must have begrudged us. While I was still in the cadet classification, her parents gave Thelxinoe in marriage to a young Spartan named Androcles, who was already, in fact, in love with Thelxinoe. At first the girl contrived numerous pretexts to postpone the marriage, and finally, when she found an opportunity to meet with me, she agreed to leave Lacedaemonia with me by night. We attired ourselves in the garb of young men, and I even shore Thelxinoe of her hair. On the very night of the marriage we departed from the city and proceeded to Argos and Corinth, and there we took ship and sailed to Sicily. When the Lacedaemonians learned of the flight they condemned us to death.

"We, for our part, lived our lives here, in actual want of necessities, yet in great happiness and as if we enjoyed abundance of all things, because we were together. Here, not long ago, Thelxinoe died. Her body is not buried; I keep it with me, and always I kiss it and consort with it." So saying, he led Habrocomes into an inner room and showed him Thelxinoe, who was quite an old woman; but in Aigialeus' eyes she was still the beautiful girl. Her body the old man had embalmed in the Egyptian manner, for he understood the technique. "With her, Habrocomes, my child," the old man continued, "I always talk as if she were alive, and I lie by her side, and I take my meals with her; and whenever I come home weary from my fishing she looks at me affectionately and comforts me. Not as she looks to you now does she appear in my sight. I conceive of her, my child, just as she was in Lacedaemonia, just as she was when we eloped; I conceive of her as she was on that festival vigil; I conceive of her as she was when we pledged our troth."

Even while Aigialeus was yet speaking Habrocomes began lamenting and said, "Ah, Anthia, girl unhappiest of all! When shall I ever find you, even a corpse? Aigialeus possesses a great solace for his life in the body of Thelxinoe, and now have I truly learned that true love has no limits of age. I am a vagabond over every land and sea, and yet have I not been able to hear any tidings of you. Oh, unhappy oracles! O Apollo, thou that hast foretold for us prophecies most grievous of all, do thou now take pity upon us and reveal the consummation of thine oracles!" So

sorrowing, Habrocomes passed his time in Syracuse, and Aigialeus offered him comfort, and now he shared in Aigaleus' craft.

Now Hippothoos and his company had greatly enlarged their robber
band, and they resolved to abandon Ethiopia and now to undertake
larger enterprises. No longer did Hippothoos deem it sufficient to waylay
individual travelers; now he would attack whole villages and cities. And
so he mustered his company and loaded all his baggage (he possessed
many pack animals and not a few camels), and left Ethiopia behind him.
He proceeded toward Egypt and Alexandria, with the intention of continuing to Phoenicia and again to Syria. Anthia he now believed dead.
But Amphinomos, who had kept guard over her in the pit, was deeply in
love with her, and he could not abide being separated from the girl, both
because of his affection for her and because of her imminent danger. He
therefore did not follow Hippothoos, escaping notice because of the great
multitude who did, and hid in a certain cave where he had cached a
supply of provisions. When night fell Hippothoos and his company arrived at a village of Egypt called Areia, which they meant to ravage; but
Amphinomos dug open the trench and brought Anthia out and spoke
comforting words to her. When she was still frightened and still suspi-
cious, he swore by the sun and by the gods of Egypt that he would preserve her chastity until such time as she herself should be persuaded and
willingly consent. Anthia trusted Amphinomos' pledges and followed
him; nor did the dogs leave them, for they had become used to their
company and lovingly attended them. They came then to Coptos, and
there they resolved to remain until Hippothoos and his company should
be farther on their way. They took care also that the dogs should have
plentiful food.

Hippothoos' band had now attacked the village of Areia, and had
killed many of its inhabitants and burned their houses down. Their journey they continued not by the same land route but on the Nile. They had
collected all the water craft from the intervening villages, and on these
they embarked and sailed to Schedia, where they disembarked, and then
passed through the remainder of Egypt along the banks of the Nile. In
the meanwhile the ruler of Egypt had been informed concerning the raid
on Areia and the activities of Hippothoos' brigands, and he learned also
that they were proceeding to Ethiopia. He therefore mustered a large
force of soldiers and appointed as their commander one of his own kinsmen, Polyidos by name, a young man charming in appearance and vigorous in action; him he sent against the brigands. This Polyidos and his
force encountered Hippothoos' troop near Pelusium, and a battle between them took place immediately on the banks of the river. Many fell
on either side, but when night came on the brigands turned in flight and
were all butchered, some few prisoners being taken alive. Only Hippothoos, having thrown his arms away, escaped during the night and

reached Alexandria. There he succeeded in escaping recognition, embarked on a vessel on the point of sailing, and put to sea. His great desire was to get to Sicily, for there he thought he could best avoid detection and most easily obtain a livelihood; he had heard that the island was both extensive and prosperous.

Polyidos did not think it sufficient merely to have vanquished the brigands he met in battle, but determined that all Egypt must be thoroughly searched and purged, and in particular he wished to apprehend Hippothoos or any of his company that might be at large. He took a portion of his soldiery, therefore, and those of the robbers that had been made prisoner, so that they might give information if any brigand were encountered, and sailed up the Nile, with the intention of proceeding as far as Ethiopia. The cities he passed he ransacked thoroughly, and in due course came also to Coptos, where Anthia was sojourning with Amphinomos. Anthia happened to be at home, but Amphinomos was recognized by the captive brigands, who informed Polyidos of his identity. Amphinomos was seized, and upon being interrogated recounted the story of Anthia. Upon hearing his account Polyidos ordered that Anthia be brought, and when she came he inquired who she was and whence. She on her part kept the truth concealed, but declared that she was an Egyptian and had been kidnaped by the brigands. As the conversation proceeded Polyidos too (who had a wife in Alexandria) fell deeply in love with Anthia. Being in love, he tried at first to persuade her with lavish promises; but at length, as they were approaching Alexandria and had got as far as Memphis, Polyidos attempted to use force upon Anthia. She contrived to escape and went to the temple of Isis, and there assumed the posture of a suppliant. "Do thou again save me, O my lady of Egypt," said she, "whom thou hast so frequently succored in time past. Let Polyidos, too, spare me, who for thy sake am keeping myself chaste for Habrocomes." Now Polyidos revered the goddess and also loved Anthia, whose lot moved his compassion; he therefore approached the temple unattended and swore that he would never violate Anthia and never commit any outrage against her, but would preserve her chaste for as long as she herself should wish. Sufficient for his love would it be if he could merely look at her and speak with her. By these pledges was Anthia persuaded, and she quitted the temple.

Since it had been decided to take repose in Memphis for three days, Anthia visited the shrine of Apis. This is the most celebrated temple in Egypt, and here those who wish receive oracles from the god. When the visitor has offered his prayers and made his petition to the god, he himself leaves the sanctuary, and in front of the temple Egyptian children, speaking some things in prose and some in verse, declare details of future events. Anthia, too, made her obeisance to Apis, and said, "O thou most benevolent of deities to man, thou who dost show compassion to strangers, take thou pity too upon my wretched lot, and declare unto me a true oracle concerning Habrocomes. For if I am yet destined to see him and receive him as my husband, I shall patiently continue to live, but if he has died it were well for me, too, to be quit of this troublesome life." So she said, and, suffused with tears, she issued from the temple. As she did so the children playing before the temple called out altogether, "Anthia shall soon recover her own husband Habrocomes." When she heard this she became more cheerful and rendered thanks to the gods. And then, in Polyidos' company, she proceeded to Alexandria.

But his wife had learned that Polyidos was bringing back a girl with whom he was in love, and she was afraid that she would be surpassed in rivalry with the newcomer. To Polyidos she said nothing, but in her own heart she deliberated how she might avenge herself upon the woman she thought was subverting her marriage. Now Polyidos had gone to the ruler of Egypt to render an account of his campaign, and then was occupied at his headquarters, administering the duties of his office. In his absence Rhenaia (for so was Polyidos' wife called) summoned Anthia, who was left at home, and tore her clothing and disfigured her person. "Wicked woman," said she, "you plotter against my marriage, it is in vain that you seemed fair to Polyidos; that beauty will profit you little. You may have been able to allure robbers and to lie with many young bravos when they were all well drunk. But the bed of Rhenaia you will never insult with impunity." So saying, she shore Anthia's hair off and threw her into chains and delivered her to a certain faithful slave named Clytos, with orders to embark her upon a ship, carry her to Italy, and there sell her to a brothel keeper. "Now," she cried, "you will be able to fill your lust to satiety." And so Anthia was led off by Clytos, weeping and wailing, and she said, "Ah, perfidious beauty, ah, ill-starred charm, why do you abide with me to afflict me, why have you caused me so many woes? Were not burials and murders and chains and brigands enough? Must I now be displayed before a brothel, and at a whoremaster's bidding dispose of that chastity which up to now I have preserved for Habrocomes? But oh, my master," said she falling at Clytos' knees, "do not, I pray you, carry me away to foul punishment, but kill me yourself. I cannot tolerate a whoremonger as master. My way of life, believe me, is chaste." So she besought him, and Clytos took pity upon her. So Anthia was carried off to Italy. When Polyidos came home Rhenaia told him that Anthia had run away; and Anthia's past conduct induced him to believe her.

But Anthia was put ashore at Tarentum, a city in Italy, where Clytos, faithful to Rhenaia's bidding, sold her to a brothel keeper. When he perceived such beauty as he had never before seen, he thought the girl would bring him great profit. Some days of repose he gave her to refresh herself from the voyage and from the ill-treatment she had suffered at the hands of Rhenaia. Clytos returned to Alexandria and reported to Rhenaia that her orders had been carried out.

Now Hippothoos, too, had completed his voyage and landed in Sicily—not at Syracuse, however, but at Taormina—and there he looked out for some opportunity to procure the necessities of life. As for Habrocomes, as his stay in Syracuse was prolonged, he fell into a state of discouragement and helplessness because he could find neither news of Anthia nor any means of returning safe to his own country. He therefore resolved to leave Sicily and sail over to Italy, and from there, if he failed to find the object of his search, to make the sad voyage back to Ephesus. By now the parents of both and indeed all the Ephesians sorrowed deeply, for neither had any messenger nor any letters from the young couple reached them, through they sent agents in all directions to make inquiries after them. Despair and old age rendering the parents incapable of further endurance, they found their release from life. Habrocomes was now on his way to Italy. As for Leucon and Rhode, the comrades of Habrocomes and Anthia, their master had died in Xanthos and had bequeathed to them his very considerable property. They resolved to sail to Ephesus, imagining that their masters had already returned thither in safety, and being themselves satiated with the tribulations of sojourning abroad. And so they put all their possessions aboard ship and sailed for Ephesus. After a few days' voyage they put in at Rhodes, and there they learned that Habrocomes and Anthia were not yet safely returned home, and that their parents had died. They resolved then not to continue to Ephesus but for the present to sojourn in Rhodes, until they should obtain some tidings of their young masters.

Now the brothel master who had purchased Anthia compelled her, after some days had passed, to display herself before his establishment. And so, bedizening her in ornate garments and with much gilt, he exposed her to public view at the door of the stew. She then cried out bitterly, "Alas for my afflictions! Are not my previous misfortunes sufficient—prison, brigands? Must I even be forced to play the whore? Ah, beauty deservedly contemned, why do you cling to me so unseasonably? But why do I utter these lamentations? Why do I not rather find some device by which I may preserve that chastity which I have guarded up to the present?" Amid these plaints she was brought to the brothel, her master now offering encouragement and now uttering threats. When she arrived at the stew and was put on display there was a great concourse of men who marveled at her beauty, and many were eager to pay the fee and satisfy their lust.

Finding herself in this ineluctable extremity, Anthia invented a means of escape. She fell to the ground, relaxing her limbs, and imitated the state of those who suffer from what men called "the sacred disease." All present were touched by pity and fear. They forbore their desire for intercourse, but rather wished to minister to Anthia. The brothel keeper realized that his plans had miscarried; believing that the girl was truly ill, he took her to his house and made her lie down, and tended her. When she seemed to come back to herself he asked her the cause of her illness. And Anthia said, "Even before this, master, I wished to tell you my trouble and to explain what had happened, but I kept it secret because I was ashamed. But now it is no longer difficult for me to speak to you, for you have already learned all about me. Once, when I was still a child, I strayed away from my family during the celebration of a festival vigil, and came upon the grave of a man who had recently died. There it seemed to me that someone leapt out of the grave and tried to lay hold of me. I shrieked and tried to flee. The man was frightful to look upon, and his voice was more horrible still. Finally, when day broke, he let me go, but he struck me on the chest and said that he had cast this disease into me. Beginning with that day I have been afflicted with that calamity, which takes divers forms and divers occasions. But I beg of you, master, do not be angry with me; I am not to blame for this situation. You will be able to sell me, and lose no penny of the price you paid for me." When the brothel keeper heard this he was greatly annoyed, but he forgave the girl, believing that her epilepsy was not of her own choosing.

And so Anthia, simulating illness, was nursed at the house of the brothel keeper. Now Habrocomes had sailed from Sicily and made land at Nuceria in Italy, but he was at a loss for some occupation to supply his needs. At first he went about searching for Anthia, for it was she that was the object of all his life and all his vagabondage; but when he could find nothing (for the girl was in the house of the brothel keeper in Tarentum) he hired himself out to some stonecutters. To him this work was very laborious, for his body was not inured to undergo toil so intense and demanding. Thus he found himself in a miserable state, and often did he bewail his own lot, saying, "Look now, Anthia, at your Habrocomes, a laborer in a toilsome trade, his body reduced to slavery. If I could have any hope of finding you and of living the rest of my life with you, that would comfort me with the best of all solace. But now, unhappy that I am, perhaps I toil for vanity and folly, perhaps somewhere you lie dead, out of yearning for your Habrocomes. But of this, my dearest, I am certain: never at all, even in death, have you forgotten me." Thus he grieved, and with pain bore his toil.

But to Anthia, as she lay sleeping in Tarentum, a dream appeared. It seemed to her that she was with Habrocomes, she in all her beauty and he in all his beauty, and that it was the season of the beginning of their love. There appeared then another woman, also beautiful, who dragged Habrocomes away from her. Then, when Habrocomes cried out and called her by name Anthia awoke and the dream came to an end. When she reflected on the vision she leapt up and lamented sore, and believed that what she had seen was true. "Woe is me for my afflictions!" she cried. "Here am I enduring every manner of hardship, and experiencing every variety of calamity in my misery, and inventing expedients beyond a woman's powers to preserve my chastity for Habrocomes; but you have now found some other woman fair—that, surely, is what my dream signifies. Why, then, do I linger in life? Why do I afflict myself? Better it were to perish, and to be quit of this vile existence, to be quit, too, of this unseemly disgrace and perilous servitude. But if Habrocomes has in truth transgressed his oaths, may the gods refrain from punishing him: perhaps it was under duress that he did what he did. But for me it is seemly to die chaste." Thus she said in her anguish, and she sought some expedient to compass her death.

At Taormina things went hard at first with Hippothoos the Perinthian, for he found it difficult to get a livelihood; but in course of time an old woman fell in love with him, and, being constrained by poverty, he married the old woman. With her he lived for a short space, and then she died and he succeeded to her great fortune and opulent possessions. He now had a large train of slaves, a sumptuous supply of clothing, and a lavish collection of household goods. He then resolved to voyage to Italy in order to purchase handsome slaves and maidservants and other articles of luxury, as was becoming to a nabob. The memory of Habrocomes also was ever present to him, and he prayed that he might find him, for he made it his ambition to share his life and his possessions with him. And so he set sail and arrived in Italy. There attended him a young man of high Sicilian birth, Clisthenes by name, who shared in all Hippothoos' affluence, for he was a very handsome young man.

Now that brothel keeper, when it seemed than Anthia had recovered her health, bethought him how he might sell her, and so he took her to the market place and exhibited her to purchasers. Meanwhile Hippothoos was walking about the city of Tarentum, seeking some beautiful object that he might acquire. He caught sight of Anthia and recognized her; the event astonished him greatly, and he turned the matter over in his mind: "Is she not the girl for whom I once dug a pit in Egypt, and immured therein with mastiffs, to avenge the murder of my friend Anchialos? What does this transformation mean? How did she save her life? How could she have escaped from that pit? What is this miraculous deliverance?" So saying, he approached, as if desirous of making a purchase, and when he stood near her he said, "Tell me, girl, do you not know Egypt? Did you not fall into the hands of robbers there? Did you not undergo other afflictions in that country? Do not be afraid to speak; I recognize you."

When Anthia heard mention of Egypt, and called to mind Anchialos and the robber band and the pit, she groaned and lamented, and then she looked steadfastly upon Hippothoos, whom she was altogether unable to recognize, and said, "I have indeed suffered many terrible afflictions in Egypt, stranger, whoever you may be, and I did fall into the hands of robbers. But how," she continued, "do you come to know my story? Whence do you say that you know me, that am so hapless? Much noised, indeed, and known to fame are the sufferings I have undergone; but you I do not know at all." What Hippothoos heard confirmed his recognition the more surely; for the moment he held his peace, and bought her of the brothel keeper and took her to his own quarters. There he bade her take heart and declared who he was and recalled the events in Egypt; he also explained the source of his wealth, and how he had made his own escape. She then begged his forgiveness, exculpating herself for the slaying of Anchialos by his unchaste attempt upon her, and she explained about the pit and Amphinomos and the docility of the dogs and her deliverance. Hippothoos took pity upon her, but never inquired who she was. As a result of their daily association Hippothoos, too, conceived a desire for Anthia and wished to have congress with her, and made her many promises. She on her part at first refused him upon the allegation that she was unworthy of so lordly a bed. But finally, when Hippothoos was urgent and she knew not what to do, she deemed it nobler to declare what she had as yet never revealed to him than to violate her pledges to Habrocomes. Therefore did she speak of Habrocomes, of Ephesus, of their love, of their oaths, of their calamities, of their captivities; and incessantly she moaned for Habrocomes. But when Hippothoos heard that she was indeed Anthia and the wife of the man dearest to him in all the world, he saluted her and bade her take heart, and he explained his own friendship for Habrocomes. Her he kept chaste at home, showing her every consideration out of respect to Habrocomes; he himself prosecuted a diligent investigation to find the whereabouts of Habrocomes.

Habrocomes at first worked at his painful labor in Nuceria, but at length, when he could no longer endure the toil, he resolved to take ship and sail for Ephesus. One night, then, he went down to the sea and embarked on the first boat ready to sail. This was bound back to Sicily, whence Habrocomes thought he would proceed to Crete, Cyprus, and Rhodes, and thence make his way to Ephesus; upon so long a voyage he hoped he might learn some news of Anthia. And so he sailed, with very scant supply of provisions, and arrived at Sicily, the first stage of his journey. There he found that his sometime host, Aigialeus, had died; he offered libations at his tomb and wept for him as was due, and then took ship again. He skirted Crete and arrived at Cyprus, where he lingered a few days and offered prayer to the ancestral goddess of the Cypriots. Then he sailed again and reached Rhodes, where he took lodging near the harbor. When he now found himself near Ephesus the memory of all his afflictions recurred to his mind. He thought of his country, his parents, Anthia, his servants, and he groaned deeply and said, "Alas for my tribulations! To Ephesus I come solitary, and I must show myself to my parents without Anthia. Vain, woe is me, is the voyage upon which I sail, and the story I have to recount may meet with little credence, for I have no witness to my trials. But endure manfully, Habrocomes, and when you are come to Ephesus continue in life until such time as you can raise a tomb for Anthia and bewail her and offer her libations, and then go and join her." Thus he said, and he wandered about the city distracted, at a loss for news of Anthia, at a loss for sustenance.

Now Leucon and Rhode, who were passing their time in Rhodes, dedicated a votive offering in the temple of the sun, near the golden panoply which Anthia and Habrocomes had dedicated. They set up a pillar with an inscription in honor of Habrocomes and Anthia in letters of gold, and they inscribed upon it also the names of the donors, Leucon and Rhode. Upon this pillar Habrocomes chanced, when he came to the temple to offer prayer to the god. He read the inscription and recognized the donors, and when he perceived the loyal good will of his servants and saw the panoply near by, he sat him down by the pillar and lamented: "How everything conspires to my misfortune!" he moaned. "Here I have come to the limit of my life and to the recollection of all my calamities. Lo, this panoply I dedicated with Anthia, and with Anthia I sailed from Ephesus, whither I now return without her. This pillar our companions dedicated for the happiness of us both: why then am I now alone? Where shall I find all that is dearest to me?" So he said in his lamentation.

In the meanwhile Leucon and Rhode had come to offer their customary prayers to the god, and they perceived Habrocomes sitting beside the pillar and gazing at the panoply; they did not recognize him, and wondered why a stranger should linger near the offerings of others. Then did Leucon address him: "Young man, what is the meaning of your sitting by votive offerings which do not belong to you and groaning and lamenting? What is your concern with these dedications? What connection have you with those whose names are inscribed upon them?" Habrocomes replied and said, " 'Tis for me, for me that Leucon and Rhode have made this offering. It is they whom, next to Anthia, I, the unfortunate Habrocomes, prayerfully yearn to see." When Leucon and Rhode heard these words they were struck dumb, but by degrees they recovered, and from his posture and voice, from what he said and his mention of Anthia, they recognized him and fell at his feet. Then they recounted all that had befallen them—their journey from Tyre to Syria, the fury of Manto, their transfer and sale in Lycia, the death of their owner, their acquisition of property, and their arrival in Rhodes. Thence they took Habrocomes to the house where they themselves sojourned, and delivered over to him all that they had acquired, and they took care of him and tended him, and they encouraged him to take heart. But to him nothing had value in comparison with Anthia, and for her he grieved at every turn. And so Habrocomes passed his time in Rhodes with his companions, deliberating what he should do.

But Hippothoos resolved to carry Anthia from Italy to Ephesus, in order to deliver her to her parents and there make inquiry concerning Habrocomes. All his possessions, therefore, he embarked upon a large Ephesian vessel and put to sea with Anthia. Their voyage was very prosperous, and in a few days they put in at Rhodes, landing when it was still night. There Hippothoos took lodging with a certain old woman, Althaea by name, near the sea, and put Anthia in the care of his hostess. That night he gave to repose, and the following day they busied themselves with preparations to sail on.

But the Rhodians were celebrating a magnificent public festival in honor of the sun; there was a procession and a sacrifice and a great host of citizens making festival. Leucon and Rhode were also there in attendance, not so much to participate in the festival as to make inquiries to learn tidings of Anthia. Then came to the shrine Hippothoos, bringing Anthia with him. And when she looked upon the votive offerings and fell into a reverie of the past, she said, "O thou Sun who dost look beneficently upon all mankind, passing only me, the unfortunate, when I was in Rhodes aforetime happily did I do obesiance to thee, and I offered sacrifices with Habrocomes, and even thought me blessed. Now I am a slave instead of free, a miserable captive instead of a happy girl, and I go to Ephesus alone, and must show myself to my kinsmen with no Habrocomes." Thus she said, and she wept copious tears, and she begged Hippothoos to permit her to shear some of her own tresses and consecrate them to the sun and utter a prayer for Habrocomes. Hippothoos consented, and so she cut off as many of her locks as she could, and when she found a fitting moment, when all visitors had departed, she dedicated her offering, inscribing upon it: "ON BEHALF OF HER HUSBAND, HABROCOMES, ANTHIA DEDICATES HER HAIR TO THE GOD." When she had done this and had offered her prayer, she departed with Hippothoos.

For a while Leucon and Rhode had attended the procession, but now they entered the temple and saw the dedication and recognized their mistress' name. First they caressed the hair and sorrowed as if they were looking upon Anthia herself. Then they hurried about, if perchance they might avail to find herself (for the Rhodian folk knew their names from their former sojourn). That day they found nothing, and so they returned home and reported to Habrocomes what they saw in the temple. The strangeness of the occurrence agitated Habrocomes to the soul, but he was now hopeful that he would find Anthia. On the morrow the weather was not fair for sailing and Anthia again came to the temple with Hippothoos, and sat down by the votive offerings, and wept and sighed. While she was so engaged Leucon and Rhode entered the temple; Habrocomes they had left at home because he was downhearted on the same account.

When they entered they saw Anthia, whom as yet they did not recognize; but the love she displayed, her tears, the offerings, the inscribed names, her figure, all assisted their conjecture, and so gradually they came to recognize her. Thereupon they fell at her knees and lay there speechless; she for her part wondered who they were and what they wished, for she had never hoped she would see Leucon and Rhode. But when they came to themselves they cried, "Mistress! Anthia! We are your slaves, Leucon and Rhode, who shared your travel abroad and your capture by the robbers. But what chance has brought you here? Take heart, mistress, Habrocomes is safe, and he is here, and he laments for you constantly." Anthia was so struck by what she heard that she lost her power of speech. With difficulty did she collect herself; she embraced them and saluted them and desired to hear every detail that concerned Habrocomes.

When it became known that Anthia and Habrocomes were found all the Rhodians flocked together in a crowd. Hippothoos, too, was now present; he was known to Leucon and Rhode, and himself learned who they were. Now was everything consummated to their satisfaction— except that Habrocomes himself was not yet aware of it! They ran just as they were to the house. But Habrocomes, when he heard from some Rhodian that Anthia was found, ran through the midst of the city shouting, "Anthia!"—like a man bereft of his wits did he run. And he did meet Anthia and those with her near the temple of Isis, and a great concourse of Rhodians followed after them. When they saw one another they recognized each other immediately, for this was their very soul's desire. They embraced one another, and sank to the ground. Many and various emotions commingled held them fast—pleasure, pain, fear, memory of the past, apprehension for the future. But the populace of Rhodes shouted their felicitations and uttered cries of joy and invoked the great goddess, Isis, saying, "Again we behold Habrocomes and Anthia, the beautiful pair." And they, when they recovered from their agitation, rose up and entered the shrine of Isis, saying, "O thou greatest Goddess, we thank thee for our deliverance. Because of thee, who art to us most precious of all, we have recovered one another and ourselves." In ecstasy they moved through the sacred precinct and humbled themselves before the altar.

Then did Leucon and his friends conduct them to his house, and Hippothoos transferred all his belongings to the same house, and they were ready to set sail for Ephesus. And when they had offered sacrifice during that day and had well feasted, many and varied were the tales each had to tell, so much had each suffered, so much had each done, and they protracted the banquet on and on, for it was after a wary time that they were now reunited. And when night was fallen they all went to their rest as fortune decreed—Leucon with Rhode; Hippothoos and the young man from Sicily who had followed him when he went to Italy, the handsome Clisthenes; and Anthia went to rest with Habrocomes.

Now when the others were all asleep and profound quiet reigned, Anthia embraced Habrocomes, and wept, saying, "My husband and my lord, I have recovered you after my long wandering over land and sea. I have escaped the threats of brigands, the plots of pirates, the outrages of brothel keepers, and chains, and pits, and beams, and poisons, and burial. But I come to you now, Habrocomes, my soul's master, just as I was when I departed from Tyre for Syria. No one has persuaded me to sin against you, neither Moeris in Syria, nor Perilaos in Cilicia, nor, in Egypt, Psammis and Polyidos, nor Anchialos in Ethiopia, nor my owner in Tarentum; nay, I have employed every device to preserve chastity and have remained pure for you. But you now, Habrocomes, have you abided chaste, or has some rival fair taken precedence over me? Or has anyone forced you to be forgetful of your pledges and of me?" Thus she said, and she kissed him close. But Habrocomes replied, "I swear to you by this day we have so ardently desired and so barely attained, that neither has any maiden appeared fair in my sight, nor has any other woman that I have seen won my favor: you receive Habrocomes back just such as you left him in the prison in Tyre."

With such protestations to one another they passed all that night, and easily did they persuade one another, for such was their desire. When day broke they embarked upon their ship, upon which they had laden their possessions, and all the multitude of the Rhodians came to escort them and wish them good speed. Hippothoos, too, departed with them, taking his goods and Clisthenes. And in a few days they completed their voyage and landed at Ephesus. All the city had learned of their deliverance in advance; and when they disembarked, immediately and just as they were they proceeded to the temple of Artemis and offered many prayers and performed various sacrifices, but in particular they dedicated to the goddess an inscription which recounted all that they had suffered and all that they had done. And when they had accomplished this they ascended to the city and raised large tombs for their parents (who, as it happened, had died by reason of old age and despair), and the remainder of their lives they passed with one another, keeping, as it were, continuous festival. And Leucon and Rhode shared all the good things that their comrades had; and Hippothoos, too, resolved to pass the remainder of his days in Ephesus. For Hyperanthes he had raised a great tomb when he was in Lesbos, and now Hippothoos adopted Clisthenes as his son and lived in Ephesus with Habrocomes and Anthia.

Of Xenophon's Ephesian Tale of
Anthia and Habrocomes
the end.

2

CHRISTIAN NOVELLA

The apocryphal Acts of the Apostles have been called the forgotten novels of the early church.[1] The earliest are the *Acts of John*, *Acts of Peter*, *Acts of Paul*, *Acts of Andrew*, and *Acts of Thomas*, composed by unknown authors in the late second and early third centuries A.D. Each narrative is a historical novel recounting the missionary activity of one of the twelve apostles as he travels around spreading the word of the new religion, encountering resistance, and making converts. Accordingly, the heroes of the novels are apostles, and the events are set in the first century during the infancy of Christianity. Although each of the Acts has its own character, some being more popular in nature than others, they all give the impression of being composed for the edification and entertainment of ordinary Christian readers, both men and women. As in the case of ancient Greek novels generally, however, the principal readership of the apocryphal Acts is unknown to us and has been the subject of considerable speculation, some scholars arguing that they were composed by women for women.[2]

Unlike the biblical Acts of the Apostles, which was eventually accepted into the canon of approved works, the apocryphal works were not accepted by the church; but they were not energetically rejected, either. Although they were widely read and had much influence, they were officially marginalized, in time were largely forgotten, and today survive mostly in fragments. The last person known to have held complete manuscripts of them in his hands was the Byzantine patriarch Photius in the ninth century.[3] So the apocryphal Acts of the Apostles came to constitute a sort of unofficial counterpart to the official Acts, the latter traditionally attributed to the apostle Luke, the former of unknown authorship, whence perhaps the appellation apocryphal, or "hidden." But both Acts, canonical and apocryphal, are replete with stirring and entertaining stories recounted in a popular style.[4]

The authors of the apocryphal Acts were active in the heyday of the Greek romantic novel, and the influence upon them of romantic novels, especially the simpler, nonsophistic novels such as Chariton's *Callirhoe* and Xenophon's *Ephesian Tale*, is manifest. Lovers and lustful persons in the romantic novels fall in love at first sight; similarly, female converts in the apocryphal Acts fall in love with the apostle's message at first hearing. Enamored characters in the romantic novels swoon and experience other extreme symptoms of love; women in the Christian novels exhibit the same symptoms in connection with the apostle and his message. The protagonists in the romantic novels value chastity above all, even above death, in their faithfulness to each other; the Christians in the apocryphal narratives value chastity even above their relationships to their spouses, in their faithfulness to their religion. Hostile rejected lovers, kindly helpers, women dressing as men, narrow escapes from dangerous situations in which the commitment of a character to his or her ideals is tested, and many other narrative ideas are common to both kinds of novel. Obviously the Christian authors composed their fiction in the idiom of the day, adapting the commonplaces of the romantic novel to the new genre of the apostolic novel. Of course there are many differences, too, among them the fact that the romantic novels conclude happily with a union of lovers, whereas the apostolic novels conclude with the death, usually the martyrdom, of the apostle, for the expected union of Christian and Christ lay in the future. In the Christian novels, moreover, the passion of female converts for the apostle and his message constitutes a threat to the existing social order in a way that the love of the protagonists in the romantic novels does not. If the romantic novels are post-civic, as Perry has described them,[5] the Christian novels are anti-civic.

Christian ideology in the second century was in a state of considerable flux, and different Christian groups exhibited a greater variety of practices than was later the case when the church had become more organized, effectively condemning certain beliefs and practices as heretical. The Christians to whom these novels were addressed evidently practiced total abstinence from all sexual relations, viewing sexual intercourse as a form of impurity that threatened the believer's chances for salvation; for chastity in the apocryphal Acts always means absolute continence, even within a Christian marriage. A recurrent narrative sequence in the apocryphal Acts recounts how (1) an apostle arrives in a town, where (2) a high-born woman hears him preach and (3) as a result vows to be chaste. Understandably, (4) her influential husband (or fiancé) responds negatively to her new unilateral policy, but (5) the apostle encourages his convert, (6) who perseveres. Although (7) the husband (or governor) imprisons the trouble-making apostle, (8) the woman manages to visit him in prison, and so on, until traditional male and municipal authority is defeated and the female convert emerges triumphant.[6] Along with this emphasis on absolute celibacy and on the trials of female converts, the apocryphal Acts show a more titillating interest in female nudity than do the romantic novels.[7]

A small-scale composition of this kind is *The Acts of Paul and Thecla*, associated with the apocryphal *Acts of Paul*. This intriguing work may originally have been a separate composition that was incorporated by the author of the *Acts of Paul* into his own work; or, like some other parts of the *Acts of Paul*, it may have circulated on its own as an excerpt from the larger work; or it may be that it was incorporated into the *Acts of Paul* and then became detached again. In any case it circulated as an independent novella, in part at least because of the interest in Thecla arising from her flourishing cult.

The novella recounts Paul's conversion of a remarkable maiden, Thecla, whose role then becomes more central as Paul's becomes more marginal so that she, not he, really becomes the protagonist of the drama. The events fall into two halves that are more or less parallel. In the first half Thecla, enthralled by Paul and his message, spurns a man who is amorously interested in her. The man brings her before the local authority, who condemns her to die. But she miraculously survives the attempt to execute her, is released, and goes looking for Paul, who is not around. The site of the first half is Iconium, and the third man in the triangle is her fiancé Thamyris. Thecla is so taken by Paul's message that she simply ignores Thamyris as well as everyone else. The second half takes place in Antioch (whether Pisidian or Syrian Antioch is unclear), and the interested man is a local official named Alexander. Seeing Thecla in public he evidently takes her for a prostitute and Paul for her pimp; she aborts his physical advances with vigor.

These doublets may come about from the author's combining two forms of a legend about Thecla serially into a single narrative (if there was such a legend), or (more likely, in my view) they may exemplify the sort of repetition that is found commonly in other works of popular fiction, such as Xenophon's *Ephesian Tale*, in which some events recur in different forms.[8] But the arrangement of the two trials of Thecla is not arbitrary, for there are marked changes in the heroine as she progresses through the episodes.[9] Thecla initially gives away her bracelets and her silver mirror, later cuts her hair, and finally dons male clothing.[10] As she gives up female things and adopts male things her behavior becomes more aggressive. In Iconium she is silent, whereas in Antioch she is combative and vocal. Earlier she declares her wish to follow Paul and to be baptized by him; later she baptizes herself and preaches on her own.

Paul's lack of support makes him an unattractive figure. If it is understandable that he does not remain in Iconium during Thecla's attempted

execution since he has been forcibly expelled from the city, it is less com-
prehensible why he does not linger in Antioch during Thecla's second
ordeal, and it is cowardice when, in response to Alexander's inquiry, he
denies even knowing Thecla. After exciting her religious passion Paul
proves to be a feckless mentor.[11] Within this apostolic vacuum the whole
feminine gender coalesces across the species to show its support for
Thecla. In the second act the kindly and generous stepmother, Tryphaena, replaces Thecla's intolerant mother, Theocleia; the women of
Antioch rally around her; and a lioness defends her against the other
beasts in the arena.

The first reader to comment on the *Acts of Paul* is Tertullian in his
essay *On Baptism* (ca. A.D. 200), in which he rails against women who
claim the right not only to preach but also to baptize.[12]

> But if the *Acts of Paul*, which was written in falsehood, brings forth the
> example of Thecla in connection with the right of women to preach and to
> baptize, let men know that the presbyter in Asia Minor who composed this
> document, as if he might add something to the reknown of Paul, has been
> found out, admitted that he did so from his love of Paul, and no longer holds
> office.

Among the interesting bits of information in this passage is that certain
women knew the story of Thecla, either from the novel or from oral
tradition, accepted it as historical, and cited Thecla as a precedent for the
rights and roles of women in the church. Since Thecla baptized herself,
the administration of baptism by women must be valid, and since Paul
gave Thecla leave to teach the word of God and she did so, women must
have the right to preach. Tertullian implies that these inferences are in-
valid because the author of the *Acts of Paul* wrote without any real authority.

The Acts of Paul and Thecla, probably the best-known portion of all
the apocryphal Acts, was translated into many languages, including Latin
(at least four independent translations into Latin were made), Syriac,
Coptic, Arabic, and Slavic. The text was sometimes treated with some
freedom, especially the account of Thecla's death, which varied according to where the writer believed, or wished, the remains of Thecla to
abide. In the text translated here, Thecla ends her days at Seleucia, where
her cult flourished from the fourth to the sixth century. In the fifth century a resident of Seleucia composed in Greek a *Life and Miracles of Saint
Thecla*, containing accounts of forty-six miracles attributed to her.[13] The
militant maiden had entered the mainstream as a saint for Christians of
all sorts. Churches were built for her in different cities, and artists represented scenes from her life.[14]

In the translation that follows, angle brackets enclose words that are missing in part of the manuscript tradition, and square brackets signify that the enclosed words are found in only part of the tradition and probably are secondary.

NOTES

1. MacDonald 1986. On the apocryphal Acts, see Schneemelcher and Wilson 1992 2:75–411; Davies 1980; Bovon et al. 1981; Hägg 1983:154–165; MacDonald 1983; *Semeia* 38 (1986), which is entirely devoted to the apocryphal Acts; Burrus 1987; Pervo 1994 and 1996.

2. See Bowie 1996 for a discussion and list of earlier studies; for the view that the apocryphal Acts were written by women, see Davies 1980.

3. Junod 1981:12.

4. On both the canonical and the apocryphal Acts as works of popular literature, see Pervo 1987.

5. Perry 1967:59.

6. For a discussion of this recurrent narrative sequence, see Tissot 1981:114–116 and Burrus 1987:31–66, from the latter of whom I have adapted my account of the pattern.

7. Cf. Pervo 1996:693, Miles 1989.

8. See, e.g., Pervo 1987:133–134.

9. See Dagron 1978:36–40 and Petropoulos 1995. Burrus correctly points out that the narrative is constructed in part upon an international folktale (1987: 53–57).

10. On early Christian women who assumed a male identity, see Miles 1989:53–77 and Castelli 1991.

11. Petropoulos 1995:135.

12. Tertullian, *De baptismo* 17. The text is uncertain in places.

13. The Greek text and a French translation are given in Dagron 1978. Since there is no independent evidence for a legend of Thecla or for Thecla as a historical person, everything we know about Thecla rests ultimately upon *The Acts of Paul and Thecla*.

14. For the cult of Thecla, see MacDonald 1983:90–96. Many illustrations of Thecla are reproduced in Carlé 1980:116–128.

LITERATURE

Carlé 1980. Dagron 1978. Haight, Elizabeth Hazelton, "A Christian Greek Romance: The Acts of Paul and Thecla," in Haight 1945:48–65. Schneemelcher and Wilson 1992 2:213–270. Petropoulos 1995. Rordorf 1986.

ANONYMOUS

The Acts of Paul and Thecla

translated by R. McL. Wilson

1. As Paul went up to Iconium after his flight from Antioch, his travelling companions were Demas and Hermogenes the copper-smith, who were full of hypocrisy and flattered Paul as if they loved him. But Paul, who had eyes only for the goodness of Christ, did them no evil, but loved them greatly, so that he sought to make sweet to them all the words of the Lord, [of the doctrine and of the interpretation of the Gospel], both of the birth and of the resurrection of the Beloved, and he related to them word for word the great acts of Christ as they had been revealed to him.

2. And a man named Onesiphorus, who had heard that Paul was come to Iconium, went out with his children Simmias and Zeno and his wife Lectra to meet Paul, that he might receive him to his house. For Titus had told him what Paul looked like. For (hitherto) he had not seen him in the flesh, but only in the spirit. 3. And he went along the royal road which leads to Lystra, and stood there waiting for him, and looked at (all) who came, according to Titus' description. And he saw Paul coming, a man small of stature, with a bald head and crooked legs, in a good state of body, with eyebrows meeting and nose somewhat hooked, full of friendliness; for now he appeared like a man, and now he had the face of an angel.

4. And when Paul saw Onesiphorus he smiled; and Onesiphorus said: "Greeting, thou servant of the blessed God!" And he replied: "Grace be with thee and thy house!" But Demas and Hermogenes grew jealous, and went even further in their hypocrisy; so that Demas said: "Are we then not (servants) of the Blessed, that thou didst not greet us thus?" And Onesiphorus said: "I do not see in you any fruit of righteousness; but if ye are anything, come ye also into my house and rest yourselves!"

5. And when Paul was entered into the house of Onesiphorus there was great joy, and bowing of knees and breaking of bread, and the word of God concerning continence and the resurrection, as Paul said:

"Blessed are the pure in heart, for they shall see God.
Blessed are they who have kept the flesh pure, for they shall become a temple of God.
Blessed are the continent, for to them will God speak.

Blessed are they who have renounced this world, for they shall be well
pleasing unto God.

Blessed are they who have wives as if they had them not, for they shall be
heirs to God.

Blessed are they who have fear of God, for they shall become angels of God.

6. Blessed are they who tremble at the words of God, for they shall be
comforted.

Blessed are they who have received (the) wisdom of Jesus Christ, for they
shall be called sons of the Most High.

Blessed are they who have kept their baptism secure, for they shall rest with
the Father and the Son.

Blessed are they who have laid hold upon the understanding of Jesus Christ,
for they shall be in light.

Blessed are they who through love of God have departed from the form of
this world, for they shall judge angels and at the right hand of the Father
they shall be blessed.

Blessed are the merciful, for they shall obtain mercy, and shall not see the
bitter day of judgment.

Blessed are the bodies of the virgins, for they shall be well pleasing to God,
and shall not lose the reward of their purity.

For the word of the Father shall be for them a work of salvation in the day
of his Son, and they shall have rest for ever and ever."

7. And while Paul was thus speaking in the midst of the assembly
in the house of Onesiphorus, a virgin (named) Thecla—her mother was
Theocleia—who was betrothed to a man (named) Thamyris, sat at a
near-by window and listened night and day to the word of the virgin life
as it was spoken by Paul; and she did not turn away from the window
but pressed on in the faith rejoicing exceedingly. Moreover, when she
saw many women and virgins going in to Paul she desired to be counted
worthy herself to stand in Paul's presence and hear the word of Christ;
for she had not yet seen Paul in person, but only heard his word. 8. Since
however she did not move from the window, her mother sent to Thamyris. He came in great joy as if he were already taking her in marriage.
So Thamyris said to Theocleia "Where is my Thecla, that I may see her?"
And Theocleia said: "I have a new tale to tell thee, Thamyris. For indeed
for three days and three nights Thecla has not risen from the window
either to eat or to drink, but gazing steadily as if on some joyful spectacle
she so devotes herself to a strange man who teaches deceptive and subtle
words that I wonder how a maiden [of such modesty] as she is can be so
sorely troubled.

9. Thamyris, this man is upsetting the city of the Iconians, and thy
Thecla in addition; for all the women and young people go in to him,
and are taught by him. 'You must' he says, 'fear one single God only, and
live chastely.' And my daughter also, who sticks to the window like a
spider, is (moved) by his words (and) gripped by a new desire and a

fearful passion; for the maiden hangs upon the things he says, and is taken captive. But go thou to her and speak to her, for she is betrothed to thee." 10. And Thamyris went to her, at one and the same time loving her and yet afraid of her distraction, and said: "Thecla, my betrothed, why dost thou sit thus? And what is this passion that holds thee distracted? Turn to thy Thamyris and be ashamed." And her mother also said the same: "Child, why dost thou sit thus looking down and making no answer, but like one stricken?" And those who were in the house wept bitterly, Thamyris for the loss of a wife, Theocleia for that of a daughter, the maidservants for that of a mistress. So there was a great confusion of mourning in the house. And while this was going on (all around her) Thecla did not turn away, but gave her whole attention to Paul's word.

11. But Thamyris sprang up and went out into the street, and closely watched all who went in to Paul and came out. And he saw two men quarrelling bitterly with one another, and said to them: "You men, who are you, tell me, and who is he that is inside with you, [the false teacher] who deceives the souls of young men and maidens, that they should not marry but remain as they are? I promise now to give you much money if you will tell me about him; for I am the first man of this city." 12. And Demas and Hermogenes said to him: "Who this man is, we do not know. But he deprives young men of wives and maidens of husbands, saying: 'Otherwise there is no resurrection for you, except ye remain chaste and do not defile the flesh, but keep it pure.'" 13. And Thamyris said to them: "Come into my house, you men, and rest with me." And they went off to a sumptuous banquet, with much wine, great wealth and a splendid table. And Thamyris gave them to drink, for he loved Thecla and wished to have her for his wife. And during the dinner Thamyris said: "Tell me, you men, what is his teaching, that I also may know it; for I am greatly distressed about Thecla because she so loves the stranger, and I am deprived of my marriage." 14. But Demas and Hermogenes said: "Bring him before the governor Castellius, on the ground that he is seducing the crowds to the new doctrine of the Christians, and so he will have him executed and thou shalt have thy wife Thecla. And we shall teach thee concerning the resurrection which he says is to come, that it has already taken place in the children whom we have, and that we are risen again in that we have come to know the true God."

15. When Thamyris had heard this from them, he rose up early in the morning full of jealousy and wrath and went to the house of Onesiphorus with the rulers and officers and a great crowd with cudgels, and said to Paul: "Thou hast destroyed the city of the Iconians, and my betrothed, so that she will not have me. Let us go to the governor Castellius!" And the whole crowd shouted: "Away with the sorcerer! For he has corrupted all our wives." And the multitude let themselves be persuaded. 16. And Thamyris stood before the judgment-seat and cried

aloud: "Proconsul, this man—we know not whence he is—who does not allow maidens to marry, let him declare before thee for what cause he teaches these things." And Demas and Hermogenes said to Thamyris: "Say that he is a Christian, and so thou wilt destroy him." But the governor was not easily to be swayed, and he called Paul, saying to him: "Who art thou, and what dost thou teach? For it is no light accusation that they bring against thee." 17. And Paul lifted up his voice and said: "If I today am examined as to what I teach, then listen, Proconsul. The living God, the God of vengeance, the jealous God, the God who has need of nothing, has sent me since he desires the salvation of men, that I may draw them away from corruption and impurity, all pleasure and death, that they may sin no more. For this cause God sent His own Son, whom I preach and teach that in him men have hope, who alone had compassion upon a world in error; that men may no longer be under judgment but have faith, and fear of God, and knowledge of propriety, and love of truth. If then I teach the things revealed to me by God, what wrong do I do, Proconsul?" When the governor heard this, he commanded Paul to be bound and led off to prison until he should find leisure to give him a more attentive hearing. 18. But Thecla in the night took off her bracelets and gave them to the door-keeper, and when the door was opened for her she went off to the prison. To the gaoler she gave a silver mirror, and so went in to Paul and sat at his feet and heard (him proclaim) the mighty acts of God. And Paul feared nothing, but comported himself with full confidence in God; and her faith also was increased, as she kissed his fetters. 19. But when Thecla was sought for by her own people and by Thamyris, they hunted her through the streets as one lost; and one of the door-keeper's fellow slaves betrayed that she had gone out by night. And they questioned the door-keeper, and he told them: "She has gone to the stranger in the prison." And they went as he had told them and found her, so to speak, bound with him in affection. And they went thence, rallied the crowd about them, and disclosed to the governor what had happened.

20. He commanded Paul to be brought to the judgment-seat; but Thecla rolled herself upon the place where Paul taught as he sat in the prison. The governor commanded her also to be brought to the judgment seat, and she went off with joy exulting. But when Paul was brought forward again, the crowd shouted out even louder: "He is a sorcerer! Away with him!" But the governor heard Paul gladly concerning the holy works of Christ; and when he had taken counsel he called Thecla and said: "Why dost thou not marry Thamyris according to the law of the Iconians?" But she stood there looking steadily at Paul. And when she did not answer, Theocleia her mother cried out, saying: "Burn the lawless one! Burn her that is no bride in the midst of the theatre, that all the women who have been taught by this man may be afraid!" 21. And the

governor was greatly affected. He had Paul scourged and drove him out of the city, but Thecla he condemned to be burned. And forthwith the governor arose and went off to the theatre, and all the crowd went out to the unavoidable spectacle. But Thecla sought for Paul, as a lamb in the wilderness looks about for the shepherd. And when she looked upon the crowd, she saw the Lord sitting in the form of Paul and said: "As if I were not able to endure, Paul has come to look after me." And she looked steadily at him; but he departed into the heavens. 22. Now the young men and maidens brought wood and straw that Thecla might be burned. And as she was brought in naked, the governor wept and marvelled at the power that was in her. The executioners laid out the wood and bade her mount the pyre; and making the sign of the Cross she climbed up on on the wood. They kindled it, and although a great fire blazed up the fire did not touch her. For God in compassion caused a noise beneath the earth and a cloud above, full of rain and hail, overshadowed (the theatre) and its whole content poured out, so that many were in danger and died, and the fire was quenched and Thecla saved. 23. But Paul was fasting with Onesiphorus and his wife and the children in an open tomb on the way by which they go from Iconium to Daphne. And when many days were past, as they were fasting the boys said to Paul: "We are hungry." And they had nothing with which to buy bread, for Onesiphorus had left the things of the world and followed Paul with all his house. But Paul took off his outer garment and said: "Go, my child, <sell this and> buy several loaves and bring them here." But while the boy was buying he saw his neighbour Thecla, and was astonished and said: "Thecla, where art thou going?" And she said: "I am seeking after Paul, for I was saved from the fire." And the boy said: "Come, I will take thee to him, for he has been mourning for thee and praying and fasting six days already." 24. But when she came to the tomb Paul had bent his knees and was praying and saying: "Father of Christ, let not the fire touch Thecla, but be merciful to her, for she is thine!" But she standing behind him cried out: "Father, who didst make heaven and earth, the Father of thy beloved Son <Jesus Christ>, I praise thee that thou didst save me from the fire, that I might see Paul!" And as Paul arose he saw her and said: "O God the knower of hearts, Father of our Lord Jesus Christ, I praise thee that thou hast so speedily <accomplished> what I asked, and hast hearkened unto me." 25. And within the tomb there was much love, Paul rejoicing, and Onesiphorus and all of them. But they had five loaves, and vegetables, and water, and they were joyful over the holy works of Christ. And Thecla said to Paul: "I will cut my hair short and follow thee wherever thou goest." But he said: "The season is unfavourable, and thou art comely. May no other temptation come upon thee, worse than the first, and thou endure not and play the coward!" And Thecla said: "Only give me the seal in Christ, and temptation shall not touch me." And Paul said: "Have patience, Thecla, and thou shalt receive the water."

26. And Paul sent away Onesiphorus with all his family to Iconium, and so taking Thecla came into Antioch. But immediately as they entered a Syrian by the name of Alexander, one of the first of the Antiochenes, seeing Thecla fell in love with her, and sought to win over Paul with money and gifts. But Paul said: "I do not know the woman of whom thou dost speak, nor is she mine." But he, being a powerful man, embraced her on the open street; she however would not endure it, but looked about for Paul and cried out bitterly saying: "Force not the stranger, force not the handmaid of God! Among the Iconians I am one of the first, and because I did not wish to marry Thamyris I have been cast out of the city." And taking hold of Alexander she ripped his cloak, took off the crown from his head, and made him a laughing-stock. 27. But he, partly out of love for her and partly in shame at what had befallen him, brought her before the governor; and when she confessed that she had done these things, he condemned her to the beasts, <since Alexander was arranging games>. But the women were panic-stricken, and cried out before the judgment-seat: "An evil judgment! A godless judgment!" But Thecla asked of the governor that she might remain pure until she was to fight with the beasts. And a rich woman named Tryphaena, whose daughter had died, took her under her protection and found comfort in her. 28. When the beasts were led in procession, they bound her to a fierce lioness, and the queen Tryphaena followed her. And as Thecla sat upon her back, the lioness licked her feet, and all the crowd was amazed. Now the charge upon her superscription was: Guilty of Sacrilege. But the women with their children cried out from above, saying: "O God, an impious judgment is come to pass in this city!" And after the procession Tryphaena took her again; for her daughter who was dead had spoken to her in a dream: "Mother, thou shalt have in my place the stranger, the desolate Thecla, that she may pray for me and I be translated to the place of the just". 29. So when Tryphaena received her back from the procession she was at once sorrowful, because she was to fight with the beasts on the following day, but at the same time loved her dearly like her own daughter Falconilla; and she said: "Thecla, my second child, come and pray for my child, that she may live; for this I saw in my dream." And she without delay lifted up her voice and said: "Thou God of heaven, Son of the Most High, grant to her according to her wish, that her daughter Falconilla may live for ever!" And when Thecla said this, Tryphaena mourned, considering that such beauty was to be thrown to the beasts. 30. And when it was dawn, Alexander came to take her away—for he himself was arranging the games—and he said: "The governor has taken his place, and the crowd is clamouring for us. Give me her that is to fight the beasts, that I may take her away." But Tryphaena cried out so that he fled, say-

ing: "A second mourning for my Falconilla is come upon my house, and
there is none to help; neither child, for she is dead, nor kinsman, for I am
a widow. O God of Thecla my child, help thou Thecla." 31. And the
governor sent soldiers to fetch Thecla. Tryphaena however did not stand
aloof, but taking her hand herself led her up, saying: "My daughter Falconilla I brought to the tomb; but thee, Thecla, I bring to fight the
beasts." And Thecla wept bitterly and sighed to the Lord, saying: "Lord
God, in whom I trust, with whom I have taken refuge, who didst deliver
me from the fire, reward thou Tryphaena, who had compassion upon thy
handmaid, and because she preserved me pure." 32. Then there was a
tumult, and roaring of the beasts, and a shouting of the people and of
the women who sat together, some saying: "Bring in the sacrilegious
one!" but others: "May the city perish for this lawlessness! Slay us all,
Proconsul! A bitter sight, an evil judgment!" 33. But Thecla was taken
out of Tryphaena's hands and stripped, and was given a girdle and flung
into the stadium. And lions and bears were set upon her, and a fierce
lioness ran to her and lay down at her feet. And the crowd of the women
raised a great shout. And a bear ran upon her, but the lioness ran and
met it, and tore the bear asunder. And again a lion trained against men,
which belonged to Alexander, ran upon her; and the lioness grappled
with the lion, and perished with it. And the women mourned the more,
since the lioness which helped her was dead. 34. Then they sent in many
beasts, while she stood and stretched out her hands and prayed. And
when she had finished her prayer, she turned and saw a great pit full of
water, and said: "Now is the time for me to wash." And she threw herself
in, saying: "In the name of Jesus Christ I baptize myself on the last day!"
And when they saw it, the women and all the people wept, saying: "Cast
not thyself into the water!"; so that even the governor wept that such
beauty should be devoured by seals. So, then she threw herself into the
water in the name of Jesus Christ; but the seals, seeing the light of a
lightning-flash, floated dead on the surface. And there was about her a
cloud of fire, so that neither could the beasts touch her nor could she be
seen naked. 35. But as other more terrible beasts were let loose, the
women cried aloud, and some threw petals, others nard, others cassia,
others amomum, so that there was an abundance of perfumes. And all
the beasts let loose were overpowered as if by sleep, and did not touch
her. So Alexander said to the governor: "I have some very fearsome
bulls—let us tie her to them." The governor frowning gave his consent,
saying: "Do what thou wilt." And they bound her by the feet between
the bulls, and set red-hot irons beneath their bellies that being the more
enraged they might kill her. The bulls indeed leaped forward, but the
flame that blazed around her burned through the ropes, and she was as
if she were not bound. 36. But Tryphaena fainted as she stood beside the
arena, so that her handmaids said: "The queen Tryphaena is dead!" And

the governor took note of it, and the whole city was alarmed. And Alexander fell down at the governor's feet and said: "Have mercy upon me, and on the city, and set the prisoner free, lest the city also perish with her. For if Caesar should hear this he will probably destroy both us and the city as well, because his kinswoman Tryphaena has died at the circus gates."

37. And the governor summoned Thecla from among the beasts, and said to her: "Who art thou? And what hast thou about thee, that not one of the beasts touched thee?" She answered: "I am a handmaid of the living God. As to what I have about me, I have believed in him in whom God is well pleased, His Son. For his sake not one of the beasts touched me. For he alone is the goal of salvation and the foundation of immortal life. To the storm-tossed he is a refuge, to the oppressed relief, to the despairing shelter; in a word, whoever does not believe in him shall not live, but die for ever." 38. When the governor heard this, he commanded garments to be brought, and said: "Put on these garments." But she said: "He who clothed me when I was naked among the beasts shall clothe me with salvation in the day of judgment." And taking the garments she put them on.

And straightway the governor issued a decree, saying: "I release to you Thecla, the pious handmaid of God." But all the women cried out with a loud voice, and as with one mouth gave praise to God, saying: "One is God, who has delivered Thecla!", so that all the city was shaken by the sound. 39. And Tryphaena when she was told the good news came to meet her with a crowd, and embraced Thecla and said: "Now I believe that the dead are raised up! Now I believe that my child lives! Come inside, and I will assign to thee all that is mine." So Thecla went in with her and rested in her house for eight days, instructing her in the word of God, so that the majority of the maidservants also believed; and there was great joy in the house.

40. But Thecla yearned for Paul and sought after him, sending in every direction. And it was reported to her that he was in Myra. So she took young men and maidservants and girded herself, and sewed her mantle into a cloak after the fashion of men, and went off to Myra, and found Paul speaking the word of God and went to him. But he was astonished when he saw her and the crowd that was with her, pondering whether another temptation was not upon her. But observing this she said to him: "I have taken the bath, Paul; for he who worked with thee for the Gospel has also worked with me for my baptism." 41. And taking her by the hand Paul led her into the house of Hermias, and heard from her everything (that had happened), so that Paul marvelled greatly and the hearers were confirmed and prayed for Tryphaena. And Thecla arose and said to Paul: "I am going to Iconium." But Paul said: "Go and teach the word of God!" Now Tryphaena sent her much clothing and gold, so

that she could leave (some of it) for the service of the poor. 42. But she herself went away to Iconium and went into the house of Onesiphorus, and threw herself down on the floor where Paul had sat and taught the oracles of God, and wept, saying: "My God, and God of this house where the light shone upon me, Christ Jesus the Son of God, my helper in prison, my helper before governors, my helper in the fire, my helper among the beasts, thou art God, and to thee be the glory for ever. Amen." 43. And she found Thamyris dead, but her mother still alive; and calling her mother to her she said to her: "Theocleia my mother, canst thou believe that the Lord lives in heaven? For whether thou dost desire money, the Lord will give it thee through me; or thy child, see, I stand beside thee."

And when she had borne this witness she went away to Seleucia; and after enlightening many with the word of God she slept with a noble sleep.

3

WISDOM LITERATURE

Wisdom literature has a long history, especially in the Near East, where the earliest wisdom texts date to the third millenium B.C. Although the utterances they contain are regularly attributed to well-known sages or other prominent men, the compositions themselves are mostly anonymous. For example, various sections of the Old Testament book of Proverbs are said to be the sayings of different persons, mostly kings, and of kings mostly Solomon, famous for his wisdom. Typical Mesopotamian and Egyptian wisdom compositions consist of exhortations or miscellaneous advice concerning the living of one's life and the conduct of one's affairs, allegedly given on a particular occasion by a father to his son. Well known is *The Story of Ahikar*, a Mesopotamian work of about the sixth century B.C. that was translated into several ancient languages, including Greek, and continued to circulate for many centuries, even into modern times. It recounts how the Assyrian counselor and sage Ahikar, having no son of his own, adopts his nephew Nadin and trains him to be his successor at the court of Esarhaddon. But Nadin treacherously turns the king against his benefactor Ahikar, whom the king now orders to be executed. Ahikar, however, is secretly saved, and when a crisis arises in which his talents are required, he is restored to the monarch's favor and Nadin's duplicity is revealed. Thereupon Ahikar lectures Nadin at length in wisdom. This didactic portion of the work comprises over a hundred fables, aphorisms, and the like.[1] So the conventional strategy of a Near Eastern author composing a literary work of wisdom was to attribute wise utterances to a particular prominent man of the past, providing the utterances with a frame that could be as slight as a sentence of attribution, as in Proverbs, or as elaborate as a fully developed narrative, as in *Ahikar*.

In Greece, extant wisdom literature begins with Hesiod's *Works and*

Days (ca. 700 B.C.), a poem made up partly of admonitions from Hesiod to his brother Perses and partly of general advice on agriculture and other matters. The misbehavior of Perses and local officials in the matter of the brothers' inheritance provides the alleged occasion for Hesiod's exhortations, just as Nadin's misbehavior provides the occasion for those of Ahikar.[2]

When Hesiod composed his poem, Greek popular and learned works were essentially one and the same. But later works on wisdom and philosophy could vary considerably in their nature and difficulty. On one hand, intellectual philosophic writings were produced—the works of the pre-Socratic philosophers, the dialogues of Plato, the treatises and dialogues of Aristotle, and so on—that must have struck many readers, especially less sophisticated readers, as abstruse and inaccessible. On the other hand, balancing these productions was fare of a lighter nature offering wisdom and philosophy in simpler and more entertaining forms. Certainly some of the ancient collections of fables and of anecdotes were composed in this spirit, the latter often consisting of notable remarks made by philosophers on various occasions.

Secundus the Silent Philosopher, or the *Life of Secundus*, or the *Life of Secundus the Philosopher*, is an anonymous piece of wisdom literature written for unsophisticated readers and dating to around the second century A.D.[3] In the manner of Near Eastern wisdom literature it is partly narration and partly instruction. Although no Athenian philosopher Secundus is known to us, the name itself was common in the Imperial period, and a conversation between an Athenian sage and the emperor Hadrian (A.D. 117–138) is a plausible historical event, for the emperor was a philhellene who enjoyed meeting Greek intellectuals.

The first part of the work luridly recounts how Secundus came to live a life of self-imposed silence. Wishing to test the assertion that every woman is a whore, he disguises himself and persuades his own mother to sleep with him in return for an amount of money. After he reveals his identity to her, she hangs herself from shame and he, blaming his tongue for her death, resolves never again to speak.

This narrative is a reflex of an international story that is attested from Europe to India to China. For example, an Indian story appearing in the *Jatakas* begins with the statement that all women are lecherous, then recounts how a young Brahman, in order that he might learn of the lecherous nature of women, is told to seduce his teacher's aged mother. She is willing, even eager, but when she is exposed, she dies on the spot from shame, and the student renounces the world, becoming a hermit.[4] So both versions begin with (1) an assertion of the lechery or faithlessness of women, (2) the truth of which is tested in the ensuing events, in which (3) a young sage succeeds in seducing his mother (or his master's mother), although the act of seduction leads to (4) her death from shame and to (5) his own disillusioned rejection of the world.

Secundus's silence is the link that joins the two parts of the composition together, for presently the silent philosopher comes to the attention of the emperor Hadrian, who during a visit to Athens summons him to an interview. The confrontation of ruler and sage is a beloved situation of Greek lore and literature, a few such encounters becoming classics, such as the dealings of Solon the Athenian and King Croesus of Lydia and the chance meeting of Diogenes the Cynic and Alexander the Great.[5]

But in this case the meeting is more than a meeting of wisdom and power, for Hadrian immediately threatens to have Secundus executed if he will not even speak with the emperor. Unmoved by the threat, Secundus is prepared to die. Fortunately Hadrian secretly admires Secundus's commitment and so privately instructs his executioner to let the philosopher live if he does *not* speak. The narrative thus slips into martyrology, recounting how a person is prepared to defy the state and accept death in defense of his ideals.[6] A philosopher of Secundus's day could take as his model no less a person than Socrates, and the unknown author of the *Life of Secundus* was writing at a time when martyrdom flourished as a theme of popular literature. There were accounts of the martyrdom of Alexandrian patriots who lost their lives defiantly protesting Roman misrule abroad, and among Christians there were the apocryphal Acts of the Apostles, which recounted how the missionaries of the nascent Christian religion bravely met their deaths.

Secundus's interview with the emperor builds up to a series of twenty philosophical questions posed by Hadrian together with the catechistic answers that Secundus gives in writing. The questions are of the sort "What is such and such (e.g., cosmos, woman, beauty)?" Secundus's replies mostly take the form of two-word definitions in the Greek (the English renderings generally require more words), several to each question, and tend to the cynical and flippant.[7] For example, number 9:

WHAT IS BEAUTY?

A picture drawn by Nature, a self-made blessing, a short-lived piece of good fortune, a possession that does not stay with us, the pious man's ruin, an accident of the flesh, the minister to pleasures, a flower that withers, an uncompounded product, the desire of men.

A number of independent compositions consisting of questions and answers of exactly this sort have survived, and this kind of question and answer is known to have formed a part of lower-level training in Pythagorean philosophy.[8] Somewhat similar questions and answers are attributed to the sages Niloxenus and Solon, as reported by Plutarch in his

Symposium of the Seven Sages.[9] For example: "What is most beautiful? The cosmos, for everything that is ordered is part of it."

Overall the *Life of Secundus* is a tale of sensational extremes. If it is unseemly for a mother to play the whore, it is unthinkable for a son so to test her. Their reactions to the results of the test are—characteristically, we assume—immoderate: suicide for one and muteness for the other. But presently the tables are turned as Secundus himself becomes the subject of a test when someone else, Hadrian, becomes the experimenter. The philosopher's remaining silent in the face of death reveals a strength of purpose that his mother lacked.

Although little notice of the *Life of Secundus* was taken by the ancients, it went on to become an international folkbook and may have influenced such well-known Oriental folkbooks as the *Book of Sindbad* and the *Arabian Nights*.[10] Its misogynism posed no obstacle to its diffusion, and indeed this attitude may have facilitated its warm acceptance among adherents of the three monotheistic religions.[11] From the seventh to the seventeenth centuries, translations and retellings were made in Armenian, Syriac, Arabic, Ethiopic, Latin, and many of the European vernaculars (Spanish, French, Italian, German, Icelandic, etc.). As usual with such works, copyists and translators treated it freely, so that different versions of the book developed that show variations in the details of the story and in the number of questions.

NOTES

1. See Lindenberger 1985 and the introduction to selection 5, *The Aesop Romance*.

2. See West 1978:3–59 on wisdom literature in general and on Hesiod's poem in particular.

3. Perry 1964:1.

4. See Krappe 1927 for the Indian parallel; however, in other respects Krappe's discussion of the *Life of Secundus* is outdated.

5. See further Hansen 1997b.

6. Daly 1939:51; Perry 1964:6–7, citing C. Bradford Welles, "A Yale Fragment of the Acts of Appian," *TAPA* 67 (1936) 7–23, and Herbert A. Musurillo, ed. and comm., *The Acts of the Pagan Martyrs: Acta Alexandrinorum* (Oxford: Clarendon Press, 1954), esp. 236–246.

7. Daly and Suchier 1939:54.

8. Perry 1964:5, 9; Daly's monograph (1939), supplemented by Suchier's texts, gives a detailed history of the question-and-answer dialogue as a popular literary genre from antiquity onward.

9. Plutarch, *Moralia* 153A–D.

10. Perry 1959:84–89.

11. Krappe 1927:183.

Daly and Suchier 1939. Perry 1964.

ANONYMOUS

Secundus the Silent Philosopher

translated by Ben E. Perry

Secundus was a philosopher. This man cultivated wisdom all his days and observed silence religiously, having chosen the Pythagorean way of life. What caused his silence was this: When he was a small boy he was sent away from home by his parents to be educated, and, while he was still occupied with his studies, it happened that his father died. He had often heard this byword, that "every woman can be bought; the chaste one is only she who has escaped notice." Now when he had grown to manhood and had returned to his homeland, he put himself forward as a follower of the Cynic discipline, carrying a stick and a leathern wallet about with him, letting the hair on his head grow long, and cultivating a beard. He took an apartment in his own father's house, without any of the servants recognizing him, nor even his own mother. Wishing to satisfy himself concerning that proposition about women, to see whether it was really true or not, he called one of the maidservants aside and promised to give her six gold pieces (if she would arrange a meeting for him) on the pretense that he was in love with her mistress, his own mother. The maid, accepting the money, was able to persuade her mistress by promising her fifty gold pieces; and the latter made an agreement with the maid, saying, "At nightfall I will have him enter secretly, and I will lie with him." Having this notice from the maid, the philosopher sent provisions for a dinner. Now after the two had finished dinner, and when they had started to go to bed, she was expecting to have carnal intercourse with him; but he put his arms around her as he would around his own mother, and, fixing his eyes upon the breasts that had suckled him, he lay down and slept until early morning. When the first light of dawn appeared Secundus rose up with the intention of going out, but she laid hands on him and said, "Did you do this only in order to convict me?" And he answered, "No, lady mother, I refrained because it is not right for me to defile that place from which I came forth at birth. God forbid." Then she asked him who he was, and he said to her, "I am Secundus, your son." And she, condemning herself and unable to bear the sense of shame, hanged herself. Secundus, having concluded that it was on account of his own talking that his mother's death had come about, put a ban upon himself, resolving not to say anything the rest of his life. And he practiced silence to the day of his death . . .

About that time the Emperor Hadrian, having arrived in Athens, heard about Secundus and summoned him into his presence; for no good thing escaped this emperor's notice. When Secundus entered, Hadrian, wishing to test him in order to see whether he was really committed to silence or not, rose up first and greeted him. Secundus, however, maintained his customary silence. Then Hadrian said to him, "Speak, philosopher, so we may come to know you. It is not possible to observe the wisdom in you when you say nothing." But in spite of this, Secundus kept still. And Hadrian said, "Secundus, before I came to you it was a good thing for you to maintain silence, since you had no listener more distinguished than yourself, nor one who could converse with you on equal terms. But now I am here before you, and I demand it of you; speak out, bring forth your eloquence to the top level of its quality." Still Secundus was not abashed, nor afraid of the emperor. Then Hadrian, losing all patience, said to one of his followers, a tribune, "Make the philosopher say a word to us." The tribune answered according to the truth by saying, "It is possible to persuade lions and leopards and other wild beasts to speak with human voices, but not a philosopher against his will." Then he summoned an executioner, who was a Greek, and said to him, "I do not want any man to live who refuses to speak to the emperor Hadrian. Take him away and punish him." Hadrian, however, called the executioner aside privately and said to him, "When you are leading the philosopher away, talk to him along the road and encourage him to speak. If you persuade him to make an answer, cut off his head; but if he does not answer, bring him back here unharmed." Secundus was led away in silence, and the executioner taking him in charge proceeded down to the Piraeus, for that was the place where men customarily were punished. And the executioner said to him, "Secundus, why do you die by persisting in your silence? Speak, and you shall live. Grant yourself the gift of life by a word. Behold, the swan sings near the end of his life, and all the other winged creatures give forth sound with the voice that nature has given them. There is no living thing that does not have a voice. So reconsider, and change your purpose. The time that you will have gained thereby will be ample for your silence." With these and many other words he sought to encourage Secundus and to lure him into the trap. But Secundus despised life itself and silently waited for death, unmoved by what had been said to him. After bringing him to the custom-ary place the executioner said, "Secundus, hold out your neck and receive the sword through it." Secundus held out his neck and took leave of life in silence. Then the executioner showed him the naked sword and said, "Secundus, buy off your death with speech." But Secundus did not speak. Thereupon the executioner took him and went back to Hadrian and said, "My lord Caesar, I have brought back Secundus to you the same as he was when you handed him over to me, silent unto death." Hadrian mar-veled at the philosopher's strength of purpose and rising up said, "Secun-dus, in observing silence you have imposed upon yourself a kind of law, and that law of yours I was unable to break down. Now, therefore, take this tablet, write on it, and converse with me by means of your hands." Secundus took the tablet and wrote as follows:

"For my part, Hadrian, I shall not stand in fear of you on account of death. You have the power of putting me to death, because you are the ruler of today. But that is all. Over my utterance and the words I choose to speak you have no power." Hadrian read this and said, "Your stand in self-defense is good; but come, answer me on a number of other matters. I have twenty questions to put before you and the first of them is this: What is the universe?"

Again Secundus wrote down his reply. "The universe, Hadrian, is the system of the heavens and the earth and all things in them, and of this I shall speak a little later on, if you pay heed to what is now being said. You, too, Hadrian, are a human being like all the rest of us, subject to every kind of accident, mere dust and corruption. The life of brute beasts is even such. Some are clothed with scales, others with shaggy hair; some are blind, some are adorned with beauty; all have the clothing and the means of protection with which they were born and which nature has given them. But you, Hadrian, as it happens, are full of fears and appre-hensions. *In the bellowing wind of winter you are disturbed too much by cold and shivering, and in the summer time you are too much op-pressed by the heat. You are puffed up and full of holes, like a sponge. For you have termites in your body and herds of lice, that draw furrows through your entrails; and grooves have been burned into you, as it were, like the lines made by the fire of encaustic painters.* Being a short-lived creature and full of infirmities, you foresee yourself being cut and torn apart, roasted by the sun and chilled by the wintry wind. Your laughter is only the preface to grief, for it turns about and passes into tears. What about the necessity that controls our lives? Is it destiny decreed by Heaven or the whimsy of personal luck? We know not whence it comes. Today is already passing us by, and what the morrow will be we do not know. Think not lightly, therefore, O Hadrian, of what I am saying. Boast not that you alone have encircled the world in your travels, for it is only the sun and the moon and the stars that really make the journey around it. Moreover, do not think of yourself as being beautiful and great and rich and the ruler of the inhabited world. Know you not that, being a man, you were born to be Life's plaything, helpless in the hands of Fortune and Destiny, sometimes exalted, sometimes humbled lower than the grave? Will you not be able to learn what life is, Hadrian, in the light of many examples? Consider how rich with his golden nails was the king of the Lydians. Great as a commander of armies was the king of the Danaäns, Agamemnon; daring and hardy was Alexander, king of the Macedonians. Heracles was fearless, the Cyclops wild and untamed, Odysseus shrewd and subtle, and Achilles beautiful to look upon. If Fortune took away from these men the distinctions that were peculiarly their own, how much more likely is she to take them away from you? For you are not beautiful like Achilles, nor shrewd as was Odysseus, nor untamed like the Cyclops, nor fearless like Heracles, nor hardy and daring like Alexander, nor such a commander of armies as Agamemnon, nor yet rich like Gyges, the king of the Lydians. These things, Hadrian, I have written by way of a preface. Now let us proceed according to your questions:

I
What is the Universe?
A circumference beyond our reach, a theoretic structure, an eminence not easily perceived in its entirety, a self-generated object of contemplation, a conformation with many aspects, an eternal establishment, nourishing ether, a globe that does not wander from its place, the light of the sun, day, stars, darkness, night, earth, air, water.

2
What is the Ocean?
The thing that embraces the world, the frontier by which the world is crowned, a girdle of brine, the Atlantic bond, a circuit embracing all nature, a mirror to reflect the sun's light (?), the holder of the inhabited world.

3
What is God?
A self-formed good, an image of many shapes, an eminence too lofty to be seen, a conformation with many aspects, a problem hard to understand, immortal intelligence, an all-pervading spirit, an eye that never closes in sleep, a power known by many names, light that prevails over all.

4
What is the Day?
A stadium of toil, a twelve-hour course, the daily beginning, a reminder to get one's living, prolongation unto evening, lively contact with

people, an everlasting reckoning on the calendar, Nature's mirror, back-running reminiscence.

5
What is the Sun?

The eye of the heavens, the adversary of night, a globe in the ether, the indicator of the cosmos, unsullied flame, unceasing light, a torch freely supplied, a traveler through the sky, the ornament of the day.

6
What is the Moon?

The crimson of the heavens, night-time consolation, an all-night vigil for sailors, encouragement for travelers, alternate to the sun, the enemy of evil-doers, the heralder of festivals, the cycle of the months.

7
What is the Earth?

The base of the sky, the middle of the universe, a stage-scene without a foundation, a thing rooted in midair, [an immeasurable circumference], the arena of life's struggle, a system established by God, the object of the moon's nightlong vigil, a spectacle that cannot be seen all at once, the nurse of the rains, the protection of the crops and their mother, the covering of Hades, a region occupied by many inhabitants, the origin of all things and their final repository.

8
What is Man?

Mind clothed in flesh, a vessel containing a spirit, a receptacle for sense-perception, a toil-ridden spirit, a temporary dwelling-place, a phantom in the mirror of time, an organism fitted with bones, a scout on the trail of life, Fortune's plaything, a good thing that does not last, one of life's expenditures, an exile from life, a deserter of the light, something that earth will reclaim, a corpse forever.

9
What is Beauty?

A picture drawn by Nature, a self-made blessing, a short-lived piece of good fortune, a possession that does not stay with us, the pious man's ruin, an accident of the flesh, the minister to pleasures, a flower that withers, an uncompounded product, the desire of men.

10
What is Woman?

A man's desire, a wild beast that shares one's board, the worry with which one rises in the morning, intertwining lustfulness, a lioness sharing one's bed, a viper in clothes, a battle voluntarily chosen, incontinence in the form of bed-partner, a daily loss, a storm in the house, a hindrance to serenity, the wreck of an incontinent man, the stock-in-trade of adulterers, the sacking of one's estate, an expensive war, an evil creature, too much of a burden, a nine-wind tempest, a venomous asp, a service rendered in the procreation of men, a necessary evil.

11
What is a Friend?
A sought-after name, a man nowhere evident, a possession hard to find, an encouragement in time of distress, the refuge of misfortune, an arm for misery to lean upon, an observer of life, a man beyond reach, a substantial and valuable possession, unattainable good fortune.

12
What is a Farmer?
A servant to the crops, a judge of rains, the companion of solitude, a merchant having no business on the sea, an adversary to the woodland, a tender of the food supply, an improver of the fields, physician to the earth, a planter of trees, trainer of the mountain lands, one habituated to toil and hardship.

13
What is a Gladiator?
Death on sale, a sacrificial offering made by the master of the show, [gluttonous appetite,] doom according to instructions, a bloody art, Fortune's mistake, speedy death, doom heralded by the trumpet, death ever at hand, a bad victory.

14
What is a Boat?
A sea-tossed affair, a house without a foundation, a ready-made tomb, a three-dimensional timber, transportation by the winds, a prison in winged flight, fate bound up in a package, the plaything of the winds, a floating death, a bird made of wood, a seagoing horse, an open weasel-trap, uncertain safety, death in prospect, a traveler amid the waves.

15
What is a Sailor?
One who travels through the waves, a courier on the sea, one who follows on the track of the winds, a fellow traveler with the winds, a stranger to the inhabited world, a deserter of the land, the opponent of the storm, a marine gladiator, one who is unsure of his safety, a neighbor to death, a lover of the sea.

16
What is Wealth?

A burden of gold, the minister to pleasures, fear mingled with hope, a senseless reaping of profits, envy sharing one's board, a source of daily pother, an unstable thing, a beloved piece of misfortune, a thing full of insidious snares, desire that can never be sated, a much longed-for hardship, a high place to fall from, a value conventionally reckoned in terms of money, transitory good luck.

17
What is Poverty?

A good thing that is hated, the mother of health, a hindrance to pleasures, a way of life free of worry, a possession hard to cast off, the teacher of inventions, the finder of wisdom, a business that nobody envies, property unassessed, merchandise not subject to tariff, profit not to be reckoned in terms of cash, a possession not interfered with by informers, non-evident good fortune, good fortune free of care.

18
What is Old Age?

An evil easy to acquire, a living death, a healthy disease, fate in prospect, a timeworn object of laughter, unstrung judgment, a breathing corpse, a stranger to love, the prospect of death, a corpse in movement.

19
What is Sleep?

Rest from toil, the success of physicians, the release of those who are bound, the wisdom of the wakeful, what sick men pray for, an image of death, the desire of those who toil in hardship, the rest of all the spirit, a principal occupation of the rich, [the idle chatter of poor men,] a daily object of concern.

20
What is Death?

Everlasting sleep, the dissolution of the body, the desire of those who suffer, the departure of the spirit, the fear of rich men, the desire of paupers, the undoing of the limbs, flight from life and the loss of its possession, the father of sleep, an appointed day sure to be met, the breakup of all things."

Thereupon Hadrian, after reading these things, and after learning the reason why he had made silence a philosophical practice, gave orders that his books should be deposited in the sacred library under the name of Secundus the Philosopher.

For him who wrote this with his fingers, for the possessor of this book and for him who reads it with piety—may the thrice-blessed Trinity preserve all three.

4

COMIC NOVEL

Lucius or the Ass (or, more properly, *Lucius, or the Ass*, for these are alternative titles) is a ribald literary treatment of an international oral tale, the story of a man who is magically transformed into a donkey and has a number of experiences in that form before managing to regain his human shape. Although its content, or at least its frame, is folkloric, its literary form is that of the contemporary novel.[1]

The text we possess is an abridgment of the original Greek work, *Metamorphoseis* (that is, *Transformations*), which has not survived. We do not know the identity either of the author or of the epitomist, although some scholars suppose the former to be the second-century satirist Lucian of Samosata. The abridgment has been transmitted to us among the works of Lucian, but it seems unlikely that Lucian himself made the epitome, regardless of whether he authored the original novel or not, since the abridgment is not particularly skillful and contains linguistic forms of a sort that are uncharacteristic of Lucian's Attic Greek. Whatever the truth of the matter is, the author of the epitome is conventionally known nowadays as Pseudo-Lucian. The fertile lost novel also spawned a Latin reworking, *Metamorphoses* (also called *The Golden Ass*), by the Roman novelist Apuleius, who greatly increased the size of the original by the insertion of many new episodes. So the original work has not survived, but we have both shrunken and expanded versions of it.[2]

Evidence suggests that the epitomist of *Lucius or the Ass* may have reduced the work by about one-third of its original length, largely by omitting some episodes, a procedure that creates a slight awkwardness here and there when the narrative refers to a detail as known to the reader that in fact is not familiar because it presumably was mentioned in a passage that the abridger has excised. We can only guess why the unknown epitomist condensed the novel. Perhaps, as Helmut van Thiel imagines, the abridgment was made in order to produce a shorter and cheaper edition for the book market. He points out, for example, that the long account of the lovemaking of the protagonist and the athletic maid Palaestra (her name signifies "wresting school"), which may have been thought to appeal to buyers, seems to be relatively intact.[3]

Even in its abridged form the novel is the most polished and sophisticated of the fictional works included in the present volume. It makes an impression of much greater unity and coherence than than does, say, the comic biography of Aesop, in which the individual stories that are strung together tend to be relatively self-contained and capable of standing alone as adventures of independent interest, doubtless because in many cases they were in fact derived from originally independent oral tales.

The work is intended to entertain the reader with an amusing and engaging tale of comic adventure, a fantastic occurrence set in a realistic world and recounted in a realistic manner. If the original was essentially light, undemanding fiction, the condensed version made by the unknown reworker with occasional carelessness and informal diction resembles all the more an incipient folkbook. The novel recounts how a certain Lucius, a Roman author of prominent family dwelling in the Greek city of Patrae, travels to Thessaly in northern Greece in his passion for witnessing the magic and witchcraft for which the region was famous. While lodging in the household of a witch he makes love to a maidservant in the hope of gaining access to her mistress's secrets. But the careless handling of a magical salve leads to his being changed into a donkey, although he retains his human faculties, and in this manner he passes from owner to owner, all of whom deliciously reveal their true selves to the reader with complete honesty, since naturally they see no reason to pretend before an ass to be anything other than what they are.

The protagonist is probably meant to be understood as a familiar type, a Roman male of good family, an eager and educated but not particularly bright or sophisticated young man. The name Lucius was so typical that the Romans themselves employed it generically, as we might say Jack or John.[4] The quality that most characterizes him is his persistent curiosity and meddling, a trait the Greeks called *periergia*.[5] He is obsessively curious about magic, in particular about the possible metamorphoses of humans into animals, wishing to learn moreover whether the human mind changes or remains intact after bodily transformations of this sort.

Ben Perry argues, persuasively in my view, that although the comedy and realism of the novel may express a kind of playful reaction to the romantic fiction of the day such as Xenophon's *An Ephesian Tale* with its seriousness and idealism, the primary intent of *Lucius or the Ass* is simply to be a comic story, not a parody of romance as a genre.[6] To the extent that the novel may also be satiric, Perry suggests that it is a gentle satire on the sort of person its protagonist represents, a writer who is drawn to marvels, whom Perry not unreasonably imagines to be a para-doxographer, a literary compiler of marvels.[7] Other critics posit other parodistic targets, such as that Lucius's quest makes fun of "the restless quest for wisdom," a theme found in a number of Greek popular works in which an author gives an account in the first person of the alleged difficult quest he has undertaken in order to acquire the arcane knowledge that he is about to set forth for the reader in his book. Of course, in Lucius's case the restless quest backfires.[8] Alex Scobie sees a possible parody, at least in Apuleius's expansion, of the doctrine of metempsychosis, or the transmigration of souls, pointing to the Platonic doctrine that the souls of persons given to gluttony, violence, or drunkenness may pass into the bodies of asses (Plato, *Phaedo* 81e).[9] The description certainly fits also the Lucius of *Lucius or the Ass*, who indulges an appetite for sex, food, and marvels. But obviously one can imagine a number of possible parodies in the novel, all or none of which may have been present in the mind of the author or of ancient readers. If there is parody, it is ancillary and unobtrusive rather than of central importance to the novel.

One thing that modern readers may wish to see but clearly is not present in the work is serious social commentary on the respective lots of the more fortunate and less fortunate in society, the wealthy as opposed to the poor, the powerful as opposed to the weak, the free as opposed to the nonfree. The experience of Lucius as a beast of burden closely resembles the daily life of a slave—the backbreaking work, the competition with fellow slaves for food, the beatings, the use as sexual object, the lack of rights and recourse, a status so low that one's very presence is scarcely acknowledged. But the novel accepts this world with its inequalities and injustices just as it is. Despite the well-born protagonist's being forced for a while to experience at first hand the conditions of servitude, he does not himself change in any way or wish to change the world in any way; nor is the reader expected to feel indignant in general at the lot of those who are owned by others. There is no basic criticism here or in other ancient novels of the structure of society. One makes one's way in the world as best one can.

As in the ancient romantic novels, especially the simpler ones, the narrative consists of a number of loosely joined episodes that are framed by an overall problem and its solution, in this case the transformation of Lucius into an ass and his eventual disenchantment. The central adventures illustrate the protagonist's troubles and his efforts toward a solution, which, as in the romances, frequently involve one close call after another: the metamorphosed Lucius anxiously escapes having his throat slit when the band of thieves who have made off with him are discovered and arrested; subsequently, he barely escapes being castrated, having his leg cut off, having to do a sexual performance in a theater, and being executed as a practitioner of magic. The framed adventures necessarily start with that in which thieves steal the enchanted ass away from his lodging, for the theft removes Lucius from the household, allowing him to experience a variety of adventures as he passes from master to master, and it concludes dramatically with the adventure of the man who exploits him for fun and profit as a performer, a scheme that facilitates the very public and undignified scene of his retransformation while also setting up the final joke concerning his sexual attractiveness to his erstwhile lover. Apart from this, the central adventures are driven by no inner necessity, and their number or order could be changed with little effect on the whole.[10] That is, apart from the adventures at the beginning and end of this series, the central events appear to be essentially a conglomerate, a more or less arbitrary arrangement of amusing experiences.

Paul Turner's translation is a lively and idiomatic rendering of this little masterpiece of comic fiction.

NOTES

1. van Thiel 1971–1972 1:190. On the oral tale see Scobie 1983:155–227.

2. My account of the interrelationship of the three novels—the lost Greek *Metamorphoseis*, the extant Greek *Lucius or the Ass*, and Apuleius's Latin *Metamorphoses*—reflects the current opinion of most scholars and rests upon arguments that are too complex to summarize here.

3. van Thiel 1971–1972 1:7.

4. So also Gaius (rendered as Caius in present translation), the name of Lucius's brother; see Perry 1967:221.

5. See, e.g., Perry 1920:49–50. Compare the comic quest in *The Aesop Romance* (chaps. 56–64) for a man who is *not* characterized by *periergia*.

6. Opinions differ here. Some scholars (e.g., van Thiel 1971–1972 1:190–194, Holzberg 1995:72–77) hold that the original was a parody of the Greek idealistic novel, whereas others (e.g., Hägg 1991:178) reject the hypothesis as unnecessary. Probably *Lucius or the Ass* shares certain features with the romantic novels, not because it parodies them, but because the author draws from the same limited pool of literary ideas as that which other writers of fiction of the time do, including the romancers and the authors of the apocryphal Acts of the Apostles.

7. Perry 1920:47–58. Toward the beginning of the novel (chap. 4) Lucius says that he wishes to witness something "marvelous" (*paradoxon*). On paradoxography see the introduction to selection 7 from the paradoxographer Phlegon of Tralles, a contemporary of the author of the *Metamorphoses*. Lucius's account of his own literary activity, however, is really too vague for us to be able to label him with any precision: he describes himself to the Governor as "a writer of *historiai* and other things" (chap. 55), which could mean either that he records information of one kind or another or that he writes stories. So he could be a paradoxographer or a historian or a novelist.

8. Winkler 1985:251–275. Lucius does refer a couple times (chap. 4) to his "quest."

9. Scobie 1983:169–170.

10. van Thiel 1971–1972 1:204.

LITERATURE

Mason 1994. Perry 1920, 1967:211–235. Scobie 1983:155–227. van Thiel 1971–1972. Winkler 1985:251–275.

PSEUDO-LUCIAN

Lucius or the Ass

translated by Paul Turner

I once had occasion to go to Thessaly on business in connection with my father's estate. I had a horse to carry me and my luggage, and one servant to look after me. On the way there I got into conversation with a party of Thessalians who were travelling back to a place called Hypata. When we finally came in sight of the town, I asked them if they happened to know a man who lived there called Hipparchus, explaining that I had a letter of introduction to him and hoped he might put me up for the night. They replied that they knew him well and would show me where he lived, but warned me that he was terribly mean, for although he had plenty of money he kept only one servant and made his wife do most of the work.

Just as we were entering the town they pointed to quite a decent little house with a garden in front of it.

"That's where he lives," they said. "So long." And off they went.

I walked up the garden-path and knocked on the front door. After a long time it was answered by a woman whom I took to be Hipparchus's wife.

"Is Hipparchus at home?" I asked.

"He is," said the woman, "but who are you, and what business is it of yours?"

"I've got a letter for him from Decrianus, Professor of Rhetoric at Patrae."

"Wait here," she snapped, and went back into the house, slamming the door behind her.

After a while she reappeared and told me to come in. I found Hipparchus sitting on a narrow bench in front of an empty table, for apparently I had interrupted them just as they were about to have dinner. I shook hands with him and gave him the letter.

"So you're one of Decrianus's students, are you?" he said, when he had read it. "A very old friend of mine—one of the best fellows in the whole of Greece. I'm delighted to hear that things are going well with him. Well, Lucius, you can see for yourself that we haven't got a very big house here, but it suits us very well, and if you're prepared to put up with it, I think we can make you reasonably comfortable. Palaestra," he added, turning to the maid, "please take my young friend to his room, and bring in his luggage, if he has any. And don't forget to show him where the bathroom is—for I expect he'd like a wash after his long journey."

Palaestra showed me into a very pleasant little room and pointed to the bed.

"You can sleep there," she said, "and I'll put a camp-bed beside it for your servant, and fetch an extra pillow."

When she had brought in the luggage, I asked her to give the horse some oats, and went off to have a wash, after which I returned to the living-room, where Hipparchus took me by the hand and made me sit down beside him. The food was not at all bad, and the wine was excellent. After dinner we went on talking and drinking, as one usually does on these occasions, until it was time for bed.

Next morning Hipparchus asked me where exactly I was trying to get to—or was I planning to spend the whole of my time at Hypata?

"Well, I'm really bound for Larissa," I replied, "but I'd like to stay here for three or four days, if I may."

I was purposely vague about the length of my stay, because I was determined not to leave until I had met one of the local witches and seen her do something spectacular, like turning a human being into a bird or a stone. With this object in view, I set off for a walk round the town. Needless to say, I had no idea where to begin my search, so I just started walking and hoped for the best.

I had not gone far before I saw a lady who showed signs of recognising me. She was young, and to judge by her clothes and jewellery, and the number of servants with her, fairly rich.

"Why, fancy meeting you here!" she exclaimed, as soon as I came up to her.

"Fancy meeting you!" I echoed politely.

"Let me introduce myself," she went on. "My name's Abroia. You must have heard your mother speak of me—I'm one of her oldest friends, and I love all her children as dearly as if they were my own—so why don't you come and stay at my house?"

"Thanks very much," I answered, "but I don't like to desert my present host. He's been very nice to me, and I've no excuse for leaving him. But in spirit, my dear lady, I'm staying with you already!"

"And where are you staying in the flesh?" she asked.

"With a man called Hipparchus."

"What, that stingy old thing?"

"Oh, you mustn't say that," I protested. "He's been quite lavish in his hospitality—in fact, some people might call it positively extravagant."

Abroia smiled, then took me by the hand and drew me aside.

"Whatever you do," she whispered, "watch out for that wife of his. She's a dangerous witch, and a sex-fiend into the bargain. She makes eyes at every young man she meets, and if they fail to respond she punishes them by magic. She's turned several of them into animals already, and killed one or two outright. Now, you're a handsome lad, just the sort that any woman might take a fancy to—and you're a stranger here, so no one's going to worry if you suddenly disappear!"

The moment I heard that the object of my long search was actually living under the same roof with me, I lost all interest in Abroia. I got away from her as soon as I could, and hurried back to the house, lecturing myself as follows:

"Now look here, you're always saying you want to see some magic. Well, here's your chance—what are you going to do about it? You'd better not start anything with the woman herself—after all, her husband's a friend of yours, quite apart from being your host. But what about that maid, Palaestra? Palaestra means a wrestling-school, doesn't it? Well, why not strip and try a fall with her? I bet if you get a good grip and roll her about a bit, you'll soon find out all you want to know. Servants are generally well acquainted with their employers' secrets."

Hipparchus and his wife were both out when I got to the house, but Palaestra was busy cooking dinner over the fire, so I set to work at once.

"What a pretty girl you are, Palaestra!" I began. "And how charmingly you waggle your hips as your stir that saucepan! I can't help moving mine in sympathy—and I'd give anything for a lucky dip in that saucepan of yours!"

Fortunately she was not at all shy, and she played up splendidly.

"You'd better be careful, young man," she replied. "If you've got any sense or any instinct of self-preservation, you'll keep well away from it. I warn you it's very hot stuff, and if you touch it you'll get badly burnt. When that happens, it won't be any good going to a doctor, for no one will be able to cure you except me. And the trouble about my treatment is that it's rather painful and definitely habit-forming—once you've had it, you'll never be able to get along without it. No matter what I do, you'll always be coming back for another dose of my bitter-sweet medicine. It's no laughing matter, I assure you. I happen to be a very good cook, and I don't confine my operations to the sort of meat I've got here—I also know how to deal with a fine big carcass like yours. I know how to slaughter it, and skin it, and chop it up into little pieces—delicious! But the part I enjoy most of all is the heart!"

"You're absolutely right," I said. "Why, even at this range you've set my heart on fire. You've started roasting it in the radiant heat that comes out of your eyes—before I've even touched you! So for God's sake give me a dose of that bitter-sweet medicine you spoke of. My carcass is entirely at your disposal—go ahead and do what you like with it."

Palaestra chuckled contentedly, and from that moment she was mine for the asking. In fact she promised to come to my room as soon as her master and mistress had gone to bed.

When Hipparchus finally turned up, we all had baths and then sat down to dinner. After the meal we went on talking over our wine until at last I pretended to be sleepy and retired to my room, where I found that Palaestra had arranged things very efficiently in advance. My servant's bed had been put outside the door, and replaced by a table with a couple of wine-glasses on it. There was also a bottle of wine, and plenty of hot and cold water. The whole room was a positive bower of roses, some scattered about on the bed-clothes and some festooned round the walls. In fact the party was all ready to begin as soon as my guest arrived, so I settled down to wait for her.

The moment she had seen her mistress into bed, Palaestra hurried along to join me, and we spent a very pleasant half-hour kissing and drinking one another's healths. When we had finally drunk ourselves into a suitable mood for the real business of the night, she addressed me sternly as follows:

"Now remember, young man, I'm not called Palaestra for nothing. You're here to do some wrestling. Now's the time to show your mettle and give a demonstration of your technique."

"Don't you worry," I replied. "You won't catch me backing out. I'm quite prepared to be put to the test, so let's strip and try a fall right away."

"Well, this is what I suggest," she said. "I'll be the trainer and sing out the instructions, and you must be ready to do whatever I say."

"Fire away then," I answered. "You'll find me a very apt pupil."

So she took off all her clothes and instructed me as follows:

"All right, my boy, strip and rub yourself with some of this perfume. Now come to grips with your opponent. Seize him by the legs and throw him down on his back. Now get on top of him and force his legs apart. Work them up and down a few times and then go into a clinch. Now push him off and pummel him all over until you get in under his guard.

That's it—don't weaken! Now pull away and make a frontal attack with your teeth. Then once more into the breach—one big push—and the moment you find the enemy giving ground, jump at him and clamp your arms round his waist. Then try not to hurry—wait a bit before you make the final assault. That's all—now you can stop."

I had no difficulty in carrying out her instructions, and when we had finished I burst out laughing and said:

"Well, sir, I hope you're satisfied with my performance. What's the next item on the programme? Please don't expect me to do anything that's not in the book of rules."

"What nonsense! Of course I won't," said Palaestra, and boxed my ears. "And mind you don't try any tricks of your own, or you'll get into serious trouble."

With these words she got up and started tidying herself. After a while she came back and knelt down on the bed.

"And now," she said, "let's see if you've enough stamina to do the hip-throw. Come on, if you call yourself a wrestler, have a try. That's right, now you've got your opponent on the hip, so give a jerk and press home your advantage. He's at your mercy—make the most of it. The first thing to do is to get a good grip on him. Then force him backwards, still holding him firmly and not allowing him any breathing-space. As soon as he shows signs of weakening, lift him up and shove him down again. Don't break out of the clinch a moment before I tell you, but keep bending him backwards until you can pull his legs from under him. Then fling him down on his back and do what you like with him. After that you can afford to relax your grip, for your opponent's down and out for a count, and all his limbs have turned to water!"

"Please, teacher," I said, laughing, "can I give the orders now for a change? And will you please do what I say? First of all, get up and sit beside me. Now pour some water over me, and rub me down, and dry me off—and now, for heaven's sake, put your arms round me and let me go to sleep!"

We had fun and games like this for several nights running, and the special beauty of these wrestling-matches was that both sides invariably won. In fact I enjoyed myself so much that I quite forgot I was supposed to be going to Larissa. But one night I suddenly remembered the original object of the exercise, and said to Palaestra:

"Darling, do let me know next time your mistress is going to do some magic—turning herself into an animal, or anything like that. I've always longed to watch it being done. Or, better still, do some yourself, if you know how to—for then I could watch you doing all kinds of wonderful things. And I'm sure you do know how—in fact it's quite obvious from my own experience, for women have always called me as hard as nails, and I've never been the slightest bit interested in any woman before, but now I'm completely under your spell. How did you manage that, if not by magic?"

"Don't be so silly," she replied. "Love's much too powerful a thing to be influenced by magic, and anyway I don't know the first thing about it. Why, I've never even learnt to read, and my mistress is terribly secretive about her methods. But if I get a chance, I'll try and let you watch her doing one of her transformations."

Having come to this arrangement, we went to sleep.

A few days later Palaestra told me that her mistress was planning to turn herself into a bird, so that she could fly off and visit her lover.

"Then now's the time," I said, "to show how much you love me. Do help me to satisfy my curiosity at last."

"Don't worry," she said. "I'm going to."

Accordingly that evening she took me to the door of my hostess's bedroom, and told me to put my eye to the keyhole. I did so, and saw that the woman was undressing. When she had taken off all her clothes, she walked over to the lamp, picked up two pieces of frankincense and holding one of them in the flame muttered some sort of incantation over it. Then she opened a big cupboard, which was full of bottles, and took one of them out. I do not know what was in it, but it looked rather like olive oil. She poured some of it into her hand, and started rubbing herself all over with it, starting at the toe-nails and working upwards. Then, quite suddenly, she began to sprout feathers. Her nose grew hooked and horny, and she developed all the outward characteristics of a bird. The next moment she was absolutely indistinguishable from an ordinary screech-owl, and as soon as she realised that she had got her wings, she uttered a fearful screech and flew out of the window.

At first I simply could not believe my eyes, and thought I must be dreaming, but having finally convinced myself that I was wide awake, I asked Palaestra to let me see if I could do it too. I was curious to know what it felt like to be turned into a bird: did one, for instance, acquire a bird's mentality?

So Palaestra stole softly into the room and fetched me the bottle. I tore off my clothes and rubbed the stuff all over me—but the result was not at all what I intended. A tail shot out behind me, my fingers and toes disappeared and were replaced by four great nails, exactly like hooves, my hands and feet lost all resemblance to human ones, my ears grew long and pointed, and my face swelled up to a monstrous size. I turned round to look at myself, and found that I was nothing more nor less than a donkey.

I could not even tell Palaestra what I thought of her, for my human voice had gone too, and the only way in which I could express my indignation was to bare my lower teeth and give her the sort of look that donkeys use to register disapproval.

"Oh dear, what an awful thing I've done!" she wailed, burying her face in her hands. "I was in such a hurry, and the bottles were all so alike that I must have brought you the wrong one. This obviously isn't meant for growing feathers. But don't worry, it's easily put right. All you've got to do is eat some roses, then you'll be my darling Lucius again. You don't mind being a donkey just for one night, do you, darling? I'll run and get you some roses first thing in the morning, and you'll be perfectly all right the moment you've eaten them."

Throughout this speech she had been tickling my ears and affection-ately patting my hide.

Well, admittedly to all appearances I had made an ass of myself, but inside I was still an intelligent human being called Lucius, even if I could not talk; so silently cursing Palaestra for her silly mistake and grinding my teeth with exasperation, I made my way to the place where I knew that my own horse and a real donkey of Hipparchus's were tethered. When they saw me coming, they immediately assumed that I wanted to eat their fodder. Their ears went back and they prepared to fight for their stomachs with their hooves. As soon as I understood what was worrying them, I went and stood well away from the feeding-trough, laughing heartily at the idea that I should want to eat oats—but my laugh sounded just like a bray.

"Oh, if only I hadn't been such a busybody!" I though. "What will happen if a wolf or some other wild beast comes along? This little adven-ture's liable to end in my being torn to pieces!"

If I had known what was really in store for me, I should have felt even worse.

In the middle of the night, when everybody was comfortably asleep and everything was quiet, I heard a slight noise on the other side of the wall, as though someone was digging through it. Someone *was* digging through it, and before long the hole was big enough for that someone to get in. The next moment he had wriggled through the hole, followed by several others, all carrying swords. After tying up Hipparchus and Pa-laestra and my servant in their respective beds, they proceeded to ransack the house at their leisure, carrying off all the money and clothes and domestic equipment they could lay their hands on. When they had col-lected everything they wanted, they got hold of me and the other donkey and the horse, and tied their plunder on our backs. Then they started making their getaway along a rough track that led up into the mountains, keeping us on the move, overloaded as we were, by beating us with sticks.

I cannot say what it was like for the other animals, but as far as I was concerned, being unshod, rather skinny, and quite unused to it, I found it absolute agony trotting over the sharp stones with a weight like that on top of me. I stumbled repeatedly, but had to keep going because every time I looked like falling down, one of them gave me a whack across the back of my legs with a stick. It was so painful that once or twice I cried, "Oh, God!" But it sounded like an ordinary donkey's bray, for the "Oh" came out with unexpected volume, and the "God" refused to come out at all. However, it did have some effect: it made them hit me all the harder, for fear I advertised their presence by my brays. So in the end I decided that it was better to suffer in silence, and at least enjoy the privilege of not being beaten so often.

By daybreak we had climbed high into the mountains, and they tied up our mouths in case we stopped to graze and spent the whole morning having breakfast instead of getting on with the journey. So for the moment I had no option but to go on being a donkey. However, about midday we came to a house which apparently belonged to some friends of theirs, for they were given a warm welcome and invited in to lunch, while some oats were provided for us animals. The other two tucked in immediately, but although I was terribly hungry I started looking round for something else to eat, as raw oats were not at all the sort of diet that I was accustomed to.

At the back of the house I soon spotted a garden full of splendid-looking vegetables, with what appeared to be roses growing at the far side of it. Nobody was watching, for the robbers and their friends were busy having lunch indoors, so I trotted round the house and into this garden, partly with the idea of eating some vegetables, and partly in the hope that the roses would turn me back into a human being. Well, the vegetables were all right, and I fairly stuffed myself with lettuces and radishes and parsley, and various other things that can be eaten raw; but the roses turned out not to be the genuine article. They were merely the flowers of a species of wild laurel, commonly known as a rhododendron—and rhododendron makes the worst lunch in the world for either a horse or a donkey, as it is a deadly poison to them.

At this point the gardener heard me, and seizing a stick came rushing out into the garden. When he saw what havoc I was making among his vegetables, he took the sort of action that you would expect from a rich householder with strong views on the rights of property who catches a burglar on his premises: he gave me a merciless thrashing on my ribs and legs, cut open both my ears, and covered my face with bruises.

After a while I could not stand it any longer. I lashed out with my back legs and sent him sprawling among his precious vegetables, and galloped off into the mountains. When he saw me escaping, he shouted to the others to set the dogs on me. There were any number of them, each about the size of a bear, and I knew they were bound to catch me and tear me to pieces, so after galloping about for a bit I decided that my wisest course was to turn round and head for the house. The dogs came rushing towards me, but their owners called them off and tied them up again, after which they proceeded to give me such a savage beating that the pain of it made me sick up all the vegetables I had eaten.

When the time came to continue our journey, they tied the largest and heaviest pieces of stolen property on my back, and off we went again. What with the beating and the weight I had to carry, and the fact that my hooves were practically worn away, I was absolutely at my last gasp, and made up my mind to fall down and refuse to get up again, even if they beat me to death. The advantage of this plan, as I saw it, was that they would be compelled to divide my load between the horse and the other donkey, and leave me to the mercy of the wolves. But some malignant power must have realised my intention and deliberately frustrated it, for at that moment the other donkey, who had probably been thinking along much the same lines, suddenly dropped in his tracks. The robbers tried to make the poor beast get up by beating him with a stick, and when he took no notice of that they attempted to rouse him by grabbing hold of his ears and tail and pulling them as hard as they could. When this had no effect either, they decided that it was a waste of time to go on fussing round a dead donkey when they were supposed to be making a getaway, so after dividing his load between me and the horse, they disposed of my poor companion in misery by hacking off his legs with a sword and pushing him, still breathing, over a precipice.

When I saw my fellow-sufferer hurtling down to his death, and realised what would have happened if I had carried out my plan, I thought I had better put up with the pain in my feet and at all costs keep going; for I told myself that I was bound to come across some roses sooner or later, and so be able to recover my human form. I also heard one of the robbers say that there was not much further to go, and that the next stop would be the end of their journey. This encouraged me to maintain a steady trot, in spite of my enormous load, and before the day was over we had reached the robbers' headquarters.

After unloading their plunder and storing it away, the robbers took us indoors, where an old woman was sitting in front of a blazing fire.

"Why are you sitting there doing nothing?" one of them shouted at her. "Hurry up and get us something to eat."

"It's all ready," she replied. "There's plenty of bread and wine, and I've cooked some meat for you as well."

"That's good," they said, and started undressing in front of the fire. Then they rubbed themselves with oil, and completed their toilet by ladling some warm water out of the copper on the hob and sloshing it over their heads. A few minutes later some other members of the gang turned up with a large haul of gold and silver and clothes and jewellery. After sharing it out between them, they stowed it away, and then performed their ablutions in much the same way as their colleagues had done. Finally they all settled down to an enormous meal, followed by a great deal of talking and drinking.

The old woman put down some oats for me and the horse, who started gulping them down as quickly as he could, from a very natural fear that I might eat more than my share; but he need not have worried, for whenever the old woman's back was turned I helped myself to bread off the table.

Next morning the robbers went out to work again, all except one young man who was left to help the old woman. I was depressed to find that he was a very efficient gaoler. The old woman presented no problem at all, for I could easily have got away without her seeing me, but this young man was very large and fierce-looking, never went anywhere without his sword, and never forgot to lock the door behind him.

Three days later the rest of the gang arrived back about midnight. This time they had not got any gold or silver with them; all they had managed to collect was a very pretty girl, who was crying as if her heart would break. They threw her down on the rushes that covered the floor, told her to cheer up, and ordered the old woman to stay indoors and keep an eye on her. The girl refused to have anything to eat or drink, and just went on crying—with the result that I was soon reduced to tears myself, for I was tethered to the feeding-trough quite close to her, and I never could bear to see a pretty girl in trouble.

Meanwhile the robbers were having dinner in the other room. Just before dawn one of the men who had been detailed to watch the roads came rushing in to report that a rich foreigner was driving past in a carriage full of valuable luggage. Immediately they all jumped up and grabbed their weapons, and after saddling me and the horse started driving us towards the road. I was so horrified at the prospect of taking part in a hold-up that I began by walking very slowly indeed, but they increased my rate of progress by their usual method—that is to say, by beating me with a stick.

They got to the road in time to hold up the carriage, and kill its owner and his servants. Then they loaded us up with the most valuable part of the stolen property, and hid all the rest in the forest. On the way back they made us go so fast that I trod on a sharp stone by mistake and cut myself very painfully on the hoof, with the result that I started limping.

"Why on earth do we keep that donkey?" asked one of the robbers. "It's always falling down. Let's throw it over a cliff, or it will bring us bad luck."

"An excellent idea," said another. "Let's make it a sort of scapegoat for all our crimes."

Everyone else agreed—so I promptly stopped limping and forgot about the pain in my foot, for the fear of death acted as a very powerful anaesthetic.

When we got back to the house, they unloaded the stolen property and stowed it carefully away, after which they sat down and finished their interrupted meal.

The following night they returned to the forest to collect the rest of the plunder.

"There's not much point in taking that wretched donkey," said one of them. "It's quite useless with that cut in its hoof. We can carry some of the stuff ourselves, and the horse can manage the rest."

So off they went, taking the horse with them.

There was a very bright moon that night, I started thinking to myself:

"You silly ass, what are you waiting for? If you stay here much longer, you'll soon be providing the vultures with an evening meal. Didn't you hear what they're planning to do? Do you really want to be thrown over a cliff? It's a bright moonlight night, and they've all gone away. Now's your chance—unless you'd prefer to be murdered!"

At this point I suddenly realised that I was not even tied up, for the strap they used for dragging me along was dangling loose from my neck. Needing no further encouragement, I promptly made a bolt for the open. When the old woman saw me escaping, she grabbed hold of my tail and held on like grim death.

"If I let an old woman like that stop me," I thought, "I'll deserve all I get."

So I merely continued to go full speed ahead, and dragged her along behind me. She shouted to her prisoner to come out and help. The girl came out all right, but when she saw the old woman attached to my rump like a sort of subsidiary tail, she rose most nobly to the occasion: she vaulted on to my back and rode away on me. I was so determined to rescue her and so anxious to get away myself, that I put on a tremendous spurt, and the old woman was soon left far behind.

"O God, please help me to escape!" I heard the girl praying. Then she put her mouth to my ear and whispered:

"You splendid creature, if you can get me safely home, I'll see that you never have to do any more work as long as you live—and I'll give you a whole bushel of oats every day for breakfast!"

Inspired by the thought of saving the girl's life as well as my own, and thus earning her eternal gratitude, I galloped along at a fantastic speed, quite unconscious of my damaged hoof. But just as we got to a place where the road split into three, we were unlucky enough to meet our enemies returning from the forest. The moonlight enabled them to spot us a long way off, and recognising us immediately they came dashing up to us and seized hold of the strap round my neck.

"My dear young lady!" said one of them. "Where on earth are you off to at this time of night? Aren't you afraid of ghosts? You'd much better come with us. We'll see you safely back home."

With these words he wrenched my head round and started pulling me back to the house—whereupon I suddenly remembered my bad foot and began to limp.

"Well, isn't that odd?" he said. "Now we've caught you, you suddenly go lame. But you were quite all right a moment ago, when you were trying to get away. You were streaking along like a racehorse then—in fact you were going so fast that you practically took off!"

The point of these remarks were driven home with a stick, and before long I had more than a sore hoof to worry about—I had a very sore leg as well.

When we got back to the house, the first thing we saw was the old woman's body dangling over the edge of a cliff. She had evidently been so frightened—as she had every reason to be—of what her masters would do to her for letting the girl escape, that she had tied a noose round her own neck and hanged herself in advance.

"Very wise of her!" was their only comment. They cut the rope and let her drop out of sight, with the noose still round her neck. Then they took the girl indoors and tied her up, after which they sat down to dinner, and discussed the situation over their wine.

"Well, what are we going to do with her?" asked one of them.

"Throw her over the cliff to join the old woman, of course," replied another. "She was trying to rob us of a valuable piece of property, and if we hadn't caught her in time, she'd have reported us to the authorities. Yes, don't you realise, if she'd once got home, she'd have had us all arrested? The whole gang would have been rounded up, and we'd all have been killed. So we simply can't afford to let her get away with it. But perhaps we shouldn't give her such an easy death as falling on the rocks. Let's think of something really slow and painful—some method of torturing her for quite a long time before she dies."

"I've got it!" said someone at last, after various proposals had been considered and turned down. "Now you must admit this is a real stroke of genius. It'll mean sacrificing the donkey, but he's always been too nervous to be very much use to us, and now he's pretending to be lame—and anyway he aided and abetted the girl in her attempt to escape. So let's slit his throat tomorrow morning, and rip open his stomach and pull out all the guts. Then we can put our young friend inside him with just her head sticking out, so that she doesn't suffocate immediately. When we've got her comfortable, we can sew up the donkey's stomach, and put them both out for the vultures. I bet they've never had such a tasty dish before. But just think what it'll be like for her! First of all having to take up residence in a dead donkey—then being cooked in a sort of oven on a hot summer's day under the blazing sun—then slowly dying of hunger, and not even being able to suffocate herself—not to speak of the other little inconveniences like the smell of the rotting carcass and the worms crawling all over her. And finally, the vultures will probably eat their way in and start tearing her to pieces while she's still alive, under the impression that she's part of the donkey."

Everyone applauded this proposal and appeared to consider it a wonderful inspiration, but I was absolutely horrified. As if it was not bad enough to have my own throat cut, my wretched body was doomed to become the grave of that poor innocent girl!

However, just as it was beginning to get light, the filthy creatures were suddenly attacked by a large body of troops, who tied them all up and marched them off for trial before the local magistrate. As it happened, the girl's fiancé was with the soldiers when they made their raid, for he was the one who had reported the location of the robbers' hideout. So he took charge of her, and led her home mounted on my back. The neighbours spotted us a long way off, and rightly interpreting my triumphant brays as a sign that we brought good news, came running out to welcome us and escorted us back to the house.

The girl made a great fuss of me, as well she might, considering what we had been through together and what a horrible fate we had narrowly escaped. She kept her promise and gave me a whole bushel of oats for breakfast, and enough hay to satisfy a camel, but I never cursed Palaestra so heartily as I did then for not turning me into a dog instead of a donkey—for the dogs were allowed to go into the kitchen and gobble up all the delicious things that were left over from the wedding-breakfast.

A few days after the wedding my mistress told her father that she was very grateful to me and wanted to give me some suitable reward for my services, so he suggested that I should be turned out to grass with the mares.

"Then he'll be completely his own master," he explained, "and have a fine old time making love to the ladies."

It sounded just the sort of thing that a donkey would like, so he sent for one of his grooms and handed me over to him. Delighted at the prospect of having no more heavy weight to carry, I cheerfully allowed the groom to introduce me to a herd of mares, and followed them out into the fields.

But apparently I am the type of person that never has any luck, for the groom soon handed me over to his wife, who set me to work grinding wheat and barley in her mill. Well, that would not have been so bad in itself: no reasonable donkey objects to making himself useful about the house. But the charming lady started hiring me out for the same purpose to all her neighbours—and there were quite a lot of them—in return for a proportion of the flour. As for the daily ration of oats that I had been promised, she used to roast them in the oven, put them in the mill for me to grind, and then bake them into oat-cakes which she gobbled up herself. All I had to eat was bran.

On the rare occasions when I was turned out to graze with the mares, I got into fearful trouble with the stallions, who suspected me of making passes at their wives. They were always chasing me about and lashing out at me with their hooves—in fact their jealous horse-play soon made life quite intolerable. The result was that I got very thin and out of condition, for most of the time I was slogging away at the mill, and the rest of it I was being persecuted by the stallions. Either way it was not much fun.

On top of all that, I was often sent up into the mountains to bring down bundles of firewood. This was quite my least favourite occupation, for it meant climbing up an almost vertical mountain-side, and with my unshod hooves I found the stony surface peculiarly painful. Worst of all, I had a beastly little boy to drive me, who thought up some new form of cruelty every time we went. To begin with, he used to beat me, even when I was trotting along as fast as I could go, not with an ordinary stick, but with a bundle of sharp twigs; and he always used to beat me on the same part of my leg, so that he very soon laid it open—but he still went on beating me on the sore place.

Then he used to load me up with enough wood to break the back of an elephant, and make me run down the steep slope with it, beating me incessantly. If he noticed my load slipping over to one side, he never did the sensible thing, which would have been to transfer some sticks from the heavier side to the lighter, and so restore the balance. Instead he would pick up some of the heavy stones that were scattered about on the ground, and tie them on to the side that was riding upwards—as if it was not bad enough having to carry all that wood, without carrying a load of useless stones as well.

On the way there and back we had to cross a stream, so to save wetting his shoes he used to clamber on to my back and sit there behind the firewood until we were safely over. But what was really unbearable was the way he treated me when I collapsed from sheer exhaustion under the weight of my load. Instead of getting off and helping me up, and if necessary reducing my load, he just sat there and started hitting me all over from my head and ears to my tail, until I somehow scrambled to my feet.

Then there was another intolerably cruel trick that he used to play on me. He would collect a bundle of sharp thistles and tie them on to my tail, so that every time I moved they banged against my legs and pricked them all over. There was absolutely no escape, for they were firmly attached to my person, and wherever I went they came too. If I tried going slowly to minimise the effect of the thistles, he thrashed me with his stick: if I tried going faster to avoid the stick, I suffered all the more from the instrument of torture at my rear. In short, that boy's one object in life was apparently to kill me.

Once, when he had been treating me even worse than usual, I lost my temper and kicked him. He never forgot that kick. A few days later he was told to move some flax from one part of the estate to another, so he got hold of me and tied the flax on to my back—or rather, he tied me to the flax, so that I could not possibly get away from it, for he was planning a really diabolical revenge. Just as we were starting off, he surreptitiously picked up a piece of burning wood from the fire, and when we were well away from the house applied it to the flax. Naturally it flared up at once, and the next moment I was carrying a bonfire on my back.

Realising that it was only a mater of seconds before I was roasted alive, I made a dash for the nearest puddle in the road and threw myself down in the wettest part of it, where I twisted and turned and rolled about in the mud, until I had put out the flames. After that I was able to continue my journey in comparative safety and comfort, for the flax was so plastered with mud that he could not set fire to it again; but when we got back, the barefaced little liar actually pretended that I had done it myself, by passing too close to the fire on our way out.

Having failed in his efforts to burn me alive, the little beast thought up something even worse. Next time he was sent into the mountains to fetch firewood, he collected an enormous load for me to carry and proceeded to sell it to a neighbouring farmer. He then took me home, and to account for the fact that I had nothing on my back, concocted a scandalous story about my goings-on.

"I don't know why we bother to keep this donkey," he said. "He's always been frightfully slow and lazy, and now he's developed a new trick—every time he sees a pretty girl or boy he kicks me over and goes rushing after them as if he'd fallen madly in love with them. Then he starts biting them—I suppose it's his way of kissing—and does his very best to mate with them. He's going to get you into a lot of trouble, for he's always knocking people down and treating them like that, and they're liable to sue you for damages. Why, just now, as we were coming back, he caught sight of a woman going into a field—so he promptly shook off every stick he was carrying, and scattered them about all over the place, then threw the woman down in the middle of the road and started trying to mate with her. Luckily there were plenty of people about and they all came running to help me, so we managed to pull him off just in time—otherwise she'd have been torn to pieces by this handsome lover of hers!"

"In that case," said the groom, "you'd better put him down. Give the offal to the dogs, and we'll have the rest cooked for dinner. If anyone asks what's happened to him, you can say he was killed by a wolf."

The little wretch was delighted, and would have cut my throat on the spot, but for the advice of a farmer who happened to be standing by—advice which saved my life, but at a fearful price.

"Oh no, don't do that," he said. "A donkey's always useful for grinding corn and carrying things about, and this particular problem's very easily solved. If you don't want him running after the girls, all you've got to do is neuter him. Then he won't have any more of these troublesome attacks. He'll grow tame and fat, and carry as much as you like without turning a hair. If you don't know how to do it, I'll come back in a day or two and perform the operation myself—and I'll guarantee to make him as gentle as a lamb."

Everyone thought this an excellent idea—everyone, that is, except me, for my eyes filled with tears at the prospect of losing what little manhood I still possessed, and I swore I would never live to be a eunuch. Rather than submit to such an indignity, I made up my mind to starve myself to death or throw myself over a precipice.

However, late that night news came from the village that the young couple to whom we all belonged had been swept away and drowned by a tidal wave, while walking along the beach the previous afternoon. So that was the end of them. In the circumstances nobody saw much point in going on being a slave, and after helping themselves to as much of their late master's property as they could carry, all the workers on the estate ran away. The groom loaded me up with all the useful things he could lay his hands on, and set off with me and the mares for Macedonia. Although I was rather annoyed at always having to do the donkey-work, I welcomed this new development, for it saved me from being neutered, if nothing else.

It was a very exhausting journey. We travelled night and day, and never stopped until we arrived, three days later, at a large town in Macedonia called Beroea. There our new owners decided to settle down, so they put us up for sale in the market-place, where a loud-voiced auctioneer advertised our charms, and prospective customers kept opening our mouths and looking at our teeth, to see how old we were. Eventually I was the only one that remained unsold, and the auctioneer told my master to take me away again.

"As you see, I've managed to sell all the others," he said, "but I can't do anything with this one."

Just then, however, Fate did one of her famous about-turns, and produced a new master for me, though not at all the type of master that I should have chosen. He was an old pervert belonging to the curious sect which worships Atargatis—that is, if you can call it worshipping when you turn your goddess into a sort of tramp and make her go from village to village begging. I was sold to this gentleman for the princely sum of thirty drachmas, and off I had to go with him, feeling very sorry for myself.

When we got to his lodgings, Philebus—for that was his name—stopped outside the door and shouted:

"Darlings, I've bought you the most heavenly slave! He's ever so strong and handsome, and he comes all the way from Cappadocia!"

The darlings, who were his fellow-perverts, all clapped their hands delightedly, thinking that his purchase was human; but when they saw that I was only a donkey, they started being very witty at his expense.

"My dear!" they screamed. "Where ever did you get that from? It's not a slave at all, it's your new boyfriend! Have a wonderful time, darling—and lots of lovely little foals just like their father!"

Next morning, however, they got down to some serious work—at least that is what they called it. Having dressed their goddess in her smartest clothes, they put her on my back, and off we went for a tour of the countryside. Whenever we came to a village, I, with my load of divinity, was made to stand still, and the musician of the party struck up an inspired little melody on his flute—whereupon the others took off their veils and started rolling their heads from side to side, gashing their arms with knives, and sticking out their tongues and cutting them, until the whole place was fairly dripping with their innocent blood. The first time I saw it I trembled violently, for fear the goddess should develop a taste for donkey-blood as well as human.

When they had finished hacking themselves to pieces, they sent a collection-plate round the circle of spectators and got it back piled high with obols and drachmas. Occasionally someone would give them some dried figs, or some cheese, or a bottle of wine, or a bushel of corn—or some oats for the donkey. So they managed to live quite comfortably on the proceeds of their piety, and were always making thank-offerings to the goddess on my back.

At one of the villages we came to, they made a convert of a handsome young fellow who lived there, and took him back to their lodgings where they proceeded to make use of him in their own peculiar way. Up to then I had always kept my opinions to myself, but this was really too much for me, and I let out a shocked "Good God!" Unfortunately it did not sound quite like that: it sounded like a loud donkey's bray.

Now, as it happened, one of the villagers had lost his donkey, and a search-party was passing the house at that very moment. Hearing my exclamation, they naturally assumed that I was the missing animal, so they marched straight into the house without knocking and caught my masters in the act. The spectacle sent them into fits of laughter and they ran off to tell the rest of the village how the holy men employed their spare time. My masters were so embarrassed at being found out that they left the village the same night.

When we got to a lonely bit of road, they started cursing and swearing at me for betraying their mysteries. Well, I should not have minded that, for I was quite used to being insulted, but I minded very much what they did next, which was to remove the goddess from my back and put her on the ground, strip off all my trappings, tie me to a large tree, and flog me practically to death with a cat-o'-nine-tails.

"That'll teach you to keep quiet in future," they said.

They even talked of cutting my throat, which they felt was the very least I deserved for ruining their reputation and seriously reducing their income. The only thing that stopped them was the look of dumb reproach on the goddess's face as she sat there in the middle of the road, deprived of all means of transport.

When they had finished flogging me, they replaced the lady on my back and started off again. Towards evening we came to the house of a rich friend of theirs, who luckily happened to be in. He agreed to put the goddess up for the night, and offered her some sort of sacrifice; but my only vivid memory of the place is that I narrowly escaped being killed there.

One of our host's friends had made him a present of a wild ass's leg, and his *chef* had carelessly allowed it to be stolen by one of the dogs that were always running in and out of the kitchen. When he found it had disappeared, he was so terrified of what his master might do to him that he decided to hang himself; but his damned busy-body of a wife had another suggestion.

"Now don't do anything desperate, darling," she said. "Just do as I tell you, and everything will be perfectly all right. Take this donkey to a place where you won't be seen, and cut its throat. Then chop off a piece of its leg to match the one that's been stolen, bring it back here, pop it in the oven, and serve it up for dinner. You can throw the rest of the carcass over a cliff somewhere, and they'll think it's just run away. As a matter of fact, it'll taste much better than the other one—you can see how plump it is."

"What an excellent idea!" said the *chef*. "How ever did you think of it? It's obviously the only way out. I'll do it right away."

They were standing quite close to me at the time, and I could see what was coming. It seemed to me only prudent to put as much distance as possible between me and his butcher's cleaver, so I broke the strap that tethered me, kicked up my heels and galloped into the dining-room, where I rushed round upsetting all the tables and lamps, while inwardly congratulating myself on my presence of mind—for I assumed that the master of the house would consider me too high-spirited to be left at large, and tell someone to lock me up. However, the only effect of this ingenious manoeuvre was to put me in even deadlier peril, for it convinced them all that I had gone mad, and every man in the room grabbed hold of a sword or a spear or a cudgel and prepared to slaughter me. Realising the gravity of the situation, I bolted into the room where my masters were going to sleep, and they slammed the door behind me and locked me in.

Early next morning our little company of pious tramps took the road again, with the goddess on my back, and eventually arrived at a large village, where they started preaching an entirely new point of doctrine, *viz.* that the goddess should not be lodged in a human dwelling, but in the temple of the chief local deity. The villagers readily agreed to billet her on their own goddess, and directed us to a poor-house.

After spending several days there, my masters decided to move on to a nearby town, and asked for their goddess to be returned. They were given permission to enter the holy precincts and fetch her out themselves, and having done so they mounted her on my back and started off. However, under cover of taking the goddess, they had also helped themselves to a golden bowl which had been placed in the temple as an offering. As soon as the villagers discovered the theft, they came galloping after us on horseback. Having overtaken us, they jumped down from their horses, seized hold of my masters and started calling them names and demanding the return of the stolen property. Everyone was searched, and the bowl was finally run to earth under the goddess's skirts; so the holy sisterhood were taken back to the village and put in prison, the goddess was presented to another temple, and the bowl was restored to its rightful owner.

Next day the villagers decided to sell all the criminals' effects, including me, and I was bought by a baker who lived in the next village. He then proceeded to buy ten bushels of corn, which he tied on to my back, and I had to carry them all the way to his house When we got there, he took me into his mill, where I saw any number of four-footed fellow-slaves, each turning a separate mill-stone; the other half of the building was piled high with sacks of flour. As I was new to the job and had just come a long way with a heavy load, he gave me a short rest before setting me to work; but next morning they tied a piece of cloth over my eyes and yoked me to the handle of one of the mill-stones. Then they started trying to make me walk round.

Well, of course I knew perfectly well how to grind corn, having done it only too often before, but I pretended not to understand what was wanted. However, it was no use, for they just stood in a circle round the mill-stone and hit me, one after another, with their sticks. As I was blindfold, I never knew where the next blow was coming from, and in my efforts to avoid them I was soon spinning round like a top. Thus I learnt from bitter experience that a slave is well-advised to use his own initiative, rather than wait for encouragement from his master.

After a few weeks of this I was nothing but skin and bone, so my master decided to sell me. This time I was bought by a market-gardener who needed transport to run his business. Every morning he used to load me up with vegetables and take me off to market. Then, as soon as they had been sold, back we would go to the garden, where he would spend

the rest of the day digging and planting and watering, while I stood about
doing nothing.

It was an absolutely wretched life. For one thing, it was winter by
this time, and my master was far too poor to buy any bedding for himself
even, let alone for me. Then I was always paddling about in wet mud, or
walking barefoot across sharp ridges of frozen soil; and we never had
anything to eat but lettuces—and very tough and bitter they were too.

One day, on our way to the garden, we met a gentleman in military
uniform who addressed us in Italian and asked the gardener where he
was taking that donkey—in other words, me. My master made no reply,
presumably because he did not understand the language. The officer was
so annoyed at being ignored that he gave the gardener a cut with his
cane, whereupon the latter made a dive at his ankles, jerked him off his
feet and laid him flat in the road. Having got his opponent down, he
started hitting him and kicking him and banging his head very hard on
the pavement. At first the officer attempted to fight back, and swore he
would draw his sword and kill him the moment he got up.

"You shouldn't have told me that," replied the gardener. "Now I
know what to do, don't I?"

With these words he drew the sword himself, threw it as far away as
he could—and went on hitting him. Finding that the situation was getting
beyond him, the officer shammed dead, which gave the gardener such a
fright that he promptly abandoned the supposed corpse, and stopping
only to pick up the sword, mounted me and galloped back to the town.
Not feeling safe even there, he asked another gardener to look after his
business, and went into hiding with me at the house of a friend of his.
Well, of course it was easy enough for him to hide in a cupboard, but I
presented a somewhat bigger problem, which they finally solved by picking me up by the legs, lugging me up a ladder, and locking me in an attic.

Meanwhile, as it later transpired, the officer had struggled to his feet
and staggered with aching head back to the town, where he met some
of his brother-officers and told them about the gardener's outrageous
behaviour. They soon found out where we were and sent for the police,
who came and banged on the door and said that everyone was to go
outside; but when all the visible occupants of the house had been lined
up in the street, my master was not among them. So they all started
arguing at the tops of their voices, the officers insisting that the gardener
and his donkey must be somewhere in the house, and the police retorting
angrily that there was no sign of either of them.

Between them they made such a noise in the narrow street that I heard
it up in my attic, and as usual my curiosity got the better of me. I poked
my head through the window to see what all the shouting was about—
and gave the whole show away. The officers spotted me immediately and
let out a view halloo, the police made a thorough search of the house,

and my master was discovered in his cupboard and haled off to prison to answer for his crime. As for me, I was brought down to earth again and handed over to the officers, who were still roaring with laughter at the way I had betrayed my presence in the attic and thus informed against my own master. In fact, that little *faux pas* of mine was probably the origin of the modern phrase: "Don't stick your neck out!"

What happened to the gardener after that I have no idea, for the officers decided to sell me, and were lucky enough to get a whole twenty-five drachmas for me. My new owner was the *chef* of a very rich man from Thessalonica, the capital of Macedonia, and he had a brother who did the baking and pastry-making in the same household. The brothers had always been great friends, and shared a room in which they kept their various implements, all jumbled up together. When I arrived, this room became my stable, but it was also a sort of larder, for every night they used to bring back all the meat and fish and bread and pastry that was left over from their master's dinner, and store it away there.

Having provided me with this delightful company, off they went to have a bath, locking the door behind them. Well, naturally I said a long farewell to the oats that they had given me, and started sampling their own exquisite handiwork. It was the first time for ages that I had tasted decent food, and I made the most of it; but I was fairly cautious to begin with, and there was so much of it that for several nights the signs of my *gourmandise* went unnoticed. Finding that they were totally unaware of what was happening, I turned my attention to the special delicacies, and generally let myself go.

Even when they did notice my depredations, their first reaction was to suspect one another; so they merely made a few pointed remarks about people who misappropriated public property, and resolved to be more careful in future about their stock-taking. In the meantime I continued to live on the fat of the land, with the result that I soon recovered my good looks, and my coat became sleek and glossy.

Eventually the honest fellows noticed the discrepancy between my excellent condition and my undiminished pile of oats, which gave them an inkling of the truth. So the next time they went out, they shut the door behind them as usual, but instead of going away they put their eyes to the key-hole and watched me having dinner.

The sight of a donkey eating his way through such an incredible menu sent them into fits of laughter, and they called all the other servants to see it too, and they burst out laughing as well. Between them they made so much noise that their master heard it in the dining-room, and asked what the joke was. When they told him, he got up from the table and applied his eye to the key-hole just in time to see me setting to work on a large helping of wild boar, at which he let out a shriek of merriment and came bursting into the room.

I was dreadfully embarrassed at being found out, for I feared he would think me a glutton as well as a thief; but he was so amused that he took me straight into the dining-room and ordered a special table to be laid for me. This was then loaded with food, of a type that would be quite unsuitable for an ordinary donkey, such as soup, fish, meat and oysters, with every conceivable dressing from mustard and olive-oil to caviar. As a matter of fact I was full up already, but finding that my luck had turned at last, I thought my only hope was to enter into the spirit of the thing, so I went up to the table and ate a hearty meal.

Everyone rocked with laughter, and eventually somebody said:

"I bet that donkey wouldn't say no to a glass of wine, if you poured it out for him!"

"Let's try and see," said my host (whose name, by the way, was Menecles), so his butler filled a glass for me, and I was only too happy to drink it.

Menecles was now convinced, as well he might be, that I was a most unusual animal. He therefore instructed his secretary to give the *chef* twice as much as he had paid for me, and told a young freedman of his to teach me as many amusing tricks as he could. He could hardly have had an easier job, for I was an extremely apt pupil. First of all he taught me to lie on a couch, propped up on one elbow like a human being. Then he taught me to wrestle with him and dance on my hind legs. Finally he taught me to nod and shake my head in answer to questions, and do various other things that I was perfectly capable of doing already.

Before long I was quite a celebrity, and everyone was talking about the wonderful donkey that wrestled and danced and drank its master's wine; but my two greatest accomplishments were answering questions by nodding or shaking my head, and catching the butler's eye when I wanted a drink. Of course, if they had known I was really a human being, they would have thought nothing of it; but luckily I was in a position to turn their ignorance to my advantage.

Besides all my other tricks, I learnt to carry my master at a very slow walking-pace, and also to trot so smoothly that he could hardly tell I was doing it. In return for this I was given some very expensive purple trappings, a bridle ornamented with silver and gold, and a harness with bells all over it, so that I had music wherever I went.

I said that Menecles came from Thessalonica, but I have not yet explained what he was doing in this part of Macedonia. The answer is that he had come to collect some gladiators for a show that he was putting on, and as soon as he had got enough he started home again. We set off early in the morning, and whenever the road was too bumpy for him to be comfortable in his carriage, I had to carry him on my back.

Eventually we reached our destination, to find that my fame had travelled ahead of me, and everyone was dying to see the donkey that did such wonderful tricks, and wrestled and danced just like a human being. However, I had to disappoint my public, for my master preferred to exhibit me at a series of private views to which only the most important people were invited, and to use me as a floor-show at his more exclusive dinner-parties.

My trainer followed suit, and converted me into a valuable source of income by locking me up in a room, and charging my fans an exorbitant fee for admission. In spite of this I had any number of visitors, and they all brought me something to eat. It was usually the type of thing that would be bound to disagree with a donkey, but I made it my policy never to refuse anything, with the result that I soon grew immensely fat.

One of my visitors was a foreign girl, who was very rich and not at all bad to look at. The moment she saw me having lunch, she fell passionately in love with me. I suppose it was partly because of my exquisite beauty, and partly because I seemed so human in other respects that she could not help wondering what I should be like in bed. Anyhow, she had a word with my trainer and offered him a large sum of money if he would let her spend the night with me. Well, obviously he could not have cared less whether the experiment was successful or not, so he took the money and agreed to do what she asked.

Sure enough, when my master had finished with me in the dining-room and sent me off to bed, I found the lady waiting for me. She had had a mattress put on the floor, complete with plenty of soft pillows, and there she was lying on it. As soon as I arrived, she told her maid to go and sleep in the corridor, and after taking off all her clothes and turning up the lamp as high as she could, she stood beside it and rubbed herself all over with perfume from an alabaster bottle. Then she rubbed some on me, especially round my nostrils, after which she gave me a kiss and murmuring the sort of endearments that women go in for on these occasions, got hold of my halter and started pulling me gently towards the bed.

I cannot say I needed much pulling, for I had drunk a lot of wine that night at dinner, the perfume had a most stimulating effect, and the girl, now I came to look at her, was extremely attractive. So I lay down on the bed; but I was very uncertain what to do next, for my donkey-career up to date had been one of complete celibacy, and I was terribly afraid I might do her a serious injury, or even be had up for murder. However, I need not have worried, for finding that I was not uninterested she started kissing me in the most seductive way, and finally lay down beside me and arranged things to my entire satisfaction.

Even then I was so nervous that I tried to back away, but she hung on to me and would not let me go. Realising at last that I was necessary to her happiness, I stopped worrying and put myself completely at her disposal.

"After all," I thought, "I can't be any worse than Pasiphae's boy-friend."

As a matter of fact she was so enthusiastic that she kept me hard at it all night.

In the morning she got up and went away, but not before she had arranged to spend another night with me on the same terms. Needless to say, my trainer was only too glad to co-operate, for not only was he getting all the pay while I did all the work, but it also meant a new trick to show his master. So he shut us up together several nights running, and she practically wore me out. Then one night he told my master about my latest accomplishment, pretending that he had taught me it himself, and Menecles came and peeped through the keyhole while I was being put through my paces. He was so delighted with the spectacle that he made up his mind to reproduce it in public.

"Don't say a word to anyone," he told my trainer, "and on the day of the show we'll put him in the middle of the arena with some female convict or other, and let him do it in front of the whole audience!"

So they got hold of a girl who would otherwise have been thrown to the lions, and told her to go into my room and start stroking me.

Finally, when the day came for my master to display his public spirit, I was the star turn on the programme. I made my entrance as follows: the girl and I lay down side by side on a huge double bed constructed of Indian tortoise-shell reinforced with gold, which was then put on a sort of trolley and wheeled into the middle of the arena, where we were greeted by a great round of applause. Then a table was put beside us and loaded with all the ingredients of a really first-class dinner, while a couple of good-looking slaves came and stood at our elbows, ready to fill our glasses from a pair of golden decanters.

When everything was ready, my trainer, who was standing just be-hind me, told me to start eating; but I did not feel much like it, for I found it most embarrassing lying there in the middle of the circus, and I was terribly afraid that a lion or a bear might suddenly leap out at me. Just then, however, an attendant walked past carrying a large bunch of flowers, among which I spotted the yellow petals of some roses.

I instantly jumped off the bed. Everyone took it for granted that I was going to do some of my famous dancing, but instead of that I galloped after the attendant and started tearing out the roses from his bouquet and gobbling them up. While the audience were still gaping in astonish-ment, my animal appearance suddenly fell away, the donkey became a thing of the past, and the real Lucius stood there naked before them.

This unrehearsed transformation-scene naturally created a tremen-dous sensation, and the circus was divided into two schools of thought, those who wanted me burnt at the stake immediately for practising black magic, and those who preferred to delay sentence until they had heard what I had to say for myself. Luckily the Governor of the province happened to be in the audience, so I ran over to his box and shouted up at him that I had been turned into a donkey by a witch's maid in Thessaly.

"Please put me in custody," I went on, "until I've satisfied you that I'm speaking the truth."

"Well, tell me your name, to start with," said the Governor, "and the names of your parents and relations, if you claim to have any, and the name of the place where you were born."

So I told him my father's name in full, and then continued:

"And my first name is Lucius, and my brother's is Caius, and our surnames are the same as my father's. I write short stories and various other things, and my brother writes poetry—he's particularly good at elegiacs. And we all come from Patrae in Achaea."

"In that case," said the Governor, "your father is one of my oldest friends. He's often had me to stay, and shown me every possible kindness. If you're his son, I'm quite sure you wouldn't lie to me."

With these words he jumped up from his chair, threw his arms round my neck and kissed me, and finally took me home with him.

Soon afterwards my brother arrived with money and clothes and everything else I needed, and there was a public hearing of my case, at which I was formally acquitted of all charges against me. When it was all over, my brother and I strolled down to the harbour, and having found a ship to take us home, arranged for our luggage to be carried on board.

Before we left, however, I thought I had better pay a call on the girl who had fallen in love with me when I was a donkey, for I hoped she would find me even more attractive as a human being. She seemed delighted to see me, though I suppose it was really my news-value that appealed to her, and asked me to have dinner and spend the night with her. I accepted her invitation, for I felt it would be asking for trouble to turn down an old admirer from my donkey-days, just because I had gone up in the world since then. So I had dinner with her, and put on a lot of her scent, and made myself a crown of roses, which were now, needless to say, my favourite flowers.

Finally, when it was time to go to bed, I jumped up and, with the idea of giving her a treat, took off all my clothes and displayed myself in the nude, fondly imagining that compared with a donkey I should be quite irresistible. But she was so disappointed to find that I was in every respect a normal human being, that she actually spat in my face.

"Get to hell out of my house!" she screamed. "Go and sleep somewhere else!"

"Why, what on earth have I done?" I asked.

"Oh, for God's sake, don't you understand?" she exclaimed. "It was the donkey I fell in love with, not you! And I did so hope that there'd be one thing left, at least, to remind me of that splendid great animal—but just look at you—you're nothing but a wretched little monkey!"

She then called her servants and told them to throw me out of the house. So, with the crown of roses still on my head, my perfumed body was dumped naked on the naked bosom of the earth, in whose cold embrace I spent the rest of the night.

Early next morning I ran back to the ship to put some clothes on, and told my brother about my ridiculous adventure. Soon afterwards we set sail with a brisk wind behind us, and a few days later arrived at Patrae, where I made a thank-offering to the gods for bringing me safe home at last, after leading me a dog's, or rather a donkey's, life for so long.

5

COMIC BIOGRAPHY

The Aesop Romance is a fictionalized treatment of the life of a supposedly historical character, the fabulist Aesop. Several recensions, or versions, of the novel exist, all going back ultimately to a single work, which in its original form has not come down to us; nor is there any evidence for the identity of its author. In short, the novel became a folkbook.

According to the recension translated here, Aesop was a Phrygian by birth who was mute of speech and deformed in body, a slave of a Greek landowner. As the result of a kindly act, he miraculously gained the ability not only to speak but to speak well. He was sold and soon came into the possession of Xanthus, a philosopher with a number of students on the island of Samos. The slave and the philosopher were at odds from the first. More clever than his master, Aesop mocked his learning, caused him problems, and occasionally rescued him from his troubles. As Aesop became more successful he gained his freedom and presently went on to save the inhabitants of Samos from an attack by Croesus of Lydia and then to win for Nectanabo of Assyria a battle of wits waged with the pharaoh of Egypt. At the height of his fame he visited Delphi, where, after insulting the Delphians as he earlier had insulted their patron deity Apollo, the locals accused him falsely of temple theft and put him to death.

Two early recensions of the novel survive, called by scholars *Vita G* and *Vita W*. Although additions, deletions, and other modifications characterize both branches of the tradition, *Vita G* generally remains closer to the original. It is also much the longer of the two (G runs to forty-three pages and W to twenty-seven pages in Perry's edition of the Greek text)[1] and is written in a more popular language. The two recensions fortunately have a complementary relationship to some extent in that matter missing from one can sometimes be supplied from the other, but ultimately they are not reconcilable and, like different performances of a folktale or of an oral epic, must each be accepted as valid expressions of the story in their own right. In addition a half-dozen or so papyrus fragments of the novel are known, some agreeing with these recensions, some not, and a Byzantine version, the *Vita Accursiana*, also exists. The present translation is based upon *Vita G* with supplements in brackets taken from *Vita W*.

We can catch a glimpse of our author at work, at least to the extent of discerning some of materials he drew upon to fashion his story. First were old traditions about Aesop. No accounts of Aesop exist from his own period, the sixth century B.C., but details about him are found in Greek authors such as Herodotus from the fifth century B.C. onward. For them Aesop was variously the inventor of fable telling, the person who brought to Greece the practice of employing fables, the inventor of certain fables, or a man who was remarkable for his use of fables.[2] In any case Aesop was renowned for having recounted simple but rhetorically effective tales, narratives that commented metaphorically on an issue at hand. He was said to be a Phrygian or sometimes a Thracian, a slave of a certain Greek named Iadmon or Xanthus and a co-slave of the famous courtesan Rhodopis. Having obtained his freedom he met his death in Delphi after he had insulted the local folk, for the Delphians secretly planted a sacred cup in his baggage, accused him of stealing it from a temple, and executed him. For this unjust act the Delphians were punished by the gods.[3] No one knows how much of this information, if any, accurately reflects the life of an historical person, but the traditions, however they came into being and however they were transmitted, manifestly formed one of the important sources used by the author of *The Aesop Romance,* for the Aesop of the novel agrees in many ways with the Aesop of tradition.

Into this framework the author fits many events that were not, so far as we know, part of the biographical tradition. Some of the episodes are recognizable as international folktales or folk-narrative structures that are adapted here to Aesop. For example, when the protagonist of a folktale sets out into the world, he or she often encounters a stranger who provides exactly the magical agent that will be required for the accomplishment of the task that lies ahead. Usually the stranger asks the hero for something, the latter responds in a kindly way, and the stranger in turn provides the hero with the sine qua non for future success. This narrative structure is known to folklorists as a *donor sequence.*[4] In *The Aesop Romance* it has clearly inspired an episode that occurs early in the novel (chaps. 4–8). As Aesop was working in the field, a stranger who had lost her way approached him and asked him to show her the road to the city. He first led the woman to a grove, where he shared his meal with her, then brought her to a spring of water and finally escorted her to the

road she sought. The grateful traveler, who proved to be a priestess of
Isis, prayed to the goddess to reward her benefactor, so that as Aesop
took his afternoon nap, Isis and the nine Muses granted him speech and
the ability to devise tales. It was this magic gift that, fairytale-like, enabled Aesop to enjoy all the success that he thereafter had.

Comic ideas and routines that were current in the author's day are
another kind of raw material that he drew upon, such as the routine in
which Aesop interprets the same abbreviation in three different ways
(chaps. 78–80). One day Aesop and Xanthus come upon a cryptic inscription: A B Δ O E Θ X. Aesop interprets it to mean: "Step off paces
four, dig, you will find a treasure of gold." In the Greek the seven words
of Aesop's sentence begin with the seven letters of the Greek inscription.
Acting upon this interpretation, Aesop takes four steps, digs a hole, and
finds the promised treasure. When Xanthus proves unwilling to share the
treasure with its finder, Aesop then declares that the inscription means:
"Return to King Dionysius what you find here, a treasure of gold." The
seven Greek words in this sentence also begin with the same seven letters.
When Xanthus finally agrees to share the treasure, Aesop confirms the
correctness of this welcome plan by means of a third reading: "Take up,
go off, divide what you find here, a treasure of gold." The comic misinter-
pretation of an abbreviation, and in particular the interpretation of a
single abbreviation in several different ways, is attested elsewhere, for
Cicero illustrates the device in a discussion of humor. When Scaurus (he
says) was prosecuting Rutilius for corrupt practices in electioneering, he
pointed to the letters A.F.P.R., which were found in Rutilius's accounts,
saying that they stood for "Acting for Publius Rutilius." Rutilius ob-
jected that they meant rather "Allocated formerly, posted recently." Then
a third man called out that neither interpretation was correct, claiming
that the true meaning was "Aemilius filched; punish Rutilius."[5]

The author's single most extensive borrowing is from a Near Eastern
literary composition, the *Ahikar Romance,* which had circulated interna-
tionally in various languages from at least the fifth century B.C.[6] The
narrative recounts the adventures of the wise Ahikar, vizier to the Assyrian king. Childless and desiring an heir, Ahikar adopted his sister's son
Nadan, taught him his craft, and instructed him in wisdom. But Ahikar's
ungrateful nephew falsely represented Ahikar to the king as being a traitor. Ahikar's execution was ordered, but the kindly executioner only pretended to do his job, concealing Ahikar in a place of safety. Subsequently
the Assyrian monarch was challenged by the king of Egypt, who bade
him accomplish several seemingly impossible tasks or, if he was unable
to do so, pay tribute to the Egyptian monarch. Since the king of Assyria
now longed again for the services of wise Ahikar, the executioner revealed that the sage was in fact still alive. After his name was cleared and
Nadan's treachery shown, Ahikar got the better of the Egyptian king.

Ahikar again instructed Nadan in wisdom, and the youth died from shame. This lively Oriental story is transferred with little change from the Assyrian sage Ahikar to the Phrygian sage Aesop (chaps. 101–123).

In the view of most critics, the author of the *Aesop Romance* has assembled these materials artlessly into a patchwork narrative unified by little more than the figure of Aesop. Episodes are tacked loosely onto one another with little regard for transition, consistency of character and action, or their place in the composition as a whole. In other words, the episodes constitute a conglomerate, existing to provide abundant reading matter rather than to play a role in a tightly organized work of art. Niklas Holzberg has challenged this view, arguing that the novel is rather an elaborately structured work reflecting definite principles of composition, including the disposition of individual episodes.[7] Whether one perceives the work as constructed casually or intricately, one must grant that it is not artless, for the author is a fine and effective raconteur.

Running thematically through the life from beginning to end is a confrontation of low culture and high culture, expressed in such ways as a tension between slave and master, vulgarity and refinement, native wit and Greek philosophy, commoner and king, Isis/Muses/Marsyas and Apollo. In return for his kindly spirit the goddess Isis and the Muses enhance Aesop's native intelligence by granting him also speech and artistry. Thus equipped he gradually rises higher and higher in the world, rescuing progressively more important persons (the philosopher Xanthus, the Samians, the ruler of Assyria) from grave threats, until in the end he faces the problem of rescuing only himself, which he is unable to do.[8] While Isis is on his side, Apollo, representing Greek aristocratic culture, is not. Aesop offends this deity when he erects a shrine to the Muses and places in it a statue of their mother Mnemosyne rather than of their leader Apollo, causing the god to become angry with him (chap. 100), and the god is still wroth when subsequently the sage comes to Delphi, Apollo's special territory, where Apollo's people, the Delphians, conspire to execute him (chap. 127).[9] Aesop loses in the end to overwhelming odds, but for most of the biography he is a man of lowly origins enjoying a superiority of wit to the powerful persons of the world. The fantasy is certainly akin to that of the lowly peasant lad who by means of wit, luck, and a good heart wins the princess and half the kingdom.

Hero and anti-hero, Aesop is multifaceted. In his ugliness and sassiness, as a lowly speaker of unpleasant truths, he is reminiscent of figures such as the deformed and outspoken Thersites in Homer's *Iliad* (2.211–277).[10] A clever slave, he is a successor to the stock character of the clever slave in ancient comedy and a predecessor of the clever slave of modern folktales.[11] In his role as narrator of fables and solver of baffling problems he is a sage.

Composed around the second century A.D., the *Aesop Romance* appears to be the work of a man of modest education, perhaps a Greek-speaking Egyptian. In many manuscripts the novel is followed by an anthology of Aesopic fables, and it is not known whether the combination is original or secondary.[12] Since the novel (chap. 100) represents Aesop as writing down his fables and depositing them in the library of King Croesus, perhaps we are supposed to view the accompanying compilation of fables as being a copy of that very book. But the compilation itself makes no such claim and ancient fable collections regularly represent their contents only as tales in the manner of Aesop.

The Aesop Romance has enjoyed widespread popularity in the past and deserves to be better known in the present. The Byzantine recension spawned Bulgarian, Serbian, and Turkish versions.[13] Two Latin renderings are known, one being a version of *Vita W* made by the Italian humanist Rinuccio da Castiglione in 1448. Heinrich Steinhöwel presently published Rinuccio's translation along with a German version in his collection of the fables of Aesop (1476–77), a famous work that became one of the best sellers among early printed books. It was translated into many other languages, among them Castilian, a rendering that was the most widely read book in Spain for at least two hundred years and probably influenced the early picaresque novel.[14]

NOTES

1. Perry 1952.

2. The ancient testimonia about Aesop are collected in Perry 1952:211–229.

3. The deception of the item planted in the visitor's luggage is employed also by the Hebrew Joseph as a ruse for the detention of his brothers in Egypt (Genesis 44) and so must have been an international story motif.

4. See Propp 1968:39–50 and Hansen 1997a:458–459.

5. Cicero, *De Oratore* 2.69.280; see also 2.59.240. I am indebted in my rendering of the Ciceronean anecdote to E. W. Sutton in his translation of *De Oratore* (Cambridge, Mass.: Harvard University Press, 1942), 1:411–413, which manages to reproduce the Latin abbreviations in English. Notice also the acronym A B Γ Δ E that Alexander the Great allegedly inscribed upon his founding of Alexandria (*Alexander Romance* 1.32).

6. See Conybeare et al. 1913 and Lindenberger 1985.

7. Holzberg 1992:33–75; 1993a; 1996. Steps in this direction are already evident in Holbek 1962 2:21–23.

8. Holzberg 1993a:7.

9. Aesop's slight to Apollo and the deity's revenge appear only in *Vita G*, in which Aesop erects a shrine to the Muses, placing an image in their midst. In Perry's text, upon which Lloyd Daly's translation is based, it is "Mnemosyne, not Apollo," whereas in the recent critical edition by Papathomopoulos (1990) it is "memorial of himself, not Apollo." Although the latter reading is closer to the

received text and perhaps gains support from the fact that presently Nectanabo also honors both Aesop and the Muses with a golden statue (chap. 123), both readings rest upon emendations of the Greek manuscript. The difference is not without significance, but the essential point in both is that Aesop slights Apollo by neglecting him.

10. See Winkler 1985:276–291, who draws in part upon Gregory Nagy, *The Best of the Achaeans* (Baltimore: Johns Hopkins University Press, 1979).

11. The African American tales concerning John and Old Marster are a striking counterpart in modern tradition to the contentious and wily relationship of Aesop and Xanthus in the novel. For modern texts, see Dorson 1967:124–171 and Abrahams 1985: 263–295.

12. *Vita G* accompanies the fable compilation known as the *Collectio Augustana,* an excerpt from which is given in this anthology (selection 8).

13. Papathomopoulos 1990:27.

14. Keller and Keating 1993:4. On the *Aesop Romance* and the Spanish picaresque novel, see Holzberg 1993a:1–2.

LITERATURE

Adrados 1979–1987, 1:661–697. Holbek 1962, 2:17–38. Holzberg 1992, 1993a, 1996. Jedrkiewicz 1989:41–215. La Penna 1962. Papathomopoulos 1990. Perry 1981 [1936], 1952. Winkler 1985:276–291. Zeitz 1936.

ANONYMOUS

The Aesop Romance

(THE BOOK OF XANTHUS THE PHILOSOPHER AND AESOP HIS SLAVE OR THE CAREER OF AESOP)

translated by Lloyd W. Daly
Notes accompanying the translation are by the translator

(1) The fabulist Aesop, the great benefactor of mankind, was by chance a slave but by origin a Phrygian of Phrygia, of loathsome aspect, worthless as a servant, potbellied, misshapen of head, snub-nosed, swarthy, dwarfish, bandy-legged, short-armed, squint-eyed, liver-lipped—a portentous monstrosity. In addition to this he had a defect more serious than his unsightliness in being speechless, for he was dumb and could not talk.

(2) His master, finding him silent under all circumstances and un-suited for service in the city, sent him to the country [to dig in one of his fields. Once when he went to visit his farm, a farm hand who had gath-ered some very fine figs brought them to Aesop's master and said, "Here, master, take this early harvest of your fruit."

The master was pleased and said, "Bless me, these are fine figs." And he said to his servant, "Agathopous, take these and keep them for me. After I have a bath and dinner, serve me the fruit."

About that time Aesop happened to quit work and came in for his daily meal. But Agathopous, who had taken the figs, began to feel hungry and ate one or two of them. *He was strongly tempted to eat all of them but did not quite dare.*] One of his fellow slaves, seeing his affliction, said to him, "Friend slave, I know you have something on your mind. You want to eat those figs."

"Yes, by Zeus, I do," said he, "but how do you know?"

He said, "I know the thought in your heart from the look on your face. Now, I'll give you an idea how the two of us can eat them."

"Well, you haven't given me a very good idea," said he, "for when the master looks for his figs and we can't produce them, what's going to happen?"

He said, "Tell him that Aesop found the storeroom door conveniently open, got in, and ate the figs. Since Aesop can't talk, he'll get a beating, and you'll get what you want."

So saying, they sat down and started to eat the figs. As they were eating they said, "Poor Aesop. He's really a sad sack, good for nothing but whipping. Let's make this bargain once and for all: Whatever gets broken or lost or spilled we'll say that Aesop did it, and we'll be unbeat-able." And so they ate the figs.

(3) At the appointed hour the master came from his bath and dinner with his mouth all set for the figs. He said, "Agathopous, give me the figs." The master, seeing that he was cheated for all his pains and learning that Aesop had eaten the figs, said, "Somebody call Aesop." He was called, and when he came, the master said to him, "You damned scoun-drel, do you have so little respect for me that you would go to the store-room and eat the figs that were set aside for me?" Aesop heard but couldn't talk because of the impediment in his speech, and seeing his accusers face to face, knowing he would get a beating, he threw himself at his master's knees and begged him to wait a bit. When the master acceded, he took a pitcher which he saw at hand and by gestures asked for some warm water. Then, putting a basin before him, he drank the water, put his fingers into his throat, retched, and threw up the water he had drunk. He hadn't eaten a thing. Then having proven his point through his resourcefulness, he asked that his fellow slaves do the same thing so that they might find out who it was that had eaten the figs. The

master was pleased with this idea and ordered the others to drink and vomit.

The other slaves said to themselves, "What shall we do, Hermas? Let's drink and not put our fingers down our throat but only in our cheek." But as soon as they drank the warm water, the figs, now mixed with bile, rose up, and they no sooner removed their fingers than out came the figs.

The master said, "Look how you've lied against a man who can't speak. Strip them." They got their beating and learned a good lesson to the effect that when you scheme up trouble for someone else, the first thing you know, you are bringing the trouble on yourself.

(4) They paid the penalty for the wrong they had done against a man who couldn't speak. [On the following day the master returned to the] city. As Aesop was digging in the field, a priestess of Isis happened to stray from the highway and came across the field where he was digging. Seeing him toiling away at his work and not knowing his misfortune she said, "Good man, if you have any pity for mortal souls, show me the road to the city, for I have lost my way."

When Aesop turned around and saw a woman wearing the raiment of a goddess, being a pious man, he bowed down to her and began to make signs with his head as much as to say, "Why have you left the highway and come to the farm?"

Seeing that he could hear but could not speak, she began to gesture and said to him, "I am a stranger in these parts and a priestess, as you see, of Isis. I beg of you to show me the way, for I am lost."

Aesop picked up the mattock with which he was digging, and taking her by the hand, he led her to a grove and put before her bread and olives from his napkin and cut wild greens and brought them to her. He pressed her to share his food, and she did. Then he took her to a spring of water and indicated that she should partake of it, too. When she had partaken of his food and drink, she offered a prayer for the finest rewards for Aesop. Then again she asked him by signs to complete his kindness by showing her the way. He took her to the highway by which the wagons traveled, and when he had pointed it out, he went back and put his mind to his work.

(5) But the priestess of Isis, having regained the road and reflecting on Aesop's friendliness, raised her hands to heaven and said, "Oh, crown of the whole world, Isis of many names, have pity on this workman, who suffers and is pious, for the piety he has shown, not to me, oh mistress, but to your appearance. And if you are unwilling to repay this man with a livelihood of many talents for what the other gods have taken from him, at least grant him the power of speech, for you have the power to bring back to light those things which have fallen into darkness." And

when the priestess had made this prayer, her mistress harkened, for word of piety quickly reaches the ears of the gods.

(6) It was very hot, and Aesop said to himself, "The overseer allows me two hours for rest. I'll sleep these hours while it's hot." He picked out a spot on the farm that was green and peaceful, a wooded, shady place where all kinds of flowers bloomed amid the green grass and where a little stream wandered among the neighboring trees. There Aesop threw his mattock on the ground, lay down on the grass and, putting his napkin and his sheepskin under his head, went to sleep. The stream whispered and, as a gentle zephyr blew, the leaves of the trees around about were stirred and exhaled a sweet and soothing breath. There was much humming of cicadas from the branches, and the song of birds of many kinds and many haunts was to be heard. There the nightingale prolonged her plaintive song, and the branches of the olive murmured musically in a sympathetic refrain. On the slenderest branch of a pine-tree the stirring of the breeze mocked the blackbird's call. And mingling with it all in harmony, Echo, the imitator of voices, uttered her answering cries. The combined sound of all these was soothing to hear and Aesop, lulled by it, drifted off into a pleasant slumber.

(7) Thereupon the goddess, our lady Isis, appeared along with the nine Muses and said, "My daughters, you see here a man who may be ill-favored in appearance but who rises above all criticism in his piety. It was he who guided my servant on her way when she was lost, and I am here with you to recompense him. I restore his voice, and do you bestow upon his voice most excellent speech." So saying, Isis herself removed from his tongue the impediment which prevented his speaking and persuaded the Muses as well to confer on him each something of her own endowment. They conferred on him the power to devise stories and the ability to conceive and elaborate tales in Greek. With a prayer that he might achieve fame the goddess went her way, and the Muses, when each had conferred her own gift, ascended to Mount Helicon.

(8) When Aesop had his sleep out, he awoke and said, "Ah! I've had a pleasant nap." And naming over things he saw—mattock, pouch, sheepskin, napkin, ox, ass, sheep—he said, "By the Muses! I speak! Where have I gotten the power of speech? *Where?* Surely it is in return for my piety toward the priestess of Isis, and piety is a good thing. I look, then, to realize good hopes from the gods."

(9) Rejoicing and taking up his mattock, he began to dig again. But the overseer of the fields came among the workers and thrashed one of Aesop's fellows with his stick. Aesop could no longer restrain himself but said, "My good man, why do you so cruelly mistreat and mercilessly beat a man who has done no wrong, though you yourself take every occasion to do wrong and are beaten by no one?"

Zenas said to himself, "What's this? Aesop is speaking! By the gods, he no sooner begins to speak than he lashes right out at me, the one who talks to him and gives him his orders. If I don't find some pretext to accuse him, he is in a position to have me removed from my stewardship, for even while he was dumb, he would make signs at me as much as to say, 'If my master comes, I'll have you removed from your stewardship. I'll accuse you by signs.' If he would lay his charges by signs, he will surely be all the more persuasive now that he is talking. So I had better forestall him."

(10) Then he mounted his horse and rode posthaste to the city. Arrived at his master's house, he sprang from the horse, and fastening the rein to the ring at the entrance, he went into the house, and when he found his master, he said, "Master—"

But the master said, "Zenas, why are you so excited?"

And Zenas said, "A monstrous thing has happened on your estate."

And he said, "A tree hasn't borne fruit out of season, has it, or an animal given birth to something that looks like a human?"

Zenas said, "No, sir."

He said, "What is it that you think is monstrous, then? Just tell me the truth."

And Zenas said, "That good-for-nothing Aesop whom you sent out to dig in the field, the potbellied—"

The master said, "What has he given birth to?"

"Nothing like that," said he, "but dumb as he is, he has spoken."

The master said, "Don't expect any thanks. Do you think this is a monstrosity?"

Zenas said, "Yes, I certainly do."

The master said, "Why? If the gods in their anger at a man deprived him of speech for a time, and now, being reconciled, have given it to him again, as is the case, do you think that monstrous?"

Zenas said, "Yes, sir. For now that he has begun to speak, everything he says is unnatural; he says the most monstrously slanderous things against me and against you, too, things my ears won't bear hearing."

(11) The master was shaken by this and said to Zenas, "Go sell him."

Zenas said, "Are you joking, master? Don't you know how unsightly he is? Who will want to buy him and have a baboon instead of a man?"

The master said, "Well then, go give him to someone. And if no one wants to take him, beat him to death."

Once Zenas had this absolute authority over Aesop, he jumped on his horse again and went back to the estate. He said to himself, "The master has given me absolute authority over Aesop: to sell him, to give him away, to kill him. What harm has he done me that I should kill him? I'll sell him." Thus all the favors granted Aesop by the gods served him in good stead.

(12) A slave dealer happened to be going by horseback from the

country to the city. Wishing to lighten his slaves' burdens, he had been looking for animals to hire in the country, but since he had found none, he was on his way back to the city. Zenas knew the man, and when he met him, he greeted him, saying, "Greetings, merchant Ophelion."

And he responded, "Greetings, farmer Zenas."

And Ophelion said to him, "Zenas, you don't have any animals to hire or sell, do you?"

And Zenas said, "No, by Zeus, I don't, but I do have a male slave to sell cheap if you want him."

And the dealer, who made his living at just this, said, "You ask me, a slave dealer, if I want to buy a slave cheap?"

Zenas said, "Come over to this next property," (13) and leading him to the field he said, "One of you slaves go out to where they're working and call Aesop."

So one of the slaves went and, finding Aesop digging, said to him, "Aesop, drop your mattock and come along, the master is calling for you."

And Aesop said, "What master? My natural master or the steward? Tell me clearly and unequivocally if you mean 'the steward' and not 'the master'; for the steward is a slave and is himself consigned to the yoke of servitude."

"Well," said the slave to himself, "how he does throw words around. But what's to become of him? Ever since he found his tongue, he's been flying high."

Aesop threw his mattock down and said, "What a wearisome thing it is being a slave to a slave! What's more, it must be evil in the sight of the gods. 'Aesop, lay the table. Aesop, heat the bath. Aesop, feed the livestock.' Anything that's unpleasant or tiresome or painful or menial, that's what Aesop is ordered to do. So I have the power of speech the gods gave me, don't I? The master will come, and I'll be right there to accuse this fellow and do him out of his stewardship. But now I must knuckle under. So lead on, my slave friend."

They went back, and the slave said, "Sir, here's Aesop."

Zenas said, "Look him over, mister dealer."

(14) As the slave dealer turned to Aesop and saw what a piece of human garbage he appeared to be, he said, "This must be the trumpeter in the battle of the cranes. Is he a turnip or a man? If he didn't have a voice, I would have said he was a pot or a jar for food or a goose egg. Zenas, I think you've treated me pretty shabbily. I could have been home already. But no, you had to drag me off as though you had something worthwhile to sell instead of this refuse." So saying, he started away.

(15) As he went, Aesop caught him by the tail of his cloak and said, "Listen."

But the merchant said, "Let me go. I wish you no luck. Why do you call me back?"

Aesop said, "Why did you come here?"

And he replied, "On account of you. To buy you."

"Well, then," said Aesop, "why don't you buy me?"

The merchant said, "Don't bother me. I don't want to buy you."

Aesop: "Buy me, sir, and by Isis, I'll be very useful to you."

Slave dealer: "And how can you be useful to me that I should change my mind and buy you?"

Aesop: "Don't you have any undisciplined fellows in your slave market who are always asking for food?"

Slave dealer: "Yes."

Aesop: "Buy me and make me their trainer. They'll be afraid of my ugly face and will stop acting so unruly."

Slave dealer: "A fine idea, by your dubious origin!" And turning to Zenas, the dealer said, "How much do you want for this sad specimen?"

"Give me three obols," said Zenas.

Slave dealer: "No fooling, how much?"

Zenas: "Give me whatever you will." The slave dealer offered a trifle and bought him.

(16) When he returned to the city, he took him into his slave market. Two boys who were in the care of their mother no sooner saw Aesop than they began to howl and hid their eyes. Aesop said to the slave dealer, "There's your proof of what I said. You've bought yourself a ready relief from unruly boys."

The slave dealer laughed and said to him, "There's the dining room where your fellow slaves are eating. Go in and say hello to them."

So Aesop went in and saw some very handsome boys, a picked lot, all regular Dionysuses and Apollos. He greeted them, saying, "Hello, my little slave friends." They all shouted back in unison.

Aesop: "Fellow slaves, I am one of you even though I am repulsive."

The slaves said to themselves, "That he is, by Nemesis. What's come over the master to buy such an ugly specimen?"

One said, "Do you know why he bought him?"

Another said, "Why?"

"To use him as a horror to protect the market from the evil eye."

(17) Then the slave dealer came in and said to the slaves, "Boys, make the most of your luck. As I hope to keep you well, I couldn't find any baggage animals either to hire or to buy. You'll have to divide the gear among you, for tomorrow we're going over into Asia."

So then they paired off and started to divide the gear up among them. But Aesop fell on his knees before them all and said, "Please, my fellow slaves, since I am newly bought and not strong, let me have the light baggage to carry."

They said, "Don't carry anything at all."

But Aesop said, "I'm ashamed to let the master see me not helping when all my fellow slaves are hard at work."

The other slaves said to themselves, "Why does he have to show off? Carry whatever you like."

(18) Aesop looked around and saw what gear the slave dealer had for the trip: a chest, reed mats, bags full of equipment, bedding, jars, baskets. Spying a basket full of bread which four men were going to carry, Aesop said, "Men, just put this basket on my shoulders."

And the slaves said to themselves, "We've never seen a worse fool than this fellow. He begged to carry the lightest load of all, and he's chosen the heaviest of all."

Another said, "He's no fool; he's starved and wants to get his hands on the bread so he can eat more than the rest. Let's give him the basket." They all gathered around and loaded the basket on him. He started out carrying the basket as though he were an Atlas, but a very shaky one.

When the slave dealer saw him, he was astonished and said, "Just see how ready that Aesop is to work and how he sets an example for the others to bear their toil in good spirit. I've already saved his price. That's a load for a mule."

(19) The others laughed at him as they paired off to pick up their burdens, for as he went out onto the road, he taught his basket to walk. When he came to a rise, he would tip the basket over and pull with his teeth until he got to the top, then on the way down he would have easy going, for he would let the basket go while he got on top and rode along with it.

After a wearisome time they came to an inn, and the slave dealer said, "Aesop, give a loaf of bread to each pair." There were enough slaves so that when he gave them their ration, the basket was half empty. They took up their burdens and started on the way again, but Aesop's step was now brisk. They came to another inn; once more he gave them bread, and the basket was emptied. Now he tossed the basket on his shoulder and ran ahead of everyone.

The slaves said to themselves, "Who is this running ahead? Is it one of us or a stranger?"

Another: "I don't know, but I think it's the newcomer, the weakling who took the basket that was too much for a mule to carry."

Another: "You underestimate the little fellow's wit."

Another: "These little fellows who are short on looks are long on brains. He asked to carry the bread that would be used up right away, but we carry the firewood and bedding and brassware, stuff that can't be used up."

Another: "Bah, the fellow ought to be crucified."

(20) They finished their trip and came to Ephesus. There the merchant

made a profitable deal of selling the slaves, but he had three left on his hands, two young bucks, one an elementary teacher and other a musician, plus Aesop. The two of them didn't bring a fair price and neither did Aesop. Then a friend of the slave dealer said, "If you want to get a price for your slaves, go over to the island of Samos; there's plenty of money there, for Xanthus the philosopher has his school there, and many come over from Asia and from Greece to study with him. Someone will buy the teacher to get a partner to share the work on his studies. Someone else will buy the musician—some playboy—to add to his good times with his young friends. Someone with whom the gods are angry will even buy this one and make him a butler or a doorman or a cook." Persuaded by his friend's advice, the merchant boarded a small vessel with his slaves and went over to Samos. There he landed, took a lodging, and dressed his slaves up for sale. (21) He dressed the musician, who was good-looking, in a white robe, put light shoes on him, combed his hair, gave him a scarf for his shoulders, and put him on the selling block. But since the teacher had spindly legs, he put a long robe and high boots on him so that the length of the robe and the protection of the boots would hide his ugly shanks, and then, when he had combed his hair and given him a scarf, he put him on the selling block. But he couldn't cover up or prettify Aesop, since he was a completely misshapen pot, and so he dressed him in a sackcloth robe, tied a strip of material around his middle, and stood him between the two handsome slaves. When the auctioneer began to announce the sale, many noticed them and said, "Bah, these fellows look fine enough, but where did this awful thing come from? He spoils their appearance, too. Take him away." Though many made cutting remarks, Aesop stood fast and didn't turn a hair.

(22) Xanthus' wife happened to pass the place, riding in a litter, and heard the auctioneer. When she got home, she went into the house, found her husband, and said, "Husband, we don't have many male slaves, and most of the time you are served by my maids. Fortunately, there are some slaves on sale. Now, you go buy me a nice slave for our family."

Xanthus said, "I will," and went out. First he met his students, and then, after they had spent some time in discussion, he left the hall, and taking the students with him, went to the market. (23) Seeing from a distance the two handsome slaves and the ugly one, he admired the slave dealer's acumen and exclaimed, "Bravo! Well done, by Hera. An acute and philosophical, indeed a marvelous, a perfect merchant!"

The students: "What are you praising, professor? What is worthy of your admiration? Let us in on it, too. Don't begrudge us a share of the beautiful."

Xanthus said, "Gentlemen and scholars, you must not think that philosophy consists only in what can be put in words but also in acts. Indeed, unspoken philosophy often surpasses that which is expressed in words. You can observe this in the case of dancers, how by the movement of their hands the continued motions themselves express an unspoken philosophy. You see, this man had two handsome boys and one ugly one. He put the ugly one between the handsome ones in order that his ugliness should make their beauty noticeable, for if the ugliness were not set in contrast to that which is superior to it, the appearance of the handsome ones would not have been put to the test."

The students: "You are marvelous, professor. How fine of you to perceive so clearly his purpose!"

Xanthus: "Very well, but come along, and let's buy one of these slaves, for I need a servant." (24) He stepped in front of the first boy and said, "Where do you come from?"

He replied, "I'm a Cappadocian."

"What's your name?"

"Liguris."

Xanthus said, "What do you know how to do?"

He said, "I know how to do everything."

Aesop stood there and burst into laughter. When the students saw him suddenly taken with a fit of laughter, [his face all drawn and contorted so that only his teeth showed, they thought they were seeing some unearthly portent. They said to one another, "Do you suppose this is a turnip with teeth?"

Another said, "What did he see to laugh at?"

Another spoke up, "He doesn't laugh, he shudders. But let's see what he has to say." He went up behind him, pulled at his robe, and said, "What were you laughing at, wise guy?"

Aesop turned around and said to him, "Go away, you silly ass." The student was nonplused at this retort and retreated.

Xanthus said to the merchant, "How much for this musician?"

He said, "A thousand denarii."

When he heard this high price, he went over to the other one and said, "Where do you come from?"

He said, "I'm a Lydian."

"And what's your name?"

He said, "Philocalus."

Xanthus said, "What do you know how to do?"

The boy said, "Everything."

Again Aesop burst out laughing, and when the students saw this, they said, "Why does he laugh at everything?"

One said, "If I want to be called a silly ass again, I'll ask him once more."

Xanthus said to the merchant, "How much will you sell the teacher for?"

He said, "Three thousand denarii."

When Xanthus heard this, he lost interest and turned to go away. But the students said, "Professor, didn't you like the slaves?"

"Yes," he said, "but it's a principle with me not to buy high-priced slaves but to be served by cheap ones."

One of the students said, "If you're determined not to pay high prices, buy the unsightly fellow. He'll serve you just as well, and we'll chip in to pay the price."

He said, "It would be ridiculous for you to pay the price and for me to buy the slave, and anyhow my wife is fussy and won't stand for having an ugly slave."

The students said, "Professor, most of your teachings are to the effect that one shouldn't pay attention to a woman."

(25) Xanthus said,] "Well, let me see if he knows anything. I don't want you to lose your money on a favor that's of no use." So Xanthus went back to Aesop and said, "Good day to you."

Aesop: "And is there anything wrong with my day?"

The students: "Fair enough, by the Muses. What was wrong with his day?" They were impressed with his apt retort.

And Xanthus said, "Where do you come from?"

Aesop: "From the flesh."

Xanthus: "That's not what I mean. Where were you born?"

Aesop: "In my mother's belly."

Xanthus: "The devil take him. That's not what I'm asking you, but in what place were you born?"

Aesop: "My mother didn't tell me whether it was in the bedroom or the dining room."

Xanthus said, "Tell me what you are by nationality."

Aesop: "A Phrygian."

Xanthus: "What do you know how to do?"

Aesop: "Nothing at all."

Xanthus: "Why do you say nothing?"

Aesop: "Because the other two boys know everything there is."

The students: "Hey! He's wonderful. These fellows' answers were no good. No man alive knows everything. That's why he said he knew nothing. That's why he laughed."

(26) Xanthus: "Do you want me to buy you?"

Aesop: "What do you mean? Do you think that you already own me as an adviser so that you can get advice from me about myself? If you want to buy me, buy me. If you don't, move on. I don't care what you do. The man who's selling me doesn't have nets to drag in unwilling customers, and no one is putting you under bond to buy me. You're entirely free to make your own choice. If you want to take me, pay the price. Undo your pursestrings. If you don't want to, don't poke fun at me."

Xanthus: "What makes you so talkative?"

Aesop: "Talking birds sell for a high price."

The students: "By Hera, this Aesop has done a neat job of muzzling the professor."

Xanthus: "I want to buy you, but—you won't run away, will you?"

Aesop: "If I intend to, I won't take you on as an adviser, as you are me. But whom does my running away depend on, you or me?"

Xanthus: "On you, obviously."

Aesop: "No, on you."

Xanthus: "Why on me?"

Aesop: "If you are good to your slaves, no one is going to run away from what is good to what is bad and condemn himself to vagrancy with the prospect of hunger and fear to face. But if you are bad to your slaves, I won't stay with you for an hour, not even for a half-hour or a minute."

Xanthus: *(aside)* "This fellow is trying to avoid having something happen to him." *(To Aesop)* "All that you say is understandable in a man, but *you* are deformed."

Aesop: "Don't look at my appearance, but examine my soul."

Xanthus: "What is appearance?"

Aesop: "It's like what often happens when we go to a wine shop to buy wine. The jars we see are ugly, but the wine tastes good."

(27) Xanthus complimented him on his pat answers and went over to the merchant. "How much," he asked, "are you selling this one for?"

The merchant: "Are you laughing at my business?"

Xanthus: "How so?"

The merchant: "Well, you've passed up these valuable slaves and gone on to this repulsive piece of human property. Buy one of them and take this one as a gift."

Xanthus: "Still, how much do you want for him?"

The merchant: "I bought him for sixty denarii, and he's cost me fifteen in expenses. Pay me what he has cost."

When the tax collectors heard that a sale of slaves had been made, they came over and wanted to know who was the seller and who was the buyer. Xanthus hesitated to say, "I bought a slave for seventy-five denarii," and the merchant was embarrassed. When they didn't say anything, Aesop bawled out, "I was sold; here's the seller, and there's the buyer. If they have nothing to say, it's plain I'm a free man."

Xanthus said: "I bought the slave for seventy-five denarii."

The tax collectors laughed, remitted the tax on Aesop to Xanthus and his students, bade them goodbye, and went away.

(28) Aesop went along with Xanthus. It was the hottest part of the day with the sun directly overhead, and since the road was deserted because of the heat, Xanthus lifted up his robe and began to urinate as he walked along. Aesop was furious when he saw this, took hold of the tail

of his master's robe and, giving it a jerk, said "Sell me, since you won't stand for my running away."

Xanthus: "Aesop, what's the matter with you?"

Aesop: "Sell me. I can't be your slave."

Xanthus: "Surely one of those people who go around upsetting decent households with their slander has prejudiced you. Someone has come to you and spoken ill of me, saying that I mistreat my slaves or beat them or am a drunkard or am irritable or irascible. Pay no attention to slander. 'Slander, pleasant to hear, provokes to anger without cause.' "

Aesop: "It was your excretion that slandered you, Xanthus. For when you, the master, who have no reason to stand in dread of anyone for fear that when you come home you may get a taste of beating or may face confinement or some worse form of punishment, but are master of your own fate—when you can't even take a little time off for the physical necessities, but urinate while you walk, what can I, a slave, do after all, when I'm sent on an errand, but defecate on the fly?"

Xanthus: "Is that what was bothering you?"

Aesop: "It certainly was."

Xanthus: "I urinated as I walked along to avoid three unpleasant consequences."

Aesop: "What are they?"

Xanthus: "The heat of the earth, the acrid smell of the urine, and the burning of the sun."

Aesop: "How's that?"

Xanthus: "You see that the sun is directly overhead and has scorched the earth with its heat, and when I stand still to urinate, the hot ground burns my feet, the acrid smell of the urine invades my nostrils, and the sun burns my head. It was because I wanted to avoid these three consequences that I urinated as I walked along."

Aesop: "You've convinced me. A very clear rationalization. Walk on."

Xanthus: "Well, I didn't realize I had bought myself a master."

(29) When they came to the house, Xanthus said to him, "Aesop, my wife is fussy. You wait here at the door until I break the news to her so that she won't take one quick look at your deformity and then ask for her dowry and leave me."

Aesop: "If you're under your wife's thumb, go and get it over with."

So Xanthus went in and said, "My dear, you no longer have cause to drum at me and say that I'm waited on by your maids. You see I've bought myself a manservant."

Xanthus' wife: "Thank you, lady Aphrodite! Great you are, and the dreams you send are true. *(To Xanthus)* As soon as I went to sleep, I had a dream in which you bought a perfectly beautiful slave and gave him to me for a gift."

Xanthus: "Just wait, my dear, and you shall see such beauty as you've never seen before. I might almost say that you shall see an Apollo or an Endymion or a Ganymede."

(30) The maids were delighted, and one of the younger girls said, "The master has bought me a husband."

Another: "Oh no, for me. I saw him in my dreams."

Another: "Someone more persuasive will get him."

"And I suppose you're more persuasive."

"Well, are you?"

And so they began to quarrel.

Xanthus' wife said, "And where is the object of this high praise of yours?"

Xanthus: "He's at the door, my dear. It's a point of training not to enter another man's house unbidden. He came with me as far as the entry and is waiting there to be called."

Xanthus' wife said, "Someone call this new acquisition."

While the other maids were quarreling, the only one of them with any sense said to herself, "I'll go out now and get myself engaged to him first." She went out and said, "Where's the new slave?"

Aesop turned around and said, "Here, girlie."

She said, "Are you the new slave?"

Aesop said, "I'm the one."

The maid: "And where's your tail?"

Aesop took a look at the girl and, realizing that she was making fun of his dog's head, said, "My tail doesn't grow behind the way you think, but here in front."

The maid said, "You stay right here. If you go in, they'll take one look at what a monstrosity you are and all run away." When she went in and saw that her companions were still fighting, she said, "Girls, I might just as well puncture your little dreams. Why are you having this boxing match over the fellow? Suppose you have a look at his beauty first."

One of them went out and say, "Where is the gentleman, the one who was bought, my beauty."

Aesop said, "Here."

The maid said, "May Aphrodite slap your ugly face! So we were fighting over you, were we, you trash? Worse luck to you. Go on in and don't touch me; don't come near me."

Aesop went in and stood before his mistress. (31) Xanthus' wife, when she saw Aesop's repulsive face, turned away and said to Xanthus, "Hah, Xanthus, you've behaved very shrewdly, like a philosopher and a gentlemen; you wanted to take another wife, and since you didn't dare to face me and say 'leave my house,' knowing how fastidious I am, you brought me this so that I wouldn't put up with having him for a servant and would run away and leave the house of my own accord. All right, give me my dowry, and I'll go my way."

Xanthus said, "Oh my, you had all that sesquipedalian verbiage for me to keep me from urinating as I walked, and now you haven't a word for her."

Aesop said, "Well, let her go her way and be damned."

Xanthus said, "Shut up, you trash. Don't you realize that I love her more than my life?"

Aesop said, "You love the woman?"

Xanthus said, "I certainly do."

Aesop said, "You want her to stay?"

Xanthus said, "I do, you contemptible fool."

Aesop said, "I'll play the role you choose." And, striking a pose, he stamped his foot and roared out, "If Xanthus the philosopher is hen-pecked, I'll show him up in the lecture halls tomorrow for the contempt-ible thing he is."

Xanthus said, "Would that be any way to behave, Aesop?"

(32) Aesop said to his mistress, "Woman, what you are after is to have your husband go out somewhere and buy a good-looking young slave with a nice face, a good eye, and blond hair."

Xanthus' wife said, "Why?"

Aesop said, "So that this handsome slave can go to the bath with you, then the handsome slave will take your clothes, then when you come out of the bath, this handsome slave will put your wrapper around you and get down and put your sandals on, then he'll play with you and look into your eyes as though you were a fellow servant who had caught his fancy, then you'll smile at him and try to look young, and you'll feel all excited and ask him to come into the bedroom to rub your feet, then in a fit of prurience you will draw him to you and kiss him passionately and do what is in keeping with your shameful impudence, and the philosopher will be disgraced and made a fool of. Well done, Euripides! Your lips should have turned to gold when you said,

Dread the anger of the waves of the sea,
Dread the blasts of river and burning fire,
Dread poverty, dread a thousand other things,
But no evil is there anywhere so dread as woman.

And you, the wife of a philosopher, an intelligent woman, with your urge to have handsome male servants, you bring no slight discredit and disrepute on your husband. It's my opinion that you are sex-crazy and don't follow your bent simply because you are afraid that I'll give you a piece of a new slave's mind, you slut."

Xanthus' wife said, "What has brought this calamity on?"

Xanthus said, "He's already said this much to you, my dear, but watch out he doesn't see you defecating or urinating, for you'll find Aesop turned a regular Demosthenes."

Xanthus' wife said, "By the Muses, the little fellow seems to be spirited and tricky. I'd better make my peace with him."

Xanthus said, "Your mistress has made her peace with you."

Aesop said, "A great accomplishment to have tamed a woman by overawing her."

Xanthus said, "Bah, you runaway!"

(33) Xanthus' wife said, "Aesop, it's obvious from what you've said that you know how to use your tongue, but I was misled by a dream, for I thought I was going to have a good-looking slave bought for me, but you're deformed."

Aesop said, "Don't be surprised, my mistress, at having been tripped up by the dream; not all dreams are true. At the request of the leader of the Muses (*i.e.* Apollo), Zeus gave him the gift of prophecy so that he excelled everyone in oracular skill. But the leader of the Muses, from being marveled at by all men and habitually looking down on everyone else, got to be too boastful in everything. This angered his superior, and since he didn't want him to have so much power among men, he contrived some true dreams that would tell men in their sleep what was going to happen. When the superior of the Muses realized that no one was going to have any use for him and his prophecy, he asked Zeus to forgive him and not to discredit his oracle. Zeus forgave him and contrived other dreams for men that would give them false indications in their sleep, so that once they had found the dreams inaccurate, they would fall back again on the original prophet. That's why it is that one of the second kind of dreams, when it comes, gives the impression of truth to what you see in your sleep. So don't be surprised if you see things one way in your sleep, and they turn out otherwise, for it wasn't the first kind you saw, but one of the lying ones come to trick you with false visions."

(34) Xanthus complimented Aesop and, realizing that he had a knack of finding the right thing to say, told him, "Take a shopping bag and come along with me. We'll buy some vegetables from the garden." Aesop put the bag on his shoulder and went along. When they came to the garden and found the gardener, Xanthus said, "Give me some cooking vegetables." The gardener took his knife and cut some cabbage, some beets, some asparagus tips, and other savory vegetables, which he arranged neatly in a small bundle and gave to Aesop. Xanthus opened his purse and was about to pay for the vegetables.

(35) The gardener said, "What's this for, professor?"

Xanthus said, "The pay for the vegetables."

The gardener said, "What do I care? As for the garden and the produce, you can wipe your feet on them. But just tell me one thing."

Xanthus said, "Well, by the Muses, I'll have neither the pay nor the vegetables until you tell me how anything I say can help you as a gardener. I'm no craftsman or smith to make you a hoe or a leek slicer; I'm a philosopher."

The gardener said, "Sir, you'll do me a great favor. There's a little question that's been bothering me and keeping me from sleeping at night. I keep puzzling and asking myself why it is that when I put plants in the ground and then hoe them and water them and give them all kinds of attention, the weeds still show up before the things I've planted."

When Xanthus heard this philosophical conundrum and couldn't, on the spur of the moment, think of an answer to it, he said, "All things are subject to the stewardship of divine providence."

(36) Aesop, who was standing behind Xanthus, began to laugh. Xanthus said, "Aesop, are you laughing with me or at me?"

Aesop said, "Oh, not at you."

Xanthus said, "Well, then, at whom?"

Aesop said, "At the professor you studied under."

Xanthus said, "You blackguard, this is blasphemy against the Hellenic world, for I studied at Athens under philosophers, rhetoricians, and philologists. And do you have the effrontery to set foot on the Muses' Helicon?"

Aesop said, "If you talk nonsense, you'll have to expect to be jeered at."

Xanthus said, "Is there any other answer to the question? Things that are at the disposal of the divine order of nature are not subject to inquiry by philosophers. I suppose you have an answer to the question, do you?"

Aesop said, "Offer to do it, and I will resolve the question for you."

(37) Xanthus was embarrassed and said, "Don't be so presumptuous. I, who have debated in many great halls, have no business arguing with you here in the garden, but come along." As they strolled along, Xanthus said to the gardener, "This boy of mine here is a fellow of vast and varied experience. Put the problem up to him, and he will answer it."

The gardener said, "Now look here, do you mean to say this ugly fellow knows his letters?"

Aesop said, "Is this any way for you to talk, you miserable wretch."

The gardener said, "I'm a miserable wretch?"

Aesop said, "You're a gardener, aren't you?"

The gardener said, "Yes."

Aesop said, "Well then, if you're a gardener, do you object to being called a miserable wretch? But you want to know why it is that you put plants in the ground, hoe them, water them, lavish care on them, and still, as you say, the uncultivated weeds come up quicker than the things you plant. [Listen and pay attention. It's just as it is with a woman who comes to a second marraige with children by her first husband and finds her husband has children by a former wife. She is mother of the children she brings with her but a stepmother to the ones she finds. And there is a great deal of difference between the two things. She lavishes affection on the rearing of the children she has borne, but out of jealousy she hates the ones produced by someone else's birth pangs. Moreover, she shortens the rations for the latter and gives them to her own children, for she naturally loves her own and hates her husband's as strangers. It's the same with the earth. She is the mother of plants that grow spontaneously, but a stepmother to the ones you plant, and by giving more nurture to her own, she makes them flourish better than the orphans you plant."

When the gardener had heard this, he said, "You've relieved me of a great deal of concern. Take the vegetables as a gift. And if you want anything else, come to the garden as though it were your own."]

[*At this point a page has been lost from the manuscript. From what is told in sections 39 and 44 it is clear that what is lost told how Aesop took the vegetables home and somehow provoked Xanthus' wife, who proceeded to trample the vegetables under foot. There is no clear indication of what else may have been lost, but whatever it was, it led up to the speech of Xanthus with which the text resumes.*]

(38) ". . . harm me by doing anything more or less than you are told. Pick up the oil flask and the towels, and let's go to the bath."

Aesop said to himself, "Masters who show an unnecessarily stern attitude about the service they want have themselves to blame for the trouble they get into. I'll give this philosopher a lesson in how to give orders." So he picked up the articles mentioned and, without putting any oil in the flask, followed Xanthus to the bath.

Xanthus got undressed, handed his robes to Aesop, and said, "Give me the oil flask."

Aesop gave it to him, and when Xanthus took it, turned it up, and found nothing in it, he said, "Aesop, where's the oil?"

Aesop said, "At home."

Xanthus said, "Why?"

Aesop said, "Because you told me to 'take the oil flask and the towels,' but you didn't mention oil. I wasn't supposed to do anything more than I was told. If I slipped up on my instructions, I was going to be answerable at the cost of a beating." That was all he said.

(39) When Xanthus found some of his friends at the bath, he told Aesop to give the robes to their servants and said to him, "Aesop, go on home, and since my wife trampled the vegetables in her temper, go out and cook us lentil. Put it in the pot, put some water in with it, put it on the cooking hearth, put some wood under it, and light it; if it starts to go out, blow on it. Now do as I say."

Aesop: "I'll do it." And he went home, went to the kitchen, put one lentil in the pot, and cooked it.

When Xanthus and his friends had had their bath, he said, "Gentlemen, will you share my simple fare? There will be lentil. We ought to judge our friends by their good will and not by the elegance of their food. On occasion the humblest dishes afford a more genial pleasure than more pretentious ones if the host serves them with a gracious welcome."

His friends said, "Let's go." (40) Xanthus took them to his house and said, "Aesop, give us something to drink for men right from the bath."

Aesop filled a pitcher straight from the bathtub and gave it to Xanthus. Xanthus said, "What's this?"

Aesop said, "Something to drink, right from the bath."

Xanthus looked sullen, and after a moment he said, "Bring me the footbath."

Aesop brought it without any water and set it down. Xanthus said, "And what's this?"

Aesop said, "You said: 'Bring me the footbath.' You didn't say: 'Put water in it, and wash my feet.' "

Xanthus said, "Take my sandals and get on with your work." Then he said to his friends, "Gentlemen, I find that I haven't bought a slave but purchased myself a teacher. Now, if you like, we'll get up and go to the table." (41) When the drink had been going around for some time, Xanthus said, "Aesop, is the lentil cooked?"

Aesop said, "Yes."

Xanthus said, "Let me see if it is done."

Aesop brought the one lentil in a spoon and gave it to Xanthus. Xanthus ate the one lentil and said, "It's all right. It's done. Bring it in and serve it." Aesop put on a plate, poured the soup, and said, "Dinner is served."

Xanthus said, "Why, this is nothing but soup you've served. Where is the lentil?"

Aesop said, "Why, you ate the lentil."

Xanthus said, "Did you just cook one?"

Aesop said, "Yes. Didn't you tell me to 'cook lentil' and not 'lentils'? The one is singular and the other plural."

(42) Xanthus said, "Just so that I won't appear to be insulting the gentlemen, go quickly and prepare with vinegar and seasoning the four pig's feet you bought."

Aesop put the feet into a kettle and started to cook them. Xanthus, looking for a pretext to thrash Aesop, got up and said to him, "Aesop, go fetch the vinegar from the pantry and put it in the kettle." Then, while Aesop was gone to the pantry, Xanthus came in, took one foot from the kettle, and hid it. When Aesop came back and saw three feet in the kettle, he realized that Xanthus had deliberately removed the foot because he wanted to have a pretext for beating him. Having noted a pig that was kept in Xanthus' yard and that was supposed to be killed for Xanthus' wife's birthday, he quickly tied up its snout with a cord and cut off one of its feet. Then, when he had singed it over the fire and scalded it, he threw it into the kettle to replace the one that had been stolen. Xanthus, suspecting that Aesop would run away if he didn't find the foot, took it out of hiding, went out, and threw it into the kettle. That made five feet. But Aesop didn't know there were five feet, and neither did Xanthus. (43) After a while, Xanthus said to Aesop, "Have you cooked the pig's feet?"

Aesop said, "Yes."

Xanthus said, "Then bring them in."

Aesop put a dish on the table, emptied the kettle, and out came five feet. When he saw this, Xanthus turned pale and said, "Aesop, how many feet did this one pig have?"

Aesop said, "It comes out all right. Here are five feet, and the pig we're feeding outside has three."

Xanthus said, "Gentlemen, this fellow will soon drive me mad."

Aesop said, "Well, you shouldn't have laid the law down to me so literally, and I would have served you properly. But don't feel sorry about it, master. The way you stated the rule for me will turn out to your advantage, for it will teach you not to make mistakes in the classroom. Statements that go too far in either inclusion or exclusion are no small errors."

Xanthus, finding no pretext for beating Aesop, held his peace.

(44) Thereafter Aesop attended him in the classroom and became a familiar figure to everyone. Once one of the students planned a dinner to which he invited Xanthus and the other students. Xanthus said to Aesop, "Get what I need for a dinner, and come along. I mean a basket, a plate, a napkin, a lantern, sandals, and anything I may have forgotten to mention." Aesop got them and went along. In the course of the dinner Xanthus took portions and gave them to Aesop. Aesop took them and put them in the basket. Xanthus turned to Aesop and said, "Do you have all the portions?"

Aesop said, "I have."

Xanthus said, "Then take them to her who loves me."

Aesop said, "I will." As he went out, Aesop said to himself, "Now is my chance to pursue my feud with the mistress and pay her back for poking fun at me and running me down just after I was bought, for tearing up and trampling the vegetables I was given by the gardener, and for not giving my gift a chance to please the master. I'll show her that a wife can't match strength with a friendly slave. Since the master said: 'Give the portion to her who loves me,' now let him see who loves him." (45) When Aesop got home and went into the house, he put the basket down before him and called Xanthus' wife. He showed her all the portions and said, "Mistress, observe carefully; nothing is missing, and nothing has been eaten."

Xanthus' wife said, "Everything is all right and in good shape, Aesop. Did your master send this to me?"

Aesop said, "No."

Xanthus' wife said, "And to whom did he send it?"

Aesop said, "To her who loves him."

Xanthus' wife said, "And who loves him, you runaway?"

Aesop said, "Just wait a little, and you'll see who loves him." Seeing the thoroughbred bitch who was a pet in the house, he called her and said, "Come, Lycaena; take this." The bitch came running, and he gave the food to her. When she had eaten it all, Aesop went back to where the dinner was being given and took his place behind the couch at Xanthus's feet.

(46) Xanthus said, "Well, Aesop, did you give it to her?"

Aesop said, "I did."

Xanthus said, "Did she eat it?"

Aesop said, "Yes, she ate it all."

Xanthus said, "Was she able to eat all of it?"

Aesop said, "Yes, she was hungry."

Xanthus said, "Did she enjoy it?"

Aesop said, "Yes, she did."

Xanthus said, "What did she say?"

Aesop said, "She didn't say anything, but in her heart she certainly expressed her gratitude."

Xanthus said, "I'll get even with her."

Xanthus' wife said to her maids, "Girls, I can't stay with Xanthus any longer. Let him give me my dowry, and I'll go away. When he prefers the dog to me, how can I live with him any longer?" So she went off in a bad mood to the bedroom.

(47) As the drinking went on, there was extended conversation, and as you might expect among men of scholarly interests, all manner of questions were brought up. One of the students said, "What circumstance will produce great consternation among men?"

Aesop, standing behind his master, said, "If the dead were to arise and demand back their property."

There was much laughter and a lot of buzzing among the students, and they said, "This is the newly bought slave, the one Xanthus bought when we were there." One of them said, "He once said I was a silly ass." Another said, "Some of the things he says are his own ideas, but the rest he learns from Xanthus."

Aesop said, "So it is with all of you."

The students said, "By the Muses, professor, do let Aesop have a drink." Xanthus gave him permission, and Aesop had a drink. (48) One of the students said to the others, "Why is it that a sheep being led to the slaughter doesn't make a sound, but a pig squeals loudly?"

When no one could find an answer to the question, Aesop said, "Because the sheep has its milk, which is useful, and its wool, which is beautiful, and when the time comes, it is shorn of its wool, which is heavy, and in getting milked is also unburdened, so that when it is led to the sacrifice, since it expects no harm, it goes along happily and doesn't try to run away when the knife is put to it. But the pig squeals so loudly because it doesn't have any wool that is useful nor any milk. No wonder it makes a big noise since it knows that it is being led off for the use that will be made of its meat."

The students said, "A clear answer, by the Muses!"

(49) When they all left, Xanthus went back home and went to the bedroom, where he began to talk sweet talk to his wife and shower her with kisses. But she turned her back on Xanthus and said, "Don't come near me, you slave-lover, or rather you dog-lover. Give me back my dowry."

Xanthus said, "Of all the bad luck. Now what has Aesop cooked up for me?"

Xanthus' wife said, "Go take her to whom you sent all the food."

Xanthus said, "Didn't I say Aesop had started a rumpus for me? Someone call Aesop." (50) Aesop came in, and Xanthus said, "Aesop, to whom did you give the food?"

Aesop said, "You told me: 'Give it to her who loves me.'"

Xanthus' wife said, "I didn't get a thing. There he is. Let him deny it to my face."

Xanthus said, "There, you runaway, she says she didn't get it."

Aesop said, "To whom did you say I should give the food?"

Xanthus said, "To her who loves me."

Aesop said, "And wherein does this woman love you?"

Xanthus said, "Well then, who does, you runaway?"

Aesop said, "Find out who loves you," and calling the dog, he said, "She loves you. Your wife says she loves you, but she doesn't. Here's your proof. This woman who you think loves you wants her dowry back and is ready to leave you for the sake of a little bit of food. Beat your dog, thrash her within an inch of her life, knock her down, drive her off, and she won't go away. She'll forget your mistreatment, she'll turn around and come back to look for her master with her tail wagging. So you ought to have said to me: 'Take it home to my wife' and not to her who loves me,' for it's not the woman who loves you but the dog."

Xanthus said, "You see, my dear, it wasn't my mistake; it was the doubletalk of this fellow who brought it. I'll find some excuse to beat him and get even for you."

[(50a) She said, "From now on I'll no longer live with you." And she sneaked out and went to her parents.

Aesop said to his master, "Didn't I tell you it was the dog who loved you, and not my mistress?"

When several days passed and she was still not reconciled, Xanthus sent some friends to urge her to come back to him. Since Xanthus was very disconsolate at being deprived of his wife, Aesop went to him and said, "Don't grieve, master, for tomorrow I'll make her come back to you of her own accord." He took some money and went to the market, where he bought some birds, some geese, and other things. He carried them with him as he passed the place where his mistress was, pretending, of course, not to know that Xanthus' wife was there. Finding one of her parents' slaves, he said to him, "Brother, I don't suppose the people in this house have any geese or anything of the sort that would be good for a wedding, do they?"

He said, "And what do you need them for?"

Aesop: "Xanthus, the philosopher, is going to take a wife tomorrow."

He ran off home and reported this to Xanthus' wife. As soon as she heard it, she hurried off to Xanthus and screamed at him, "Xanthus, you can't take up with another woman while I'm alive."]

(51) The next day Xanthus sent out invitations to the students who had entertained him at dinner and said to Aesop, "I've invited my friends to dinner; go cook the best, the finest thing imaginable."

Aesop said to himself, "I'll show him not to give me stupid orders." So he went to the butcher shop and bought the tongues of the pigs that had been slaughtered. When he came back, he prepared them all, boiling some, roasting some, and spicing some. At the appointed hour the guests arrived.

Xanthus said, "Aesop, give us something to eat." Aesop brought each a boiled tongue and served hot sauce with it.

The students said, "Hah, Xanthus, even your dinner is fraught with philosophy. You never do anything that isn't carefully worked out. At the very beginning of the dinner we're served tongues."

(52) After they had two or three drinks, Xanthus said, "Aesop, give us something to eat." Again Aesop served each a roast tongue with salt and pepper.

The students said, "Wonderful, professor, excellent, by the Muses. Every tongue is sharpened by fire, and best of all by salt and pepper, for the salt combines with the sharpness of the tongue to give it a glib and biting effect."

After they had drunk again, Xanthus said, for the third time, "Bring us food."

Aesop brought each of them a spiced tongue. One student said to another, "Democritus! I'm getting tongue-tied eating tongues."

Another student said, "Is there nothing else to eat? Whatever Aesop has a hand in will come to no good end."

When the students tried to eat the spiced tongues, they were seized with nausea. Xanthus said, "Aesop, give us each a bowl of soup."

Aesop served them tongue broth. The students didn't even touch this but said, "This is Aesop's master stroke; we admit defeat by tongue."

Xanthus said, "Aesop, do we have anything else?"

Aesop said, "We have nothing else."

(53) Xanthus said, "Nothing else, damn you? Didn't I tell you: 'Buy the finest, the most delicious thing imaginable'?"

Aesop said, "I am glad you find fault with me in the presence of scholarly gentlemen. You told me: 'Buy the finest, the most delicious, the greatest thing imaginable.' Well, what can one imagine finer or greater than the tongue? You must observe that all philosophy, all education, depends on the tongue. Without the tongue nothing gets done, neither giving, nor receiving, nor buying. By means of the tongue states are re-formed and ordinances and laws laid down. If, then, all life is ordered by the tongue, nothing is greater than the tongue."

The students said, "Yes, well put, by the Muses. It was your mistake, professor." They went home, and all night long they suffered from sei-zures of diarrhea.

(54) The next day the students took Xanthus to task. Xanthus said, "Gentlemen and scholars, it was not my fault; it was the fault of that worthless slave. But tomorrow I'll repay you your dinner, and I'll give him his orders in your presence." Then and there he called Aesop and said to him, "Since you are determined to turn my words around, go to the market and buy the most worthless, the most inferior thing there is."

When Aesop heard this, nothing daunted, he went to the butcher, and again he bought the tongues of all the pigs that had been butchered. Then he went back and prepared them for dinner. Xanthus came home with his students, and they took their places at table. After they had the first drink, he said, "Aesop, give us something to eat."

Aesop served each a pickled tongue and hot sauce. The students said, "What's this, tongues again?" Xanthus turned pale. The students said, "Maybe he wants the vinegar to help our stomachs recover from yester-day's diarrhea."

After they had another drink or two, Xanthus said, "Give us some-thing to eat." Aesop served each of them a roast tongue. The students said, "Bah, what's this? Our dunderhead of yesterday is trying to make us sick again with his tongues."

(55) Xanthus said, "What? Again, you filthy villain? Why did you buy these? Didn't I tell you: 'Go to the market, and if you can find any-thing inferior, anything worthless, buy it'?"

Aesop said, "And what is there that is bad which does not come about through the tongue? It is because of the tongue that there are enmity, plots, battles, rivalry, strife, wars. Is it not, then, true that there is nothing worse than this most abominable tongue?"

One of the students at the table said, "Professor, if you pay attention to him, he'll soon drive you mad. Like body, like mind. This abusive and malicious slave isn't worth a penny."

Aesop said, "Quiet, student. I think you're far more malicious. You don't have the distinction Xanthus has, but you fan a master's anger with your inflammatory talk and egg the master on against his slave. This isn't the way of a man who minds his own business but that of a busybody, poking your nose into another man's business."

(56) Xanthus, looking for a pretext to give Aesop a beating, said to him, "Since I have to pursue philosophic discussions with my own slave, you said my friend was a busybody; prove that he is a busybody."

Aesop said, "He certainly is a busybody. There are many men who eat and drink at the expense of others and also poke their nose into others' business, but there are men who reflect on their own troubles and do not act the busybody."

Xanthus said, "Well, if you say there is a man who is not a busybody, I'll give you another order and cancel the one I gave you before. Someone else shall prepare the dinner tomorrow. You go out and invite me to dinner a man who is not a busybody. And if he acts the busybody in any way, the first time I'll say nothing, the second time I'll let it go, the third time you'll get a hiding and take the consequences."

(57) After hearing what Xanthus said to him, Aesop went out the next day to the market and looked for a man who was not a busybody. [He found a fight going on with a crowd standing all around and one man sitting off to the side, reading. Aesop said to himself, "I'll invite him. He doesn't appear to be a busybody, and I'll avoid a beating." So he went to him and said, "Most refined sir, Xanthus the philosopher has heard of your gentility and invites you to dinner."

He said, "I shall come. You will find me at the front door."

So Aesop went home and prepared dinner. Xanthus said, "Aesop, where is the man who is not a busybody?"

He replied, "He is standing at the front door."

At the appointed hour Xanthus brought him in and gave him a place at table among his friends. (58) He ordered honeyed wine to be served to his guest first, but the guest said, "Oh, no, sir. You must drink first, then your wife, and then we, your friends."

Xanthus nodded to Aesop, "I have you once." For the guest had shown himself something of a busybody. Then a fish soup was served. Xanthus, looking for a pretext, said, "With all the condiment I've provided my cuisine is insulted; this has no spices, no oil, and the broth is curdled. The cook must be beaten."

The guest said, 'Stop, master! Nothing's amiss. Everything's all right."

Xanthus nodded to Aesop, "There's twice." Then a rich sesame cake was brought in. Xanthus tasted it and said, "Call the baker. This cake has no honey and no raisins."

Again the guest said, "The cake is fine, too, and there's nothing wrong with the dinner. Don't beat your slaves without reason."

Again Xanthus nodded at Aesop. "There's the third time."

He said, "I concede."

When the guests left after dinner, Aesop was strung up and beaten. Xanthus said to him. "That for you, and if you don't find me a man who is not a busybody, I'll put you on the rack and break you."

(59) The next day Aesop went outside the city and tried to find a man who was not a busybody. After he had watched many men pass by] he finally spotted a man who was crude in appearance but civil enough in his behavior. He was driving a little ass loaded with wood, avoiding the confusion of the throngs, and talking to his ass. Judging that this man would tend to his own business and not be a busybody, Aesop followed him.

The rustic was riding the ass, and as they went along, he kept talking to him, "Let's go. The sooner we get there and get the wood sold for a dozen farthings,* the sooner you'll get two of them for fodder. I'll take two for myself, and we'll keep the eight against bad times, for fear we'll get sick or some bad weather will come along unexpectedly and keep us from getting out; for if you eat barley today, and then some unexpected bad luck comes along, you'll have neither barley nor fodder to eat."

(60) When Aesop heard this, he said to himself, "By the Muses, I do think this man is no busybody; I'll approach him." So he went up to him and said, "Greetings, good sir." The rustic returned his greeting, and Aesop said, "How much do you want for your wood?"

The rustic said, "Twelve farthings."

Aesop said, "It's the truth; he's selling for the same price he mentioned before." Then to the rustic, "Good sir, do you know Xanthus, the philosopher?"

The rustic said, "No, son, I don't."

Aesop said, "How is that?"

The rustic said, "Because I'm not a busybody. I've heard of him, all right."

Aesop said, "Bless you, I'm his slave."

The rustic said, "Did I ask you whether you are a slave or a free man? What do I care?"

---

*The original refers to *asses*, a small Roman monetary unit current at the time the *Life* was written.

Aesop said, "He really is no busybody. Good sir, you've sold your wood. Drive your ass to Xanthus' house."

The rustic said, "But I don't know where his house is."

Aesop said, "Follow me, and you'll find out." (61) And he led him to the house, unloaded the wood, paid him, and said, "Good sir, my master asks you to have dinner with him; so leave your ass in the courtyard, and he'll be taken care of."

The rustic went in to dinner without bothering to ask why he was invited and went in just as he was with mud on his shoes. Xanthus said, "Is this the man who's no busybody." . . .*

Xanthus, seeing that Aesop made very strong claims about the man, said to his wife, "My dear, do you want to see Aesop taught a lesson?"

Xanthus' wife said, "That's what I'm praying for."

Xanthus said, "Then do as I say. Get up and take a basin over to the stranger as though you intended to wash his feet. From your appearance he'll know that you're the lady of the house and won't let you do it but will say: 'Lady, don't you have any slave to wash my feet?' He'll be shown up as a busybody, and Aesop will get a beating."

Xanthus' wife hated Aesop so much that she tied a towel around her, threw another over her arm, and took the basin over to the stranger. He saw that she was the lady of the house and said to himself, "Xanthus is a philosopher. If he wanted my feet washed by a slave, he would have ordered it, but if he has made his wife wash my feet to show me honor, I'll not disgrace myself and be a busybody. I'll just put my feet out and let them be washed." And he took his ease while they were being washed.

(62) Xanthus said, "Clever, by the Muses!" And he ordered the honeyed wine to be served to the stranger first.

The stranger said to himself, "The hosts ought to drink first, but the philosopher ordered the drink served me first to do me honor, so I'll not be a busybody." And he took it and drank it.

Xanthus told them they could serve the dinner, and a plate of fish was brought on. Xanthus told the rustic to help himself. The rustic began to gulp them down like Charybdis. Xanthus took a taste, and wishing to draw the rustic out so that he would say something to show himself a busybody, he said, "Boy, call the cook." The cook came in, and Xanthus said, "Tell me, you runaway, when you got all the ingredients, why didn't you put in any oil or sardine paste or pepper? Strip him and beat him."

The rustic said to himself, "It's well seasoned and nothing is missing. But if Xanthus is so mad at his cook that he wants to beat him, I'll not play the busybody."

The unhappy cook got his beating, and Xanthus said to himself, "I

*A few words appear to be missing.

think this man must be deaf or dumb and doesn't speak at all." Then after dinner the cake was brought in. The rustic, who had never so much as seen a picture of a cake, began to break off square chunks about the size of bricks and gulp them down.

(63) Again Xanthus took a taste and shouted, "Somebody call the baker." He came in, and Xanthus said, "Damn you, why doesn't the cake have any honey or pepper or any balsam, and why is it sour?"

The baker said, "Sir, if the cake is raw, blame me, but if it doesn't have any honey in it and is sour, it's not my fault but the mistress's. When I was making the cake, I asked her for honey, and she said: 'When I get back from the bath, I'll get some out.' Well, she was late, and since the cake didn't get honey in time, it turned out sour."

Xanthus said, "All right. If this is the result of my wife's carelessness, I'll burn her alive." To his wife he said, "Now, my dear, play your part." To Aesop he said, "Bring in some firewood, and make a pyre right here."

Aesop brought the wood in and made a big pyre. Xanthus took his wife and made her get in the midst of it, all the while watching the rustic to see if he would jump up in indignation and not let him go ahead. (64) The rustic didn't turn a hair but just sat there and finished his drink. He saw that Xanthus was trying him and said, "Sir, if you're determined to do this, wait a while till I run out to the farm and fetch my wife. You can burn the two of them."

Xanthus admired the coolness of this man who was clearly no busy-body and said, "Aesop, I admit defeat. Enough of your tricks. Give this up and serve me in good faith from now on."

Aesop: "You'll find no cause to complain of me, master, and you'll find out what a faithful servant can be."

(65) The next day Xanthus said to Aesop, "Go see if there are many people at the bath."

On the way Aesop met the governor. The governor recognized Aesop and said to him, "Aesop, where are you going?"

Aesop said, "I don't know."

The governor said, "I ask you where you're going and you say, 'I don't know'?"

Aesop said, "By the Muses, I don't know."

The governor ordered him taken off to jail.

Aesop said, "Master, you can see that I answered you fairly, for I didn't know that I was going to be taken to jail."

The governor was so taken aback that he let him go.

(66) Aesop went on to the bath and saw a great crowd of bathers. He also saw a stone lying at the entrance—just lying there for no purpose; everyone who went in stumbled over it and cursed the man who put it there, but no one moved it out of the way. As he was marveling at the stupidity of the people who were stumbling over it, one man stumbled

and said, "Damn the man who put that stone there," but he moved the stone aside and went on in.

Aesop went back to Xanthus and said, "Master, I found one man at the bath."

Xanthus said, "One? Here's a chance to bathe without being crowded. Get the things for my bath." When Xanthus went in and saw a great crowd bathing he said, "Aesop, didn't you tell me: 'I found one man at the bath'?"

Aesop said, "I certainly did. You see this stone? It was lying at the entrance, and all the bathers stumbled on it, but no one had the common sense to move it. After all of them stumbled on it, one man stumbled and then moved it so that others coming in wouldn't have the same trouble. I thought he was really a man in comparison with the other men, and I told you the truth."

Xanthus: "Aesop is never slow to give an explanation of things he does wrong."

(67) When he had finished bathing, Xanthus called Aesop to bring what he needed and went to dinner. When they had been drinking for some time, Xanthus' belly reminded him that it was time to go out to answer the call of nature. Aesop stood by with a towel and a pitcher of water. Xanthus said to him, "Can you tell me why it is that when we defecate, we often look at our own droppings?"

Aesop: "Because long ago there was a king's son, who as a result of the looseness of his bowels and his loose way of living, sat there for a long time relieving himself—for so long that before he knew it, he had passed his own wits. Ever since then when men relieve themselves, they look down for fear they, too, have passed their wits. But don't you worry about this. There's no danger of your passing your wits, for you don't have any."

(68) Returning, Xanthus took his place at the table. As the drinking went on apace and Xanthus was beginning to be more than a little drunk, they began to pose questions and conundrums, as men who are inclined to speculation will. When a fight started over the posing of the questions, Xanthus started to join in the dispute and was behaving as though he were in the lecture hall instead of at a drinking party. Aesop sensed that he was going to get into a fight and said, "When Dionysus invented wine, he mixed three cups and showed men how they should use drink: the first for pleasure, the second for good cheer, and the third for rashness. Now then, my master, since you have drunk the cup of pleasure and that of good cheer, leave that of rashness to the youngsters. You have your lecture halls where you can show off your talents."

Xanthus, who was drunk by this time, said, "Will you shut up, you swineherd? You're the devil's advocate."

Aesop: "Just wait, you'll go to the devil."

(69) One of the students, seeing that Xanthus was carried away with himself, said, "Professor, are all things possible for man?"

Xanthus: "Who turned the conversation to man? He will do anything and is capable of all things."

The student pressed the argument to the impossible and said, "Can any man drink the sea dry?"

Xanthus said, "That's easy. I'll drink it dry."

The student said, "If you don't drink it dry, what then?"

Xanthus, whose wits were the worse for all the wine he had drunk, said, "I'll stake my fortune on it, and if I don't drink it dry, I'll be destitute."

They put up their rings to guarantee the stakes. Aesop, who was standing at the foot of Xanthus' couch, rapped him on the knuckles and said, "What are you doing, master? Are you out of your mind? How can you drink the sea dry?"

Xanthus said, "Shut up, you garbage," not realizing what kind of stakes he had pledged.

(70) The next morning when Xanthus wanted to wash his face he said, "Aesop."

And Aesop said, "What is it, master?"

Xanthus: "Pour some water on my hands." Aesop took the pitcher and poured. When he had washed his face, Xanthus noticed that his ring was missing and said, "Aesop, what happened to my ring?"

Aesop: "I don't know."

Xanthus: "Bah!"

Aesop: "Well, anyhow, you'd better take whatever you can get away with of your fortune and put it away for a rainy day, for your fortune doesn't belong to you anymore."

Xanthus: "What do you mean?"

Aesop: "At the party yesterday you laid odds you could drink the sea dry, and you put up your ring as a guarantee of your fortune."

Xanthus: "And how can I drink the sea dry?"

Aesop said, "I stood there by you and said: 'Stop, master. What are you doing? It's impossible.' And you didn't believe me."

Xanthus fell at Aesop's feet and said, "Aesop, I beg of you, if your sharp wits can do it, find some pretext on which I can win or else get out of the bet."

Aesop: "Make you win I can't, but I'll see that you solve the problem."

Xanthus: "How? What's your idea?"

(71) Aesop: "When the stakeholder comes with the other party and tells you to drink the sea dry, don't say no, but now that you're sober, just repeat the terms you set when you were drunk. Bring out a table, have it put in front of you, and have servants stand by. This will make

an impression, for everyone will come running to see the show, thinking you're going to drink the sea dry. When you see the place is full, fill a cup with sea water, call the stakeholder forward and say: 'What were the terms of my agreement?' And he will say: 'That you would drink the sea dry.' You say: 'Is that all?' And he will say: 'Yes.' Then you call witnesses and say: 'My fellow citizens, there are many rivers and unfailing streams which flow into the sea. The terms of my agreement were that I would drink dry the sea only, and not the rivers that flow into it. Let the other party stop up the mouths of the rivers so that I will only have the sea to drink dry. But it's impossible to stop up the mouths of all the rivers in the world, and it's impossible for me to drink the sea dry.' So, when one impossibility is matched with another, it will break your agreement."

(72) Xanthus was astonished at the readiness of his wit and now looked forward with positive relish to the test. The man who had made the bet appeared at the front door with a group of leading citizens and challenged Xanthus, saying, "Make good your wager or turn over your fortune."

Aesop said, "You give us an account of your fortune, for we've already got the sea half-empty."

The student said, "Aesop, you're my slave. You don't belong to Xanthus any more."

Aesop: "No, you'd better hand your fortune over to my master and stop talking nonsense." So saying, he ordered the couch brought out and set up on the beach. He set the table out and some cups on it. Everybody came running, and Xanthus came down and took his place. Aesop stood by his master, filled the cups from the sea, and served them to him.

The student: "Devil take me! Is he really going to drink the sea dry?"

(73) As Xanthus was about to put the cup to his mouth, he said, "Where's the stakeholder?" He came forward, and Xanthus said to him, "What were the terms of my agreement?"

The student: "That you would drink the sea dry."

Xanthus: "Was that all?"

The stakeholder: "Yes."

Xanthus said to the people, "My fellow citizens, you know that there are many rivers and unfailing streams which flow into the sea. I only agreed to drink the sea dry, not the rivers, too. Let the other party close up the mouths of the rivers so that I won't have to drink up the rivers along with the sea." And the philosopher won the bet.

There was a great shout from the crowd in honor of Xanthus. The student fell at his feet and said, "Professor, you are a great man; you win; I concede. But I beg you to call the bet off." And they did call off the bet.

(74) Aesop said to Xanthus, "Master, I saved your fortune; I ought to get my freedom."

Xanthus: "Will you be quiet? This was not what I, at any rate, had in mind."

Aesop, aggrieved, not at failing to get his freedom but at his master's ingratitude, held his peace. [But to himself he said, "Just wait. I'll get even with you."

(75) One day Aesop lifted up his clothes and took his member in his hand so as to stimulate it. Xanthus' wife saw him and said, "Aesop! What is this?"

Aesop replied, "Lady, I was cold during the night, and it helps me if I hold it in my hand."

When the woman saw how long and thick it was, her lust was aroused, and she said to him, "Now, Aesop, if you'll do what I want, you'll have more pleasure than your master."

He replied, "Lady, you know that if the master learns of this, it will be bad for me. He'll be justified in making me pay the price for it."

She smiled and said, "If you'll go to bed with me ten times, I'll give you a shirt."

Aesop said, "Give me your oath."

She was so excited that she took the oath, and Aesop took her word. He wanted to pay his master back. He went to bed with her nine times, and then he said, "Lady, I can't do any more."

She was burning with desire and said, "If you don't do it ten times you'll not get a thing from me."

So he tried a tenth time and succeeded in letting the semen fall wide of the mark. And he said, "Give me the shirt. If you don't, I'll appeal to my master."

The wife said, "I called on you to plow my field but you crossed the property line and worked in another field. Do it once more, and take the shirt."

(76) When Xanthus came home, Aesop went to him and said, "Master, judge between me and my mistress."

Xanthus said, "What?"

Aesop said, "My mistress and I were walking in the orchard and she saw a branch of a tree which was full of apples. She said to me: 'If you can throw a rock and knock off ten apples, I'll give you a shirt.' I picked up a rock, threw it, and knocked off ten apples. But one apple fell in a manure pile, and now she won't give me the tunic."

When the woman heard this, she said to her husband, "Obviously there's no argument about the nine, but, as for the tenth one which fell in the manure pile, I'm not satisfied. Let him throw again and knock off an apple and get the shirt."

It was Xanthus' judgment that she should give Aesop the shirt, and he said to Aesop, "Let's go to the forum, and when we come back, knock off the tenth apple and get the shirt."

Xanthus' wife said: "Yes, let him do that, and I will truly give him the shirt as you direct."]

(77) Xanthus said to Aesop, "Since I can interpret omens, go out and see if there is any bird of ill omen at the door. If you see a pair of crows there in front of the door, call me, for this sign means good luck for the man who sees it."

So Aesop went out and, as luck would have it, saw a pair of crows in front of the door. He came back in and said to Xanthus, "It's time for you to go out, for there's a pair of crows there."

The master: "Let's go." But while Aesop had been gone, one crow flew away, and when the master came out and saw one crow, he said, "Damn you! Didn't I tell you: 'Call me if you see a pair of crows,' and you call me although you saw only a single crow?"

Aesop: "One flew away, master."

The master: "Now you have made a mistake. Strip him. Bring the straps."

He got a thorough licking, but while he was still getting it, a slave of one of Xanthus' friends came in to invite him to dinner.

Aesop: "Master, you beat me unjustly."

Xanthus: "What do you mean, unjustly?"

Aesop: "Because you said a pair of crows was a good sign and a lucky one. I saw a pair of crows, and while I came to tell you about it, one of them flew away. But although you went out and saw a single crow, you got invited to dinner. It was I who saw the pair of crows, and I got a beating. Well, then, aren't signs and the interpretation of omens an idle business?"

Xanthus was surprised at this, too, and said, "Let him alone. Stop beating him." And he said he would come along to dinner.

[(77a) Several days later, Xanthus called Aesop and said to him: "Make us a good dinner, for I've invited my students. When Aesop had put everything in order for the dinner, as his mistress was lying there on the couch, he said to her, "Keep an eye on the table, mistress, so that the dog doesn't get in and eat any of the food."

She said, "Go on and don't worry about it; even my behind has eyes."

Aesop got busy with another task, and when he came back, he found his mistress asleep with her back to the table. Still afraid that the dog might get in and spoil the table and recalling that his mistress had said: 'Even my behind has eyes,' he raised her robe, exposed her rear, and left her lying there.

When Xanthus and his students came, they went in to dinner. Seeing her asleep and exposed, they turned their eyes away in shame. Xanthus said to Aesop, "Damn you, what is this?"

He said, "Master, while I was busy preparing to serve you, I told the mistress to keep an eye on the table so that the dog wouldn't get in and eat anything. She said to me: 'Go on and don't worry about this; even my behind has eyes.' Well sir, she's sound asleep, as you see, and I exposed her so that the eyes in her behind would see the table."

Xanthus said, "You runaway, you've embarrassed me many a time, but you've never done a more embarrassing thing than this, disgracing me and your mistress. But out of consideration for the guests I'll not lose my temper. I'll find a time to beat you thoroughly within an inch of your life."

(77b) Not long after this Xanthus had invited some rhetoricians and philosophers, and he said to Aesop, "Stand at the front door, and don't let any ignoramuses into the house, only scholars."

At the dinner hour Aesop closed the door and sat down inside. One of the guests came, and when he knocked on the door, Aesop said, "What does the dog shake?" The man thought he was calling him a dog and went off angry. So when Aesop addressed this remark to many others, they all went away feeling that what he said was an insult. But when one man came and knocked on the door and Aesop said, "What does the dog shake?" he said, "Its tail." When Aesop heard him give the right answer, he opened the door and let him in. He went to his master and said, "Sir, not another philosopher came to dine with you except this one man."

Xanthus was very much annoyed, since he thought they had played him false. The next day when they came to his lecture, they said to Xanthus, "Professor, apparently you wanted to humiliate us and, not having the face to do it yourself, put this filthy Aesop at the door to insult us and call us dogs."

Xanthus: "Is this something you dreamed, or is it the truth?"

The students: "Unless we are sleeping now, it's the truth."

Xanthus: "Somebody call Aesop." When he came, Xanthus said, "Tell me, you piece of filth, why, instead of bringing my friends and students into the house with all due respect to share my hospitality, did you humiliate them and insult them and turn them away with disrespect?"

Aesop: "Master, didn't you tell me: 'Don't let any unlearned men into the house, only rhetoricians and philosophers'?"

And Xanthus said, "Yes, you scarecrow, and what of it? Aren't these learned men?"

Aesop: "No. They are real ignoramuses, for when they knocked at your door and I stood inside and asked them: 'What does the dog shake?' not one of them understood what I said, and because they were stupid, I didn't let them in, except for this one man who answered me intelligently." And he pointed to the man who had dined with his master. When Aesop had given this explanation, they said he was right.

(78) A few days later Xanthus] walked out with Aesop to the edge of the city in pleasant conversation, and when he came to the cemetery, he was enjoying reading the epitaphs. Aesop saw the scrambled letters A B

Δ Ο Ε Θ Χ carved on one of the tombstones and pointed them out to Xanthus, saying, "What's this?"

Xanthus tried to figure out what the inscription was and what it signified. When he couldn't fathom it, he was perplexed and said, "What does it mean, Aesop?"

Aesop, seeing that his master was racking his brain, and having himself at the same time received the wisdom of the Muses as a mark of divine favor, said, "Master, if I find a treasure of gold with the help of this monument, what will you give me?"

When he heard this, the master said, "Half of the treasure and your freedom."

(79) When Aesop heard this, he immediately picked up a good-sized potsherd, paced off four steps from the monument, dug up the earth, brought up a treasure of gold, and gave it to his master. He said, "Master, give me what you promised."

Xanthus: "No, by the gods, I won't give it to you unless you tell me how you got the idea of finding the treasure, for I'm much more interested in learning this than I am in your discovery."

Aesop said, "Master, the man who buried this treasure here, being of a philosophical turn of mind, protected it and concealed it in a number of letters. You see how he inscribed the first letters of the words, for it says: 'Α—stepping off, Β—paces, Δ—four, Ο—dig, Ε—you will find, Θ—a treasure, Χ—of gold.' "*

Xanthus: "By Zeus, since you're such a good guesser and so smart, you'll not get what I promised."

When Aesop saw that he was going to be cheated of his reward, he said, "Well then, master, I warn you here and now to give the gold back to its owner."

Xanthus said, "And who is the owner of the treasure?"

Aesop said, "The king Dionysius of Byzantium."

Xanthus: "And how did you find this out?"

Aesop: "From the letters; they show it."

Xanthus: "How?"

Aesop: "Listen to what it says: 'Α—return, Β—to king, Δ—Dionysius, Ο—what you find, Ε—here, Θ—a treasure, Χ—of gold.' "

(80) When Xanthus saw that he had a good explanation, he said, "Aesop, take half the treasure and keep quiet."

Aesop: "Don't give it to me as a favor but as a gift from the man who buried it here."

Xanthus: "How's that?"

---

*The Greek letters are, of course, the initials of the words which are given here in translation. In what follows two other sets of words with the same initials are substituted.

Aesop: "The letters indicate it, for they say: 'A—take up, B—go off, Δ—divide, O—what you find, E—here, Θ—a treasure, X—of gold.' "

Xanthus: "You're a great genius. Come on into the house where we can divide the gold, and you can get your freedom." But when he got into the house, he was afraid that if Aesop got his freedom, he would tell the king about the treasure, and so he ordered him to be tied up and locked in.

Aesop said, "Give me my freedom, and keep the gold."

Xanthus: "Very nice! And that will put you in a better position because of your rights as a freedman to demand the gold back and make your slander more credible to the king. You won't persuade me to do that."

Aesop: "Just you watch, master, and see if you don't free me of your own free will and if you aren't forced to do it."

Xanthus said, "You're stopped, so be quiet."

(81) About this time there was an election, and the citizens assembled in the theater. The Guardian of the Laws brought in the volume containing the laws of the city as well as the public seal, deposited them before the assembly, and said, "Fellow citizens, select the man you want to act as Guardian of the Laws: the keeper of the laws and the seal, the transactor of the city's business."

While they were still deliberating as to the man to whom they wanted to entrust this responsible position, an eagle swooped down, seized the seal, and flew away. The Samians were much disturbed, viewing this as a great portent which they regarded as no slight misfortune. They immediately called up seers and priests to interpret the portent that had appeared. Then, when no one could interpret the portent, an old man stood up in the crowd and said, "Men of Samos, we are on the point of paying attention to these fellows who fill their bellies from the offerings to the gods and gamble away their means under a cloak of decent behavior. You don't realize that it is no easy matter to tell the significance of a portent. If a man is not thoroughly educated, he will not properly analyze a portent. But we have Xanthus, the philosopher who is known to all of Greece, in our midst. Let us appeal to him to interpret the portent."

When he sat down, they shouted for Xanthus and appealed to him urgently to explain the portent. (82). Xanthus came forward and, when he couldn't think of what to say, requested time to get at the meaning of the portent. As the assembly was about to break up, the eagle swooped down again and dropped the seal into the lap of a public slave. They asked Xanthus to study the answer to this portent, too. Xanthus agreed and went off looking worried.

(83) He went back home and said, "I'm going to have to thank Aesop again so as to get a solution to this portent." And he went in and said,

"Call Aesop." And he came in with his chains on. Xanthus said, "Turn him loose."

Aesop said, "I don't want to be turned loose."

Xanthus: "But I am turning you loose so that you may give me a solution."

Aesop: "Then you're turning me loose for your own interest, are you?"

Xanthus said: "Stop it, Aesop. Let bygones be bygones."

When Aesop had been unshackled, he said, "What do you want, master?"

Xanthus told him about the portent. Aesop undertook the task. (84) The next day Aesop wanted to torment him and said, "Master, if it's a question of words, I have ready answers, but I can't do anything about the situation you describe, for I'm no seer."

When Xanthus heard this, he lost hope, and since he was ashamed to face the Samians, he began to think about suicide. He said, "The time has come to interpret the portent, and I can't face the shame of being a philosopher and not being able to do what I undertook." After this remark, at nightfall Xanthus got a rope and left the house.

(85) From the room where Aesop slept he saw his master going out, and realizing what he was about to do, he went after him, forgetting all about his bitterness over the gold. He watched until Xanthus got beyond the gate, fastened the rope to a tree, and was about to put his neck in the noose. Then from a distance he shouted, "Wait, master!"

The master turned around, and seeing Aesop running toward him in the moonlight, he said, "I'm caught by Aesop. Aesop, why do you call me back from the path of justice?"

Aesop: "Master, where is your philosophy? Where is your boasted education? Where is your doctrine of self-control? Come now, master, are you in such an ill-considered and cowardly rush to die that you would throw away the pleasure of life by hanging yourself? Think it over, master."

Xanthus, "Let me alone, Aesop, for I shall go through with this honorable death in preference to ingloriously claiming a life that I will have to lead in shame."

Aesop: "Put down the rope, master. I'll try to interpret the portent."
Xanthus: How?"

Aesop said, "Take me to the theater with you, and make up some plausible excuse for the crowd on the portent, something about the dignity of philosophy. Then put me forward as a pupil of yours. I'll have a solution, and at the proper moment I'll be called on to speak."

(86) With this argument he persuaded him to change his mind. When Xanthus came forward the next day, he began to speak as follows: "Since our system of logic has laid down certain limits of philosophy, I no longer

practice the interpretation of portents or omens from birds. But this service ought by all right to be performed by my household. In keeping, then, with my distinction as a philosopher, I shall give you my slave, to whom I have given philosophical instruction in such matters, and he will interpret your portent." So saying, he put Aesop forward.

(87) But when the Samians saw Aesop, they burst out laughing and shouted, "Bring us another interpreter to interpret this portent. What a monstrosity he is to look at! Is he a frog, or a hedgehog, or a potbellied jar, or a captain of monkeys, or a moulded jug, or a cook's gear, or a dog in a basket?"

Aesop heard all this without turning a hair, and when he had gotten silence, he began to speak as follows: (88) "Men of Samos, why do you joke and gape at me? You shouldn't consider my appearance but examine my wits. It's ridiculous to find fault with a man's intelligence because of the way he looks. Many men of the worst appearance have a sound mind. No one, then, should criticize the mind, which he hasn't seen, of a man whose stature he observes to be inferior. A doctor doesn't give up a sick man as soon as he sees him, but he feels his pulse and then judges his condition. When did anyone ever decide on a jar of wine by looking at it rather than by taking a taste? The Muse is judged in the theater and Aphrodite in bed. Just so, wit is judged in words."

So, when the Samians found that what he said didn't jibe with his appearance, they said to one another, "A clever fellow, by the Muses, with a real gift for speaking." And they shouted to him, "All right, interpret."

When Aesop saw that he had their favor, he seized on this opportunity to speak freely and began, (89) "Men of Samos, it is not creditable for a free people to have a slave interpret a portent. Therefore, allow me freedom of speech in what I have to say so that, if I hit the mark, I may receive the appropriate honors like a free man and that if I go wrong, I may be punished as a free man and not as a slave. If, then, you allow me to speak with the privilege of freedom, I shall proceed with what I have to say in full confidence."

(90) The Samians said to Xanthus, "We beg you, Xanthus, free Aesop." And the presiding officer said to Xanthus, "Make Aesop a free man."

Xanthus: "I shall not free a slave who has been in servitude for a very long time."

The presiding officer, seeing that Xanthus refused the proposition, said, "Accept the price you paid for him, turn him over to me, and I'll make him a freedman on behalf of the city."

When Xanthus reflected that he had bought Aesop for seventy-five denarii, in order not to appear to have refused to free Aesop because of stinginess, he brought him forward and said, "Xanthus, at the request of the people of Samos, lets Aesop go free."

(91) Once this was done, Aesop took his place before them and said, "Men of Samos, be your own allies and take council for your own freedom, for this is a portent of attack and an omen of enslavement. First, you will have a war. I tell you this, for I want you to understand that the eagle is the king of the birds and is more powerful than the others. And he flew down, removed the seal, the symbol of leadership, from the laws, and dropped it in the lap of a public slave. He moved the sure pledge of freemen to the dubious yoke of servitude. This is the interpretation of your portent. It is certain that one of the ruling kings is determined to destroy your freedom, to abrogate your laws, and set the seal of his own power upon you."

(92) Even as Aesop was saying this, there arrived from King Croesus an emissary in a white-bordered robe, asking for the officials of the Samians. When he heard that an assembly was being held, he came to the theater and presented his letter to the officers. They opened the letter and read it. The contents were the following: "Croesus, king of the Lydians, to the officers, the council, and the people of the Samians, greeting. From this moment I command you to pay public tribute and public taxes. If you will not do this, I shall do you harm to the full extent of the power of my kingdom."

(93) The officers advised the people to agree to pay so as to avoid bringing such an enemy as the king down on the city. But they honored Aesop as a true prophet of the outcome of the portent and called on him also to give them advice as to whether they should send the tribute or refuse. Aesop said to them, "Men of Samos, when your first citizens have given you the opinion that you should pay the tax to the king, do you ask me whether you should give it or not? If I say: 'Don't give it,' I'll mark myself as an enemy to King Croesus."

But the crowd shouted, "Give us your opinion."

Aesop said, "I will not give you advice but will speak in a fable. (94) Once, at the command of Zeus, Prometheus described to men two ways, one the way of freedom, and the other that of slavery. The way of freedom he pictured as rough at the beginning, narrow, steep, and waterless, full of brambles, and beset with perils everywhere, but finally a level plain amid parks, groves of fruit trees, and water courses where the struggle reaches its end in rest. The way of slavery he pictured as a level plain at the beginning, flowery and pleasant to look upon with much to delight but at its end narrow, hard, and like a cliff."

(95) The Samians recognized from what Aesop said where their interest lay and shouted with one accord to the emissary that they would take the rough road. He went back to the king and reported everything Aesop had said. When Croesus heard this, he called up his army and ordered it

to arms. His friends encouraged him, saying, "Master, let's sail for the island; let's conquer it; let's drag it off to the Atlantic Ocean and make it an example to other peoples so as to forestall anyone else getting the idea of opposing so great a king."

But a member of the royal family spoke with the king's permission. "I give you my oath by the sacred diadem which adorns your head, you will not be able to capture the Samians so long as the man called Aesop, who gave them advice, still lives. Demand of them by letter the surrender of Aesop. Say to them: 'Ask whatever you will for him, and I will give it to you.' "

(96) When Croesus had heard him, he ordered the man who gave this advice to go to Samos, for he had no ambassador who was more devoted or wiser. The man sailed without delay to Samos and, calling an assembly, persuaded the Samians to surrender Aesop rather than lose the king's friendship. And at first the people shouted, "Take him. Let the king have Aesop."

But Aesop came forward and said, "Men of Samos, I agree and would be content to die at the feet of the king, but I want to tell you a story that I wish you would have engraved on my tombstone when I'm dead. (97) When animals talked the same language as men, the wolves and the sheep started a war with one another. The wolves had the upper hand and were harassing the sheep; but then the dogs joined the sheep and routed the wolves. But while the wolves were running from the dogs, they sent an ambassador to the sheep. The wolf came and appeared before the sheep and talked like a politician. He said: 'If you want to enter into a peace treaty, surrender the dogs to us, and sleep in security with no fear of hostility.' The sheep, being stupid creatures, were persuaded and surrendered the dogs, and the wolves tore them to shreds. After a while, the wolves subjugated the sheep. According to this fable, you ought not to surrender useful men lightly."

(98) The Samians saw that the story was told for their benefit and decided to keep Aesop. But Aesop wouldn't stay and went away to Croesus with the ambassador. When the king saw Aesop, he was angry and said, "Look who prevented my subjugating a city and wouldn't let me collect taxes. It wouldn't be so bad if he were a man instead of this riddle, this monstrosity among men."

And Aesop said, "Sire, I was not brought to you by force but came of my own accord to your feet. You're like a man who has been suddenly wounded; he cries out on the spur of the moment at the suddenness of what has happened. Wounds are the business of physicians, but what I have to say will cure your temper. If I die at your feet, I will disgrace your regime, for you will always have your friends giving advice against your interest. When they figure out that those who give good counsel die, they will certainly speak contrary to the interest of your regime."

(99) The king was astonished at him and smiled and said, "Can you do me another favor and tell me stories of the ways of fortune with men?"

Aesop said, "When animals talked the same language as men, a poor fellow who was hard up for food used to catch insects that are called hummers. He would put them up in brine and sell them at a fixed price. One insect he got between his fingers and was about to kill, but it saw what was going to happen and said to him: 'Don't just idly kill me. I don't hurt the grain or the fruit or the flowers, and I don't harm the branches, but by moving my wings and feet together in harmony, I make a pleasant sound. I am a solace to the wayfarer.' The man was moved by what she said and let her go back to her native haunts. Just so I fall at your knees. Have pity on me, for I have no power to injure an army, nor am I so handsome that I might give false evidence against someone and get away with it. Poor as my body is, I utter words of commonsense and thereby benefit the life of mortals."

(100) The king liked his story and said, "I grant you your life. Ask for whatever you wish, and I will give it to you."

Aesop said, "Make peace with the Samians."

The king said, "I make peace."

Aesop fell at his feet and thanked him. Then he wrote down the stories and fables that go by his name even now and deposited them in the library. When he had gotten from the king a letter wherein he agreed to make peace with the Samians for the sake of Aesop, he sailed for Samos, taking many gifts with him. He called an assembly and read the king's letter. The Samians, recognizing that Croesus had made peace with them for the sake of Aesop, voted honors for him and named the place where he had been turned over the Aesopeum. As for Aesop, he sacrificed to the Muses and then built a shrine to them, erecting in their midst a statue of Mnemosyne and not of Apollo. Thereupon, Apollo became angry with him as he had once been with Marsyas.*

(101) After spending many years in Samos and being recognized with many honors, Aesop decided to tour the world. He lectured to audiences for a fee and, after traveling all around, came to Babylon, where Lycurgus was king. After giving an exposition of his philosophy, he was acclaimed as a great man by the Babylonians. Even the king became a great admirer of his character and wit and appointed him chamberlain. (102) In those days it was customary for kings to collect tribute from one another by means of contests in wit. They did not face one another in wars and battles but sent philosophical conundrums by letter, and the one who

---

*Another Phrygian whose story is mentioned by Ovid in the *Metamorphoses* VI 382 ff. He challenged Apollo to a musical contest, and when he lost, Apollo skinned him alive.

couldn't find the answer paid tribute to the sender. By answering the conundrums sent to Lycurgus Aesop won reputation for the king. He also provided the problems for Lycurgus to send the other kings, and they, being unable to discover answers, paid tribute. In this way the kingdom of the Babylonians expanded until it not only included barbarian nations but even most of the lands up to Greece itself were subjugated.

(103) Aesop made the acquaintance of a young man of good family at Babylon, and since he was childless, adopted him, and presented him to the king as the heir to his own wisdom. He lavished every care on his education, but the young man began to get a big head, became involved with the king's concubine, and was enjoying the sport. Aesop saw this and was so angered that he repeatedly threatened him, saying that anyone who touched the king's woman was bringing on his own death. (104) The boy was put out at what Aesop said, and at the persuasion of his friends, made a false accusation against him to the king. He wrote a false letter in Aesop's name to the king's enemies saying that Aesop was ready to help them, and sealing it with Aesop's ring, he turned it over to the king with the words, "This is your faithful friend; just see how he is plotting against your rule."

The king was convinced by the seal and in a rage ordered a captain of the guard to kill Aesop for a traitor. But the captain didn't kill him, because he was his true friend. Since no one inquired into the matter, he kept him in the prison and reported to the king, "I have put Aesop to death." Helios succeeded Aesop as chamberlain.

(105) Some time later Nectanabo, king of Egypt, heard that Aesop was dead and sent an embassy to Lycurgus with a letter and a conundrum for him to resolve, knowing that with Aesop dead no one could be found among the Babylonians who could solve it. And this was the conundrum: "Nectanabo, king of Egypt, to Lycurgus, the Babylonian, greeting. I want to build a tower high in the air, one that touches neither earth nor heaven. Send me men to build it and one to answer any question I ask, and collect three years' tribute on behalf of the royal city. But if you cannot do this, I will collect ten years' tribute on behalf of all the territory under your rule."

(106) When Lycurgus read the letter, he was very much distressed at this sudden turn of events. He summoned all his friends to appear, including Hermippus, and said to them, "Can you solve the question of the tower, or shall I chop off all your heads?"

His friends said, "We don't know how a tower can be built that touches neither heaven nor earth."

Another said, "Sire, we wish to do whatever you command, but we have no ability nor experience at such things. We beg you, therefore, for forgiveness."

But the king was furious and ordered the guard to put them all out of the way. Then he began to beat his brow and tear his hair and mourn for Aesop. And as he moaned he said, "In my stupidity I have destroyed the pillar of my kingdom." And he would take neither food nor drink.

(107) When the captain of the guard saw the king's misery, he decided to disclose his misconduct immediately and said, "Sire, I know that today is my last day."

Lycurgus said to him, "What did you say?"

He replied, "In disobeying the king's order I have laid up trouble for myself."

The king said, "What do you have on your conscience?"

He said, "Aesop is alive."

The king was overjoyed at this unexpected news and said to Hermippus, "I only wish I could make this last day you talk about an eternity for you if you're telling the truth about Aesop's being alive, for if you've kept him safe, you've been the guardian of my salvation. But I'll not let you go unrewarded; I'll proclaim you my savior." And he ordered Aesop brought before him. When he appeared all filthy, unshaven, and pallid from his long imprisonment, the king turned away and wept. Then the king ordered him to be cared for and clothed and brought to receive his embrace.

(108) When Aesop was himself again, he came and embraced the king. He explained how his adopted son had laid a false accusation against him, and he took an oath to the truth of his account. The king wanted to kill Helios for having dealt treacherously with his father, but Aesop dissuaded him, arguing that if he were dead, he would have death as a cloak for the disgrace of his life, but so long as he lived, he would be a monument of his own guilt. The king consented to let him live but said to Aesop, "Take this letter from the king of the Egyptians and read it."

He read the requirement and said with a smile, "Answer him this way: 'I will send you men to build your tower and answer your questions when the winter is over.' " The king wrote as he directed and sent the letter by his ambassadors to Egypt. He restored Aesop to his original position of responsibility and turned Helios over to him.

He took the young man and lectured him. And this was what he said, (109) "Helios, my son, listen to my words even though you were brought up on them and yet repaid me with a gratitude I did not deserve. But now keep these precepts as a trust. First, reverence God as is right. Honor your king, for his power deserves the same honor as that of God. Honor your professor as your parents, for you are naturally obliged to treat them well, but you should be doubly grateful to him whose affection is freely bestowed. Take good food for the day as well as you can so that you may be ready for the work of the next day and keep your health. At the king's court let whatever you hear perish within you so that you may not quickly perish yourself. Let your relations with your wife be worthy so that she may not wish to have experience of another man, for woman-kind is a vain thing and less likely to go astray when flattered. When in your cups do not discuss serious matters to show off your learning, for you will be tripped up in an off moment and get yourself laughed at. Keep ahead of your tongue. Do not envy those who are successful, but rejoice with them, and you will share in their good fortune, for he who is jealous unwittingly harms himself. Take care of your slaves, and share what you have with them so that they may not only obey you as their master but also honor you as their benefactor. Rule your passions. If you learn a thing later than you should, do not be ashamed, for it is better to be called a late learner than a dolt. Keep your councils from your wife, and reveal no secrets to her, for womankind is a rival in married life, and she will sit all day plotting and scheming how to get you under her con-trol. (110) Strive to put away something for tomorrow from what you get today, for it is better to leave something behind for your enemies than to go begging of your friends while you live. Be affable and courteous to those you meet, knowing that a dog's tail gets him food and his mouth, beatings. Be proud of your character and not of your wealth, for chance may rob you of the latter, but the former cannot be taken away. If you prosper, bear no grudge toward your enemies; rather treat them well so that they may have a change of heart when they realize what kind of a man they have wronged. If you are able to be charitable, do not hesitate, but give with a will, knowing that fortune does not tarry. If you find a man to be a gossip and a slanderer, cast him out in time even though he be your brother, for he does not behave so out of good will but rather in order to reveal to others what you say and do. Rejoice not at great wealth, and grieve not at small." When he had said these things to the young man, he left him. But Helios, grieving at the wrong he had done him and at being tongue-lashed by him, ended his life by refusing food. And Aesop mourned him and gave him a splendid funeral.

(111) After the funeral he called some fowlers and ordered them to catch four eagles. When the eagles were caught, he pulled out the last row of wing feathers, with which they are supposed to fly, and gave orders for them to be brought up and taught to carry boys. When they were full-grown, they would carry the boys, and with this burden they would fly up into the air with cords attached to them so that they were under the boys' control and would go wherever the boys wished. When summer came, he said goodbye to the king and set sail with his boys and his eagles, accompanied by many servants and much equipment calculated to impress the Egyptians.

(112) When he came to Memphis, it was announced to king Necta-nabo that Aesop had arrived. Displeased at this news, he summoned his friends and said, "Men, I have been trapped by the news of Aesop's death. I have challenged Lycurgus by letter." So saying, he gave orders

for Aesop to debark. The next day Aesop came and presented his respects to the king. Nectanabo ordered his generals and governors to put on white robes, he himself put on a pure white linen robe and horns on his head. As he sat thus on his throne, he ordered Aesop to enter.

[(113) As he entered and saw this regalia, he made obeisance. Nectanabo said to him, "What likeness do you see in me and my attendants?"

Aesop said, "I would liken you to the moon in its fullness and those about you to the stars, for as the moon surpasses the other stars so you too have the appearance of the moon in this horned guise and your officials that of the stars about it." When Nectanabo heard this, he was amazed and gave him gifts.

(114) The next day Nectanabo dressed in shining purple, took his place, carrying many flowers, amid his courtiers and ordered Aesop to enter. When he came in, the king questioned him, saying, "What likeness do you see in me and my attendants?"

Aesop said, "I would liken you to the sun in springtime and those about you to the fruits of the earth, for like a king you delight the eye with your purple splendor, and you gather to yourself the flowering fruits." Again the king was amazed at his intellect and gave him gifts.]

(115) The next day Nectanabo dressed in white, clothed his friends in scarlet robes, and mounted his throne. When Aesop came, he asked him, "What do I resemble?"

Aesop said, "You are like the sun and those about you like its rays, for as the sun is bright and undefiled, so you too present yourself pure to men who wish to behold you and are brilliant as the sun, and these are flaming red like the rays of the sun."

The king was amazed and said to him, "So long as my kingdom continues thus, it follows that Lycurgus is nothing."

Aesop smiled and said, "Don't take his name recklessly in vain, for Lycurgus is as far above you as Zeus is above things of the earth. Zeus makes the sun and the moon to shine and to keep the seasons in order. If it pleases him to be angered, he makes his own shrine to tremble, causing terrifying thunder and dread lightning and setting earthquakes in motion. Just so, Lycurgus by the brilliance of his kingdom makes your brilliance dim and obscure, for he humbles everyone with his preëminence."

(116) Nectanabo, observing his sagacity and the readiness of his tongue, said to him, "Have you brought me men to build my tower?"

Aesop said, "They are ready when you point out the place."

The king in wonderment went outside the city with Aesop and gave the measurements for the building. Aesop stationed the eagles at the corners of the assigned space and ordered the boys to mount and fly up into the air. When they got aloft, they shouted, "Give us the mud and bricks and wood and whatever is required for the building."

Nectanabo: "Where did you trump up these winged men?"

Aesop said, "Oh, Lycurgus has winged men. And do you, who are only a man, want to match yourself against a king who is on a footing with the gods?"

Nectanabo said, "Aesop, I have lost. But answer me one question."

Aesop said, "Speak up; whatever you like."

(117) Nectanabo said, "I imported brood mares from Greece, and when they hear the horses in Babylon neighing, they miscarry."

Aesop said, "I'll give you my answer on this tomorrow." Then Aesop went to his quarters and ordered his men to catch a cat alive. [They caught him a great big one and began to whip it in public.] When the Egyptians saw this, they ran to Aesop's house and raised a shout against him. Aesop then ordered the cat released. But the Egyptians went to the king with their outcry against Aesop. The king summoned Aesop and, when he arrived, said to him, "You've done a bad thing. The animal is a symbol of the sacred goddess of Bubastis, and the Egyptians show it reverence."

(118) Aesop said, "Yes, but Lycurgus was wronged by it this night. He had a young rooster, a fighting cock—what's more, it told him the time—and the cat killed it tonight."

Nectanabo said to Aesop, "Aren't you ashamed of such a barefaced lie? How could a cat get from Egypt to Babylon in one night?"

Aesop said, "How can your mares here hear the horses at home and miscarry?"

The king, seeing his wit, began to be afraid that he would be bested and have to pay tribute to King Lycurgus.

(119) He immediately summoned prophets from Heliopolis who had knowledge of the questions of natural philosophy. When they had discussed Aesop with him, he invited them to dinner along with Aesop. They arrived at the appointed hour and took their places for dinner. One of the Heliopolitans said to Aesop, "We are sent by god to propose to you certain statements for your interpretation."

Aesop said, "You give the lie to yourselves and your god, for if he is a god he ought to know the thought of each and every man. But say on as you like."

(120) They said, "There is a temple and in it one column, and atop the column are twelve cities, and each of these is roofed with thirty beams, and about each of them run two women."

Aesop said, "Among us, children solve this conundrum. The temple is the universe, for it embraces all things; the column is the year, for it stands firm; the cities upon it are the twelve months, for they are continuously populated; the thirty beams are the thirty days of the month which embrace the year; and the two women moving around are night and day, for one follows the other." With this they arose from the dinner.

(121) The next day King Nectanabo held a council with his close

associates and said, "As I can see, because of this ill-favored and accursed fellow, I am going to have to send tribute to King Lycurgus."

But one of his friends said, "Let's pose him a problem in these words: 'What is there which we have neither seen nor heard?' and no matter what clever answer he gives, we'll tell him we've heard it and seen it. He'll be stopped by this and admit defeat."

When the king heard this, he was overjoyed, thinking he had found a way to win. When Aesop presented himself, King Nectanabo said to him, "Answer us this one more question, and I will pay the tribute to Lycurgus. Tell us something we have never either seen or heard."

Aesop said, "Give me three days, and I will give you your answer." He left the king and reasoned with himself, "They will say they have seen whatever I mention." (122) But Aesop, ever resourceful in such affairs, sat down and drafted himself a note of a loan in this form: "Lent to Nectanabo by Lycurgus, a thousand talents of gold." And he inserted an indication of the time that had passed since the loan. Then, after three days, Aesop went to Nectanabo and found him with his friends, expecting him to be at a loss. But Aesop brought out the note and said, "Read this agreement."

King Nectanabo's friends lied and said, "We've seen this and heard of it many times."

Aesop said, "I'm glad you authenticate it. Let him pay the money on the spot, for the due date is past."

King Nectanabo said, "How can you be witnesses to a debt I don't owe?"

They said, "We've never seen or heard of it."

Aesop said, "If that's your answer, the problem is solved."

(123) Nectanabo said, "Lycurgus is truly fortunate to have such wisdom in his kingdom." He gave Aesop the tribute for three years and sent him back with a peaceful letter. When Aesop arrived in Babylon, he told Lycurgus all that had happened in Egypt and gave him the money. Lycurgus then ordered the erection of a golden statue of Aesop with the Muses, and he held a great celebration in honor of Aesop's wisdom.

(124) But Aesop wished to go to Delphi, and so he said goodbye to the king, swearing to return and spend the rest of his life in Babylon. He went to other cities and gave demonstrations of his wisdom and learning. And when he came to Delphi, he undertook to give an exhibition there, too, and the people enjoyed hearing him at first but gave him nothing. Seeing that the men were as pale as potherbs, Aesop said to them,

Even as the leaves of the trees such is the race of men.*

(125) Still jibing at them he said, "Men of Delphi, you are like a piece of driftwood floating on the sea; when we see it at a great distance, toss-

*Iliad VI, 146.

ing on the waves, we think it is something worthwhile, but then when we approach and come to it, we find that it is a very insignificant thing of no value. So it has been with me; when I was far away from your city, I was impressed with you as men of wealth and generosity, but now that I see you are inferior to other men in your breeding and in your city, I recognize that I was mistaken. I shall carry away a bad impression of you, for I see that you act in no way unworthy of your ancestors."

(126) When the Delphians heard this, they said to him, "And who are our ancestors?"

Aesop said, "Slaves, and if you don't know this, let me tell you about it. Long ago it was the custom among the Greeks when they captured a city to send a tenth of the spoils to Apollo. For example, out of a hundred oxen they would send ten, and the same with goats and everything else— with money, with men, with women. You, being born of them as slaves, are like men in bondage, for by your birth you are marked as slaves of all the Greeks." So saying, he made preparation for his departure.

(127) But the officials, seeing how abusive he was, reasoned to themselves, "If we let him go away, he'll go around to other cities and damage our reputation." So they plotted to kill him by a trick. With the connivance of Apollo, who was angry with Aesop because of the insult on Samos in not setting him up along with the Muses, the Delphians, not waiting for a reasonable pretext, devised a villainous scheme so that the other visitors could not help him. They kept a watch on the slave at his door, and when they caught him asleep, they did their work. They brought a golden cup from the temple and hid it in his baggage. Unaware of what had been done, Aesop set off for Phocis.

(128) Some Delphians overtook him, tied him up, and dragged him back to the city. When he demanded in a loud voice, "Why are you taking me prisoner?" they replied, "You have stolen treasures from the temple."

Aesop, whose conscience was clear, said with tears in his eyes, "I am ready to die if I am found guilty of such a thing."

The Delphians ransacked his baggage and found the cup. They showed it off to the city and loudly and violently made a spectacle of him. Aesop reasoned that it must have been hidden there as part of a plot and asked the Delphians about it, but they wouldn't listen to him. He said, "Mortals that you are, be not wiser than the gods." But they locked him up in the prison to hold him for punishment. Finding no means of saving himself, Aesop said, "Now how can I, a mortal man, escape what is to be?"

(129) A friend of his came and with the permission of the guards went in to him. With tears in his eyes the friend said, "What have we come to?"

And Aesop told him a fable. "A woman who had buried her husband was sitting beside his tomb and weeping uncontrollably. A man who was plowing saw her and conceived a desire for her. He left his oxen standing with the plow and went over to her, pretending to weep himself. She paused and asked him: 'Why are you weeping?'

"The plowman said: 'I have buried a good and wise wife, and when I weep I find it lightens my grief.'

"She said: 'I, too, have lost a good husband, and when I do as you do, I lighten the burden of my grief.'

"He said to her: 'Well now, since we have both suffered the same fate and fortune, why don't we get to know one another? I'll love you as I did her, and you shall love me as you did your husband.' With this he persuaded the woman. But while he took his pleasure of her, someone drove off his oxen. When the plowman returned and didn't find his oxen, he began to weep and shout in earnest. The woman said: 'What are you wailing about?'

"The plowman said: 'Woman, now *I've* got something to mourn.'

"And you ask me why I'm grieving when you can see the pass fortune has brought me to?"

(130) The friend sorrowfully said to him, "Why in the world did you have to insult them in their own land and city, and do it when you were at their mercy? Where was your training? Where was your learning? You have given advice to cities and peoples, but you have turned out witless in your own cause."

But Aesop offered him another fable. (131) "A woman had a simple-minded daughter. She prayed to all the gods to give her daughter some sense, and the daughter often heard her praying. Then once they went out to the country. The girl left her mother and went outside the farmyard, where she saw a man coupling with a mule. She said to the man: 'What are you doing?'

"He said: 'I'm putting some sense in her.'

"The simple girl remembered her mother's prayer and said: 'Put some in me.'

"In his state he refused, saying; 'Nothing is more thankless than a woman.'

"But she said: 'Oh, don't worry, sir, my mother will thank you and will pay you whatever you want. She prays for me to get some sense.'

"And so the man deflowered her. She was overjoyed and ran home to her mother and said: 'Mother, I have some sense.'

"And the mother said: 'How did you get sense, child?'

"The simple girl told her mother the story. 'A man put it in me with a long, sinewy, red thing that ran in and out.'

"When the mother heard her daughter tell this, she said: 'My child, you've lost what sense you had.'

"It's turned out the same way for me, my friend, for I've lost what sense I had in coming to Delphi."

After many tears, the friend left him.

(132) The Delphians came in to Aesop and said, "You are to be thrown from the cliff today, for this is the way they voted to put you to death as a temple thief and a blasphemer who does not deserve the dignity of a burial. Prepare yourself."

Seeing that they were threatening him, Aesop said, "Let me tell you a story." And they gave him leave to speak.

Aesop said, (133) "Once when the animals all spoke the same language, a mouse made friends with a frog and invited him to dinner. He took him into a very well-stocked storeroom where there was bread, meat, cheese, olives, figs. And he said: 'Eat.'

"When he had helped himself generously, the frog said: 'You must come to my house for dinner, too, and let me give you a good reception.' He took the mouse to his pool and said: 'Dive in.'

"But the mouse said: 'I don't know how to dive.'

"The frog said: 'I'll teach you.' And he tied the mouse's foot to his own with a string and jumped into the pool, pulling the mouse with him.

"As the mouse drowned he said: 'Even though I'm dead, I'll pay you off.' Just as he said this the frog dove under and drowned him. As the mouse lay floating on the water a water bird carried him off with the frog tied to him, and when he had finished eating the mouse, he got his claws into the frog. This is the way the mouse punished the frog. Just so, gentlemen, if I die, I will be your doom. The Lydians, the Babylonians, and practically the whole of Greece will reap the harvest of my death."

(134) When he had said this and the Delphians still paid him no heed but were taking him off to the cliff, Aesop took refuge in the shrine of the Muses. Even so they showed him no mercy, but as he was being dragged off against his will, he said, "Men of Delphi, do not scorn this shrine. (135) It was just so that the rabbit, who was being chased by the eagle, took refuge with the tumblebug and begged the bug to save him. The tumblebug pleaded with the eagle not to disregard his request, adjuring him by Zeus not to despise his smallness. But the eagle brushed the tumblebug aside with his wing, carried off the rabbit, tore him to bits, and ate him.

(136) "The tumblebug was infuriated and flew off after the eagle. It spied out the nest where the eagle had its clutch of eggs and came back and smashed them. When the eagle returned, he was very much wrought up and started to find out who was responsible for this to tear him limb from limb. When the season came around, the eagle laid an egg in a higher place. The tumblebug came back, repeated his performance, and was gone. The eagle mourned its children, saying that this was the wrath of Zeus, sent to make the race of eagles even rarer.

(137) "When the time came around again, the eagle was so unhappy it didn't keep its eggs in its nest any more but went up to Olympus and deposited its eggs on the lap of Zeus and said: 'Twice my eggs have disappeared; the third time I'm leaving them with you to have you protect them.'

"But the tumblebug found this out, loaded himself up with manure, and went up to Zeus. He flew past Zeus' face, and Zeus was so startled to see the filthy thing that he jumped up. Forgetting that he had the eggs in his lap, he smashed them.

(138) "After this Zeus learned that the tumblebug had been wronged, and when the eagle returned, he said: 'You deserved to lose your children for the wrong you did the tumblebug.'

"The tumblebug said: 'He not only wronged me, but he was very impious toward you, for although I adjured him in your name, he had no fear but killed my suppliant. I shall never stop until I have punished him to the fullest extent.'

(139) "Since Zeus did not want the breed of eagles to die out, he tried to persuade the tumblebug to be reconciled. When the tumblebug would not hear of this, he changed the nesting season for the eagle to a time when the tumblebug is not to be seen on earth.

"So, do not, men of Delphi, dishonor this shrine where I have taken refuge, even though the temple is small, but remember the tumblebug and reverence Zeus, the god of strangers and Olympus."

(140) The Delphians were not deterred but took him off and stood him on the cliff. When he saw the fate that was prepared for him, he said, "Since I've used all kinds of arguments without persuading you, let me tell you this story. A farmer who had grown old in the country and had never seen the city begged his children to let him go and see the city before he died. They hitched the donkeys to the wagon themselves and told him: 'Just drive them, and they'll take you to the city.'

"On the way a storm came up, it got dark, the donkeys lost their way and came to a place surrounded by cliffs. Seeing the danger he was in, he said: 'Oh Zeus, what wrong have I done that I should die this way, without even horses, but only these miserable donkeys, to blame it on?' So it is that I am annoyed to die not at the hands of reputable men but of miserable slaves."

(141) As he was on the point of being thrown over the cliff, he told still another fable. ["A man fell in love with his own daughter, and suffering from this wound, he sent his wife off to the country and forced himself upon his daughter. She said: 'Father, this is an unholy thing you are doing. I would rather have submitted to a hundred men than to you.' This is the way I feel toward you, men of Delphi. I would rather drag my way through Syria, Phoenicia, and Judaea than die at your hands here, where one would least expect it."] But they did not change their minds.

(142) Aesop cursed them, called on the leader of the Muses to witness that his death was unjust, and threw himself over the cliff. And so he ended his life.

When the Delphians were afflicted with a famine, they received an oracle from Zeus that they should expiate the death of Aesop. Later, when word reached them, the peoples of Greece, Babylon, and Samos avenged Aesop's death.

6

HISTORICAL NOVEL

The Alexander Romance, or more properly *The Life and Deeds of Alexander of Macedon,* has been called antiquity's most successful novel, and if the success of a work of fiction can be judged by the number of versions in which it eventually existed (eighty), the number of languages into which it was translated (twenty-four), the length of time it has appealed to readers (from its composition in antiquity well into the age of printing), and the number of literary works it inspired, this estimate is certainly true.[1]

> The storie of Alisaundre is so commune
> That every wight that hath discrecioun
> Hath herd somwhat or al of his fortune.

So declares the monk in Chaucer's *Canterbury Tales.*[2]

The historical Alexander (356–323 B.C.) was the son of King Philip II of Macedon and his wife, Olympias. Like his father, Alexander was politically ambitious and a brilliant military strategist, and as a prince he was tutored by the Greek philospher Aristotle. Upon Philip's death in 336 B.C. he succeeded to the throne, inheriting his father's conquests, which effectively included Greece. Soon he led a large army of Macedonian and other troops across the Hellespont, where he challenged the forces of the Persian Empire, winning decisive battles and occupying major cities. He presently became master of Egypt and Mesopotamia, and after the fleeing Persian monarch Darius III was murdered by members of his own entourage, Alexander ruled the Persian Empire. From Persia he moved on into India, where he overcame an Indian king, Porus, and continued eastward until his men refused to proceed any farther. The invincible Alexander died soon thereafter, allegedly by poisoning.

Desirous that his achievements should be recorded, Alexander brought with him on his Eastern campaigns a cluster of court historians, among them Callisthenes, to whom some manuscripts of *The Alexander Romance* credit the authorship of the romance. But the attribution is impossible, since Callisthenes died before Alexander did. The works of these first-generation historians of Alexander do not survive, but derivative historians drew upon them, fashioning different accounts of Alexander.

While historians busied themselves writing histories of Alexander, an unknown author of the Hellenistic or the Imperial era composed a novelized biography of the Macedonian conqueror. This author's knowledge of and interest in Egypt suggests that he was an Egyptian, and his writing implies that he was a person of modest education. We do not know when he lived, only that the novel necessarily came into being sometime after the death of Alexander and before about A.D. 300, when Julius Valerius (consul in A.D. 338) turned it into Latin, the first of many translations. Fictionalized treatments of historical figures were fashionable in the Hellenistic and Roman periods when novelizations of the lives of foreign rulers as well as of the fabulist Aesop were composed, and the genre reaches back at least to *The Education of Cyrus* by Xenophon of Athens, an idealized biography of a Persian prince.[3]

In creating his novel the author reworked a variety of sources.[4] One was the historical tradition going back ultimately to Alexander's court historians. The romancer, however, was not much interested in the historical details of Alexander's career or in the military aspects of his battles, regardless of their brilliance or human impact. Indeed, the battles do not even occur in their proper chronological sequence; nor does the author always grasp the relevant geography. Clearly what was important to him was not so much the facts of Alexander's career as their drama and the intriguing meanings they could be made to bear.

A second kind of source was folk narrative, that is, traditional oral stories that the author or someone else attached to Alexander. A familiar example is the account of the death of Nektanebos in the novel (1.14). Alexander's mother, Olympias, summoned Nektanebos and asked him what treatment she might expect from her husband Philip, and Nektanebos made various astrological calculations. When Alexander inquired whether these stars might not actually be seen in the sky, Nektanebos took Alexander outside the city to a solitary place in the evening and showed him the stars. Alexander led Nektanebos by the hand to a pit in the ground, and the astrologer fell into it. When Nektanebos asked Alexander why he had done that, the youth told him to blame himself, for though he studied the heavens he was ignorant of things on earth. Shortly afterward, the man died.

Underlying this odd episode is a simple traditional story that had long been well known in Greece.

> An astrologer had the habit of going outside every evening to observe the stars. Once as he was walking around in the outskirts of the town with his mind wholly given over to the heavens he fell into a well that he had failed to notice. As he wailed and called out, a passerby heard his groans, came up to him, and after learning what had happened said to him: "Fellow, while you are trying to see what is in the heavens, don't you see what is on the earth?"

So runs the Aesopic fable, and the same story was told of the philosopher Thales, who for the Greeks was the classic type of the intellectual.[5] In other words, it is a tale of the absent-minded intellectual who, while his thoughts are on things impractical, does not notice the obvious. Although the anecdote, taken by itself, is a perfectly coherent narrative, it does not rest with complete comfort in its novelistic adaptation, for the author does not equip Alexander with a clear motive for wishing to harm Nektanebos, and his allegation, borrowed from the original tale, that Nektanebos himself is to blame, is hardly just, since it is Alexander himself who engineers the man's fatal fall. On the other hand, there is definitely a ruthless side to Alexander, who enjoys winning and does not always play fair. The incident also introduces an important theme that recurs in the novel. Just as Nektanebos's death is devised by his own son, Darius also is slain by traitors in his own camp, and in the end Alexander himself is given a poisoned drink by one of his own men. Powerful and brilliant though they be, these men each find death, not nobly on a battlefield nor peacefully in old age, but in the unexpected treachery of those whom they trust.

The historical Nektanebos was the last native pharaoh of Egypt. In the novel he flees Egypt for Macedon, where he deceives and seduces Olympias, fathering on her a child, Alexander.[6] Accordingly, the Macedonian Philip is represented as being merely the putative father of Alexander, whose rule in Egypt becomes a continuation of native, pharaonic rule. In the popular mind Nektanebos was the generic Egyptian pharaoh, for we find him as well in *The Aesop Romance*, even though that work is set at a much earlier time.

Into this roughly historical framework of events the author worked a third kind of preexisting material—fictional letters, most of them apparently deriving from an early epistolary novel consisting of exchanges between Alexander and other persons, such as his military opponents Darius and Poros. Other correspondence that comes perhaps from the same epistolary novel are letters to or from the Gymnosophists, or Naked Philosophers, Queen Kandake, and the Amazons.[7] This novel in letters, whose author is not known and which has not independently survived except for a few papyrus fragments, was in existence no later than the first century B.C. Presumably it attempted to portray the respective characters of Alexander and his correspondents, as the epistolographer imagined them to be, through letters allegedly written by them. The letters do so unsubtly, representing Darius, for example, as the braggart barbarian soon to be humbled and Alexander as the noble Hellene who treats the captive family of his enemy with generosity.[8] A second series of fictional letters, descriptions of various marvels addressed by Alexander to his mother, Olympias, and to his tutor Aristotle, also predate the novel, and their original composer is likewise unknown.[9]

The Alexander Romance offers an impressive variety of moods and material, including adventure, marvels, cunning, and nobility. We consort with monarchs, the Amazons, the Brahmans of distant India; we glimpse the heights of heaven, the depths of the sea, and the far end of the world; we marvel at oracles and strange beings; we smile at bold deceptions; we admire noble behavior; we are pained when the protagonist comes close to obtaining such rare and precious things as the Water of Life, only to lose them. Most of all, we wonder at Alexander's refusal to accept human limitations, his yearning to go places where no human before him has gone, his longing to experience and learn things that no one previously has experienced or learned.

Like *The Aesop Romance,* the novelized life of Alexander is an odd mix of art and artlessness. The appeal of both works, written in quite ordinary and uneven prose, lies in their content rather than in the pleasure of their language. Both give the impression of a kind of casual composition with inconsistencies, abrupt transitions, and illogicalities of various sorts, while at the same time they burst with energy, with bold and memorable stories effectively recounted, and with delicious fantasies of astounding personal success. In one work a trickster of humble origins outsmarts and discomfits his social betters and rises to enjoy tremendous worldly acclaim; in the other work a proud prince challenges and wins the known world by means of his brilliance and bravery, an Achilles on the battlefield, an Odysseus in exotic lands.

Although the original *Life and Deeds of Alexander,* written sometime between the third century B.C. and the third century A.D., is lost, reworkings of it survive in astonishing variety, forming a complex network of densely interrelated texts.[10] In a sense there is no *Alexander Romance,* only *Alexander Romances.* The first recension, represented in Greek by a single manuscript, A, is believed to be the closest of the extant versions to the lost original. Since a text belonging to this recension was rendered into Latin by Julius Valerius around A.D. 300, the recension was in existence by that time.[11]

Recension B evidently arose after A.D. 300 and represents a different line of development from the original novel. Its author revised the diction, reworked some of the historical inaccuracies, treated occasional verse passages in the original novel as prose, and increased the element of wonder. In the fifth or sixth century A.D. when an Armenian translation of the novel was made, the translator had before him texts of both recensions; accordingly, the second recension must have developed by this date.[12] Recension B was in turn reworked by various writers in different ways, creating a number of subrecensions. The present translation of the novel by Ken Dowden is a rendering of *The Alexander Romance* as it is realized in manuscript L of Recension B, with a number of corrections made by the translator in the direction of Recension A.[13]

Reworkings in Greek of *The Alexander Romance* continued to be made, and in the tenth century a second translation into Latin was made, this one by Archpresbyter Leo of Naples, which formed the basis for other Latin recensions.[14] But I shall not follow the trail of reworkings further than this. Suffice it to say that Greek versions continued, including eventually folkbooks in Modern Greek; that as the novel worked its way eastward, Oriental renderings (Syriac, Arabic, Ethiopic, Pahlavi, Hebrew, etc.) were made of the Greek as well as from other Oriental translations; and that the Latin versions deriving from Leo formed the basis of many vernacular treatments of Alexander in the West, including printed folkbooks. In addition, parts of the novel circulated independently, sometimes in a fuller form than in the novel itself. The novelized life of Alexander, like Alexander himself, enjoyed an astonishing career of conquest, different Alexanders for different eras and for different regions of the world.

NOTES

1. The figures come from Ken Dowden, in Reardon 1989:650. Different manuscripts of the novel bear different titles, but among moderns the work is usually referred to as *The Alexander Romance* or, in languages such as French and German that do not label early novels as romances, as *The Alexander Novel*.

2. Chaucer, *The Monk's Tale* 7.2631–33.

3. For the fragments of the novels about the Assyrian Ninus and the Egyptian Sesonchosis, see Stephens and Winkler 1995.

4. The basic discussion is that of Merkelbach 1954. See also Fraser 1972 1:675–687 for a discussion of the mix of Greek and Egyptian elements in the composition.

5. For the fable see Perry 1952:337, no. 40; for the Thales anecdote see Plato, *Theaetetus* 174a, and Diogenes Laertius, *Lives of the Philosophers* 1.34. The tale remains part of Greek folklore, recounted nowadays of a hungry fox who falls into a pit because he focuses all his attention upon the birds up in the trees; see Megas 1970:9, no. 7.

6. Nektanebos's seduction of Olympias by impersonating a god is also attested outside the novel as a comic and ribald story told of different characters in Greek and other traditions; see Weinreich 1911.

7. The exchange with Darius begins at 1.36 and that with Poros at 2.19. For the Naked Philosophers, see 3.5; for Queen Kandake, 3.18; and for the Amazons, 3.25–26. On ancient fictitious and forged letters in general, see Stirewalt 1993:20–42, and for ancient epistolary fiction, see Rosenmeyer 1994 and Holzberg 1994. On the Naked Philosophers, or Brahmans, in *The Alexander Romance,* see Stoneman 1995.

8. Merkelbach 1954:32–40.

9. *The Alexander Romance* 2.23–41, 3.27–28; see further Merkelbach 1954:40–50, Gunderson 1980.

10. See especially Stoneman 1996.

11. For an English translation of manuscript A, see Haight 1955.

12. For an English rendering of the Armenian version, see Wolohojian 1969.

13. For a different rendering of manuscript L into English with other supplements from other versions, see Stoneman 1991.

14. For an English translation of these recensions, see Kratz 1991.

LITERATURE

Hägg 1983:125–143. Haight 1945:1–47. Köhler and Schenda 1975. Merkelbach 1954. Stoneman 1994a, 1994b, 1996. van Thiel 1974.

———

PSEUDO-CALLISTHENES

The Alexander Romance

translated by Ken Dowden
Notes accompanying the translation are by the translator

Book One

1. No finer or more courageous man is held to have existed than Alexander, king of Macedon. He had a special way of doing everything and found his own qualities always had Providence for a partner. In fact, his wars and battles with any one nation were over before historians had time to gather full information on its cities. The deeds of Alexander, the excellences of his body and of his soul, his success in his actions, his

bravery, are our present subject. We begin with his family—and the identity of his father. People generally are under the misapprehension that he was the son of King Philip. This is quite wrong. He was not the child of Philip but rather, as the wisest Egyptians assert, the son of Nektanebos,[1] conceived after he had been driven from his throne.

This Nektanebos was an expert in the art of magic, and since his magic gave him the advantage over all nations, by the use of this power he lived in peace. If ever an enemy force attacked him, he did not start preparing armies or constructing engines of war or readying a weapon transport or bothering his officers about battle dispositions. Instead he would set down a dish and practice dish divining. He would pour springwater into the dish, form wax models of ships and men in his hands, and put them in the dish. Then, he would don the robes of a prophet, holding a staff of ebony in his hand; and, standing, he invoked the "gods"[2] of his spells—spirits of the air and demons of the earth beneath—and at his spell the model men came alive. In this way he sank the model ships in the dish, and immediately, as they were being sunk, the ships at sea belonging to the enemy attacking him were destroyed through the man's expertise in magic. So then, his kingdom remained at peace.

2. After some time had passed, some *exploratores* (which is what the Romans call spies) came to Nektanebos and reported to him that a great war cloud, armies of innumerable warriors, was advancing on Egypt. Nektanebos's general came to him and said: "O King, live long! Dismiss now all your ways of peace and get ready for the dispositions of war: a great cloud of barbarians is attacking us. It is not just one nation that is advancing upon us, but millions of people. Advancing on us are Indians, Nokimaians, Oxydrakai, Iberians, Kauchones, Lelapes, Bosporoi, Bastranoi, Azanoi, Chalybes, and all the other great nations of the East,

1. Nektanebo(s) II was the last native Egyptian king of Egypt. Coming to the throne in 360 B.C., he repulsed the attack around 350 B.C. of Artaxerxes III Ochus, king of Persia. But in 343 Artaxerxes led a better-prepared invasion force, spearheaded by Greek mercenaries, and overwhelmed Egypt. Nektanebos lost heart early and fled—south to Ethiopia, never to return and never to become father of Alexander. This King Arthur, as it were, of Egypt figures in a papyrus fragment of the second century B.C. that has been thought to cast some light on the origins of the Greek novel. The papyrus preserves the so-called *Dream of Nektanebos*, part of an Egyptian story translated into Greek, which seems to tell how the gods turned against Nektanebos. It could have continued by making Nektanebos Alexander's father. To be legitimized as ruler of Egypt, Alexander would need to be son of Nektanebos and also son of Ammon.

2. *The Alexander Romance* appears to have been written from a pagan point of view, though the term "Providence above," which otherwise first gains favor with the early Christian fathers, is embedded in the novel. Our manuscript L extends the use of this Christian term and likes to emphasize that Nektanebos's gods are only so-called gods. In a later recension one even finds Ammon, who appears in a dream to Alexander at 2.13, replaced by the prophet Jeremiah!

armies of innumerable warriors advancing against Egypt.[3] So postpone your other business and consider your position."

At these words of the general, King Nektanebos laughed long and said to him: "From the point of view of carrying out the responsibilities of your post, what you say is fine and reasonable; but it is still a cowardly and unsoldierlike statement. Power is not a matter of numbers; war is a matter of drive. After all, it only takes one lion to overpower many deer, and one wolf to ravage many flocks of sheep. So you go with the armies under your command and maintain your position! With one word I shall engulf the innumerable host of barbarians in the sea." And with that Nektanebos dismissed the general from his presence.

3. He himself, however, arose and went into the palace. When he was quite alone, he used the same invocation and looked into the dish. And there he saw the gods of Egypt steering the vessels of his foreign enemies and their armies being guided by the gods themselves. Nektanebos was a man of much experience in magic and accustomed to talking with his gods, and, learning from them that the end of the kingdom of Egypt was at hand, he put in his pocket a large quantity of gold, shaved off his hair and his beard, changed his appearance, and fled via Pelusion. After a voyage he reached Pella in Macedonia and set himself up there at a particular place as an Egyptian prophet, with a thriving business in astrology.

Meanwhile, the Egyptians were asking their "gods" whatever had become of the king of Egypt (by now the whole of Egypt had been devastated by the foreigners), and their "god" in the sanctum of the Sarapeion uttered an oracle to them in these words.

> This king who has fled will come again to Egypt, not in age but in youth, and our enemy the Persians he shall subdue.[4]

They debated the meaning of what had been said to them, but finding no solution, they inscribed the oracle given to them on the pedestal of Nektanebos's statue.

4. After his arrival in Macedonia, Nektanebos became well known to everyone. His calculations were of such accuracy that even the queen, Olympias, heard of him and came to him by night while her husband Philip was away at war. And she learned from him what she had been

---

3. This overwhelming list of frighteningly exotic barbarian tribes fails to mention the Persians who were actually conducting the invasion: our author is concerned more with effect than accuracy.

4. An oracle to the effect that Nektanebos would return to rule again is apparently presented in the Egyptian "Demotic Chronicle" (third century B.C.). The implication of our oracle should be that he will return as the youthful Alexander. The Sarapeion is the shrine of the god Sarapis.

seeking, and left. A few days later, she sent for him and told him to come to her. When he saw how beautiful she was, Nektanebos was filled with desire for her loveliness and, reaching out his hand, said, "Greetings, Queen of the Macedonians!"

"Greetings to you also, most excellent prophet!" she replied. "Come here and sit down." She continued: "You are the Egyptian teacher whose complete reliability has been established by those who have tried you. Even I have been convinced by you. By what method can you command true predictions?"

He replied: "There is a wide choice of method, O Queen. There are horoscope casters, sign solvers, dream specialists, oracular ventriloquists, bird observers, birth-date examiners, and those called magoi, who have the gift of prophecy." And with that he looked up fiercely at Olympias.

Olympias said to him. "Prophet, has your gaze become fixed at the sight of me?"

"Yes, lady," he replied. "I was reminded of an oracle given to me by my own gods that I must be consulted by a queen, and, look, it has come true. So now tell me what you wish."

Putting his hand in his pocket, he took out a little tablet, which mere words could not describe. It was made up of gold and ivory, with seven stars and the ascendant. The sun was of crystal, the moon adamant, Jupiter aerial jasper, Mars bloodred hematite, Saturn serpentine, Venus sapphire, Mercury emerald, and the ascendant white marble. Olympias, fascinated by so precious a tablet, sat down beside Nektanebos and, dismissing all the servants, said to him: "Prophet, cast my horoscope and Philip's"; for there was a rumor concerning her that if Philip returned from the war, he would divorce her and marry another.

Nektanebos replied, "Tell me your date of birth and tell me Philip's." And what did Nektanebos do next? He put his own date of birth with that of Olympias and, having completed his calculations, said to her, "The rumor you have heard about yourself is not wrong; but, as an Egyptian prophet, I can help you avoid being divorced by Philip."

"How can you?" she asked.

He replied, "You must have intercourse with a god on earth, conceive by him, bear a son and rear him, and have him to avenge you for the wrongs Philip has done you."

"What god?" Olympias asked.

"Ammon of Libya," he told her.

"And what is this god like, then?" Olympias asked him.

"Middle-aged," he replied, "with golden hair and beard and with horns growing from his forehead—these too just like gold. So you must get yourself ready like a queen for him, because today in a dream you shall see this god have intercourse with you."

And she said to him, "If I see this dream, I shall revere you not as a magos, but as a god."

5. So Nektanebos left the queen and picked from the wasteland herbs he knew for bringing dreams and extracted their juices. Then he made a wax model in the shape of a woman and wrote on it the name of Olympias. He lit lamps and, sprinkling the juice from the herbs over them, invoked with oaths the demons appointed to this function so that Olympias had a vision. And she saw the god Ammon embracing her that night and as he arose from her, saying to her, "Woman, you have a male child in your womb to be your avenger!"

6. Olympias arose from her sleep in amazement and with all speed sent for Nektanebos, and when he came, said to him: "I have seen the dream and the god Ammon you told me about. I beg of you, Prophet, bring me together with him again. And do be careful about when he is going to come to me, so that I may be better prepared for my bridegroom."

He replied: "First of all, mistress, what you saw was a dream. When the god comes in person into our sight, he will see to your needs. But if Your Majesty commands, give me a room to sleep in, so that I may intercede with him on your behalf."

"Here," she said, "have a room in my quarters. And if I manage to become pregnant by this god, I shall honor you greatly, as a queen can, and treat you as though you were the child's father."

Nektanebos said to her: "There is something you must know, mistress. Before the god enters, there is this sign: when you are sitting in your room in the evening, if you see a snake gliding towards you, dismiss the servants but do not douse the lamps that I now give you, having prepared them expertly to be lit in honor of the god. Instead, go back to your royal bed and get ready: cover your face and do not look directly at the god you saw coming to you in your dreams."

So saying, Nektanebos left, and the next day Olympias gave him a bedroom immediately next to hers.

7. Nektanebos got ready for himself a very soft ram's fleece, complete with the horns on its temples, and an ebony scepter and white clothing and a cloak of the exact color of a snake, and went into the bedroom where Olympias was lying covered upon the bed. But she was looking out of the corner of her eye: she saw him coming and was not afraid, since she was expecting him to be as he had appeared in the dream. The lamps lit up, and Olympias covered her face. Nektanebos, setting down his scepter, got into her bed and lay with her. And he said to her: "Have strength, woman! You have in your womb a male child to be your avenger and king and sovereign of the whole world." Then Nektanebos took his scepter and left the bedroom and hid all the props he had.

In the morning Olympias awoke, went into the room of Nektanebos, and roused him from his sleep. He rose and said: "Greetings, Queen! What news do you bring me?"

"I am surprised, Prophet," she replied, "that you do not already know. Will this god be coming back to me? I had such pleasure from him."

"Listen to me, Queen," he said to her. "I am the prophet of this god. So, when you wish, provide me with this place to sleep undisturbed so that I may perform the purification appropriate to him. Then he will come to you."

She replied, "Have this place from now on," and gave instructions that he was to be given the keys of the bedroom.

He put his props away in a secret place and went to her as often as Olympias wanted—with her thinking he was the god Ammon.

Day by day her stomach enlarged, and Olympias asked Nektanebos, "If Philip comes home and finds me pregnant, what am I to say?"

"Have no fear, mistress," Nektanebos replied to her. "The god Ammon will help you with this by appearing to Philip in his dreams and letting him know what has happened. As a result, Philip will be unable to find fault with you."

In this way, then Olympias was taken in by Nektanebos, thanks to his magical powers.

8. Presently Nektanebos took a sea hawk and enchanted it. He told it everything he wanted said to Philip in a dream, using the black arts of magic to prepare it. And the sea hawk, released by Nektanebos, flew through the night to the place where Philip was, and spoke to him in a dream. Philip, seeing the hawk speak to him, woke greatly disturbed. So without delay he sent for a dream interpreter, a distinguished Babylonian, and related the marvel to him, saying: "I saw a god in a dream. He was very handsome, with grey hair and beard, and he had horns on his temples, both like gold; and in his hand he held a scepter. It was night, and he was going to my wife, Olympias, lying down, and having intercourse with her. Then, as he rose, he said to her: 'Woman, you have conceived a male child who shall tend you and shall avenge the death of his father.' And I thought I used papyrus thread to sew her up and that I put my seal upon her. And the seal ring was of gold, containing a stone with a relief of sun, lion's head, and spear. While I was having these impressions, I seemed to see a hawk perched over me, waking me from my sleep with its wings. What does all this mean for me?"

So the dream interpreter said to him: "King Philip, live long! What you saw in your dream is true. Sealing your wife's womb is indicative of your confidence that your wife has actually conceived: people seal a full vessel, not an empty one. As for your sewing her up with papyrus, papyrus is produced nowhere else except in Egypt. So the seed is Egyptian, and not lowly, but dazzling and glorious, as the gold ring shows: what, after all, is more glorious than gold, a medium through which men worship the gods? As regards the seal with the sun, a lion's head beneath, and a spear: this child who is going to be born will reach the rising sun, waging war with all—like a lion—and capturing cities by force—on account of the spear beneath. As for your having seen a god with ram's horns and grey hair, this is the god of Libya, Ammon." This was the interpretation of the expert, and Philip did not like what he heard.

9. Now Olympias was in distress, as she had little confidence in Nektanebos's arrangement to deal with Philip, and when Philip returned from the war, he saw his wife was upset and said to her: "Wife, why are you upset at what has happened? It is someone else's fault—that has been shown to me in a dream—so you cannot be blamed. We kings have power over all, but we do not have power over the gods. Your affair was not with one of the people, but with one of the most magnificent beings." With these words, Philip cheered Olympias, and she thanked the prophet who had let her have advance knowledge of Philip's experiences.

10. A few days later Philip was with Olympias and said to her, "You have deceived me, wife: you were made pregnant not by a god, but by someone else—and he is going to fall into my hands!" Nektanebos heard this. There was a great banquet in the palace, and everyone was feasting with King Philip to celebrate his return. King Philip alone was downcast—because Olympias, his wife, was pregnant. So, in front of everyone, Nektanebos turned himself into a serpent larger than the original one and came into the middle of the dining hall and hissed so hideously that the foundations of the palace shook. The king's guest leapt up in panic at the sight of the serpent; Olympias, however, recognized her bridegroom and reached out her right hand to him. And the serpent stirred himself to rest his head in her hand and coiled down to Olympias's knees and, putting out his forked tongue, kissed her—a token of his love for the benefit of the onlookers. And while Philip was simultaneously protesting and yet gazing insatiably in amazement, the serpent changed himself into an eagle; and where he went, it would be pointless to say.

Regaining his composure, Philip said: "Wife, I have seen the god coming to your assistance in peril, and that proves his concern for you. But I do not at present know the identity of the god: he has displayed to me the shape of the god Ammon and of Apollo and of Asklepios."

Olympias replied, "As he revealed to me in person when he came to me, he is the god of all Libya, Ammon."

Philip counted himself lucky at what he had seen: the child his wife bore was going to be known as the seed of a god.

11. Some days later, Philip was sitting in one of the royal gardens, when a mass of birds of various kinds was feeding there. Then, suddenly, one bird leapt into King Philip's lap and laid an egg; but it rolled off his lap and broke as it fell on the ground. From it sprang a tiny serpent that

coiled around the shell and then attempted to reenter where it had emerged; but, having got its head inside, it died. King Philip was disturbed at this, sent for an interpreter, and outlined to him what had happened. The interpreter, inspired by God, said: "King, you will have a son who will go around the whole world, bringing everyone under his sway. But, turning back towards his own kingdom, he will die young; for the serpent is a royal beast, and the egg from which the serpent came is like the world. So, having encircled the world and wanting to return where he had come from, he did not reach it but died instead." So then the interpreter, having resolved the problem, was duly rewarded by King Philip and left.

12. When the time came for Olympias to give birth, she sat on the birthing stool and labored. Nektanebos stood beside her and, calculating the courses of the heavenly bodies, distracted her from delivering too quickly. Using his magical powers violently to adjust the celestial bodies, he learned what the situation was and said to her: "Woman, hold yourself back and defeat the situation nature presents. If you give birth now, you will produce servile prisoner or a monster."

When again the woman was in distress from her labor and was no longer able to hold out against the intensity of the contractions, Nektanebos said: "Preserve a little longer, woman. If you give birth now, your offspring will be a eunuch and a failure." In addition, with encouragement and kindly words he instructed Olympias how to hold her hands over the paths of nature and himself used his magic to restrain the woman's delivery.

Now once more observing the courses in heaven of the celestial bodies, he realized that the whole cosmos was at its zenith; and he saw a brilliance shining from heaven, as from the sun at its zenith, and said to Olympias, "Now give out the birth cry!" Indeed, he himself urged on her delivery and said to her, "You are on the point of bearing a king who will rule the world." and Olympias, bellowing louder than a cow, gave birth with good fortune to a male child. As the child fell to the ground, there were continual thunderclaps and lightning flashes stirring the whole world.

13. In the morning, Philip saw Olympias's newborn child and said: "I had wanted not to rear it, as it was not my offspring; but since I see that the seed came from a god and that the birth has been specially marked by heaven, he shall be raised in memory of my son by my previous wife, who died; and he shall be called Alexander." That was what Philip said, and the child received every attention. And garlands were worn throughout Macedonia, Pella, and Thrace.

I do not want to take long over Alexander's upbringing: he was weaned, and he grew older. When he became a man, his appearance was not like Philip's and, indeed, not even like his mother Olympias's or his real father's—he was a type all of his own. Indeed, he had the shape of a man, but he had the mane of a lion and eyes of different colors—the right eye black, the left grey—and teeth as sharp as a serpent's; he displayed the energy of a lion. And there was no doubt of how his nature would turn out.[5]

His nurse was Lanike (the sister of Kleitos the Black); his school attendant and governor, Leonidas; his primary teacher, Polyneikes; his music teacher, Leukippos of Lemnos; his teacher of geometry, Menippos from the Peloponnese; of rhetoric, Anaximenes of Lampsakos, son of Aristokiles; of philosophy, Aristotle of Stageira, son of Nikomachos.[6]

Having followed the entire curriculum, even astronomy, and being released from his studies, Alexander began in turn to teach his classmates. He drilled them for war and, standing apart, set them fighting, and when he saw one side being defeated by the other, he would go over to the losing side and help them out; and it would start winning again—so it was clear that he was victory. This, then, was Alexander's upbringing.

Now, one day Philip's horse breeders brought a colt of outstanding size from his studs and presented him to King Philip, with the words: "Lord King, we have found this horse born in the royal studs of a beauty that exceeds that of Pegasus. So we bring it to you, master." Looking at its size and beauty, King Philip was amazed. It needed the strength of them all to hold it back, and the horse breeders added, "Lord King, it is a man-eater!' "This really does show," King Philip replied, "the truth of the Greek proverb 'Close to good stands evil.' But since you have already brought him, I will take him." And he instructed his attendants to make an iron cage and to lock the horse in there without a bit "and any who are disobedient to my rule and require punishment after disobeying the law or being convicted of piracy[7] shall be thrown to him." And the king's instructions were carried out.

14. Alexander grew older, and when he was twelve, he started accompanying his father on troop maneuvers: he armed himself, swept along with the armies, leapt on the horses. As a result, Philip, seeing him, said, "Alexander, my boy, I like your character and your bravery, if not your appearance—because it is not like mine."

All of this was upsetting for Olympias; so she called Nektanebos to her and said to him, "Investigate what Philip intends to do with me." He

---

5. L makes no sense of this sentence: I have substituted the version of A.

6. This list of teachers came from Favorinus's *Universal History* and provides the *terminus post quem* for the dating of the romance (circa A.D. 140).

7. A rather illogical alternative, an example of thoughtless rewriting in our manuscript; A has "so that we may throw to him those who require punishment by law, convicted of piracy or murder."

set out his tablet and investigated her stars as Alexander sat by them. And Alexander said to him, "Sir, can't these stars you are talking about be seen in the sky?" "Of course they can, boy!" he replied. And Alexander said to him "Can I not know about them?" "Yes, boy," he replied, "you can when evening falls."

So in the evening Nektanebos collected Alexander and took him outside the city to a solitary spot and, looking up to the sky, showed Alexander the stars in the heavens. But Alexander took him by the hand, led him to a pit in the ground, and let him fall. Nektanebos, as he fell, took a fearful blow on the back of his head and cried: "Ah, Alexander, my boy, why did you decide to do that?"

Alexander replied, "Blame yourself, astrologer!"

"Why, boy?" he asked.

"Because," said Alexander, "you make a study of the heavens in ignorance of things on earth."

"Boy," said Nektanebos to him, "I am badly wounded. But there is no way that any mortal can overcome his fate."

"Why?" asked Alexander.

"Because I had read my own fate," said Nektanebos to him. "I was to be slain by my own child, and I have not escaped my fate: I have been slain by you."

"Am I your son then?" asked Alexander.

Then Nektanebos told him how he had been king in Egypt, had fled from Egypt, had come to live in Pella, had met Olympias and cast her horoscope, and how he had gone to her as the god Ammon and had had intercourse with her. With these words, he breathed out his spirit.

Alexander heard him say this and, being convinced that he had killed his father, was heartbroken and did not leave him in the pit for fear that he might become food for the beasts (it was night, and it was a solitary place). Moved by filial affection, he girt himself up and lifted him bravely onto his shoulders; then he took him to his mother, Olympias. At this sight Olympias said to Alexander, "What is this, my child?" And he replied, "I am another Aeneas and carry my Anchises," and proceeded to relate to her in detail everything he had heard from Nektanebos. She was astonished and blamed herself for having been deceived by him and his evil magical skills into adultery. But moved by affection, she buried him as befitted the father of Alexander, and, constructing a tomb, she had him placed there. It is one of Providence's notable marvels that Nektanebos, an Egyptian, received a funeral in the Greek style in Macedonia, but that Alexander, a Macedonian, received a funeral in the Egyptian style.

15. On his return from abroad Philip went off to Delphi to consult the oracle on who would succeed him as king. And the Pythia at Delphi

tasted the Kastalian spring and with an oracle of the earth replied as follows:[8]

> Philip, he shall be king over the whole world and shall subject all to his power, whosoever shall leap upon the horse Bucephalus and ride through the center of Pella.

(It was called Bucephalus because its shank was branded with the head [*cephale*] of an ox [*bus*].) Philip, hearing the oracle, was expecting another Hercules.

16. Alexander had Aristotle as his sole teacher. Many other children were studying with Aristotle, among them the sons of kings, and one day Aristotle asked one of them, "If you inherit your father's kingdom, what will you give me, your teacher?" He replied, "You shall hold a unique position of power as my companion, and I shall make you famous everywhere."

He asked another, "If you, boy, succeed to your father's kingdom, how will you treat me, your teacher?" He replied, "I shall make you a minister and consult you on all matters that require my decision."

And he also asked Alexander, "If you, Alexander, boy, succeed to the kingdom of your father Philip, how will you treat me, your teacher?" Alexander replied: "Are you asking me now about future matters, though you have no certainty about tomorrow? I shall give you your reward when the time and opportunity arrive." And Aristotle said to him, "Hail Alexander, world ruler: you shall be the greatest king."

Everyone liked Alexander, since he was intelligent and a good warrior. Only Philip had mixed feelings: it gave him pleasure to see such a warlike spirit in the boy, but it pained him to see that the boy was unlike him.

17. Alexander was fifteen when by chance one day he was passing the place where the horse Bucephalus was caged. He heard a terrifying neigh and, turning to the attendants, asked "What is this neighing?" In reply, the general Ptolemy said, "Master, this is the horse Bucephalus that your father caged because he was a man-eater." But the horse, hearing the sound of Alexander's voice, neighed again, not in a terrifying manner as on all previous occasions, but sweetly and clearly as though instructed by God. And when Alexander went up to the cage, straightaway the horse extended its forefeet to Alexander and licked him, indicating who its master was. Alexander observed the striking appearance of the horse

---

8. The Pythia's trance was usually attributed to the effect of fumes supposed to issue from the ground, but here is ascribed to drinking the springwater of Kastalia. The phrase "with an oracle of the earth" is odd and may result from rewriting of an earlier version of this recension.

and the remains of numerous slaughtered men at its feet, but elbowed aside the horse's guards and opened the cage. He grasped its mane;[9] it obeyed him, and he leapt on it without a bridle, then rode through the center of the city of Pella. One of the horse breeders ran and informed King Philip, who was outside the city of Pella, and Philip, remembering the oracle, went to meet Alexander and greeted him with the words "Hail, Alexander, world ruler." And thereafter thought of the child's future made Philip glad.

18. Now one day Alexander found his father at leisure and, giving him a kiss, said, "Father, please, will you let me sail to Pisa for the Olympic Games—because I would like to take part."

"You want to go?" asked Philip. "So what sport have you been training in?"

"I want to enter the chariot race," replied Alexander.

"My boy," he said, "I shall now see to suitable horses for you from my stables. So they will be taken care of; but you, my boy, must train yourself more seriously—it is a prestigious competition."

Alexander replied, "Father, you just let me go to the competition: I have horses that I have reared for myself since they were young."

Philip gave Alexander a kiss and, astounded at his determination, said to him, "Boy, this is what you want; so go with my blessing."

Alexander went off to the harbor and gave instructions for a brand new ship to be built and for the horses complete with their chariots to be put aboard. Alexander embarked together with his friend Hephaistion and after a voyage reached Pisa. On disembarkation, he received numerous gifts and instructed the lads to rub down the horses. Himself, he went for a walk with his friend Hephaistion, and they ran into Nikolaos, son of King Andreas of Akarnania,[10] a man proud of his wealth and good fortune—two unstable gods—and confident in his physical strength. He went up to Alexander and hailed him with the words "Greetings, young man!"

"Greetings to you too," he replied, "whoever you are and wherever you come from."

Nikolaos said to Alexander, "I am Nikolaos, king of Akarnania."

But Alexander said to him, "Do not be so proud, King Nikolaos, or preen yourself in the opinion that you are well equipped to deal with your life tomorrow: Fortune does not stay in one place, and change shows up the worthlessness of braggarts."

9. "Mane" according to A; "halter" according to the Armenian, which adds that Alexander used brute strength rather than good luck to tame the horse; "tendon" (?) according to L. In Plutarch *Life of Alexander* 6 Alexander takes the *rein* and turns Bucephalus towards the sun because he is worried by his shadow. The sense of this story had been lost by either our author or the recensions.

10. Nikolaos is invented by our author—and Akarnania was not ruled by a king!

Nikolaos replied: "What you say is right, but what you imply is not. Why are you here? As a spectator or a competitor? I understand that you are the son of Philip of Macedon."

"I may be young," Alexander replied, "but I am here to compete with you in the horse-racing."

"You should rather," said Nikolaos, "have come for the wrestling, the boxing, or the all-in fighting."[11]

Alexander replied, "I want to take part in the chariot-racing."

Then Nikolaos boiled over with rage and contempt for Alexander, observing how young he was but not having discovered the capacity of his soul, and spat in his face, saying: "May no good come to you! See what the stadium of Pisa has sunk to!"

But Alexander, taught by nature to control his feelings, wiped off the spit that insulted him and, with a smile that meant death, said, "Nikolaos, I shall defeat you forthwith, and in your homeland of Akarnania I shall take you prisoner." And they parted as enemies.

19. A few days later the time for the competition arrived. Nine men had entered for the chariot race, four of them sons of kings: Nikolaos the Akarnanian himself, Xanthias the Boeotian, Kimon the Corinthian, and Alexander the Macedonian.[12] The rest were sons of satraps and of generals. Everything for the competition was in place, including the urn, from which the lots were now drawn. Nikolaos drew first place, Xanthias second, Kimon third, Kleitomachos fourth, Aristippos of Olynthos fifth, Pieros of Phokaia sixth, Kimon of Lindos seventh, Alexander of Macedon eighth, Nikomachos of Lokroi ninth. Next they took up position for the race. The trumpet rang out the signal to begin. The starting gates on the stalls were opened up. They all leapt forward at an enormous pace—first lap, second and third and fourth. Now those at the back slackened as their horses gave out; but Alexander was driving in fourth position, and behind him was Nikolaos, not so much trying to win as to kill Alexander: Nikolaos's father had been killed by Philip in a war. Alexander had the intelligence to realize this, and when the leading drivers caused each other to fall, he let Nikolaos get past. And Nikolaos, unaware of the trap, overtook him, with his thoughts on the crown of victory. Now he was driving in first position, but, two laps further on,

11. A contest (*pankration*) combining traits of boxing and wrestling, sometimes compared to judo. Biting and gouging were not allowed, but dislocation of limbs and bone breaking were—clearly not a sport for aristocrats. Plutarch remarks how Alexander never instituted contests in boxing or all-in fighting; he also reports an anecdote in which Alexander declines to take part in foot-racing on the grounds that he would not have kings for competitors. These are the materials out of which this episode has been invented.

12. The names of the participants other than Alexander appear to be fictional.

the right-hand horse of Nikolaos stumbled against the front of the chariot, and the front horses came down together with it, and Nikolaos fell. Alexander hurtled forward, thanks to the pace of his own horses, and as he passed, seized the pole of Nikolaos's rear horses, and the whole of Nikolaos's chariot collapsed together with the charioteer, and Nikolaos was killed. Now Alexander and no one else was left, and the man who died suffered what the proverb says: "Whoever makes trouble for another, makes trouble for himself."

Now Alexander was crowned and, wearing his victory crown of wild olive, went up to the temple of Olympian Zeus. And the prophet of Zeus said to him: "Alexander, Olympian Zeus makes this prediction for you: 'Be of good cheer! As you have defeated Nikolaos, so shall you defeat many in your wars.' "[13]

20. Alexander, receiving this omen, returned victorious to Macedonia to find that his mother, Olympias, had been divorced by King Philip and that Philip had married the sister of Lysias, by name Kleopatra. Philip's wedding was taking place that very day, and Alexander, wearing his Olympic victory crown, entered the banquet and said to King Philip: "Father, accept the victory crown of my first exertions. And when in turn I give my mother, Olympias, to another king, I shall invite you to Olympias's wedding." So saying, Alexander reclined opposite his father, Philip, but Philip was hurt by Alexander's words.

21. Then Lysias, a joker who was reclining at table, said to Philip, "King Philip, ruler over every city, now we celebrate your wedding with Kleopatra, an honorable lady, by whom you have legitimate children, not the product of adultery—and they will look like you." Hearing Lysias say this made Alexander angry, and he reacted instantly, hurling his goblet at Lysias; it hit him on the temple and killed him. Philip, seeing what had happened, stood up, sword in hand—pointed in fury at Alexander—and fell over, tripping against the bottom of the couch. Alexander laughed and said to Philip, "Here is the man eager to take over the whole of Asia and subjugate Europe to its very foundations—and you are not capable of taking a single step." And with these words Alexander seized the sword from Philip, his father, and left all the guests half-slaughtered. It was just like watching the story of the Centaurs: some fled under the couches; some used tables for cover; others hid in dark areas. The result was that you could see Alexander as another, latter-day, Odysseus killing the suitors of Penelope.

Then Alexander went off and brought his mother, Olympias, into the palace, becoming an avenger of her marriage, but Lysias's sister Kleopa-

---

13. It is probably relevant that Niko-laos means literally "defeat people."

tra he drove into exile. The bodyguards took up King Philip and laid him down on the couch—in extremely bad condition.[14]

22. Ten days later, Alexander went in to Philip and, sitting down by him, said to him, "King Philip—I shall call you by your name so that you may not have the displeasure of being called Father by me—I have come to you not as your son, but as your friend to intervene in your unfair treatment of your wife."

Philip said to him, "You did a bad thing, Alexander by killing Lysias for the improper words he uttered."

"But you," replied Alexander, "did a fine thing by standing up sword raised against your child, wanting to kill me, and by wanting to marry another though your previous wife, Olympias, had done you no wrong? So get up and pull yourself together—I know what is making your body sluggish[15]—and let us forget these errors. I shall now appeal to Olympias, my mother, to be reconciled to you: she will be persuaded by her son— even if you are not prepared to be called my father!"

With these words Alexander left and, going to his mother, Olympias, said to her: "Mother, do not be angry at what your husband has done. He does not know about your indiscretion, whereas I, the son of an Egyptian father, am the living evidence against you. So go and appeal to him to be reconciled to you: it is the decent thing for a wife to take second place to her husband." And he took his mother to King Philip, his father, and said: "Father, turn to face your wife—I shall now call you Father, as you for your part follow the advice of your child. My mother stands at your side as a result of the many appeals I have made to her to come in to you and forget what has been done. Now embrace each other: there is no shame in your doing so in front of me—I was, after all, born from you." So saying, he reconciled his parents, and all the Macedonians were amazed by him. And from then on people who were getting married avoided mentioning the name of Lysias, in case by the mention of his name[16] they should be parted.

23. The city of Methone had rebelled against Philip. So Philip sent Alexander with a larger army to conduct the war. But Alexander, on his

14. This overcolored episode of the marriage banquet rather inverts historical truth. In 337 B.C. Philip married Kleopatra, his sixth wife, who, as a native Macedonian, posed a special threat to the position of Olympias (who came from Epirus), though there was no question of divorce. At the banquet, Attalos, a Macedonian general and uncle of Kleopatra, played the role assigned here to Lysias. But Alexander did not proceed to slaughter the wedding guests: rather, he fled with Olympias to Epirus, and was only able to return after a negotiated reconciliation. In 335 B.C. Olympias murdered the baby daughter of Philip and Kleopatra and caused Kleopatra to commit suicide.

15. The fuller version of A may make this clearer: "I know why you are sluggish: it is not your body I am talking about, but you are anguished in your soul at your errors."

16. Lysias means "he who parts."

arrival at Methone, persuaded them by clever argument to resume their allegiance.[17]

On his return from Methone, having gone in to his father Philip, he was standing and saw ahead of him men dressed in foreign costume. He asked about them, "Who are these people?" and was given the reply "Satraps of Darius, king of Persia."

Alexander asked them, "What are you here for?"

"To demand from your father the usual tribute," they replied to him.

"On whose behalf," Alexander asked them, "do you demand tribute?"

The satraps of Darius replied to him, "On behalf of Darius, king of the Earth."

"If the gods," said Alexander to them, "have given men the earth as a gift for their sustenance, is Darius taking a percentage of the gods' gift?" And again he said, testing them, "What would you want to take?"

"One hundred golden eggs," they told him, "made from twenty pounds of gold."

In reply Alexander said to them, "It is not right for Philip, king of the Macedonians, to pay tribute to barbarians: it is not open to anyone who so wishes to make Greeks his subjects." So Alexander told the satraps of Darius, "Go back and tell Darius, 'Alexander, son of Philip, hereby informs you, "When Philip was on his own, he used to pay you tribute. But now he has begotten a son, Alexander, he no longer pays you tribute, and, indeed, the tribute that you have taken from him I shall come in person and take back." ' " And with these words he sent away the emissaries, not even deigning to write to the king who had sent them. Philip, king of the Greeks, was pleased at this, seeing the style of Alexander's daring.[18]

The emissaries, however, took some money and gave it to a Greek friend of theirs who was a painter, and he did them a miniature portrait of Alexander, which they took to Darius in Babylon when they reported back to him everything Alexander had said to them.

Now another city in Thrace revolted from Philip, and he sent Alexander with a large number of soldiers to make war on it.

24. There was a man called Pausanias in Pella, a man of importance and great wealth who was the leader of all the Thessalonicans.[19] Now,

17. Methone had in fact been destroyed by Philip in 354 B.C., when Alexander was two.

18. The episode of the Persian emissaries is based on a tale (Plutarch *Life of Alexander* 5) of how Alexander once entertained Persian envoys while Philip was away, asking them useful questions about their empire. Demands for tribute and haughty dismissal are fictional amplifications.

19. Thessalonike, the second city of modern Greece, was founded about 316 B.C., seven years after Alexander's death. Pausanias was in fact an aristocrat from the western

this man had fallen in love with Olympias, Alexander's mother, and sent some people to her to persuade her to leave Philip, her husband, and marry him, sending her many gifts. But Olympias refused; so Pausanias headed for the place where Philip was, having discovered that Alexander was away at war, and arrived as a stage competition was being held. Philip was conducting proceedings in the Olympic theater when Pausanias appeared, sword in hand, in the theater with a number of other brave men, with the intention of killing Philip so that he could seize Olympias. He attacked him and struck him in the side with his sword but failed to kill him. Pandemonium resulted in the theater. And Pausanias rushed off to the palace to seize Olympias.

Now it just so happened that Alexander returned victorious from the war on the same day and saw massive uproar in the city. He asked what had happened and was told, "Pausanias is in the place intending to seize Olympias, your mother." And immediately he went in with those of his guards he had with him and found Pausanias violently restraining Olympias as she screamed. Alexander wanted to strike him with a spear but was afraid he might hit his mother too: he was keeping hold of her with considerable force. But Alexander tore Pausanias away from his mother and used the spear he was holding to strike him. Discovering Philip was still alive, he went to him and asked, "Father, what do you want done with Pausanias?" "Bring him here to me," he replied. And when they brought him, Alexander took a dagger, put it in the hand of Philip, his father, and brought Pausanias up to him. And Philip took hold of him and cut his throat. And Philip said to Alexander: "Alexander, my boy, it is no sorrow to me that I am dying: I have had vengeance, killing my enemy like this. So Ammon the god of Libya was right when he said to Olympias, your mother, 'You shall have in your womb a male child who shall avenge the death of his father.' " So saying, Philip expired. He had a king's funeral, and the whole of Macedonia attended.

25. When calm had been restored in Pella, Alexander went up to his father Philip's statue and at the top of his voice cried out, "Sons of the Pellaians and Macedonians and Greeks and Amphiktyons[20] and Spartans

---

fringe of Macedonia who had become a royal bodyguard. He was said by Aristotle to have killed Philip because of a personal grudge, but it has seemed suggestive that his homeland had originally been under the influence of Epirus, Olympias's home. His passion for Olympias is romantic fiction; and he was apprehended not by Alexander, but by three bodyguards as he tripped over a vine root.

20. The Amphiktyonic League was a loose confederation of the states of central Greece, between Macedonia and Attica (the territory of Athens). It was prompt to recognize Alexander as Philip's successor. Philip had already federated the Greeks (except the unwilling Spartans) at Corinth in 337 B.C. for a campaign against Persia and became leader of this "League of Corinth." Alexander took over his leadership and reaffirmed the intention to invade the Persian Empire, at Corinth in 335 B.C., and that is where he would have made this sort of speech—not at Pella. This event is referred to at the end of 1.27.

and Corinthians, join with me, your comrade-in-arms, and pledge yourselves to me, to campaign against the barbarians and free ourselves from
slavery to the Persians so that we who are Greeks may cease to be slaves
to barbarians." And having made this speech, Alexander issued royal
edicts in every city. Then men mustered from all the states and arrived in
Macedonia—volunteers, all of them, as though summoned by a god-sent
voice—to join the campaign. Alexander opened his father's armory and
issued the young men with full military equipment. And in addition he
brought all the guards of his father, Philip, by now old men, and said
to them, "Veterans and mighty comrades-in-arms, consent to add your
distinction to the Macedonian campaign and march with us to war!"

"King Alexander," they replied, "we have grown old marching with
your father, King Philip and our bodies are no longer strong enough to
match our adversaries. Consequently, we seek to be excused from cam-
paigning under you."

"But I am all the more keen," replied Alexander to them, "to march
with you if you are old: age is often stronger than youth. Indeed, on
many occasions youth, trusting in the effectiveness of the body, deviates
into ill-advised action and finds the scales weighted against it and encounters sudden peril, whereas the old man thinks first and acts later,
using judgment to avoid peril. So you, sirs, march with us; you will not
be lined up against the enemy but will show your mettle by encouraging
the young men. The contribution of both is necessary; so lend the support
of your minds to the army: the conduct of war too needs intelligence. The
fact is, if you will consider the battle, it is clear that your own security too
depends on victory for the homeland: if we are defeated, the enemy will
have no opposition save those unfit through age; whereas if we win, the
victory reflects on the judgment of the advisers." So saying, Alexander
persuaded all the veterans by his words to follow him.

26. So Alexander succeeded to the kingdom of Philip, his father, at
the age of eighteen. And the disturbance occasioned by Philip's death was
quelled by Antipatros, a clever man and a fast thinker. He took Alexander armed with a breastplate into the theater and developed a number of
arguments in his appeal to the Macedonians to support Alexander.

Alexander was, it seems, more fortunate than his father, Philip, and
immediately took upon himself great affairs. He brought together all his
father's soldiers, counted them, and found there were 20,000 horsemen
(including 8,000 armed with breastplates), 15,000 infantry, 5,000 Thra-
cians, 30,000 Amphiktyons, Spartans, Corinthians, and Thessalonicans.
He found the total of all those present was 70,000, and 6,590 archers.

27. As the Illyrians, Paionians, and Triballoi had rebelled, he
marched against them, but while he was fighting these nations, Greece
revolted. A rumor had got about that Alexander, king of the Macedonians, had been killed in the war, and it is said that Demosthenes brought

a wounded man before the Athenian assembly who claimed he had seen Alexander lying dead. When the Thebans discovered this, they cut down the garrison that Philip had put in the Kadmeia after the battle of Chaironeia.[21] According to the story, Demosthenes persuaded them to do this. Alexander in anger attacked the Thebans. And the Thebans had signs of the misfortunes that lay in store for them: a spider wove its web over the shrine of Demeter and the water of the spring "Dirke" turned bloody. The king took and demolished the whole city, sparing only the house of Pindar. And he is supposed also to have compelled the flautist Ismenias to play to the demolition of the city. So the Greeks took fright: they elected Alexander their leader and handed over to him the rule of Greece.

28. Back in Macedonia, he got everything ready for the expedition across Asia, constructing Liburnian cruisers and triremes[22] and a very large number of battleships. He embarked all his troops and wagons, together with all manner of arms. And, taking 50,000 talents of gold,[23] he gave the order and came to the region of Thrace, where he took 5,000 picked men and 500 talents of gold. And all the cities received him with garlands.

At the Hellespont, he took the ships and reached Asia from Europe. There he fixed his spear in the ground and claimed Asia by right of conquest. From there Alexander came to the river Granikos, as it is called: the satraps of Darius were defending this. After a mighty battle, Alexander was victorious. He took spoils and sent them to the Athenians and to his mother, Olympias, as a gift. He decided first to subdue the coastal areas and so took possession of Ionia and after that Caria, after which he took Lydia and the treasures at Sardis. And he captured Phrygia, Lycia, and Pamphylia—where something amazing happened: Alexander had no ships with him, but part of the sea receded to let his infantry cross.[24]

29. Pressing on, he rendezvoused with his fleet and crossed to Sicily.[25] Subduing some people who opposed him, he crossed to the land of

21. Philip decisively defeated the joint forces of Athens and Thebes at Chaironeia in 338 B.C., establishing his supremacy over Greece. Alexander destroyed Thebes in 335 B.C. L tells of the destruction twice over, here and at 1.46. The other recensions omit most of 1.27–29.

22. Liburnian ships were fast warships with two banks of oars, which become important only after Octavian (Augustus) deployed them at the battle of Actium in 31 B.C. Triremes had three banks of oars.

23. A talent was the largest weight in Greek currency, roughly the weight a man can carry, about fifty pounds.

24. By Mt. Klimax in Lydia; the coastal area was only passable when northerlies blew—as they did on Alexander's arrival.

25. Alexander never went to Sicily, Italy, or Africa, though a western expedition was alleged to be among his last plans, and "What if he had?" later became a popular debating topic. On the other hand, envoys from Europe and Africa met Alexander on his return from India to Babylon, wisely, to offer congratulations, and one witness claimed that Romans were among them, something not impossible.

Italy. And the Roman generals sent Marcus, one of their generals, with a crown of pearls and another of precious stones, saying to him. "We add to your crowns, Alexander, king of the Romans and of every land," bringing him also five hundred pounds of gold. Alexander, accepting their gifts, promised to make them great and powerful and took from them two thousand archers and four hundred talents.

From there he crossed over to Africa. And the African generals met him and begged him to keep away from their city, Carthage. But Alexander despised their weakness and said to them, "Either become stronger or pay tribute to those stronger than you."

Setting off from there, he crossed the whole of Libya and reached the shrine of Ammon.[26] (He put most of his troops aboard ship and instructed them to sail away to the island of Proteus and await him there, while he himself went off to sacrifice to Ammon on the supposition that he had been begotten by Ammon.) He prayed to him in these words. "Father Ammon, if she who bore me tells the truth when she says that I was begotten by you, give me an oracle!" And Alexander saw Ammon embracing his mother, Olympias, and saying to him, "Alexander, my child, you are my seed." Discovering the actual power of Ammon, Alexander renovated his shrine and gilded his idol and consecrated it with this inscription.

DEDICATION OF ALEXANDER
TO HIS FATHER, THE GOD AMMON.

He also asked to receive an oracle from him on where he might found a city named after him so that it might last in perpetual memory of him. And he saw Ammon, aged, golden-haired, with ram's horns on his temples, saying to him:

O King, you the ram-horned Phoebus addresses:
If you wish through ages unsullied[27] to retain your youth,
Found your city greatly famed opposite the Isle of Proteus,
Over which presides Time, son of Wealth, himself its lord,
Turning the boundless world on his five-peaked ridges.[28]

26. As pharaoh of Egypt, Alexander became son of Ammon and was apparently greeted as such at Ammon's shrine at the oasis Siwah (in the depths of the Egyptian desert). This chapter, which accepts the parentage by Ammon, is of course inconsistent with the tale of the trickery of Nektanebos in 1.7, which maintains continuity with pharaonic rule in a different way.

27. A has "through centuries unaging," more plausibly.

28. Phoebus here denotes the sun-god (Egyptian, Ra) with whom Ammon was identified. The city to be founded is, of course, the Egyptian Alexandria, perpetuating Alexander's name. Proteus, an elusive god who could transform his appearance, lived according to Homer (*Odyssey* 4.351ff.) on Pharos. "Time, son of Wealth" refers to Sarapis, the great god developed at Alexandria for the use of Greek Egypt. The final line depicts the site as

Receiving this oracle, Alexander tried to work out what island was meant by "the Isle of Proteus" and who the god was that presided over it. And as Alexander tried to work this out, he made another sacrifice to Ammon and journeyed to a village in Libya, where he let his troops rest.

31. As Alexander was taking a walk there, an enormous deer ran by and entered some undergrowth. Alexander called out to an archer and instructed him to shoot the beast. The archer drew his bow but did not hit the deer, and Alexander said to him, "Fellow, that was a miss [*paratonon*]"; and as a result of this, that place was called Paratone on account of Alexander's exclamation. So he built a small town there, and, inviting certain local people of good class, he gave them houses there, calling the place Paratone.

Traveling on from there, he came to Taphosirion.[29] Then he questioned the locals on the reason for this name, and they told him that the shrine was the grave [*taphos*] of Osiris. So, having sacrificed there too, he reached the end of his journey and came to the land of present-day Alexandria and saw a huge area stretching as far as the eye could see, containing twelve villages. Alexander marked out the length of the city from Pandysis, as it is called, to the Herakleotic mouth; and its width from the district of Mendes up to the small Hormoupolis (it was called Hormoupolis, not Hermoupolis, because everyone coming down the Nile put in [*pros-hormein*] there).[30] So it was as far as that locality that King Alexander marked out the city, and up to the present day it is registered as the territory of the Alexandrians.

King Alexander was advised by Kleomenes of Naukratis and Deinokrates of Rhodes not to found the city on so great a scale, "because you will not be able to find enough people to fill it; and even if you do, the administration will be unable to supply the food it would need. In addition, the inhabitants of the city will be at war with each other because of its excessive and boundless size: it is small cities that think constructively together and form constructive plans for the good of the city; whereas if you build it on the enormous scale you have planned, there will be differences and dissension among its inhabitants, as the population will be

---

the center of the universe; van Thiel refers the five peaks to five elements in Perisan lore, as there are in fact no mountains at the site.

29. More accurately, Taposiris, the modern Abusir, thirty miles west of Alexandria. The derivation of this native Egyptian place-name from the Greek word for "grave" is naturally false. Osiris was the Egyptian god of the underworld, with whom the dead pharaoh was identified.

30. Pandysis was to the west of Alexandria, and the Herakleotic mouth of the Nile was at Kanobos, twenty miles to the east. The lesser Hermoupolis ("city of Hermes" in Greek, referring to the Egyptian god Thoth, who was identified with Hermes) was thirty miles upstream from Kanobos; Mendes (L mistakenly talks of the "shrine of Bendis" instead) was in the northeast area of the delta. This fictional first plan of Alexander would have put New York and Greater London to shame.

boundless." Alexander was persuaded and commissioned the architects to lay out the city on the scale they wanted, and they, under King Alexander's instructions, marked out the length of the city from the river Drakon at the spit of land with Taphosirion on it up to the river Agathodaimon at Kanobos, and the width from the district of Mendes to Eurylochion and Melanthion. And Alexander ordered those who lived in this area within thirty miles of the city to move into the districts of the city, granting them areas of land and entitling them to be called Alexandrians. The chief officials of the districts were Eurylochos and Melanthos—which is where the names came from.

Alexander consulted other master builders for the city too, including Noumenios the stonemason, Kleomenes of Naukratis the engineer, and Krateros of Olynthos. Noumenios had a brother called Hyponomos: this man advised Alexander to build the city on proper foundations and to install water channels and sewers discharging into the sea—and it is called a hyponomos because he divised it.[31]

32. [From the land he saw an island in the sea and asked what it was called. "Pharos," the locals replied. "Proteus lived there. And we have his tomb also, which we worship, on a high mountain." They took him to what is now called the Hero's Shrine and showed him the coffin. He sacrificed to the hero Proteus and, seeing the tomb had in the course of time fallen into disrepair, gave instructions for it swiftly to be restored.]

Alexander ordered the perimeter of the city to be marked out so that he could take a look at it. So the workmen marked the city out with wheat meal, but all sorts of birds flew down, ate up the meal, and flew off. Alexander was very disturbed at what this sign might mean; so he sent for the interpreters and told them what had happened. Their reply was, "The city that you, King, have ordered to be built will nourish the whole world, and men born in it will be found everywhere: birds fly round the whole world."[32]

So he gave instructions for the building of the city. When he had laid the foundations for the most part of the city and marked it out, Alexander inscribed five letters—A B Γ Δ E—A for "Alexander," B for "King" [Basileus], Γ for "of the Race" [genos], Δ for "of Zeus" [Dios], E for "has founded [ektisen] an inimitable city."[33] Donkeys and mules were

---

31. Another false etymology: *hyponomos* is just Greek for "something that runs underground." The bracketed paragraph that follows is omitted by L and restored by Van Thiel from A.

32. L now omits a paragraph in which a snake troubling the workmen is caught and killed, and Alexander orders a shrine to be built for it—it is the Good Spirit (in Greek, Agathos Daimon). This is the shrine referred to in the next paragraph.

33. This is a colorful explanation for the fact that Alexandria was divided into 5 districts, lettered A, B, Γ, Δ, E. One may compare divisions of modern cities for postal purposes.

working away. But as the gateway of the shrine was being erected, an enormous and very ancient slab, covered with letters, suddenly fell, and a large number of snakes came out of it and crept into the entrances of the houses, whose foundations had by now been laid. (Alexander was still present to found the city on the new moon of the month Tybi—that is, January—including the actual shrine.)[34] And this is why doorkeepers revere these snakes as Good Spirits entering the houses (they are not poisonous); and they garland their working animals and let them rest. This is why up to the present day the Alexandrians have kept the custom of holding the festival on the twenty-fifth of Tybi.

33. Alexander found a cult statue stationed on the high hills, together with the Pillars of Helion and the Hero's Shrine.[35] In addition he looked for the Sarapeion, in accordance with the oracle given to him by Ammon. (He had spoken to him in an oracle like this.

> O king, you the ram-horned Phoebus addresses:
> If you wish through ages unsullied to retain your youth,
> Found your city greatly famed opposite the Isle of Proteus,
> Over which presides Time, son of Wealth, himself its lord,
> Turning the boundless world on his five-peaked ridges.

So Alexander was looking for him who beholds all.)[36] He constructed opposite the Hero's Shrine a great altar, now called the Altar of Alexander, at which he celebrated a costly sacrifice. And he offered this prayer. "You are the god who takes care of this land and beholds the boundless world—this is clear. Yourself now accept my sacrifice and be my helper in the wars." So saying, he put the victims on the altar. Then suddenly a huge eagle flew down and snatched the entrails of the offering, carried them off through the air and dropped them at another altar. Alexander, observing the spot, went there quickly and saw the entrails lying on the altar. The altar, he saw, had been set up by men of olden times. There was a precinct, with a wooden idol presiding inside. With its right hand it was soothing a beast of many shapes,[37] in its left hand it held a scepter.

---

34. The sentence in parentheses seems to belong a few lines later.

35. The nonexistent "high hills" have been invented on the basis of the oracle. The Hero's Shrine is that of Proteus. The Pillars of Helion are puzzling: they may refer to obelisks at the Kaisareion, but they sound like Pillars of the Sun and their function here, set on high mountains, may be to mark the center of the universe as indicated in the last line of the oracle.

36. The author seems to have thought that the rare word for "turning" in the last line of the oracle meant "beholding."

37. The "beast of many shapes" is the three-headed dog, Cerberus, who guards the entrance to the underworld. In the standard iconography Sarapis, who controls the underworld, is depicted seated with scepter and with Cerberus, both of which details appear only in recension B. The "maiden" is Sarapis's consort Isis. Sarapis and Isis, when translated into traditional Greek mythology, have the status of Zeus and Hera.

And beside the idol was a huge statue of a maiden. So he asked the people that lived there who the god of the place was. They replied that they did not know, but had received a tradition from their forefathers that it was a shrine of Zeus and Hera.

Here too he saw the obelisks that stand to this day in the Sarapeion, outside the present precinct. On these there were hieroglyphic letters inscribed, of the following content.[38]

[I, Sesonchosis, King of Egypt and world ruler, built and dedicated this to Sarapis, the first god revealed to this land. (Sarapis then appears in a dream to Alexander, prophesies that Alexandria will indeed perpetuate the memory of Alexander and its name will not be changed, and tells of its future prosperity. A phrase then tries to smooth over the omission in the manuscript.)] The reward of the actual city [will be]: (and the manuscript continues) . . . possessed of fine temples, exceptional in the huge size of its population, superior in its healthy climate. And I shall be its champion and stop hardships, either famine or earthquake, from taking hold: instead, they shall pass swiftly through the city, like a dream. Many kings shall come to it, not to bring war, but to pay homage. And when you become a god, your body will constantly receive homage and gifts from many kings, and you shall live in the city, dead and yet not dead: for you shall have the city that you are founding as your tomb.

Receive now, Alexander, a concise proof of my identity: add twice one hundred [S][39] and one [A]; then another hundred [R] and one [A]; then four times twenty [P] and ten [I]; and, taking the first letter, put it at the end— then you will understand who has appeared to you.

Having delivered this oracle, he withdrew. Alexander, recalling the oracle, realized it was SARAPIS. The layout of the city is as Alexander arranged it, and the city was established, growing stronger day by day.

34. Alexander took his armies and hurried on to Egypt. When he arrived at the city of Memphis, the Egyptians enthroned him as king of Egypt on the throne of Hephaistos.[40] In Memphis Alexander saw a tall statue of black stone with the following inscription on its pedestal.

---

38. Recension B here omits about two pages, scarcely deliberately. I indicate in the text the content of what intervened. When the recension resumes, Sarapis is delivering a prophecy, but B does not notice it is in verse and, paraphrasing, destroys the meter.

There is some confusion between the names Sesonchosis and Sesostris, and the reference here is in fact to Sesostris III (1877–1839 B.C.), whose fabulous conquests, supposedly as far as Scythia and Thrace, are reported already in Herodotos and were invented, it seems, to restore the Egyptian ego by outdoing the conquests of Darius I of Persia (521–486 B.C.). In the generation after Alexander they were extended to outdo Alexander's exploits. Our author may have borrowed material from a Sesonchosis novel (of which fragments survive), and in any case he uses him here as a forerunner of Alexander.

39. Greeks, not having arabic numerals, used letters of the alphabet instead, so that 200, for instance, is S. Cf. Heliodoros 9.22.

40. The Egyptian god Ptah, god of craftsmen, like the Greek Hephaistos.

THIS KING WHO HAS FLED WILL COME AGAIN TO EGYPT, NOT IN AGE BUT IN YOUTH, AND OUR ENEMY THE PERSIANS HE SHALL SUBJECT TO US.

Alexander asked whose statue this was and the prophets told him: "This statue is of the last king of Egypt, Nektanebos. When the Persians were coming to devastate Egypt, he saw by his magical powers the gods of Egypt guiding the armies of the enemy towards us and Egypt being destroyed by them. He then realized their impending betrayal and fled. But when we conducted a search for him and inquired of the gods where our king, Nektanebos, had fled to, they gave us this response.

> This king who has fled will come again to Egypt, not in age but in youth, and your enemy the Persians he shall subject to you.

When Alexander heard this, he leapt onto the statue and embraced it, saying: "This is my father—I am his son. What the oracle told you was not false. But what amazes me is that you were taken over by the barbarians even though you have invincible walls that could not be pulled down by the enemy. This must be the working of Providence above and the justice of the gods, so that you, who have a productive land and a natural river to fertilize it, are subjected to and ruled by people who do not have these advantages; otherwise, through not having them the barbarians would perish." And so saying, he demanded from them the tribute they used to pay to Darius, saying this to them, "It is not so that I may collect it for my own treasury, but rather so that I may spend it on your city, the Egyptian Alexandria, capital of the world." When he had put it this way, the Egyptians were glad to give him great quantities of money; and it was with awe and full honors that they escorted him on his departure at Pelousion.

35. He took his armies and marched for Syria. There he enlisted two thousand armored cavalry and arrived at Tyre. The Tyrians formed up against him to prevent his passing through their city, because of an ancient oracle that had been given to them, as follows.

> When a king comes against you, men of Tyre, your city shall be razed to the ground.

This is why they offered opposition to his entry into their city. So they formed up against him, having walled the entire city, and in the violent battle between them the Tyrians killed many of the Macedonians. Alexander retired, defeated, to Gaza. When he had recovered his strength, he tried to work out how to sack Tyre. Then in a dream Alexander saw someone saying to him, "Alexander, do not consider going yourself as a messenger to Tyre." So when he awoke from his sleep, he sent emissaries to Tyre with a letter of the following content.

King Alexander, son of Ammon and King Philip, I who am Greatest King of Europe and the whole of Asia, of Egypt and Libya, to the Tyrians, who no longer exist:

Journeying to the regions of Syria in peace and lawfulness, I wished to enter your land. But if you Tyrians are the first to oppose our entrance as we journey, then it is only by your example that others will learn the strength of the Macedonians in the face of your mindless action and shall cower in obedience to us. And you may rely on the oracle you have been given: I shall come through your city.

Farewell, men of sense—or, otherwise, farewell men of misfortune!

Having read the king's letter, their government ordered the messengers King Alexander had sent to be flogged, asking them, "Which of you is Alexander?" And when they replied that none of them was, they crucified them.

So Alexander was trying to work out what route to enter by and how to strike down the Tyrians—he had discounted his defeat. And he saw in his sleep a satyr, one of the attendants of Dionysos, offering him a cheese [*tyros*] made from milk; he took it and trampled it under his feet. On waking, Alexander related the dream to a dream interpreter, and he said to him, "You shall be king over all Tyre, and it shall be under your control, because the satyr [*sa Tyros*, 'your Tyre'] gave you *tyros* ['cheese' or 'Tyre'], and you trampled it under your feet."

Three days later, Alexander collected his troops and, together with the three neighboring villages, who had fought bravely with Alexander, in the night opened up the gates in the walls, entering and killing the guards. Alexander sacked the whole of Tyre and razed it to the ground, and the byword "The ills of Tyre" continues to the present day. As for the three villages that had fought with him, he combined them into one city and called it Tripoli ["triple city"].

36. Appointing a satrap of Phoenicia at Tyre, Alexander broke camp and followed the coast of Syria. Emissaries of Darius came to meet him, bringing him a letter, a strap, a ball, and a money box of gold. Alexander accepted the letter of Darius, king of Persia, and, on reading it, found its contents were these.

King of Kings, kinsman of the gods, I who rise to heaven with the Sun, a god myself, I Darius to my servant Alexander give these orders:

I instruct you to return to your parents, to be my slave, and to sleep in the lap of your mother, Olympias: that is how old you are—you need to be corrected and nursed. So I have sent you a strap, a ball, and a money box of gold, and you can take whatever you like first. I sent the strap to let you know you still need correction. I sent the ball so that you can play with children your own age and not mislead so many young men at such an arrogant age into going around with you, like a brigand chief, and disturbing the peace of the cities: not even if this whole world is brought together by a single man, will it be able to overthrow the kingdom of the Persians. I have such huge numbers of troops that, like grains of sand, no one could even count them; and I have enough gold and silver to fill the whole earth. I have also sent you a money box full of gold so that should you run out of food to give your fellow brigands, you may give them each the wherewithal to go back to their own homeland.

But if you do not obey my instructions, I shall send a force after you, and the result will be that you will be arrested by my soldiers—and you will not be educated as the son of Philip but crucified as a rebel.

37. Alexander read this out before all his troops, and they were all frightened. Alexander noticed their fright and said to them: "Men of Macedonia and comrades-in-arms, why are you upset at what Darius has written, as though his boastful letter had real power? There are some dogs too who make up for being small by barking loud, as though they could give the illusion of being powerful by their barking. That is what Darius is like: in practice he is powerless, though in what he writes he seems to be someone to reckon with, just like the dogs with their barking. But even let us admit that what he says is true: it illuminates for us who it is that we must fight courageously for victory, to help us avoid the shame of defeat."

With these words, he gave instructions for Darius's letter carriers to have their arms tied behind their backs and to be taken away to be crucified. They said: "What harm have *we* done you, King Alexander? We are messengers: why do you give instructions for us to be killed miserably?"

Alexander replied, "Blame King Darius, not me: Darius sent you with a letter like that, as though it were to a brigand chief, not to a king. So I am killing you as though you had come to a ruthless man, not a king."

"Darius," they said, "had seen nothing when he wrote you that sort of letter. But we see such an array before us and realize that the son of King Philip is a very great and intelligent king. We implore you, Greatest King and Master, grant us life!"

Alexander said to them: "Now you have shown cowardice in the face of your punishment and beg not to die, I shall—for that reason[41]—release you. I am not of a mind to kill you, but only to show the difference between a Greek king and a barbarian one. So do not expect any ill-treatment at my hands: a king does not kill a messenger."

Having spoken to them in this way, Alexander told them, as dinner was being prepared, to join him at table. The letter carriers wanted to tell Alexander how, when it came to war against Darius, he could capture Darius in an ambush; but he said to them: "Do not tell me anything: if you had not been returning to him, I would have wanted to know about

41. A stresses that it is not for that reason (which makes more sense.)

this from you. But as you are making your way back to him, I am not prepared to, in case any of you should report what has been said to Darius, and I should be found to deserve punishment as much as you.[42] So be quiet and let us calmly pass over this point." The letter carriers of Darius spoke much in his praise, and the whole mass of troops cheered him.

38. Three days later, Alexander wrote a letter to Darius, which he also read in full to his own troops in the absence of Darius's letter carriers. And its content were as follows.

King Alexander, son of King Philip and his mother, Olympias, to the King of Kings, enthroned with the gods, who rises to heaven with the Sun, a Great God, King of the Persians, greetings:

It is a disgrace if someone priding himself on such great power and "rising with the Sun" eventually falls into base slavery to a man, Alexander. The titles of the gods, when they come into the possession of men, do not confer great power or sense upon them. For how can names of the immortal gods take up residence in destructible bodies? Note how we have condemned you for this also: you have no power over us, but usurp the title of the gods and attribute their powers on earth to yourself. I am going to wage war on you in the view that you are mortal, and which way victory goes depends on Providence above.

Why did you write also to tell us that you have in your possession all this gold and silver? So that, on discovering the fact, we would fight the war more courageously so as to capture it? For my part, I shall be famous when I have defeated you, and I shall be a great king among Greeks and barbarians because I have killed Darius, such a mighty king. But if you defeat me, you will not have achieved anything remarkable: you will have defeated a brigand—according to your letter to me; but I shall have defeated the "King of Kings, great god, Darius."

You also sent me a strap, a ball, and a money box of gold, having a joke at my expense. Well, I have received these, counting them good messages. I have taken the strap so that I may flay the barbarians with my spears and weapons and reduce them by my hands to servitude. As for the ball, you are indicating to me that I shall gain control over the whole world: the world is spherical and round. The money box of gold you sent me is an important symbol: you will be defeated by me and pay me tribute!

39. Having read this to his troops and sealed it, King Alexander gave it to Darius's letter carriers and gave them as a present the gold they had brought. Having experienced the magnanimity of Alexander, they withdrew and returned to Darius.

Darius read the letter of Alexander and realized the forcefulness in it.

42. A adds "for allowing you to escape punishment at my hands," which reveals the author's thought.

And he asked detailed questions about Alexander's intelligence and his preparations for war. This disturbed him, and he wrote his satraps a letter with the following contents.

> King Darius to the generals beyond the Taurus, greetings:
> I have received a report that Alexander, the son of Philip, his risen up against me. Arrest him and bring him to me, without doing him any physical harm, so that I can strip him of the purple and flog him before sending him back to his homeland, Macedonia, to his mother, Olympias, with a rattle and dice (which is how the Macedonian children play). And I shall send with him men who teach all aspects of correct behavior. And sink his ships in the depths of the sea and put the generals that accompany him in irons and send them to us. Send the remaining soldiers to the Red Sea to make their homes there. The horses and all the pack animals I give to you.
> Good health.

The satraps too wrote to Darius, in these terms.

> To the Great God, King Darius, greetings:
> So large an army is advancing on us that we are astonished that you did not know about it before now. We have sent you those of them we have found astray, but have not dared to interrogate them before you. So come quickly with a large force so that we do not become spoils of war.

Darius received this letter at Babylon in Persia and, reading it, wrote them this reply.

> King of Kings, Great God Darius, to all his satraps and generals, greetings:
> Do not expect any help from me—just show your renowned bravery! What sort of beast has sprung upon you and panicked you—you who can quench lightning bolts but cannot take the roaring of a low born man?[43] What have you to say for yourselves? Has one of you fallen in battle? What policy am I to adopt with you, who hold my kingdom and make excuses for a brigand because you are not prepared to have him arrested? But now, as you said, I shall come and arrest him myself.

Learning that Alexander was nearby, Darius encamped by the river Pinaros[44] and wrote a letter to Alexander in these terms.

---

43. This sentence makes little sense in any recension (I present a stopgap). Clearly, in an earlier letter in the epistolary novel (see the Introduction), not, however, incorporated in our novel, the satraps had boasted they could quench lightning bolts.

44. The river at Issos, a town on the coats of Cilicia, in modern Turkey somewhat north of Iskenderun and around thirty miles from the Syrian frontier. The battle of Issos (333 B.C.) was Alexander's second major battle, after the Granikos (1.28).

King of Kings, Great God Darius and Lord of the Nations, to Alexander, who has plundered the cities:

You are apparently unaware of the name of Darius, which the gods have honored and have decreed should share their thrones. In addition, you have not considered it happiness to escape notice as ruler of Macedonia without my authority: instead, you have passed through obscure countries and alien cities, proclaiming yourself king there and collecting desperadoes like yourself. And you fight wars against inexperienced cities, whose lordship I have always refrained from assuming and which I have considered unimportant because of their isolation; whereas you have sought tribute from them as though you were taking a collection. Are you convinced then that we are like you? But you shall not boast of your possession of the places you have taken. So you have misjudged the situation badly. In the first place you should have made amends for your foolish errors and come to me, your lord, Darius, and not continued accumulating forces of brigands. I have written to you to come and do obeisance to King Darius—and I swear to you by Zeus, the greatest god and my father, that I will not hold against you what you have done. But you persist in another, foolish, course; so I shall punish you[45] with an indescribable death; and those with you who have failed to install good sense in you shall suffer worse than you.

41. When Alexander received the letter of Darius and read it, he was not incensed at Darius's haughty words.

Darius mustered a large force and came down with his children, his wife, and his mother; and around him were the ten thousand "Immortals" (they were called Immortals because their number was kept up, and new men were brought in to replace those that died).

Alexander made his way through the Cilician Taurus Mountains and came to Tarsos, the capital of Cilicia. There he saw the river Kydnos, which flows below it, and as he was pouring with sweat from the march, he took off his breastplate and took a swim in the river. But he caught a chill and became very seriously ill and was only with difficulty cured. The man who cured him was Philip, a famous doctor. Having regained his strength, he pressed on against Darius. And Darius was encamped at the place called Issos in Cilicia.[46]

Provoked, Alexander hurried to do battle in the plain and drew up his forces opposite Darius. But as Darius's officers saw Alexander bring the might of his army against them at the point where he could hear Darius, they positioned the chariots and arranged the whole battle lineup. Indeed, as both sides were standing ready to engage in battle,

45. A has, more sensibly, "But if you persist in another, foolish, course, I shall punish you."

46. The last two paragraphs are found only in recension B and disturb the order of the novel. Darius has already arrived at Issos at 1.40 *init.*, and the incident concerning the doctor Philip is told in full later (2.8).

Alexander was not prepared to let them break through inside the phalanx or to ride through and attack his rear (the majority of the chariots, pinned down on every side, were destroyed and dispersed). Mounting his horse, Alexander gave the order for the trumpeters to play the war signal, and with a huge roar from the armies a fierce battle began.

There was a lengthy engagement with missiles at the ends of the wings, where they used their spears and, struck by each other, were driven here and there. They parted, then, with each side claiming victory. But Alexander's company pressed on that of Darius and by main force broke them, so that they were routed and stumbled over each other because of the mass of soldiers. Nothing could be seen there except horses lying dead on the ground and slain men; and it was impossible to distinguish Persian from Macedonian, allies from satraps, infantry from cavalry, for the clouds of dust; for the sky was not visible, and the earth could not be made out for all the gore. Even the sun felt sympathy at what was happening, and refusing to contemplate all that pollution, clouded over. But it was the Persians, forcefully driven back, who began to flee. With them was Amyntas of Antioch,[47] who had fled to Darius, having previously been dictator of Macedon. When evening fell, Darius, afraid, got away with difficulty and kept going.[48] But the royal chariot was conspicuous; so, leaving behind his own chariot, he mounted a horse and fled. Alexander was eager to capture Darius and went after him to prevent someone killing him. After pursuing him for seven miles Alexander captured Darius's chariot, bow and arrows, his wife, daughters, and mother; but Darius himself was saved by darkness; and in addition he got a fresh horse and fled.

Alexander captured Darius's tent and used it for himself. He had defeated the enemy and made himself a great reputation, but he did nothing extravagant: he simply gave instructions for the bravest and noble Persians who had died to be buried. Darius's mother, wife, and children he took with him and treated honorably. In the same way he spoke to the other prisoners too and encouraged them. The number of the fallen Persians was enormous; the fallen Macedonians were found to number 500 infantry and 1600 cavalry, with 308 wounded; of the barbarians, there were 20,000, with around 4,000 men taken as slaves.

42. Darius, having got away safely, began enrolling more forces. And he wrote to the nations under his control to come to him with a large force. One of Alexander's spies found out that Darius was mustering

47. Actually, as our author probably wrote, "Amyntas, son of Antiochos." Recension B alone preserves the detail that he had "previously been dictator," confusing him with his associate Amyntas IV, who had been child king until his regent, Philip II, deposed him. Alexander naturally had him murdered.
48. There is something amiss in this area of the text; I have improvised this sentence.

armies and wrote to Alexander about the situation. On hearing this, Alexander wrote to his general Skamandros in these terms.

Alexander the King to our general Skamandros, greetings:
Take the phalanxes under your command and all your forces and come with all speed to us: the barbarians are said not to be far off.[49]

Alexander himself took the force he had and marched onward. Crossing the Taurus, he fixed a massive spear in the ground and said, "If any mighty king, Greek, barbarian, or other, lifts this spear, it will be an evil sign for him: his city shall be lifted from its foundations."[50]

He came next to the city of Pieria in Bebrykia,[51] where there was a temple and a statue of Orpheus, and also the Pierian Muses and the animals standing next to his statue. As Alexander looked at it, the idol of Orpheus sweated all over. Alexander tried to find out the meaning of this sign, and Melampous the interpreter told him: "You will have to work hard, King Alexander, with sweat and toil to bring barbarian nations and Greek cities under your control. Just as Orpheus through playing the lyre and singing won over Greeks, brought barbarians round, and tamed beasts, so you too, toiling with your spear, will subject all to your rule." Hearing this, Alexander rewarded the interpreter richly and dismissed him.

And he reached Phrygia. Coming to the river Skamandros, where Achilles had leapt in, he himself leapt in too.[52] Seeing the seven-layered shield, not very big, nor as striking as Homer had described it, he said, "Happy are you men who have found a herald such as Homer: in his poems you have become great, but from what we can see you are not worthy of what he wrote." And a poet came up to him and said, "King Alexander, we will write of your deeds better than Homer." But Alexander replied, "I would sooner be a Thersites in Homer than an Agamemnon in your writing."

49. There was no general named Skamandros (the *river* Skamandros is mentioned a few lines later). Perhaps Kassandros is meant: he came to Alexander at Babylon in 324 B.C., shortly before Alexander's death; later (305–297 B.C.) he was king of Macedonia. In any case, this letter makes no sense in this context.

50. This is an elaboration of the authentic spear story, told in its right place at 1.28 by recension B.

51. The Bebrykes were a tribe in northern Turkey mentioned only in legend. Pieria is a region of Macedonia that includes the town Leibethra, where this episode, interpreted by the seer Aristandros, is said to have occurred before Alexander set out.

52. In the Armenian recension, and probably the author's original, Alexander does not leap in; instead, the smallness of the Skamandros is emphasized. Before this, there seems to have been a scene where Alexander makes a dedication at Achilles' tomb and connects himself with Achilles in a genealogical poem. Afterward, Olympias (!) returns home with a retinue of distinguished prisoners.

43. From there he came to Pyle,[53] where he mustered the Macedonian army, together with the prisoners he had taken in the battle with Darius, and marched on to Abdera. But the inhabitants of Abdera shut the gates of their city. Alexander, enraged at this, instructed his general to burn the city. They sent him representatives, saying: "We have not closed our gates to oppose your power, but in fear of the kingdom of Persia: if Darius stays in power, he might sack our city for having received you. So come when you have defeated Darius and open the gates of the city: we will be subjects of the stronger king."

Alexander smiled at what he heard and told the representatives that had been sent to him: "You are afraid of Darius's royal power—that he will remain king and at a later date sack your city? Go back, open the gates, and live undisturbed! I am not going to enter your city until I have defeated Darius, the king you fear; then I will take you as my subjects." With these words for the representatives, he marched on his way.

44. In two days he had reached Bottiaia and Olynthos[54] and devastated the whole land of the Chalkidians and killed those in the neighborhood. From there he came to the Black Sea and subjected all the cities next to it.[55] But the Macedonians' food supplies were running out, so that they were all about to die of starvation. Alexander devised a tremendously intelligent solution. He searched out all the horses of the cavalry, slaughtered them, flayed them, and gave instructions for them to be roasted and eaten. This filled them, and they recovered from their hunger. But some of them said: "Why has Alexander decided to kill our horses? Look, for the present we are filled with food, but we are unprepared for battle with cavalry." Alexander heard this, went into the camp, and said: "Comrades-in-arms, we have slaughtered the horses, despite the fact they are vital for war, so that we may be filled with food: when an evil is replaced by a lesser evil, it is less painful. When we come to another land, we shall easily find other horses; but if we die from starvation, we shall not presently find other Macedonians." Having calmed the soldiers, he marched on to another city.

[Recension B omits 1.45, in which Alexander is associated with Hercules by an oracle—maybe that at Delphi. It also omits 1.46, but some manuscripts, including L, restore this highlight to the text.]

46. And from there he marched on to the Thebans. He sought men

53. It is difficult to determine what place the author has in mind (Amphipolis?), especially as his account is proceeding backwards. Abdera, on the coast, two-thirds of the way from Thessalonike to the Turkish border, had in fact been under Macedonian control since 352 B.C.

54. Bottiaia was a region of Macedonia. Olynthos, in the Chalkidike, was destroyed by Philip in 348 B.C.

55. Now, in fuller versions, Alexander reaches the Sea of Azov and land so cold it is impenetrable.

from them to join his campaign, but they closed the gates in the walls and did not even send representatives to him; instead, they lined up and armed themselves, ready to fight Alexander. And they sent 500 men to him to tell him. "Either fight or keep away from our city." Alexander smiled and said to them: "Brave Thebans, why do you lock yourselves away inside your gates and bid King Alexander fight you? Indeed, I will fight, but it will not be against brave men with experience of war, but against amateurs and women brimming with cowardice: shutting yourselves away like little women inside your walls, you address those outside."

So saying, he instructed 1,000 cavalry to ride across outside the walls and shoot those standing on the walls and another 1,000 to use double axes and beams to dig out the foundations of the wall, to set fire to the gates, and to use battering rams to demolish the walls (these are appliances on wheels, heaved vigorously by a team of soldiers—they are launched at the walls from a distance and demolish even the best-constructed walling). Alexander hurried across with another 1,000 slingers and spearmen. Fire was everywhere; and stones, missiles, and spears were being cast. The Thebans fell wounded from the walls, unable to form up against Alexander.

For three days, the whole city of Thebes was besieged. The first gate to be broken through was the Kadmean, at which Alexander was standing; and without hesitation Alexander was the first to get in, inflicting wounds on them, striking panic and confusion into them. But masses of soldiers followed him in through the other gates too—the whole horde was about 4,000 men. They killed everyone and demolished the walls: it was with the utmost rapidity that the Macedonian soldiers used to carry out all Alexander's orders. Great quantities of human gore drenched the earth. Many Thebans fell to the ground with the towers. And as their city burned furiously in the fires, the Thebans were killed by Macedonian hands.

46a.   Then it was that one of the Thebans, a professional flute player and a man of intelligence, saw Thebes cast to the ground and people of every age being killed. He groaned for his native city but realized that he stood out for his expertise in the flute; so he decided to fall down before Alexander and throw himself at his mercy. He came to Alexander's feet and, sinking to his knees, played a melancholy, fearful, and pitiful theme. In this way, playing a lament and entreaty by flute, he was able to placate Alexander with his many tears. And he began to speak as follows.

Great King Alexander, now learn we by experience thy godlike head to worship. . . .

[Recension B now omits a substantial section, replaced by 1.27. Ismenias's lament, in origin a rhetorical set piece, continues for four pages.

In response, Alexander denounces Thebes and the Thebans and has the city destroyed; but (1.47) at the Isthmian Games the Theban fighter Kleitomachos so impresses him that he orders Thebes to be refounded.

Book 2 begins with Alexander at Plataia, removing its Athenian commander (!) from office. His conflict with Athens is resolved after letters and much debate among Athenian statesmen. Spartan opposition too (2.6) is ineffective, and Alexander sets off for Asia.]

Book Two

6. Immediately Alexander took his armies and set out via Cilicia for the land of the barbarians.

7. Darius gathered together the leaders of the Persians and consulted them on the question of what they should do. Darius said: "As I can see, the war is becoming increasingly serious. I thought Alexander had a brigand's ambitions, but he is undertaking the business of kings. And we Persians may think we are great men, but Alexander is greater because of his considerable intelligence—and we sent him a strap and a ball for his play and correction! So let us consider what would serve to put things right again, in case by dismissing Alexander as worthless (because we are elated by this great Persian kingdom), we are defeated across the whole face of the earth. My worry is that the greater may be discovered inferior to the lesser, if circumstances and Providence allow the crown to change hands. It is now in our interest to rule over our own nations of barbarians and not, by seeking to redeem Greece, to lose Persia into the bargain."

Oxyathres, Darius's brother, addressed him. "That means you are doing Alexander a great favor and providing him with the confidence to march on Persia by conceding Greece to him. You yourself should emulate Alexander—that is the way you will maintain control of your kingdom. He has not delegated the war to generals and satraps as you have: he is first to rush into battles and fights at the head of his troops and by fighting sets aside his kingship; and when he was won, he takes up his crown again."

Darius asked him, "Why should I emulate him?"

Another general replied: "By doing this, Alexander is supreme in everything, postpones nothing, does everything with resolution, because he has courage. He even looks exactly like a lion."

"How do you know that?" asked Darius.

"When I was sent by you, King, to Philip," he replied. "I saw the awe in which Alexander was held in Macedonia, and his appearance, intelligence, and character. So in your turn, King, you should send for your satraps and all the nations you rule—Persians, Parthians, Medes,

Elamites, and Babylonians in Mesopotamia[56] and the land of the Odynoi, not to mention the names of the Baktrians and Indians (you rule many nations)—and levy troops from them. If it is possible for you to have the gods as allies to help defeat the Greeks, then well and good; all the same, we will dumfound our enemies with the massive size of our forces."

Darius, hearing this, said, "Your advice is good, but inappropriate: one Greek idea confounds hordes of barbarians, just as one wolf heads off a herd of sheep." And with that Darius gave orders for his hordes to be mustered.

8. Alexander, having made his way through Cilicia, came to the river "Ocean." The water was clear, and Alexander, as he saw it, wanted to bathe in the river. He stripped and leapt into it, but the water was very cold, and it brought him no relief. The chill gave him a headache and internal pains, an he was in a bad way. As Alexander lay there suffering, the Macedonians themselves contracted illness in their souls, worrying that Darius might learn of Alexander's illness and attack them. So it was that the one soul of Alexander broke so many souls of his troops.

At this point a man called Philip, who was a doctor,[57] prescribed Alexander a medicine that would cure his illness. Alexander was keen to take it, and Philip was making up the prescription, but a letter was handed to Alexander, sent by Parmenion, a general of King Alexander's, which ran

> Darius told the doctor Philip to poison you when he had the opportunity, promising to give him his sister in marriage and to make him a partner in his kingdom; and Philip agreed to do this. So be on your guard, King, against Philip.

Alexander took the letter, but reading it did not upset him: he knew the attitude Philip had towards him. So he put the letter under his pillow. The doctor Philip came up and gave King Alexander the cup of medicine to drink, with the words "Drink, Lord King, and be rid of your illness." Alexander took the cup and said, "Look, I am drinking it," and drank it straight down. After drinking it, he then gave him the letter. Philip read the letter on his own and said, "King Alexander, you will not find this an accurate picture of me."

When he had recovered from his illness, Alexander embraced Philip and said to him: "You now know my opinion of you, Philip. I received

56. This part of the list of tribes has been thought to be drawn from Acts of the Apostles 2.9 and to show that our author was a Christian.

57. This episode, duplicated in our recension at 1.41, belongs to 333 B.C. Philip the Akarnanian had been Alexander's personal doctor since youth. Parmenion, Alexander's elderly and expert second-in-command, in fact remained in his post until his execution in 330 B.C., following his son's involvement in a plot against Alexander.

the letter before the medicine and then proceeded to drink the medicine, entrusting myself to your name: I knew a Philip had planned no evil against Alexander."

"Lord King," Philip replied, "now you should punish the one who sent you the letter—Parmenion—as he deserves. The fact is that he himself has on many occasions tried to persuade me to poison you, the terms being that I should have Darius's sister Dadipharta in marriage. And when I refused, you can see what a dreadful situation he tried to put me in." Alexander investigated the matter, and, finding Philip to be innocent, he relieved Parmenion of his command.

9. From here Alexander took his armies and reached the land of the Medes. He was in a hurry to capture Greater Armenia.[58] Having subjugated it, he marched for quite some days into waterless territory, full of ravines, and, passing through the Aryan land, he reached the river Euphrates. This he bridged with arches and iron spokes,[59] and then he ordered his troops to cross. But as he saw they were afraid to, he gave orders for the animals, the carts, and everyone's food to be taken across first, and only then the troops. But they were afraid, when they saw the current of the river, that the arches might come adrift. As they did not dare cross, Alexander took his guards with him and went over first. And so his whole army followed.

Immediately he gave orders for the bridges over the river Euphrates to be broken up. The whole army took this badly, and they were even more afraid, saying, "King Alexander, if it should happen that when we fight, we are routed by the barbarians, how are we going to get away safely and cross the river?"

Alexander, seeing their panic and hearing the mutterings among them, brought together all his troops and made a statement to them as follows. "Comrades-in-arms, you present fine hopes of victory, entertaining thoughts of defeat and retreat. It was for this reason that I ordered the bridge to be cut down—so that you would fight and win, or if you lost, not run away: war is not for those who run away but for those who pursue! Let us, after all, make our return to Macedonia together and return victorious. Engaging in battle is mere play for us!"

Following this statement of Alexander's, the troops cheered him, entered upon the war with confidence, and pitched camp.

Likewise, Darius's army was encamped above the river Tigris. They met each other in battle, and both sides fought valiantly against each other. One of the Persians came up behind Alexander—he had got Mace-

58. Armenia was divided into Greater and Lesser 150 years after Alexander. Greater Armenia in fact lay east of the Euphrates.

59. Alexander used rafts and chains. The reader may speculate on how one might use "arches and iron spokes."

donian armor and looked like one of the Macedonian allies—and struck Alexander on the head, breaking his helmet. He was instantly arrested by Alexander' soldiers and presented to him in chains. Alexander, under the impression that he was a Macedonian, said to him, "My good man, what made you do this?"

"King Alexander," he replied, "do not let my Macedonian armor deceive you: I am a Persian, a satrap of Darius's. I had gone up to him and said, 'If I bring you the head of Alexander, what favor will you grant me?' And he promised me a kingdom and his daughter in marriage. So I came to you and acquired Macedonian costume, and, having failed, I stand in chains before you."

On hearing this, Alexander sent for his whole army and, with everyone watching, freed him. And he said to his own army, "Men of Macedonia, this is what soldiers should be like: daring in war."

10. The barbarians were now without food supplies and made a detour into Baktria, but Alexander stayed on there and took control of the whole area. Another of Darius's satraps came to Alexander and said: "I am a satrap of Darius's and have brought about some great successes for him in wars, but have received no thanks from him. So give me ten thousand armed soldiers, and I shall give you my king, Darius."

Alexander replied to him, "Go and assist your king, Darius: I am not entrusting other people's men to you who are attempting to betray your own."

Now, the satraps of those regions reported on Alexander as follows.

To Darius, Great King, greetings:
   We had previously informed you urgently of the assault that Alexander was making on our people. We now in turn inform you that he has arrived. He has laid siege to our territory; he has killed many of our Persians, and we ourselves are in mortal danger. So make speed with a large force to reach here before he does and do not give him the chance to advance on you: the Macedonian army is powerful and enormous and is stronger than us.
   Farewell.

Darius received and read their letter and then sent a letter to Alexander along the following lines.

I call upon the great god Zeus to witness what you have done to me. My mother I consider has gone to join the gods; my wife I consider I never had; my children I deem not to have been born. Myself, I shall never cease to follow up the outrage done to me. In the letter to me, it says that your behavior to my family is just and respectful. But if you were in fact acting justly, you would have acted justly towards me. You can be merciless to my family; maltreat them and take your vengeance—they are enemy children.

Being kind to them will not make me your friend, nor will being cruel to them make me your enemy.

Alexander received and read Darius's letter: he smiled and wrote him this reply.

King Alexander to Darius, greetings:
Your pointless stupidity, your gabbling and ineffectual talk, the gods utterly and completely detest. Are you not ashamed at such evil words and pointless thoughts? It is not out of fear of you that I have treated those who were formerly yours with courtesy, nor in the hope that I may come to a settlement with you, so that on my arrival you might show your gratitude to us. And do not come to us: my crown is not of the same value as yours. You will certainly not impede the respect I show everyone—I shall display even more extreme kindness to those who were once yours.
This is my last letter to you.

11. Having written this letter to Darius, Alexander prepared for war and wrote to all his satraps.

King Alexander to all the satraps under him, those of Phrygia, Cappadocia, Paphlagonia, Arabia, and to all the others, greetings:
I want you to supply tunics for a very large army and dispatch them to us at Antioch in Syria.[60] And send us the supplies of arms that you have built up. Three thousand camels have been provided between the river Euphrates and Antioch in Syria to assist in carrying out our orders so that work proceeds on schedule. So be quick to join us.

Darius's satraps also wrote.

To Darius, Great King:
We hesitate to write to you in this way but are obliged to by circumstances. Know, King, that the Macedonian leader, Alexander, has slain two of us lords and that some of the lords have gone over to Alexander together with their harems.

Learning of this, Darius wrote to the nearest generals and satraps to get ready and set up camp. He also wrote to the kings nearest him.

Darius, King of Kings, greetings:
We are to fight a miserable nation, the Macedonians, and it will be like wiping off sweat.

60. Antioch was founded in 300 B.C.

The Persian army too he instructed to be in readiness, and he wrote also to Poros, king of India, requesting assistance from him.[61]

12. King Poros, on receipt of Darius's letter, read of the misfortunes that had befallen him and was distressed. He replied to him as follows.

> Poros, King of India, to Darius, King of Persia, greetings:
> I was greatly distressed to read what you write but am in an impossible situation, because although I want to join you and offer advice on what might help, I am prevented from so doing by the illness that has a grip on me. So keep your spirits up, just as though we were with you, unable to tolerate this outrage. Write to us for anything you want: my forces are at your disposal—even the remoter nations will follow my orders.

Learning about this,[62] Darius's mother sent to Darius, writing to him secretly like this.

> To Darius, my child, greetings:
> I hear you are gathering nations and wanting to engage in another battle with Alexander. Do not inflict chaos on the world, child: the future is unclear. Give up your hopes for an improvement in the situation and do not, when you are in doubt, act inflexibly and lose your life. After all, we receive the greatest respect from King Alexander: he has not treated me as the mother of an enemy, but with great courtesy, and as a result I hope that a decent agreement will be reached.

Darius read and wept, remembering his family bonds; but at the same time he was in confusion and came down on the side of war.

13. Alexander arrived with a large force in Persia. The city walls were high and could be seen by the Macedonians from far off. Now, the intelligent Alexander thought up a scheme. Taking the goats that were grazing there and chopping down branches from the trees, he tied the branches to the backs of the goats, and the goats followed behind the soldiers. As they were dragged along the ground, the branches disturbed the dust, and the cloud rose to Olympus, so that the Persians looking from the walls thought the mass of soldiers was beyond counting. When evening fell, he gave orders for torches and candles to be attached to the horns of the goats and for these to be lit and burn—the region was flat—and the whole plain looked like burning fire, and the Persians were afraid.

---

61. The chronological order of these letters from the epistolary novel (see the Introduction) is disturbed. A letter corresponding to these stated contents is included at 2.19. Alexander came into conflict with Poros, a king in the Punjab, in 326 B.C., but there is no reason to suppose Darius was in contact with him.

62. Namely, "that Darius was preparing to fight another battle with Alexander" (from Leo's Latin translation).

So they came within about five miles of the city of Persis,[63] and Alexander was looking for someone to send to Darius to declare to him when they would engage in battle. Now, Alexander was asleep that night and saw in a dream Ammon standing by him in the shape of Hermes, with his herald's wand, cloak, staff, and a Macedonian cap on his head, saying to him: "Alexander, my boy, when it is time for assistance, I am by your side. If you send a messenger to Darius, he will betray you: you yourself must become a messenger and go on your way in the dress you see me in."

"It is dangerous," Alexander replied to him, "for me, a king, to be my own messenger."

Ammon said, "But with a god to aid you, no harm shall befall you."

Alexander, having received this divine message, rose in good spirits and shared it with his satraps; but they advised him against doing this.

14. Taking with him a satrap by the name of Eumelos and collecting three horses, he set out without delay and reached the river Stranga.[64] This river freezes in icy weather to such an extent that it forms a rock-hard surface, and beasts and wagons go over it. Then, days later, it thaws and becomes deep enough to sweep away with its current those caught trying to cross. Well, Alexander found the river frozen over, and, putting on the dress he had seen Ammon wearing in his dream, he sat on his horse and crossed alone. And when Eumelos urged him to cross together with him in case he should need help, Alexander said: "Stay here with the two horses. I have the help of him who gave me the oracle to put on this dress and travel on my own." The river was about two hundred yards wide. At the other side, Alexander went on his way and came right up to the gates of Persis. The guards there, seeing him in such dress, thought he was a god, but they held him and asked him who he was. "Take me to King Darius," replied Alexander. "I will report who I am to him."

Darius was outside the city on a hill, constructing roads and training his troops in phalanx formation as though they were Macedonians.[65] Alexander turned all heads towards him because of his strange appearance, and Darius all but fell down before him, thinking him a god descended from Olympus and that he had been adorned with barbarian robes. Da-

---

63. The author thinks wrongly that there is a city called Persis that is the capital of Persia. Similarly at 3.17, the land Prasiake is though to be a capital city. Our manuscript even presents Macedonia as a city at 3.32.

64. In some later recensions this river possesses the fairy-tale attribute of freezing for the night and thawing for the day; the author must surely have intended this originally—that is why Alexander travels at night. The satrap Eumelos is equally fictional.

65. "As though they were Macedonians" is my guess at the author's meaning, as the various recensions are muddled. What follows in L is ungrammatical, and in other important recensions it is Alexander who thinks Darius a god.

rius was sitting, wearing a crown of precious stones, a silken robe with Babylonian gold embroidery and the royal purple, and golden shoes with precious stones inset up to the leggings. And he had scepters on either side and thousands upon thousands of men around him.

Darius inquired of him who he might be, observing him wearing a costume he had never seen before. Alexander replied, "I am the messenger of King Alexander."

King Darius asked him, "And why have you come to us?"

Alexander replied: "I declare to you that Alexander is here and ask when you are going to engage in battle. You must realize, King Darius, that a king who is slow to join battle has already revealed to his adversary that his battle spirit is weak. So do not be careless but announce to me when you wish to engage in battle."

Darius was angered and asked Alexander: "Is it you I am joining battle with or is it Alexander? You display enough audacity to be Alexander himself, and you reply boldly as though you were a companion of mine. But I shall proceed to my usual dinner, and you shall dine with me, seeing that Alexander himself also gave dinner to my letter bearers." And so speaking, Darius took Alexander by the hand and went inside his palace. And this action Alexander took as a good omen, being guided by the tyrant. Entering his palace, immediately Alexander was the first to recline at Darius's banquet.

15. The Persians looked in amazement at Alexander's small stature, not realizing that in a small vessel was contained the glory of heavenly Fortune. As the drinks came round more frequently, Alexander thought up this scheme: all the cups he got, he put in his pocket. People saw him and told Darius, and Darius stood up and asked, "My good man, why are you putting these in your pocket when you are at a banquet?" Then Alexander used his ingenuity and said, "Greatest King, this is what Alexander does when he gives a dinner for his officers and guards—he makes a present of the cups—and I thought you were like him."[66] So the Persians were astonished and amazed at what Alexander said: for every story, if it carries conviction, always has its audience enthralled.

A deep silence fell, and a man called Pasarges, who was a leader in Persis, examined Alexander. In fact he knew Alexander by sight: when he had first gone to Pella in Macedonia, sent as an emissary by Darius to demand the tribute, and had been prevented by Alexander, he took note of him. And having taken a reasonably long look at Alexander, he said to himself, "This is Philip's son, even if he has changed his appearance:

---

66. I have omitted here an incomprehensible clause. There was in fact such a custom among the Macedonians, though the author evidently supposes there was not and glorifies the crafty acquisitiveness of Alexander.

many men can be recognized by their voice, even though they remain in darkness." Convinced by his awareness that it was Alexander himself, he leaned over to Darius and said to him, "Greatest King Darius and lord over every land, this emissary of Alexander is Alexander himself, king of Macedon, son of the late Philip, displaying his valor."

Darius and the feasters were very drunk. So Alexander, hearing what Pasarges had said to Darius at the meal and realizing that he had been recognized, outwitted them all, jumped up with the golden cups in his pockets, and left stealthily. Mounting his horse to escape the danger and finding a Persian guard at the gate with torches in his hands, he killed him and took them, leaving the city of Persis. When Darius found out, he sent armed Persians to arrest Alexander. But Alexander urged on his horse, guiding his path: it was the depths of night, and darkness had fallen from Olympus. A very large number pursued him, but they did not catch him: he managed to keep to the road surface, but the others stumbled in the darkness over cliff edges. Alexander was like a beaming star in heaven that rises alone, and as he fled he led the Persians to destruction.

Darius sat on his couch in misery and in addition saw an omen. A portrait of King Xerxes of which Darius was particularly fond (because it was a very fine piece of painting) fell suddenly from the roof.

Alexander got away and, continuing through that night, came at dawn to the river Stranga. He had scarcely crossed it, with his horse reaching the bank and putting its forefeet on the land, when the river melted at the sun's rays. The horse was snatched by the water and swept away, but it threw Alexander onto the land. The Persians in their pursuit of Alexander came to the river when he had already crossed and, as they were unable to cross, turned back—no man could cross the river. So the Persians turned round and reported to Darius Alexander's good luck. Darius, dumbfounded by the unexpected omen, was greatly pained. Alexander, making his way by foot from the river, found Eumelos sitting with the two horses he had left behind, and told him everything he had done.

16. Returning to the camp of his troops, he immediately ordered the Greek phalanxes, by their names, to arms in readiness to attack Darius. He himself stood in the midst of them, encouraging them. When he had mustered all the troops, he found the number to be 120,000. Standing at a high point, he exhorted them in these words. "Comrades-in-arms, even if our number is small, all the same we have great sense, spirit, and power—more than the Persians, our opposition. So let the thoughts of none of you admit any weakness when you see the mass of the barbarians: one of you, baring his sword, will kill thousands of the enemy. Let none of you be afraid: there are millions of flies crowding the meadow, but when wasps buzz at them, they scare them away with their wings. In just this way, massive numbers do not bear comparison with intelligence:

when wasps come, flies count for nothing." So speaking, Alexander encouraged his troops, and his troops showed themselves good men and cheered Alexander.

Proceeding on his way, then, he came to the region of the river Stranga, that is, to its banks. Darius, collecting his force, came himself also to the Stranga; and as he saw it was very slight and frozen, he crossed it and pressed on, sweeping through the middle of the desert. His intention was to take Alexander's troops by surprise[67] so as to find them unprepared and rout them. And criers went into their midst and called out for the best fighters for the battle, and Darius's whole army put on its full armor. Darius was on a high chariot, and his satraps sat in chariots equipped with sickles; others brought fiendish weapons and artillery. The Macedonian troops were led by Alexander mounted on the horse Bucephalus—and no one could approach this horse.

Once both sides had sounded the signal for battle, some flung stones, some shot arrows like a rainstorm sweeping down from heaven, some flung spears, others again used slings with leaden shot so as to obscure the light of day. Confusion reigned as men struck and were stricken. Many, wounded by missiles, died; others lay half-dead. The air was dark and full of blood. When many Persians had met their grim end, Darius panicked and turned the reins on the sickle chariots, and as they rotated, he mowed down the vast hordes of the Persians, like farmhands shearing corn in a field.

When Darius came to the river Stranga in his flight, he himself and his companions crossed over, finding the river frozen. But the hordes of Persians and barbarians wanting to cross the river and get away came onto it in all their numbers, and it gave way and took all it found. The remaining Persians were killed by the Macedonians.

Darius came, a fugitive, to his own palace and threw himself on the floor, wailing and tearfully lamenting for himself, having lost so huge a number of soldiers and having emptied the whole of Persia. In the grip of such calamities, he mourned to himself, saying: "Darius, so great a king, with so many nations under my control and all the cities subject to me, I who shared the thrones of the gods and rose with the Sun—now I am a solitary fugitive. It is a fact that no one plans securely for the future: Fortune only needs a slight tilt, and it raises the lowly above the clouds and draws those in the heights down to Hell."

17. Darius, then, lay bereft of men, he who had been the king of so many nations. Recovering a little, standing up, and regaining his composure, he wrote a letter and sent it to Alexander. Its content was as follows.

---

67. The motif of surprise, of which no effective use is made, is peculiar to recension B. The battle in question is the final great battle against Darius—Gaugamela (or Arbela) of 331 B.C.

Darius to my master Alexander, greetings:

He who showed me the light of glory, in haughtiness of mind, conceived a great passion to invade Greece, unsatisfied with the gold and other riches that we have inherited from our ancestors.[68] He died after losing much gold and silver and many tents, though he had been richer than Croesus of Lydia, and he did not escape the death that awaited him. So, Alexander, you in your turn, as you have observed luck and its nemesis, set aside grandiose thoughts. Pity us who come to you for refuge, by Zeus of Suppliants and our common descent from Perseus,[69] and give me back my wife, mother, and children, recalling to your mind the hopes a father has. In return for this I undertake to give you the treasures that our ancestors deposited in the earth in the land of Minaia and at Susa and in Baktria. I also undertake that you may be lord of the lands of the Persians, Medes, and the other nations for all time.

Farewell.

Having learned the content of this letter, Alexander gathered together his whole army and his lords and ordered Darius's letter to be read out to them. And when this letter had been read out, one of the generals, by name Parmenion, said, "King Alexander, I would have taken the money and the land he has offered you; and I would have returned Darius his mother, children, and wife, after sleeping with them."

Alexander smiled and said to him: "I, Parmenion, am taking everything from him. I am amazed that Darius thought he could ransom his own family, using my money, but much more amazed that he undertakes to hand over my own land to me. Darius fails to realize that if he does not defeat me in battle, this is all mine, together with his family. However, it is a disgrace, an outright disgrace, for the man who has defeated men manfully to be miserably overcome by women. The battle we press upon him is for what is ours: I would not have come into Asia in the first place if I had not supposed it to be mine. And if he ruled it first, he should consider that his gain, in that he held someone else's land for so long and did not suffer for it."[70]

This is what Alexander said, and he told the emissaries of Darius to go back and report this themselves to Darius, without giving them a letter. Then Alexander gave instructions for the soldiers wounded in the battle to be tended with all care and for the dead to be mourned and buried. Staying there for the winter, he ordered Xerxes' palace, the finest in that land, to be burned down; but shortly after, he changed his mind and instructed them to stop.

68. Darius refers to his ancestor Xerxes, who invaded Greece in 480 B.C.
69. "By Zeus . . . Perseus" is corrupted in all recensions; a papyrus of the epistolary novel preserves the original.
70. The more celebrated reply, which no recension preserves accurately, was "And so would I if I were Parmenion." See Plutarch *Alexander* 29.

18. He also saw the tombs of the Persians, decorated with great quantities of gold. And he saw also the tomb of Nebuchadnezzar (who is called Nabuchodonosor in Greek) and the offerings of the Jews that were kept there and gold mixing bowls, like those of heroes to look at. Nearby he saw the tomb of Cyrus too: it was a twelve-story tower of stone, and he lay in a golden sarcophagus on the top floor, with glass round him so that his hair and whole body could be seen through the glass.

There were Greeks here, with their feet or noses or ears mutilated, bound by shackles and nailed to the tomb of Xerxes, men of Athens, and they shouted to Alexander to save them. Alexander, seeing them, wept: it was a terrible sight. So he was deeply upset at this and ordered them to be released and to be given a thousand didrachms and to be returned each of them to his own country. But they took the money and asked Alexander to grant them an area of land in that place and not to be sent off to their home countries—in their present condition they would bring embarrassment upon their relatives. So he gave instructions for an area of land to be granted to them and for a gift to be made to them of corn and seed and six oxen each and sheep and everything useful for farming among other things.

19. Darius was preparing to engage Alexander in another battle. And he wrote to Poros, king of India, as follows.

King Darius, to Poros, King of India, greetings:
A disaster has befallen my house in these days, and now I inform you of it—the Macedonian king has attacked me and, with the feelings of a wild beast, is not prepared to return me my mother, wife, and children. I have offered him treasures and much else besides, but he will not take them. So as a result, to destroy him for what he has done, I am preparing another campaign against him, until I have vengeance on him and his nation.
It is only right, then, that you should be annoyed at what I have suffered and that you should march out to avenge the outrage done to me, remembering our traditional obligations to each other. So assemble as many nations as possible at the Caspian Gates and supply the mustered men with plenty of gold, corn, and fodder. And I shall grant you half of all the spoils I take from the enemy and the horse Bucephalus, together with the royal lands and his concubines.
On receipt of our letter muster your hordes in great haste and send them to us.
Farewell.

Alexander learned about this from one of Darius's men who had fled to him, and as soon as he had read it, he took his whole force and marched to Media. He heard that Darius was at Ekbatana at the Caspian Gates and made his pursuit intense and more audacious.

20. Darius's satraps, Bessos and Ariobarzanes, realized Alexander

was near, and, with an insane change of mind, these men planned to kill Darius. They said to each other, "If we kill Darius, we shall receive much money from Alexander for having killed his enemy." So, having formed their evil plan, sword in hand they attacked Darius. And when Darius saw these men setting upon him with swords, he said to them: "Masters of mine who were my slaves before, what wrong have I done you that you should kill me with barbarian audacity? Do not do any more than the Macedonians have: leave me cast down like this in my palace to lament the inconstancy of Fortune; for if Alexander, king of Macedon, comes now and finds me slaughtered, as a king he will avenge a king's blood." But they paid no attention to Darius's pleading and repaid him with murder. Darius used both hands: with the left he took hold of Bessos and brought his knee up into his groin; he checked Ariobarzanes with his right hand and held him in such a way that he could not bring his sword down on him. So their blows missed. And as the criminals no longer had the strength to kill him, they wrestled with him—he was a strong man.

Now, the Macedonians, finding the river Stranga frozen, crossed it, and Alexander entered Darius's palace. The criminals learned of Alexander's arrival and fled, laving Darius behind, half-dead. And coming to King Darius, Alexander found him half-dead, the blood pouring from his wounds; over him he raised a lament to match his grief, poured tears upon him, and covered the body of Darius with his cloak. And laying his hands upon Darius's breast, he spoke over him words laden with pity.

"Arise, King Darius, and rule over your land and be master of what is yours! Take your crown as lord over the Persian people: keep the greatness of your realm. I swear to you by Providence above, I speak the truth to you, not fabrications. Who are they who struck you? Declare them to me, so that I may now give you rest."

And at these words of Alexander Darius groaned and, stretching out his hand, drew Alexander to him. Embracing him, he said: "King Alexander, never exult in your royal position. When you succeed in a project of divine scale and want to reach heaven with your hands, consider the future: Fortune knows no king, though he rule a vast people; with indiscriminate mind she comes down on any side. You see what I was and what I have become.

"When I die, Alexander, bury me with your own hands. Let Macedonians and Persians conduct my funeral. Darius and Alexander shall be of one family. I entrust my mother to you as though she were your mother; pity my wife as though she were your sister. My daughter Roxana I give to you as wife, so that you may leave children in remembrance for endless ages; and rejoicing in them, as we rejoice in our children, you yourself will perpetuate the memory of Philip and Roxana will perpetuate that of

Darius, as time passes and you grow old together."[71] So spoke Darius, and, holding onto Alexander's neck, he breathed his last.[72]

21. Alexander wailed and wept with feeling for Darius, then gave instructions for him to be buried in the Persian manner. He ordered the Persians to lead the procession, then all the Macedonians to follow in arms. Alexander put his shoulder to the bier of Darius and carried it together with the satraps. Everyone wept and keened, not so much for Darius as for Alexander, seeing him bearing the bier. Having conducted the funeral in accordance with the Persian usages, he dismissed the crowds.

Immediately an edict was published in each city, containing the following.

I, Alexander, son of King Philip and Queen Olympias, to those who inhabit the cities and lands of Persia, give these instructions.

I do not wish such vast numbers of men to come to an evil end. The goodwill of heaven makes me victorious over the Persians; so I thank Providence above. Now recognize that I intend to appoint satraps over you, whom you are obliged to obey, as under Darius. And recognize no other king but Alexander. Keep your own customs and your usual festivals, sacrifices, and carnivals, as under Darius. Each of you shall live in his own city; but if anyone leaves his own city or land and takes up residence in a foreign place, he shall be food for the dogs. Each of you shall have control over his own property except gold and silver: I instruct that the gold and silver should be brought to our cities and lands, but the coinage you have we allow you each to keep as your own property. I order all weapons of war to be brought to my armories. The satraps shall remain in their posts. No longer shall any nation approach you except for trade. And I intend to bring prosperity to your lands and to see that the roads of Persia are used for trade and business in total peace, so that people from Greece may trade with you and you with them: from the Euphrates and the crossing to the river Tigris up to Babylon I shall build roads and construct signs to indicate where the road leads.

It was not I who killed Darius; who his killers were, I do not know. I owe it to them to reward them richly and grant them extensive lands, as they killed our enemy.

At these words of Alexander, the Persians were bewildered, thinking Alexander was going to destroy Persis utterly. But Alexander, realizing the distress of the crowd, told them: "Why do you think, Persians, that I am looking for the men who killed Darius? If Darius had been alive, he

---

71. The Roxana whom Alexander married was not the daughter of Darius but a Baktrian princess whom he met later in the campaign.

72. Arrian (*Anabasis* 3.21) says that Darius died before Alexander saw him.

would have launched a campaign against me, but, as it is, war has totally ceased. Accordingly, whether the man who killed him is a Macedonian or a Persian, let him come to me confidently and receive whatever he asks from me; for I swear by Providence above and by the life of my mother, Olympias, that I shall see they are marked out and notable before all mankind."

And at this oath of Alexander's the crowd broke into tears, but Bessos and Ariobarzanes came up to Alexander, expecting to receive large gifts from him and said, "Master, we are the men who killed Darius." And straightaway Alexander ordered them to be arrested and to be crucified at Darius's grave. They cried out and said: "Did you not swear that you would see the killers of Darius were marked out and notable? How is it that you now break your oath and order us to be crucified?" To which Alexander replied: "It is not for your sake, you miserable wretches, that I shall justify myself, but for the mass of troops. Otherwise it would not have been possible to find you so easily or bring you into the open, had I not for a short while applauded the death of Darius. This is what I was praying for: the chance to sentence his killers to the severest punishment. After all, how are men who have slain their own master going to spare me? And as far as you go, you miserable men, I have not broken my oath: I swore I would see you were marked out and notable before everyone, that is, that you would be crucified for everyone to see." At these words everyone cheered him, and the detestable murderers were crucified at Darius's grave.

22. Alexander, having restored the whole land to peace, said to them, "Whom would you like to be viceroy of your city?" and they replied, "Adulites, the brother of Darius." And he gave orders that he should be appointed.

He had left Darius's mother, wife, and daughter in a city two days' journey away and he wrote to them like this.

King Alexander to Stateira and Rodogoune and my wife, Roxana, greetings:
Though we drew our forces up against Darius, we did not take vengeance upon him. It was instead the opposite: I prayed to have him alive under my supremacy but found him mortally wounded, and in pity covered him over with my cloak. I tried to establish from him who had struck him; however, he said nothing to me except this: "I entrust to you my mother and my wife, and particularly Roxana, my daughter and your wife." He did not manage to disclose to me what had happened to him. But those responsible for his death I have punished appropriately. He instructed us to bury him by the graves of his fathers, and this has been done.
I imagine you too have heard all this. So bring an end to your grief for him: I shall restore you to your royal prerogatives. But for the time being, remain where you are, until we have arranged everything here properly. And in accordance with Darius's instructions, I intend that Roxana, my wife,

shall share my throne, providing you find this acceptable. I also wish and order her to receive obeisance from now on as Alexander's wife.

Farewell.

Rodogoune and Stateira received Alexander's letter and wrote him this reply.

To King Alexander, greetings:

We have prayed to the heavenly gods who have laid low the name of Darius and the pride of the Persians that they appoint you eternal king of the world, so full are you of reason, wisdom, and power. We know that in your arms we have not been treated as prisoners. So we pray also to Providence above to give you, moreover, all that is best so that you may rule for immeasurable time. And your deeds show that you belong to a superior race. But now we are no longer like prisoners, and we know that Alexander is another Darius for us. We do obeisance to Alexander, who has not shamed us, and we have sent letters everwhere saying, "People of Persia, look how Darius at his death has found Alexander to succeed him as Greatest King: Fortune gives Roxana in marriage to Alexander, king of the whole world. So all of you must bring proper thanks to Alexander because the pride of the Persians has now been raised even higher. Rejoice, then, with us, proclaiming Alexander Greatest King." This, then, is what we have declared to the Persians.

Farewell.

Alexander received their letter and wrote this reply.

I applaud your sentiment. And I will struggle to act worthily of your affection—since even I am a mortal man.

Farewell.

And in another letter he wrote to Roxana of his decisions.

He also wrote this letter to his mother, Olympias.

King Alexander, to my sweetest mother, greetings:

I am writing to you to send me the women's jewelry and clothing of Darius's mother and his wife, and the royal attire for Roxana, Darius's daughter and my wife.

On receipt of his letter, his mother sent him all her royal clothing and all the jewelry, made from gold and precious stones. When he had received these things, Alexander got preparations for the wedding in Darius's palace under way. And who could adequately describe the joy there at that time?

23. After this, Alexander wrote this letter to his mother.

King Alexander, to my much-beloved mother and to Aristotle, my most-esteemed teacher, greetings:

I thought it necessary to write to you of the battle I had with Darius. Hearing he was at the Gulf of Issos with a mass of soldiers and other kings, I took a large number of goats and fastened torches to their horns, then set out and marched by night. They saw the torches in the distance and thought it was an innumerable army, as a result of which their thoughts turned to panic and they were defeated. This was how I gained the victory against them. At that spot I founded a city which I called Aigai;[73] and I founded another city on the Gulf of Issos, calling it Alexandria. Darius was abandoned, captured, and wounded by his own satraps, and I was extremely distressed about him: having defeated him, I did not want to murder him but to have him under my command. I came upon him still alive and took off the cloak I had on and covered him. Then, recognizing the uncertainty of Fortune, as displayed in Darius's case, I lamented him. I gave him a royal funeral and ordered the ears and noses of those guarding his tomb to be cut off, following the native custom. And I ordered the killers of Darius to be crucified at Darius's grave. Leaving there, I won control of the kingdom of Ariobarzan and Manazakes; I subjugated Media and Armenia, Iberia and the whole territory of Persia that Darius ruled over.[74]

[Recension C contains a narrative converted from a different letter, including chapters 24–32, in which Alexander shows respect for Jewish religion, captures Egypt, where he is crowned by the statue of Nektanebos, and founds Alexandria—again, but now his monotheism (!) is highlighted. Now follow giant ants, a river in which sand flows, Lilliputians, and a statue of Sesonchosis whose inscription denies the possibility of going further—Alexander covers it up!]

32. Picking up guides there, I wanted to go into the interior of the desert, following the Plough, but they advised me against going there because of the large number of wild animals that live in those places. All the same, I ignored what they said and began the journey. So we came to a region full of ravines, where the road was very narrow, and we traveled along it for eight days. We saw strange animals in those places, the like of which we had never known before. When we had crossed that region, we came to another, more dismal, one. We found there a great forest of trees called anaphanda, with odd and peculiar fruit: they were enormous apples like the largest melons. And there were men too in that forest called Phytoi ["plantmen"], 24 cubits tall, with necks 1 1/2 cubits long, and likewise with long feet. Their arms and hands were like saws. When they saw us, they rushed at the army. I was beside

73. *Aiges* is Greek for "goats," and Aigai a common enough name for a town.
74. Manazakes is probably the Mazaios who surrendered Babylon after Gaugamela; Ariobarzanes surrendered after Darius's death (but the Ariobarzanes of chapter 20 = Satibarzanes, satrap of Areia). Alexander never visited Armenia or Iberia (a region north of Armenia in the Caucasus).

myself, seeing them. So I ordered one of them to be caught. But when we rushed at them with cries and the sound of trumpets, they ran away. We killed thirty-two of them, but they killed one hundred of our soldiers. So we stayed there, eating the fruit from the trees.

33. Setting out from there, we came to a green land where there were wild men like giants, round bodied with fiery faces, who looked like lions. There were some others with them called Ochlitai ["mobmen"] who had no hair at all, four cubits high and a spear's length across. And seeing us, they ran at us. They wore lion skins and were extremely strong and quite ready to fight without weapons. We struck them, and they struck us with staves, killing a considerable number of us. I was afraid they were going to rout us; so I gave instructions to set fire to the wood. And when they saw the fire, those fine specimens of men ran away. They killed 180 soldiers of ours. On the following day I decided to visit their caves. We found beasts like lions tethered at their entrances—and they had three eyes. And we saw fleas there leaping about like our frogs.

Moving on from there, we came to a place where an abundant spring rose. I ordered my chariot to be halted there, and we stayed there two months.

Leaving there, we came to the Melophagoi ["apple eaters"]. There we saw a man whose whole body was covered with hair, a huge man, and we were terrified. I ordered him to be taken, and when he was taken he glared savagely at us. I gave orders for a naked woman to be brought to him: he took her and started eating her. And when the soldiers rushed in to get her away, he gabbled in his language. His neighbors heard him and came at us from the marsh, maybe 10,000 men, but our army was 40,000 strong, and I ordered the marsh to be set on fire. And when they saw the fire, they fled. We chased them and caught three of them, who would not take any food and died after eight days. They did not have human intelligence but barked like dogs.

[In recension C, Alexander now comes to the Pillars of Hercules and Semiramis and meets further monsters. Then come the gymnosophists— whom we meet at 3.5ff.]

36. Setting out from there, we came to a river. So I gave orders to pitch camp and for the soldiers to disarm in the usual way. There were trees in the river, and as the sun rose, they grew until midday; after midday, they grew smaller until they could not be seen at all. They gave off droplets like Persian oil of myrrh, with a very sweet and fine scent. I gave instructions for incisions to be made in the trees and the drops to be caught with sponges, but suddenly the collectors were whipped by an invisible divinity. We heard the sound of them being whipped and saw the weals rising on their backs, but we could not see who was striking them. And a voice came, saying not to make incisions or collect the liquid, "and if you do not stop, the army will be struck dumb!" I was afraid and forebade any of them to make incisions or collect the liquid.

There were black stones in the river; everyone who touched these stones turned the same color as the stones. There were also many snakes in the river and many types of fish—which were not boiled above a fire, but in cold spring water. One of the soldiers caught one, washed it, and dropped it in a container—and found the fish cooked. There were birds on the river, very like our birds, but if anyone touched them, fire came from it.

37. The following day we became lost. The guides said to me: "We do not know where we are going, Lord King Alexander. Let us return so that we do not stumble into worse places." But I was not prepared to return. We came across many animals: six-footed ones, three-eyed ones, five-eyed ones ten cubits long, and many other kinds of animals. Some of them ran away; others leapt at us. We came to a sandy place, from which emerged animals like wild asses of more than twenty cubits. And they had not two eyes each but six each, but only saw with the two; they were not aggressive but tame. Many others too the soldiers shot with arrows.

Moving on from there, we came to a place where there were men without heads, though they spoke as men do in their own language; they were hairy, wore skins, ate fish. They caught sea fish and brought us them from the sea they lived next to. Others brought truffles from the land weighing twenty-five pounds each. We saw a great many large seals crawling on the land. And my friends persistently advised me to turn back, but I would not, because I wanted to see the end of the earth.

38. Pressing on from there, we traveled through uninhabited land to the sea, no longer seeing anything—not bird nor beast—only the sky and the earth. We no longer saw the sun; the air was dark for ten days. We came to a place on the coast and pitched our tents and made camp there, staying very many days. In the middle of that sea there was an island, and I was keen to find out about the interior of it. I ordered a very large number of boats to be constructed. Around a thousand men boarded those boats, and we sailed to the island, which was not far from the land. And on it we heard the voices of men saying in Greek

> Son of Philip, seed of Egypt,
> The name you received indicates the future
> Success you shall achieve courageously:
> From the womb you have been called ALEXANDER.
> You have warded off [ALEX-] men [ANDR-] by chasing them off
> And scaring kings away from their possessions.
> But you shall swiftly in any case become an ex-man [EX-ANDR-]
> When you complete the second letter
> Of your name, which is called lambda [= 30, i.e., 30 years old].

We heard these words but did not see who spoke them. Some soldiers risked their lives to dive in and swim from the boats to the island to find out about it; and straightaway crabs emerged, dragging them into the water and killing them. We were afraid and turned back to land.

When we had disembarked from the boats and were walking about on the seashore, we found a crab emerging from the water onto the dry land. It was the size of a breastplate and its front feet, the so-called pincers, were each six feet long. Seeing it, we took spears and killed it with a struggle, because the iron would not penetrate its shell, and it smashed our spears with its front feet. When we had killed and shelled it, we found inside its shell seven pearls of great value—no man has ever seen such pearls. Seeing them, I realized they must be formed at the bottom of the unsailed sea. So I had the idea of taking a large iron cage and putting an enormous glass demijohn inside the cage, a cubit and a half thick; and I ordered a hole to be sited in the base of the demijohn to take a man's hand, because I wanted to go down and discover what was at the bottom of this sea. My intention was to keep the hole at the base of the demijohn closed from inside, but when I got down immediately to open it up, put my hand through the hole, and pick up from the sand beside it whatever I found at the bottom of this sea, then to bring my hand back in and straightaway to seal off the hole. And that is what I did. So I ordered a chain of 308 fathoms to be made and gave instructions that I was not to be pulled back up until there was a tug on the chain. "When I have been down on the bottom, I will immediately shake the demijohn for you to bring me up."

When everything had been prepared, I entered the glass demijohn to attempt the impossible. When I had entered it, the entry was immediately sealed with a leaden cap. I had descended 120 cubits when a passing fish shook the cage with its tail, and they brought me up because the chain had been tugged. I descended again, and the same thing happened to me. Going down for the third time, around 308 cubits, I saw all sorts of fish swimming around me, when, lo and behold, the biggest fish of them all came and seized me and my cage in its mouth and took me far off to the land a mile away. Now, in the boats there were the 360 men who were managing my descent: the fish took all of them with it and the four boats as well. Having reached dry land, it crushed the cage with its teeth, then cast it aside. I was scarcely breathing and frightened to death. And I fell down and worshipped Providence above who had preserved me from the terrifying beast. And I said to myself, "Alexander, give up attempting the impossible, in case by investigating the deep you lose your life." Immediately I instructed the army to move on from there and to proceed onward.

Traveling again, we came in two days to a region where the sun does not shine. There lies the Land of the Blest. As I wanted to find out about and see that region, I attempted to take my own slaves and advance there, but my friend Kallisthenes recommended that I should advance with 40 friends, 100 slaves, and 1,200 soldiers—only the reliable ones. So, leaving behind the infantry, together with the old and the women, I took soldiers, all young and handpicked, and marched on with them, having given orders that no old man should march with us. But one inquisitive old man, with two brave sons who were real soldiers, said to them: "Children, listen to the voice of your father and take me with you—you shall not find me useless on the march. After all, look, in time of crisis King Alexander will be looking for an old man. So if you are found to have me with you, you will be greatly rewarded."

But they replied, "Father, we fear the king's threats and do not want to be found to have contravened his orders and lose not just the chance of this expedition, but even our lives."

The old man replied, "Get up and shave my chin and alter my appearance. I will march with you in the midst of the army, and in time of need I shall be a great help to you." And they did what their father told them.

So, traveling on from there for three days, we found a misty place. We could not go further, because there were no paths or tracks, and pitched our tents there. On the following day I took a thousand armed men and went with them to investigate if the end of the earth was here. We went leftward (there was more light on that side) and journeyed through rocky ground with steep drops up to midday (this I did not work out by the sun; rather, by measuring out ropes in accordance with the science of surveying I calculated the distance and the time). After this we were afraid and returned because the route was impassable. I wanted to set out again and go to the right: it was an extremely level plain, but it was dark and murky. But I was in an impossible position because the young men all advised me not to proceed into that area, in case the horses got separated because of the darkness and the distance, and we were unable to get back. I said to them: "O brave men, all of you, in war! Now you realize that there is no such thing as great bravery without planning and intelligence. If an old man had come with us, he would have given us advice on how to advance into this murky area. But who among you is brave enough to go back to the camp and fetch me an old man? I will give a reward of ten pounds of gold." No one was found to do this because of the length of the journey and because the atmosphere was without light.

Now, the old man's sons came up to me and said, "If you will listen to us with forebearance, master, we will tell you something."

I replied, "Tell me whatever you wish—I swear by Providence above I shall do you no harm."

They straightaway explained about their father and how they had come to bring him; then they ran off and presented the old man himself. Seeing him, I embraced him and asked him to give us his advice. And the old man replied: "King Alexander, you must realize that unless you go there with horses, you will never see the light again. So pick out mares with foals and leave the foals here while you go off with the mares; then they will bring you out because of the foals." Having searched throughout the army, we only found 100 mares with foals. So I took these and another 100 select horses, as well as some other horses to carry what we needed, and went off, following the old man's plan, and left the foals behind.

The old man instructed his sons to collect anything they found lying on the ground after they set out, and drop it in their saddlebags. So 360 soldiers set out, and I gave orders for the 160 infantry to march in front. So it was that we journeyed about fifteen schoinoi [perhaps seventy-five miles]. We found a place, and in it there was a translucent spring, whose water flashed like lightning, and very many other sources of water. The air too in that place was fragrant, and it was not entirely dark. I became hungry and wanted to have some food; and I called over the cook, who was called Andreas, and said to him, "Prepare us a meal." He took salt fish and went to the translucent water of the spring to wash the food. But the moment it was doused in the water, it came to life and escaped the cook's hands. In his fear he did not report to me what had happened but took some of the water and drank it, then put some in a silver container and kept it. The whole place abounded in springs, and we all drank from them. Alas for my ill luck, that it was not ordained for me to drink from that immortal spring that brought life to the lifeless and was not denied to my cook!

40. After taking food, we rose and traveled on more or less 230 schoinoi [circa 1,100 miles!]. After that we traveled on and saw light, but not from sun, moon, or stars. And I saw two birds flying, and they had human faces; they were crying in Greek: "Alexander, why do you tread the land that is God's alone? Turn back, poor man, turn back; you will not be able to tread the Isles of the Blest. Turn back, human being; tread the land that is granted you and do not bring trouble upon yourself!" I shivered and swiftly obeyed the instruction the birds had given me. The other bird in turn spoke in Greek. "The East," it said, "calls you, and the kingdom of Poros shall be assigned in victory to you." So speaking, the bird flew off. I succeeded in persuading the guide to stand aside and put the mares at the front of us; then with their mothers leading us back[75] we returned in twenty-two days to the cries of the foals.

41. Now, many individual soldiers brought back what they had found. But in particular the old man's sons filled their saddlebags, following their father's instructions. And when we got back to the light, they were discovered to have collected pure gold and pearls of great value. At the sight of this there was regret—among those who had collected something that they had not collected more, and among those who had not that they had not. And we all expressed deep gratitude to the old man for giving us such excellent advice.

After our return, the cook told what had happened to him at the spring. Hearing this, I was overwhelmed with grief and punished him severely. All the same, I said to myself, "What good does it do you, Alexander, to have regrets over a matter that is past?" But I did not know that he had drunk the water or kept some; he had only admitted that the salt fish had come to life. But the cook approached my daughter by the concubine Ounna, Kale by name, and seduced her by promising to give her water from the immortal spring—and this he did. On learning of this—I will tell you the truth—I envied them their immortality. I summoned my daughter and told her: "Take your clothes and depart from my presence: you have, after all, evidently gained immortality and become a spirit. And you shall be called a Neraïd, since you received eternity [aïdion] from the water [neron]."[76] She departed from my presence, weeping and wailing, and went to live with the spirits in

75. I have emended the text of L at this point; it oddly refers to following the Great Bear simultaneously.

76. The author of this episode, then, explains the name Nereid—a nymph of the sea, daughter of Nereus, known since Homer—by misspelling it and deriving it from a word for "water" that no ancient Greek had ever heard.

uninhabited regions. As for the cook, I ordered a millstone to be tied to his neck and that he should be cast into the sea. There he became a spirit and went off to live in a part of the sea, which was called Andreas after him. So much then about the cook and my daughter.

As a result of all this, I formed the opinion that here was the end of the earth. And I gave orders for a huge arch to be built in that place and for it to be inscribed as follows.

YOU WHO WISH TO ENTER THE LAND OF THE BLEST,
TRAVEL TO THE RIGHT AND AVOID DESTRUCTION.[77]

But I had second thoughts and wondered whether the end of the earth was really here and whether the sky sloped down [i.e., to meet the earth] here. So I decided to find out the truth. So I ordered two of the birds from that place to be caught. They were huge white birds, extremely powerful and tame: they did not fly away when they saw us. Some of the soldiers mounted their necks, and they flew up, carrying them. They eat carrion, and this is why a very large number of these birds came to us—because of the horses that were dying. So I ordered two of them to be caught and not to be given food for three days. And on the third day I gave instructions for something like a yoke to be made of timber and for it to be attached to their necks. Then I made a sort of basket from oxhide and got into the basket myself, holding a spear about seven cubits long with horse liver on its tip. So straightaway the birds flew up to eat the liver, and I was carried up with them into the air, until I considered I was near the sky. I shivered all over because of the extreme cold of the air being beaten by the birds' wings. At that point a flying creature in the shape of a man met me and said to me: "Alexander, do you investigate the things of heaven when you have not grasped things on earth? So return swiftly to the earth and avoid becoming food for these birds!" And again he spoke to me, "Alexander, direct your gaze to the earth below." I did so with fear and saw there before me a large coiled snake and, in the middle of the snake, a tiny disk. And the creature that had met me said to me, "Turn your spear, then, against the disk—it is the world, because the snake is the sea that encircles the earth."

I turned back and by the wish of Providence above came down to earth seven days from the camp. I was utterly drained and half-dead. I found there a satrap under my power and, with three hundred cavalry from him, came to my camp. And I resolved never again to attempt the impossible.

[In recension C, chapter 42 tells of a sweet-tasting lake and a fish with a stone in its stomach that can be used as a torch. Women emerge at night from the lake, singing; and there is a battle with Centaurs. Chapter 43 contains a letter to Olympias summarizing Alexander's fantastic

77. Some ancient mystics thought it important that the dead man's soul should keep to the right on arrival below. Tablets with such instructions have been discovered in tombs.

adventures. In chapter 44, downcast by a prophecy of his early death, Alexander is cheered by a dwarf's foolery.]

Book Three

1. After all this, Alexander marched with his forces against Poros, king of India. Having marched through much uninhabited land, through terrain without water and full of ravines, the army commanders said to their troops: "It is enough for us to have waged war as far as Persis and to have subjugated Darius for demanding tribute from the Greeks. Why then do we laboriously march against Indians, into the haunts of wild animals, no concern of Greece? If Alexander, with his great spirit, is a man of war and wants to subjugate nations of barbarians, why are we following him? Let him march and fight wars on his own!"[78] Hearing this, Alexander separated the Persian troops from the Macedonians and other Greeks and said to the Macedonians and Greeks: "Comrades-in-arms and allies, Macedonians and all you lords of the Greeks—these Persians are your enemies and mine—so why are you grumbling now? You have instructed me to march to war and fight the barbarians on my own. I will, however, remind you of this: I have won the previous wars on my own too; and, taking with me all the Persians I want, I shall win on my own again. A single idea of mine encouraged the souls of you all for the battle, when you were already weakening against the hordes of Darius. Was I not there with my shield at the head of the army in the battles? Did I not go as my own messenger to Darius? Did I not expose myself to danger? So take your own counsel and march to Macedonia on your own and get yourselves back safely and do not have any disputes with each other—so that you may learn that an army is powerless without the intelligence of a king." So spoke Alexander, and they pleaded with him to set aside his anger and to keep them with him right to the end.

2. When he arrived with all his forces at the border of India, letter bearers sent by Poros, king of India, met him and gave him the letter of Poros's. Alexander took it and read it out before his army. Its contents were these.

King Poros of India, to Alexander, who plunders cities:
  I instruct you to withdraw. What can you, a mere man, achieve against a god? Is it because you have destroyed the good fortune of others by meet-

---

78. The author here blends the two mutinies: (a) in 326 B.C., after the defeat of Poros, the army refused to cross the river Hyphasis (Beas or Sutlej) into India and demanded to turn back; (b) in 324 B.C., at Opis (near Babylon), the Macedonians rebelled at the inclusion of Persians in privileged positions in Alexander's army, but later begged forgiveness.

ing weaker men in battle that you think yourself more mighty than me?[79] But I am invincible: not only am I the king of men, but even of gods—when Dionysos (who they say is a god) came here, the Indians used their own power to drive him away. So not only do I advise you, but also I instruct you, to set off for Greece with all speed. I am not going to be frightened by your battle with Darius or by all the good fortune you had in the face of the weakness of other nations. But you think you are more mighty. So set off for Greece. Because if we had needed Greece, we Indians would have subjected it long before Xerxes; but as it is, we have paid no attention to it, because it is a useless nation, and there is nothing among them worth the regard of a king—everyone desires what is better.

So Alexander, having read out Poros's letter in public before his soldiers, said to them: "Comrades-in-arms, do not be upset again at the letter of Poros's that I have read out. Remember what Darius wrote too. It is a fact that the only state of mind barbarians have is obtuseness. Like the animals under them—tigers, lions, elephants, which exult in their courage but are easily hunted thanks to man's nature—the kings of the barbarians too exult in the numbers of their armies but are easily defeated by the intelligence of the Greeks."

Having given this declaration to encourage his army, Alexander wrote in reply to Poros.

> King Alexander, to King Poros, greetings:
> You have made us even more eager to be spurred on to battle against you by saying that Greece has nothing worth the regard of a king but that you Indians have everything—lands and cities. And I know that every man desires to seize what is better rather than to keep what is worse. Since, then, we Greeks do not have these things and you barbarians possess them, we desire what is better and wish to have them from you. You write to me that you are king of gods and of all men even to the extent of having more power than the god. But I am engaging in war with a loudmouthed man and an absolute barbarian, not with a god. The whole world could not stand up to a god in full armor—the rumble of thunder, the flash of lightning, or the anger of the bolt. So the nations I have defeated in war cause you no astonishment, and neither do boastful words on your part make me a coward.

3. Poros, receiving Alexander's letter and reading it, was very much spurred on and immediately mustered the barbarian hordes and the elephants and many other animals that used to fight beside the Indians. When the Macedonians and Persians came close, Alexander saw Poros's line and was afraid not of his numbers but of the animals. He was aston-

---

79. In this and the following sentence L makes insufficient sense: I have translated A with slight alterations.

ished to see the strangeness of the animals: he was accustomed to fighting men, not animals.

So once more Alexander became his own messenger and entered the city where Poros was, dressed as a soldier buying provisions. Seeing him, the Indians straightaway presented him to King Poros, and Poros asked him, "How is Alexander?"

"He is alive and well," he replied, "and keen to see such a king as Poros."

Then he went out with Alexander and showed him the number of his animals and said to Alexander, "Go to Alexander and tell him, 'I am bringing animals like you to fight with you.' "

Alexander replied, "King Poros, Alexander has heard what you have said before I return to him."

"From whom?" asked Poros.

"From Poros," said he. "Being the son of a god, he cannot fail to know what is said."

So Poros sent him away with gifts.

As Alexander left Poros, he saw the lineup of animals and exercised his mind with much hard thinking. So what did the intelligent man do next? He took all the bronze statues he had and the suits of armor won in battle and had these carefully heated until the bronze was red-hot, and ordered them to be placed at the front of the battle line, like a wall. They sounded the signal for battle. Poros immediately ordered the animals to be released. So the animals, sweeping in, sprang at the statues and clutched them; immediately they burnt their mouths, and thereafter they touched no one. So in this way clever Alexander eliminated the attack of the beasts. The Persians were overpowering the Indians and pursued them with arrowshots and battles on horseback, and great was the battle as men slew and were slain. And there fell Alexander's horse, Bucephalus, its judgment having weakened.[80] And at this event, Alexander neglected the battle; for twenty days they continued fighting with each other. And Alexander's side was beginning to surrender through fear.

4. So realizing that he was about to be forced into surrender, Alexander ordered a halt in the battle and made a declaration to King Poros, saying: "This is not royal power, if, whichever of us wins, our armies perish between us. But this is our nobility of body, if each of us stops the army and enters a single combat for the kingship." Poros was delighted and promised Alexander he would fight a single combat with him, seeing Alexander's body was no match for his own body—Poros was five cubits

---

80. In A, more sensibly, Alexander's judgment weakens, not the horse's: he saves the corpse of the horse and neglects the fighting.

high, but Alexander not even three.[81] So each side took up position to watch Poros and Alexander. But suddenly there was a disturbance in the camp of King Poros. So Poros turned round, worried, to see what the noise was. But Alexander pulled the feet from under him, leapt on him, and drove his sword into his flank, instantly killing Poros, king of India.[82]

Both armies set to fighting each other, but Alexander said to the Indians, "Poor Indians, why are you fighting, when your king has been slain?"

They replied, "We are fighting to avoid being taken prisoner."

Alexander said to them: "Stop fighting; turn round and go to your city as free men. It was not you who recklessly attacked my army, but Poros." He said this, knowing that his army was not capable of fighting the Indians.

Immediately he gave instructions for King Poros to receive a royal burial. Then he took all the treasures from his palace and marched for the Brahmans, or Oxydrakai, not because they were warlike and numerous, but because they were gymnosophists who lived in huts and caves.[83]

5. The Brahmans, on learning that King Alexander was coming to see them, sent their best philosophers to meet him with a letter. Receiving and reading the letter, Alexander found its contents to be as follows.

> The Gymnosophists, to the man Alexander, write this letter:
> If you come to us in war, you will not profit from it: you will not have anything to take away from us. But if you want to take what we have, there is no need for war, only for a request—not to us, but to Providence above. If you want to know who we are, the answer is: naked men who have devoted their lives to philosophy, fashioned not by ourselves, but by Providence above. War is your companion, philosophy ours.

Reading this, King Alexander traveled to them in peace. And he saw many woods and many extremely beautiful trees with all sorts of fruit and a river encircling that whole land, whose water was translucent, white as milk, and countless palm trees laden with fruit, and the vine rods with a thousand bunches of grapes, gorgeous and enticing. And Al-

81. A cubit was eighteen inches in Athens, fourteen in Macedonia. Poros was said by historians to be five cubits high, and Alexander to be too short for Darius's throne (though he was doubtless more than three feet six inches).

82. There was no single combat; and Poros, though wounded in the battle, survived to retain his kingdom under Alexander's overlordship and to hold others won by Alexander.

83. In 326 B.C. at Taxila (near Islamabad), before the battle with Poros, Alexander had Onesikritos, a pupil of the Cynic philosopher Diogenes, meet Indian ascetics, for whom Taxila seems to have been a center. Greeks, always impressed by exotic wisdoms, had a word for them: *gymnosophistai*, "naked philosophers." One, Kalanos, joined Alexander's party, but Alexander's supposed meeting with the community became a favorite part of the romantic tradition (even in a Buddhist text, the *Sayings of Milinda*).

exander saw the sages with no clothes living in huts and caves. Away at a great distance from them, he saw their women and children grazing the flocks.

6. Alexander inquired of them, "Do you not have graves?"

They replied: "This area where we live is our grave as well: here we take our rest on the earth and bury ourselves for sleep. The earth begets us, the earth feeds us, and when we die, we lie beneath the earth in eternal sleep."

He asked another question. "Who are more numerous, the living or the dead?"

They replied, "Those who have died are more numerous, but as they no longer exist, they cannot be counted—those who can be seen are more numerous than those who cannot."

He posed another question. "Which is stronger, death or life?"

They replied, "Life, because the sun has bright rays when it rises, but is weaker to the sight when it is setting."

Again he asked, "What is greater, the land or the sea?"

They replied, "The land: even the sea itself is confined by the land."

He asked another question. "Which is the most dangerous of all animals?"

They replied, "Man."

He asked, "How?"

They replied, "Your own case will convince you: you are an animal, and look how many animals you have with you so that you alone can rob the other animals of life."

He was not angry but smiled. He asked something else. "What is kingship?"

They replied, "An immoral force for superior power, daring maintained by opportunity, a golden burden."

He asked another question. "What came first, night or day?"

They replied, "Night: creatures being born develop in the darkness of the womb and are then delivered to receive the light of day."

He posed another question. "Which side is better, the right or the left?"

They replied: "The right: the sun himself rises on the right and travels to the leftward regions of the sky. And a woman suckles first on the right breast."

Then Alexander proceeded to ask them, "Do you have a lord?"

They replied, "Yes, we have a leader."

He said, "I should like to greet him."

And they pointed out Dandames to him, who was lying on the ground, with lots of tree leaves strewn over him and with cucumbers and other produce laid out before him. Seeing him, Alexander greeted him, and he in his turn said to Alexander, "Hail," but did not rise or give him the honors due to a king.

Alexander asked him if they had property.

He replied: "Our property is the land, the trees that bear fruit, the light, sun, moon, the troupe of stars, the water. When we are hungry, we go to the leafy trees and eat the fruit that grows of its own accord. As the moon waxes, all our trees produce fruit. And we have too the great river Euphrates, and whenever we are thirsty, we go to it, drink water, and are gladdened. We have, each of us, our own wife, and, during the waxing moon, each of us goes and has intercourse with his own partner, until she bears two children. We reckon one to replace the father; the other, the mother.

Hearing this, Alexander said to them all, "Ask me for what you want, and I shall grant it to you."

And they all shouted out, "Give us immortality."

Alexander replied, "I do not have power over that: I too am mortal."

"Why, then," they asked, "if you are mortal, do you wage so many wars? To win everything and carry it off somewhere? Are you not in your turn going to leave these things behind for the others?"

"That," said Alexander, "is managed by Providence above, so that we may be slaves and servants of their [the gods'] commands. The sea does not stir if no wind blows upon it, nor do trees if no wind blows. The fact is that man displays no activity but for Providence above. I too would like to stop conducting wars; only, the master of my mind does not allow me. But in fact if we were all of one mind, the world would be a dull place: the sea would not be sailed, the earth not worked, marriages not celebrated, children not born. Think how many have met misfortune in the wars I have been responsible for and have lost what they had! Yet, others have had good fortune from other people's property. Everyone takes things from everyone else and delivers them up to others: nothing belongs to anyone."

So saying, Alexander brought Dandames gold, bread, wine, and olive oil. "Take these, old man, to remember us by." But Dandames laughed and replied, "These are no use to us, but so as not to seem proud, we will take the oil from you." He made a pile of wood, set fire to it, and poured the oil into the fire before Alexander.

[Chapters 7–16: Recension A now inserts a booklet partly by Palladius (circa A.D. 364–430), *On the Tribes of India, and the Brahmans*.]

17. After this, Alexander left them. So he returned along the river Hyphasis, which leads to Prasiake, which is held to be the capital of India and was where Poros was king.[84] And all Poros's subjects received

84. "Along the river Hyphasis" is an emendation of L, though Alexander actually re-

Alexander. He had managed all affairs along the Hyphasis, and the Indians eagerly gathered. And some of them said to Alexander, "Greatest King, you will take marvelous cities and kingdoms and mountains on which no king of the living has ever set foot." And some of the sages came to Alexander and said, "King, we have something amazing and worth your attention to show you: we will show you plants speaking with human voice." So they brought Alexander to where a shrine of the Sun and Moon was. There was an enclosure to protect them and two trees like cypresses: encircling them were trees like the myrobalanos of Egypt—their fruit too. The two trees in the middle of the garden spoke, one in a male voice, the other in a female. The name of the male one was Sun, and of the female Moon, which they called in their own language Mithras and Mao.[85] The two trees had been clothed in skins of various animals, the male one with skins of male animals, the female with female. In their vicinity there was no iron, bronze, or tin, and not even potter's clay. When Alexander asked what sort of skins were covering them, they replied by saying they were lion and leopard skins.

Alexander sought to learn more about the trees, and they told him: "In the morning when the sun rises, a voice comes from the tree, and when it is at its zenith, and a third time when it is on the point of setting. And the same thing happens in the case of the moon." And men who were clearly priests came up to Alexander and said, "Enter in purity, worship, and you will receive an oracle." But the priests said, "King Alexander, no iron is allowed in the shrine." So he ordered swords to be laid down outside the precinct. A considerable number of men went in with Alexander, and he ordered them to form a ring and keep watch on the place. Then he called over some of the Indians who were attending him so that they could act as interpreters for him. And he swore to them that "if the sun sets and I do not hear the voice of the oracle, I shall burn you alive!"

But it happened as the sun set: an Indian voice came from the tree, but the Indians with him were afraid and did not want to translate. After some thought, Alexander took them aside individually. And they whispered in his ear, "King Alexander, soon you must die at the hands of your own people." All present were thunderstruck, but Alexander wanted to receive another oracle. Having heard the future, he went in and asked

---

turned by the river Hydaspes (Indus), of which the Hyphasis (Sutlej) is a tributary. Prasiake was in fact the land of the Prasioi (Sanskrit for "Easterners"), whose capital was Pali(m)bothra (near today's Patna, on the Ganges 150 miles west of the Bangladeshi border)—unvisited, of course, by Alexander, and far from Poros.

In other recensions 3.17 is the *Letter to Aristotle*. Recension B omits a number of marvels and monsters at the beginning and converts the rest into narrative.

85. This emendation (of "Mutheamatus") produces Iranian words for "sun" and "moon."

that he might embrace his mother, Olympias. And when the moon rose, the tree said in Greek, "King Alexander, you must die in Babylon and you will be killed by your own people and you will not be able to return to your mother, Olympias."

Alexander was amazed and wanted to put magnificent garlands on the trees, but the priests told him: "This is not permitted. But if you are going to use force, do what you will: for a king every law is canceled." Alexander was very upset, and, rising at first light, he went back into the shrine with the priests, his friends, and the Indians. After a prayer, he went up with the priest and, placing his hand on the tree, asked if the years of his life were complete—as this was what he wanted to know. And as soon as the sun began to rise and cast its rays on the top of the tree, a voice came out, explicitly declaring: "The years of your life are complete, and you will not be able to return to your mother, Olympias; instead, you must die in Babylon. And shortly afterwards your mother and your wife will die miserably at the hands of your own people. Ask no further questions about these matters: you shall not hear anything more." On hearing this, he was very upset. And on his departure from there, he broke camp and left India. And he came to Persia.

18. He hurried to see the palace of Semiramis—it was famous.[86] There had become queen of that whole country a woman of sublime beauty in middle age. So Alexander sent her a letter with the following content.

> King Alexander, to Queen Kandake at Meroë and the princes under her, greetings:
>   On my travels to Egypt I heard from the priests there about your dwellings and graves, and that for some time you had ruled Egypt. So I have sent to you. Take advice and send what seems appropriate to you.
>   Farewell

Kandake replied as follows.

> Queen Kandake of Meroë and all the princes, to King Alexander, greetings:
>   Do not think the worse of us for the color of our skin. We are purer in soul than the whitest of your people. We are in number 80 squadrons ready to do harm to aggressors. The emissaries sent by us bring you 100 solid gold ingots, 500 Ethiopians not yet mature, 200 chimpanzees, an emerald crown

---

86. Semiramis, a legendary queen of Babylon, so appealed to Greek imagination that she seems even to have been the heroine of the early (ca. 100 B.C.?) *Ninos Romance*. The author seems to think Semiramis's city is the same as Kandake's Meroë. Meroë, on the Nile in central Sudan, was the capital of the Nubian kingdom of Napata, and Kandake was the regular name of its queens. But for Greeks the land beyond Egypt was Ethiopia and was perceived as lying to the southeast—even up to India; hence maybe our author's confusion. It has been thought that the Kandake episode was in origin a separate novelette.

of a thousand pounds of gold, 10 sealed necklaces of unpierced pearls, 80 ivory caskets, and various kinds of animals from our country: 5 elephants, 10 tame leopards, in the cages 30 man-eating hounds, 30 fighting bulls, 300 elephant tusks, 300 leopard skins, 3,000 ebony staves. So send us immediately the men you want to receive the presents. And write to us about yourself when you have become king of the whole world.

Farewell.

Receiving Queen Kandake's letter and reading it, Alexander sent Kleomenes, an Egyptian,[87] to receive the presents. Kandake, on hearing how Alexander was defeating such important kings, called one of her people, a Greek painter, and gave him instructions to go and meet him and secretly to paint a likeness of Alexander. And he did so. Receiving the likeness of him, Kandake hid it away.

Some days later it happened that Kandake's son, Kandaules, in the company of some riders, was attacked by the prince of the Bebrykians,[88] and Kandaules, the son of Kandake, rode in to Alexander's tents in his flight. The guards arrested him and brought him before Ptolemy, surnamed Soter, who was second-in-command to Alexander (King Alexander was asleep). Ptolemy questioned him, "Who are you and your companions?"

He replied, "I am the son of Queen Kandake."

Ptolemy asked him, "Why have you come here, then?"

He replied: "Together with my wife and a few soldiers I was on my way to celebrate the annual mystery rite among the Amazons. But the prince of the Bebrykians saw my wife and came out with a huge force; he seized my wife and killed most of my soldiers. So I am returning to collect a larger force and burn the land of the Bebrykians."

Having heard this, Ptolemy went in to Alexander, woke him, and outlined to him what Kandake's son had told him. Alexander listened and straightaway rose. He took his crown and put it on Ptolemy, put his mantle on him and said to him, "Sit on the throne as though you were Alexander and say this to the secretary, 'Call Antigonos, the principal guard.' And when I come, relate to me what you have told me and ask me, 'What policy are we to adopt here? Give me your advice.'"

So Ptolemy sat on the throne, dressed in the royal robes—and the troops, seeing him, worriedly discussed what new plan Alexander had thought up. But the son of Kandake, seeing him in the royal robes, was afraid he would order his execution—he thought it was Alexander. Then

87. Kleomenes of Naukratis, recognized as satrap of Egypt by Alexander, but later subordinated to Ptolemy and executed by him.

88. The names connect this story with Asia Minor: the Bebrykians are a legendary people of Bithynia; Kandaules, a king of Lydia; Amazons have several important Asia Minor connections; the real Antigonos was satrap in Asia Minor.

Ptolemy gave the order "Call Antigonos, my principal guard." And when Alexander came, Ptolemy said to him: "Antigonos, this is the son of Queen Kandake. His wife has been seized by the prince of the Bebrykians. What action would you advise?"

"I would advise you, King Alexander," he replied, "to arm the troops and make war on the Bebrykians so that we may free his wife and return her to him out of respect for his mother." Kandaules, the son of Kandake, was pleased to hear this. And Ptolemy said: "If this is what you want, Antigonos, go ahead and do this as my guard. Instruct the army to prepare."

20. Ptolemy gave instructions, as though he were Alexander, to Antigonos, and this was done. Antigonos reached the region of the prince in one day together with Ptolemy. And Antigonos said to Ptolemy: "King Alexander, let us not be seen by the Bebrykians by day, in case the prince discovers and kills the woman. So let us break into the city by night and set fire to the houses: then the masses will rise and return Kandaules his wife. Our battle is not about the kingdom, but about demanding back the woman."

As Antigonos said this, Kandaules fell down before him and said: "Ah, your intelligence, Antigonos! I wish you were Alexander and not a guard of Alexander."

So then they broke into the city by night, while the people were asleep, and set fire to the suburbs. And as they woke up and asked why the city was being set on fire, Alexander had the shout raised "It is King Kandaules with a massive force, demanding you return his wife before I set your whole city on fire." They were surrounded and all advanced to the prince's palace and by force of numbers broke it open. Kandaules' wife was in bed with the prince: they dragged her away and returned her to Kandaules, and they killed the prince.

Kandaules thanked Antigonos for his advice and idea and, embracing Antigonos, said, "Put yourself in my hands so that I can take you to my mother, Kandake, and give you the royal presents you deserve." Alexander was overjoyed and said to him: "Ask King Alexander to release me. I too would like to see your country." So Alexander sent a message to Ptolemy to send him with Kandaules as his messenger. And Ptolemy said to Kandaules: "I wish to greet your mother by letter. So take my messenger Antigonos with you and bring him back safe here to me, in the same way that I restore you and your wife safe to your mother." Kandaules replied: "King, I take this man as though he were Alexander himself. And I shall send him back to you with royal gifts."

21. So then Kandaules set out and took with him Alexander, a considerable number of soldiers, beasts, wagons, and many presents. On the way Alexander marveled at mountains marked out with veins of quartz that reached up to the clouds of heaven and at the towering trees laden

with fruit—not of the Greek sort, but a marvel in themselves: they were apple trees glinting gold with fruit the size of citrons in Greece. And there were enormous bunches of grapes and nuts with the girth of melons and full-grown apes the size of bears and other animals of various colors and strange shapes. And there were some rocky places with downward passages. And Kandaules said, "Antigonos, these here are called the dwellings of the gods." So they journeyed on and reached the palace. He was met by his mother and brothers; but when they were about to embrace him, Kandaules said, "Do not embrace me before you have greeted the man who has saved me and been so good to my wife, Antigonos, the messenger of King Alexander." And they asked him, "In what way did he save you?" Then, when Kandaules had told them about the prince of the Bebrykians seizing his wife and the assistance Alexander had given him, the brothers and their mother, Kandake, embraced him. And there was a splendid banquet in the palace.

22. The next day, Kandake came forward in the royal crown, displaying enormous stature and having the appearance of a demigod, so much so that Alexander thought it was his own mother, Olympias. And he looked at the palace glittering with its golden ceilings and marble walls. And there were cushions of woven silk with contrasting gold embroidery on couches with legs of gold and reclining chairs with golden webbing. The tables were studded with ivory inlays, and ebony colors gleamed from the capitals of Median columns. There were countless statues of bronze and sickle-bearing chariots sculpted from porphyry complete with the horses so that you might think they were alive and running; and there were elephants sculpted from the same stone, trampling enemies underfoot and sweeping over opponents with their trunks; and there were whole temples complete with columns sculpted from a single stone. Seeing this, then, Alexander was filled with amazement. And he ate with the brothers of Kandaules. Kandaules called his mother over and asked her to give Alexander's messenger the gifts he deserved for his good sense and to release him.

The next day, Kandake took Antigonos by the right hand and showed him translucent chambers made of indescribable stone that made one think the sun was rising inside and shining through the marble. Among the rooms she showed him a dining room of imperishable timbers, and a house not built firmly on foundations on the ground, but fixed on massive square timbers and drawn on wheels by twenty elephants. And wherever the king went in order to make war on a city, he stayed in it.

Alexander said to Kandake, "This would all be astonishing if it were among the Greeks rather than in your country, where you have mountains with such varied stone."

Kandake replied angrily, "You are right, Alexander."

Addressed by the name Alexander, he turned round and said, "Lady, my name is Antigonos. I am Alexander's messenger."

"All right," replied Kandake, "your name is Antigonos—but I am not calling you that: you are King Alexander. And now I will show you the evidence." And she took him by the hand into a chamber and brought him the portrait of him. She asked, "Do you recognize your appearance?"

Alexander recognized his picture and was disconcerted and trembled.

Kandake asked him: "Alexander, why are you trembling and disconcerted? The destroyer of Persia, the destroyer of India, he who tore down the trophies of the Medes and Parthians and overthrew the whole East, now without battle and army you have fallen under the control of Kandake. So you must now realize, Alexander, that whenever a man thinks that he is brilliant, there will be another man still more brilliant than him. Kandake's mind has been more than a match for your ingenious plan, Alexander."

Alexander was furious and gnashed his teeth. Kandake said to him: "Are you gnashing your teeth? What can you do? Such an important king and you are in the power of a single woman!"

Alexander wanted to kill himself and Kandake with a sword, but Kandake said to him: "Very brave and royal! Do not agonize, Alexander, my boy. Just as you have saved my son and his wife from the Bebrykians, I in my turn shall protect you from the barbarians—by calling you Antigonos; for if they recognize you as Alexander, they will immediately kill you, because you killed Poros, king of India. The wife of my younger son is a daughter of Poros's. So I shall call you Antigonos: I shall protect your secret."

23. Having said this, Kandake went out with him and said: "Kandaules, my boy, and you, my daughter Marpessa, if you had not found Alexander's army at the right time, I would not have seen you again, and you would not have found your wife. So let us treat Alexander's messenger properly and give him presents." And the other son, the younger one, said to her: "Alexander saved my brother and his wife. But my wife is in sorrow because her father, Poros, was killed by Alexander, and as he is here in her power, she wants to kill Antigonos, his messenger." But Kandake said: "And what good would it do you, my boy? If you murder him, do you defeat Alexander?" And Kandaules said to his brother: "He saved me and my wife: I in my turn will save him and send him to Alexander. So are we on this man's account to join in battle here with each other?" And his brother said, "I, my brother, for my part, do not want to; but if you do, I am readier than you." With these words, they went to start a single combat with each other.

Kandake was in anguish at the prospect of her children fighting each other. She took Alexander aside and said to him, "You are an intelligent man and have dealt with so many matters—can you not use your intelligence to devise a way of stopping my children fighting each other on your account?"

"I will go," replied Alexander, "and make peace between them." And Alexander went between them and said: "Listen, Karagos, and you, Kandaules! If you kill me here, it will not matter to Alexander: messengers that people send are not very valuable compared with the battles of kings. So if you kill me here, Alexander has more messengers. But if you want through me to take your enemy Alexander prisoner, promise to give me a share of the gifts here; in this way I will be able to stay with you and get Alexander to come here on the grounds that you want to give him the gifts you have prepared for him in person. Then, having got your enemy in your power and having avenged yourselves, you will have your cure."

He convinced the brothers, and they were reconciled. Kandake admired Alexander's intelligence and said to him, "Antigonos, I wish you were my son—through you I would have controlled all nations: you would not have defeated the enemy and their cities by war, but by your sharp mind." Alexander was delighted at the respect shown him, and Kandake resolutely kept Alexander's secret. Ten days later he set off, and Kandake gave him royal presents: a precious diamond crown, a breastplate with pearls and beryls, and a cloak of purple, star-bright with gold work. And she sent him on his way with a large escort and his own soldiers.

24. Having traveled the set number of days, he came to the place where Kandaules had told him the gods dwelt. Going inside with a few soldiers, he saw a semblance of figures and a flash of fire. Alexander, caught at the front, was frightened but stayed on to see what would happen. He saw some men reclining with a sort of torchlight gleaming from their eyes, and he saw one of them say to him: "Greetings, Alexander! Do you know who I am? I am Sesonchosis, the world ruler,[89] but I did not have your luck: you have an immortal name through founding that loved city in Egypt, Alexandria."

Alexander asked him, "How many years will I live?"

He replied, "It is good for a living man not to know when he is to die; through awaiting that hour, he has died from the moment he learns. But for the living man to be in ignorance provides him with the forgetfulness of not having in his mind whether he will even die at all. But as for the city you found, famous among all mankind, many kings will step upon its ground worshiping you as a god. And you shall live in it dead and not dead: for you shall have the city you are founding as your tomb."

89. In other recensions Sesonchosis (see note 38 on 1.33) shows to Alexander the creator and omnipresent god Sarapis, who then delivers the prophecy.

25. When he had said this, Alexander left. Taking his men, he marched back to his army. The satraps met him and gave him the royal clothing. From there he marched to the Amazons; and when he had reached them, he sent them a letter of the following contents.

King Alexander, to the Amazons, greetings:
I think you will have heard about the battle with Darius. After that I campaigned against the Indians and defeated their leaders and subjected the people, thanks to Providence above. After that we journeyed to the Brahmans, the so-called gymnosophists. Taking tribute from them, we allowed them to stay in their own regions, on their request, and left them in peace. After that we are marching to you. Meet us with joy; we do not come to do you ill, but to see your country and at the same time to do you good.
Farewell.

Receiving Alexander's letter and reading it, they wrote Alexander this reply.

The leading Amazons and the mightiest, to Alexander, greetings:
We have written to you so that you may be informed before you set foot on our land and not have to withdraw ignominiously. By our letter we shall make clear the nature of our country and of ourselves, who have a way of life to be reckoned with.
We are on the other side of the river Amazon, but we live on an island:[90] the perimeter of our land is a river with no starting point, whose circuit takes a year to travel. There is a single road into our land. We virgins who live here are under arms and number 270,000. There is nothing male among us: our men live on the other side of the river and graze the land. Every year we keep a festival and make a horse sacrifice to Zeus, Poseidon, Hephaistos, and Ares, which lasts thirty days. All of us who wish to end our virginity stay with the men. But they send all the female children they bear across to us when they reach the age of seven. But when an enemy marches against our country, 120,000 of us ride out on horseback, while the rest guard the island. And we go to the border to meet them, with the men drawn up behind following us. And anyone who is wounded in the war receives adoration from our proud hearts, is garlanded, and is remembered forever. If anyone dies in battle fighting for their country, her next of kin receives no small sum of money. If anyone brings the body of an enemy to the island, the reward for this is gold, silver, and maintenance for life. So we compete for our individual reputations. If we defeat the enemy or they just run away, a terrible disgrace stays with them for all time; but if they defeat us, they will be in a situation of having defeated women. So, King Alexander, see that the same thing does not happen to you.

90. I have adopted the Armenian version of this sentence, in the absence of sense from L or A. According to the historian Diodoros (3.53.4), the Amazons lived on an island in a marsh near Ethiopia.

When you have reached a decision, write us a reply; you will find our camp on the border.

26. Alexander read their letter and with a smile wrote them this reply.

King Alexander, to the Amazons, greetings:
We have taken control of three-quarters of the world, and we have not stopped setting up monuments of our victories over every nation. A legacy of shame will be left to us if we fail to campaign against you. Now if you want to be killed and want your land to be uninhabited, stay at the border. But if you want to live in your own land rather than to try your luck in battle, cross your river and be seen by us. The men likewise are to remain on the plain. And if you do this, I swear by my father and my mother, Olympias, that I shall not harm you but shall take from you the amount of tribute you wish to give and shall not enter your land. Send whomever you select on horseback to us; and we shall give each person you send an allowance of a stater of gold per month and maintenance. After a year, these will return, and you must send replacements.
When you have reached a decision, write us a reply.
Farewell.

On receiving and reading Alexander's letter, they held an assembly and after a debate wrote him this reply.

The leading Amazons and the mightiest, to King Alexander, greetings:
We give you permission to come to us and see our country. And we undertake to give you 100 talents of gold a year and have sent you the 500 mightiest of us to meet you, bringing you the money and 100 thoroughbred horses. You will have these women, then, for a year. But if any of them loses their virginity to a foreigner, she shall remain with you; you will inform us in writing how many stay with you; send the others back, and you will receive replacements. We accept allegiance to you, in your presence and in your absence—we have heard of your exceptional qualities and your bravery. We are people who dwell beside the world, but you have come to us as our master.[91] We have decided to write to you, to live in our own land, and to be subject to you as master.
Farewell.

27. After this exchange of letters, Alexander wrote his mother, Olympias, this account of his deeds.

King Alexander, to my dearest mother, Olympias, greetings:
After drawing up my army against the Amazons, I marched to the city

91. This line only makes sense in a fuller recension: "We are nothing in comparison with the whole world you have traversed to make it worth your intervening in our affairs."

Prasiake.[92] On my arrival in the suburbs I saw a river there, full of animals. The soldiers became very despondent. Although it was already midsummer, the rain over the land had not ceased, and many of the infantry had sore feet. There were also enormous claps of thunder and lightning flashes and bolts. As we were about to cross the river Prytanis, as it was called, it happened that many of the local inhabitants were killed by the soldiers.

Then we came to the river Thermodon, as it was called, which flows out into a flat and fertile land inhabited by the Amazons, women of exceptional height, much taller than other women, notable for their attractiveness and strength, wearing bright clothes. They used silver weapons and axes—they did not have iron or bronze. But they were drawn up with intelligence and ingenuity. When we reached the river where the Amazons lived—it is a large river that cannot be crossed and is full of animals—anyway, they crossed and formed up against us; but we persuaded them by our letters to become subject to us.

28. Taking tribute from them, we withdrew to the Red Sea and to the strait. And from there we came to the river Atlas. There it was impossible to see either earth or heaven, but there were many races of all kinds living there. We saw men with the heads of dogs and men with no heads at all who had their eyes and mouths on their chests; and further men with six hands, with the faces of bulls; troglodytes who lived in caves and wild men with straps for legs; and others again as shaggy as goats and with the faces of lions; and animals of every sort, various in appearance.

We sailed off from that river and came to a large island, 120 stades [15 miles] from land. And we found the City of the Sun there. There were twelve towers built of gold and emeralds, and the wall of that city was in the Indian style. In the middle was an altar built of gold and emerald, with sixty steps, and on top of it stood a chariot with horses, and the charioteer was of gold and emeralds, but it was not easy to see him for the mist. The priest of the Sun was an Ethiopian dressed in pure linen. He spoke to us in a barbarian language to the effect that we should leave that place. Leaving there, we walked along the road for seven days. Then we found darkness, and not even fire was to be seen in that region.

Leaving there, we came to the meadow of Nysa, and we came across a very high mountain;[93] I went to it and saw fine houses laden with gold and silver. And I saw a large precinct wall of sapphire with 108 steps leading up

---

92. This is a muddled chapter: the Amazons occur twice over, as does a river full of animals. I have introduced "the city Prasiake" from the Armenian (L has instead the "river Prytanis," but rivers do not have suburbs). Even so, the city Prasiake fits badly with 3.17. The river Prytanis (a few lines later) is presumably a mistake for the river Hyphasis. These problems result from adding an independent (and incompatible) letter to Olympias to the narrative.

93. An emendation of L here gives us Nysa, the mythical birthplace of the god Dionysos, but also a real town encountered by Alexander in Afghanistan, east of Kabul. The mountain is the world mountain of Indian mythology, Mt. Meru. The decorative figures belong to Greek Dionysian religion and art; Maron, a son or grandson of Dionysos, is confused with Silenos, the old reveler-companion of Dionysos who educated Maron.

to a round temple with 100 sapphire columns forming a circle. Inside and out were figures carved in relief as though by demigods: bacchae, satyrs, women initiates playing the flute and dancing ecstatically. And the old man Maron was on a donkey. In the middle of the temple lay a couch with golden legs, made up with cushions, on which there was a man dressed in silken cloth. I did not see what he looked like, as he was covered up, but I did see his strength and the heftiness of his body. And in the middle of the shrine there was hanging a one-hundred-pound golden chain and a golden wreath. Instead of fire, precious stone provided light that illuminated that whole place. A quail cage of gold was suspended from the ceiling, in which there was a bird the size of a dove, and as though with human voice, it cried out to me in Greek, saying, "Alexander, from now on stop matching yourself with the gods: return to your own palace and do not rush head over heels into the ascent to the paths of heaven." I wanted to take it and the chandelier down to send you, but I saw the man on the couch stirring, evidently to rise, and my friends said to me, "Don't, King—it is sacred." Going out into the precinct I saw there two mixing bowls of chased gold with a capacity of sixty firkins—we measured them out at the banquet. I gave orders for the whole camp to be there for a feast. There was a large, well-equipped building there and striking goblets to grace any level of elegance, carved from stone. As we and the troops were taking our places for the feast, suddenly there was a sort of violent thunder of countless flutes, cymbals, Pan-pipes, trumpets, drums, and lyres. And there was smoke all over the mountain, as though we had been hit by a storm of lightning bolts.

We were afraid and left that region, proceeding to Cyrus's palace. We found many cities deserted, including one noteworthy city with a large building where the king used to give audiences. They told me there was a bird there that spoke with human voice. When I went into the building I saw many amazing sights: it was entirely of gold, and in the middle of the ceiling there hung a gold quail cage like the first one, and inside was a golden bird like a dove. They told me it spoke to kings in whatever language was needed. I also saw there a large mixing bowl of chased gold—these things were inside Cyrus's palace—with a capacity of 160 firkins. And it was quite amazing in its decoration: on its rim it had statues, and on the top band a sea battle; its center had a blessing, and its outside was of chased gold. They told me this was from Egypt, from the city of Memphis, and had been brought from there when the Persians took control. The building where the king himself used to give audiences was constructed in the Greek style, and on it was a relief of Xerxes' naval battle. Also in the building was a throne decorated with gold and precious stones and a lyre that played itself. And around the throne was a goblet cabinet sixteen cubits long with eight shelves, and above it stood an eagle overshadowing the whole circle with its wings. And there was a climbing vine of gold with seven branches, and everything was worked in gold. As for the other sights, what point is there in my attempting to tell you so much? They are such that their number prevents me from expressing their outstanding quality.

Farewell.

[Chapter 29 is missing in manuscript L. Other manuscripts include at this point an account of how Alexander encountered "vile peoples" who ate human corpses; to avoid contamination he enclosed them within an area surrounded by high mountains.]

30. Alexander also wrote another letter to his mother, Olympias, when he was in Babylon the Great and would presently leave the life of men, as follows.[94]

Great they say is the foresight of the divine powers. One of the native women gave birth to a child, the upper part of whose body, as far as the flanks, was all natural and human; but from the thighs downward there were animal heads so as to make the child just like the Scylla—there were the heads of lions and of wild dogs. And the forms moved, and everyone could make them out and recognize what each was, but the child's head was stillborn. Once the woman had given birth to the baby, she put it into the cloth and, having covered it up, arrived at Alexander's palace. She told his announcer, "Inform King Alexander that I have come concerning an amazing matter—I wish to show him something." It was midday, and Alexander was taking a siesta in his bedroom, but when he woke, he was told about the woman and ordered her to be brought in. When she came, the king dismissed all present, and when they had all gone, the woman showed him the monster that had been born, adding that she herself had given birth to it.

Seeing this, Alexander was astounded and immediately gave instructions for expert interpreters and magicians to be brought. When they came, he ordered them to deliver an interpretation of this portent that had been born, threatening them with death if they failed to tell him the truth. Of the Chaldaians, there were five who had the greatest reputation and intelligence, and one of them was much superior to them all in skill, but he, so it happened, was not in the city. Those who were in fact present said that Alexander would be stronger than all others in his wars and would become master over all mankind. The animals, they said, were the mightiest nations, subject to man's body—and this was what they indicated.

After them, the other Chaldaian too came to Alexander and, seeing what the omen was like, screamed out aloud in tears and tore his clothing apart from sorrow. Alexander grieved not a little to see him so distressed and told him to have confidence and tell him what he saw in the sign. He made this reply to him, "King, one can no longer count you among the living."

Alexander pressed him for the details of his interpretation of the sign,

---

94. There is no further letter to Olympias: what follows is not a letter (first person) but narrative (third person). This mistake occurs also in some other versions.

and he replied: "King, most powerful of all men, you are the human shape; the animal forms are those around you. Now if the upper part was alive and moving like the animals under it, then you would have gone on to rule over all men. But just as it has departed life, so have you, King. And those around you are just like the animals under it: they have no sense and in fact are savage to men, and those around you are disposed in just this way to you." With this the Chaldaian left. As for the baby, the Chaldaian said it should be burned forthwith. After hearing this Alexander put his affairs in order daily.

31. Antipatros rose against Olympias, Alexander's mother, and treated her as he wished.[95] Alexander's mother wrote to him about Antipatros on many occasions (as Alexander's mother, she was distressed) and wanted to go across to Epirus, but Antipatros prevented her. When Alexander received the letters of his mother, Olympias, and learned from them of the pain she was experiencing, he sent a man called Krateros to Antipatros in Macedonia to be governor of it. Antipatros realized what Alexander's plan was; he knew Krateros was coming and that the soldiers were returning from Alexander to Macedonia and Thessaly on his account. He was frightened and decided to assassinate Alexander, fearing, after his treatment of Olympias, that he might be humiliatingly punished. He had, indeed, heard that Alexander had become very haughty as a result of the successes he had achieved. With this in mind, he prepared a poison, which no vessel could contain without immediately breaking—not bronze nor glass nor earthenware. So Antipatros put the poison in a lead casket, and, covering it up with another casket, of iron, he gave it to his son and sent him to Babylon to Iollas, butler of King Alexander,[96] after having told him about how terrible and lethal the poison was, so that if anything happened to him in the wars at the hands of the enemy, he might take it and end it all.

Arriving in Babylon, Antipatros's son told Iollas, Alexander's butler, secretly about the giving of the poison. Now Iollas had a grudge against Alexander: a few days earlier Iollas had made a mistake, and Alexander had beaten him on the head with a staff, injuring him badly. So, as a result, Iollas, in his anger at Alexander, agreed to help Antipatros's son with the crime. Iollas took in with him a man called Medios who had been badly treated like him. And they arranged among themselves how

95. Antipatros, the aged former minister of Philip II, was left in charge of Macedonia and Greece while Alexander was in the East. The friction with Olympias is historical, and Krateros was indeed to replace him. In the end (316 B.C.) Antipatros's son Kassandros killed Olympias.

96. Iollas (Iolaos) was actually a son of Antipatros, thus Kassandros's brother. Alexander in fact cannot have been poisoned and probably died of malaria. Medios was a Thessalian aristocrat, a Companion of Alexander's. The plot as presented recalls the unsuccessful Conspiracy of the Pages (327 B.C.).

they would give Alexander the poison to drink. Alexander was resting one day after a large dinner, and the next day Medios came to him with an invitation to come to his house. Alexander accepted Medios's invitation and came to dinner with him. Others too dined with King Alexander. The plot to murder him by poison was unknown to Perdikkas, Ptolemy, Olkias, Lysimachos, Eumenios, and Kassandros; but all the others dining with Alexander were implicated in the criminal deed and had made an agreement with Iollas, King Alexander's butler, having sworn oaths to each other; by now they had ambitions on Alexander's powers. When Alexander had reclined with them, Iollas brought him an ordinary goblet of wine. There was a conversation to pass the time, and the drinking had by now been going on for a considerable time when Iollas gave him another goblet containing the poison. Alexander, as chance would have it, took the cup and upon drinking it suddenly screamed as though he had been struck through the liver by an arrow. He waited a short time and endured the pain, but then went to his own house, instructing those present to continue with the dinner.

32. But they were upset and immediately brought the dinner to a close and waited outside to see what would happen. Alexander, losing control of himself, said, "Roxana, lend me your help a little."[97] and supported by her returned to his palace and lay down.

At daybreak he ordered Perdikkas and Ptolemy and Lysimachos to come to him and said that no one else should come in with them until he had made his will. Suddenly there was a roar from the Macedonians and a rush upon the courtyard of Alexander's palace to kill his bodyguards if they did not show them the king. Alexander asked about the noise; so Perdikkas came up to him and informed him of what was being said by the Macedonians. Alexander gave instructions for his bed to be raised to a place where the whole army could file past, see him, and go out through another door. Perdikkas carried out King Alexander's instructions, and the Macedonians alone filed in and saw him. And not one of them failed to weep at Alexander, so great a king, lying near to death on his bed. And one of them, a man not undistinguished in appearance, but an ordinary man, came close to Alexander's bed and said: "It was for the good, King Alexander, that your father, Philip, ruled and for the good that you too have ruled, my king. You are abandoning us; and it would be good for us in our turn to die together with you who have made the city of Macedonia free." Alexander wept and stretched out his right hand in a sign of consolation.[98]

97. The unabridged version is more sensational: Roxana intercepts Alexander leaving to drown himself in the Euphrates, and Alexander complains that she is robbing him of glory for little benefit to herself.

98. The procession of soldiers is historical; Alexander by now could not speak.

33. He ordered his registrar to come in and told him, concerning his wife, Roxana: "If a male child is born to me by my wife, Roxana, let him be king of the Macedonians. But if a female child is born, let them choose whomever they wish as king." And he instructed him to write to his mother as follows.[99]

> King Alexander to my dearest mother, greetings:
> When you receive this, my last letter, prepare an expensive meal to thank Providence above for having given you such a son. But if you wish to do me honor, go on your own and collect together all men, great and humble, rich and poor, for the meal, saying to them: "See, the meal is prepared! Come and feast! But no one who now or in the past has experienced suffering should come, as I have prepared a meal not of suffering but of joy."
> Farewell, Mother.

Olympias did this, but no one came to the meal—neither great nor humble, not rich, not poor, could be discovered without suffering. So immediately his mother recognized his wisdom and realized that Alexander there had departed from the living and had written this to console her, on the grounds that it was nothing strange that had happened to him, but something that had happened and continued to happen to everyone.

When Alexander had said this and much more, a mist formed in the air, and a great star appeared, shooting from heaven to the sea, and together with it an eagle; and the statue in Babylon that they said was of Zeus stirred. The star returned back up to heaven, and the eagle followed it too. And when the star was lost from view in the heavens, immediately Alexander sank into the eternal sleep.

34. The Persians fought with the Macedonians to take Alexander's body back with them and to proclaim him as Mithras. The Macedonians on the other hand wanted to take him back to Macedonia. Ptolemy told them, "There is an oracle of Babylonian Zeus; so we will seek an oracle from him telling us where we are to place Alexander's body." And the oracle of Zeus gave them this response.

> I shall say what will benefit all. There is in Egypt a city called Memphis. There enthrone him.

After the oracle, there was no further discussion; they assented to Ptolemy's proposal that they should march and convey his embalmed body in a lead coffin to the city of Memphis. Ptolemy put him on a wagon and made the journey from Babylon to Egypt. And the people of Memphis heard of this and came to meet Alexander's body and escorted it into

---

99. The banquet episode appears only in L of the major manuscripts. A has Alexander's last will and testament, at great length.

Memphis. But the archprophet of the temple at Memphis said: "Do not settle it here, but at the city he founded in Rhakotis. For wherever this body shall be, that city shall continuously be in turmoil from wars and battles." So immediately Ptolemy took it to Alexandria and erected a tomb in the shrine called The Body of Alexander and rested Alexander's remains there.[100]

35. Alexander lived thirty-two years. His life was as follows. From the age of twenty he was king; and he fought wars for twelve years—and won the wars he fought. He subdued twenty-two barbarian nations and fourteen Greek tribes. He founded twelve cities, namely, Alexandria in Egypt, Alexandria by the Horpes, Alexandria at Issos, Scythian Alexandria, Alexandria on the river Granikos, Alexandria in the Troad, Alexandria at Babylon, Alexandria in Persia, the Alexandria named after the horse Bucephalus, Alexandria named after Poros, Alexandria at the river Tigris, Alexandria by the Massagetai.[101]

Alexander was born on the new moon of the month of January, at sunrise, and died on the new moon of the month of April, at sunset. And they called the day of his death Neomaga[102] because Alexander died young. Alexander died in the year of the world 5176, at the end of the one hundred and thirteenth Olympiad [325–324 B.C.] (the Olympiad is four years, and the first Olympiad began in the 4th year of the reign of Ahaz.)[103] From the death of Alexander to the incarnation of the Divine Logos by the Virgin is three hundred and twenty four years.

100. After two years of preparations, Alexander's body was being sent to Macedonia, but Ptolemy diverted it and after displaying it in Memphis took it to Alexandria.

101. Alexander founded many more than twelve cities. The list of names is somewhat garbled, and I have restored sense where I can. Alexandria at Issos = Iskenderun in Turkey; Alexandria Bucephalus = Jalalpur in Pakistan; Alexandria by the Massagetai may be Alexandria Eschate ("remotest") = Leninabad (formerly Khojent) in Turkestan (USSR).

102. Neomaga probably represents some Egyptian word in which Greeks thought their own words *neos* ("young") was present.

103. Ahaz was king of Judah (733–718 B.C.). The first Olympiad was in 776 B.C. Alexander died on 10 June 323 B.C.

PART TWO

Popular Compilations

7

WONDERS

Phlegon of Tralles was a Greek who served on the staff of the emperor Hadrian (A.D. 117–138) in Rome. He was one of several educated Greek freedmen employed by the emperor, a man drawn to Greek culture and converse with Greek intellectuals. In *Secundus the Silent Philosopher* (see selection 3), the philhellene Hadrian is represented as seeking out the company of the Greek philosopher Secundus during a visit to Athens.

Beyond this we know little of Phlegon's life other than the titles of the books he wrote. They include *A Description of Sicily*, *The Festivals of the Romans*, *A Topography of Rome*, *Long-Lived Persons*, and *Olympiads*. Although these works no longer survive, we do have substantial fragments of *Long-Lived Persons* and *Olympiads* from which to form an idea of their nature. The former consisted mostly of classified lists of persons who had lived a hundred years or longer, concluding with the Sibyl of Cumae, a prophetess who, according to tradition, had lived around a thousand years. The latter work provided the names of the victors at each Olympic festival from the First Olympiad in 776 B.C. to Phlegon's own lifetime together with a digest of important historical events that had occurred during each Olympiad. This compilation was intended for the use of Greek historians, for whom the Olympiads served as a convenient system of absolute dating. From these titles and fragments it appears that Phlegon's literary talents and interests lay primarily in making learned compilations from a variety of sources. Appreciating a good fact, we may suppose, and not inclined by temperament to speculation or interpretation, he produced reference works of useful or interesting information.[1]

Happily his most remarkable work survives almost entire. *On Marvels*, rendered here as *Book of Marvels*, is a collection of wondrous facts and events, and consistent with his other literary output, it consists largely of information compiled from earlier written sources. The book belongs to a literary genre that was well established in Phlegon's day, notices of wonders and marvels found in different realms of the natural world, in different geographical regions, or among different peoples. Such compilations were partly an outgrowth of the work of Aristotle and the Peripatetic school of philosophers, who made extensive collections of data in the course of their systematic researches into different fields of learning. When this learned passion for making and publishing compilations of raw data met with the ever-growing fascination of Greek authors for the element of the marvelous in nature and in human behavior, the result was *paradoxography*, or writing about marvels.[2]

The first work of independent paradoxography for which we have clear information is *A Collection of Wonders from the Entire Earth Arranged by Locality* by Callimachus of Cyrene, the Alexandrian poet and scholar who is better known in literary history as the author of carefully crafted hymns, epigrams, and other poems.[3] But Callimachus, a member of the staff of the great library at Alexandria, also produced a number of scholarly works including his influential compilation, *Tables of Illustrious Persons in Every Branch of Learning Together with a List of Their Works*. Although his collection of wonders has not survived, it found in antiquity many imitators, or at least successors. From the third century B.C., when Callimachus made his collection, to the third century A.D., over twenty Greek and several Roman paradoxographers were active.[4] Including Phlegon's, seven of these works survive to our day more or less complete. Since they have met with scorn by modern scholars, who dismiss the genre as science gone astray, they receive little notice in histories of Greek literature and have almost never been translated into modern languages. As a result this ancient literary tradition is now little known.

A typical work of Greek paradoxography consists of citations of marvelous events and facts gleaned from earlier authors. Since the interest of the writer and his readers was in the content and not in the presentation of the matter, each item was related briefly and objectively in unpretentious prose, sometimes with an acknowledgment of its source, as in this entry in the *Wondrous Researches* by the paradoxographer Apollonius (second century B.C.?).[5]

> Aristotle says in his work *On Drunkeness* that although Andron of Argos ate much dry, salty food throughout his entire life he remained free from thirst and never drank. Moreover, twice he journeyed to Ammon through waterless regions eating dry barley without the addition of any liquid. He did this throughout his entire life.

A citation of source does not necessarily mean that the compiler consulted the original work, for paradoxographers often derived their information at second hand from other compilations.

Paradoxographers arranged their material geographically (as Callimachus did), thematically, by source, or according to no apparent principle of organization at all. Since the authors saw their work strictly as compilation rather than persuasion or explanation, they rarely commented on their citations or on their own aims and principles. Their favorite topics were wonders of the natural world—marvelous regions, springs, minerals, animals, plants, and fire. This entry on a mysterious characteristic of certain islands is typical; it comes from *Collection of Marvelous Researches* by the paradoxographer Antigonus of Carystus, a younger contemporary of Callimachus.[6]

> In the Lemnian islands called Neae no partridges are born, and they perish if a person even brings them there. Some persons report something even more marvelous than this, that they perish if they even see the place.

Ethnographic items presently came to be included in the canon as well, usually the strange customs or remarkable nature of foreign peoples, as in this report by Apollonius.[7]

> Eudoxus of Rhodes says that there is a people in Celtic territory who see not during the daytime but at night.

The entries focus upon the abnormal, the surprising, the ironical, and the effect on the reader is like that of reading a series of pointed narratives such as anecdotes or jokes, each little presentation bearing a clever cognitive hit. Obviously this kind of reading does not make serious demands on the reader, asking one to savor the writer's presentation or to reflect long and hard upon the substance. Making no lofty claims to be scientific or scholarly or artistic, it is simply light reading for anyone, intellectual or nonintellectual, who enjoys being awed briefly at the wonders of the world and who does not much care if the reports are entirely reliable or not. It is amusing literature with a flavor of learning, all the more enjoyable and worthwhile because it may be true.

Most ancient Greek paradoxography consists of the same sort of things that one reads in modern publications such as *Ripley's Believe It or Not!* and the *Guinness Book of Records*. Consider these typical items from Ripley.[8]

> The smallest church in the world—near Latonia, Kentucky—only seats 3 people.

> Red snow falls in Japan.

> Every inhabitant of the village of Cervera de Buitrago, in the province of Madrid, Spain, has a multiplicity of fingers and toes. The usual number is seven.

Phlegon's *Book of Marvels* shows most of the characteristics of this literary tradition. A compilation of some thirty-five marvels, it is composed in ordinary language with occasional citation of sources and rare editorializing. What is significantly different about Phlegon's collection, apart from the fact that he sometimes copies out lengthy entries word for word from his sources instead of summarizing their content, is its sensationalism. Focusing almost entirely on human phenomena, Phlegon selects for the grotesque and the bizarre in a way that other ancient paradoxographers do not. For example:[9]

> There was also a hermaphrodite in Antioch by the Maeander River when Antipater was archon at Athens and Marcus Vinicius and Titus Statilius Taurus, surnamed Corvinus, were consuls in Rome.
>
> A maiden of prominent family, thirteen years of age, was good-looking and had many suitors. She was betrothed to the man whom her parents wished, the day of the wedding was at hand, and she was about to go forth from her house when suddenly she experienced an excruciating pain and cried out. Her relations took charge of her, treating her for stomach pains and colic, but her suffering continued for three days without a break, perplexing everyone about the nature of her illness. Her pains let up neither during the night nor during the day, and although the doctors in the city tried every kind of treatment they were unable to discover the cause of her illness. At around daybreak of the fourth day her pains became stronger, and she cried out with a great wailing. Suddenly male genitals burst forth from her, and the girl became a man.
>
> Some time later she was brought to the Emperor Claudius in Rome. Because of the portent he had an altar built on the Capitoline to Jupiter the Averter of Evil.

Phlegon's subjects are ghosts, sex changers and hermaphrodites, finds of giant bones, monstrous births, births from males, amazing multiple births, abnormally rapid development of human beings, and discoveries of live centaurs. He arranges his material thematically, moving from topic to related topic. Ghosts are creatures that imply a breakdown in the categories of the living and the dead in that they seem to be both at the same time; what ghosts are to life and death, hermaphrodites are to the equally basic and normally distinct categories of male and female; the topic of androgynes leads to reports of other physical abnormalities, first to discoveries of huge bones belonging to heroes and other giant populations that dwelled on the earth before the present time, then to human oddities from recent times such as multiheaded infants; unusual physiology yields to unusual parturition, first to births from males and then to large numbers of offspring produced by fertile women or fecund couples; the subject of birth gives way to the topic of abnormally speedy development of human beings from birth to death; and the collection ends with a description of the corpse of a centaur who had been captured alive in Arabia and sent to Rome.

There appear therefore to be two strains in Western paradoxography, one relatively quiet and modest, the other loud and outrageous. Whereas most ancient Greek paradoxography is of the former sort, the emphasis in the *Book of Marvels* places it at the other end of the paradoxographical continuum along with such Renaissance works as *On Monsters and Marvels* by the Frenchman Ambroise Paré and such modern sensationalistic and bizarre journalism as supermarket tabloids, which like Phlegon dwell upon two-headed infants, extremely young mothers, unexplained mysteries, and the like.[10]

The following selection comprises chapters 11–35 of Phlegon's *Book of Marvels*.[11]

NOTES

1. On Phlegon's life and work, see further Frank 1941, Hansen 1996.

2. On the history and nature of ancient Greek paradoxography, see Ziegler 1949, Alessandro Giannini 1963 and 1964, Fraser 1972 1:770–774, and Hansen 1996; for the Greek texts, see Alexander Giannini 1965. The term is a modern coinage; the ancients gave the tradition no special name.

3. On Callimachus as paradoxographer, see Fraser 1972 1:454–455, 770–774.

4. See Ziegler 1949. Roman authors include Varro and Cicero, whose paradoxographical works do not survive, but the *Natural History* of Pliny, though not exclusively paradoxographical, includes virtually every topic of which the paradoxographers were fond. Since the Greek paradoxographers have remained little known outside a small circle of scholars, most of the direct influence of ancient paradoxography upon later paradoxographical compilations has come through Pliny.

5. Apollonius 25.

6. Antigonus 9.

7. Apollonius 24.

8. Ripley 1946:161, 91, 256.

9. Phlegon, *Mir.* 6.

10. See Paré 1982, Bird 1992.

11. For a translation of the entire work together with commentary, see Hansen 1996. The translator has supplied the subtitles above each entry; they do not appear in the original.

LITERATURE

Frank 1941. Hansen 1996.

PHLEGON OF TRALLES

Book of Marvels

translated by William Hansen

Finds of Giant Bones

Idas

In Messene not many years ago, as Apollonius says, it happened that a storage jar made of stone broke apart in a powerful storm when it was pounded by much water, and there came out of it the triple head of a human body. It had two sets of teeth. They sought to discover whose head it was, and the inscription explained it: "Idas" was inscribed thereon. So the Messenians prepared another storage jar at public expense, placed the hero in it, and tended him more carefully, since they perceived that he was the man about whom Homer[1] says

> And of Idas, who of men on earth at that time
> Was the strongest. He drew his bow against lord Phoibos
> Apollo for the sake of his lovely-ankled bride.

The Cave of Artemis

In Dalmatia in the so-called Cave of Artemis one can see many bodies whose rib bones exceed eleven cubits.[2]

A Giant Tooth

Apollonius the grammarian reports that in the time of Tiberius Nero there was an earthquake in which many notable cities of Asia Minor utterly disappeared, which Tiberius subsequently rebuilt at his own expense. On account of this the people constructed and dedicated to him a colossus beside the temple of Aphrodite, which is in the Roman forum, and also set up statues in a row next to it from each of the cities.

Among the places that suffered from the earthquake were numerous cities in Sicily as well as the regions around Rhegium, and numerous peoples in Pontus were also struck. In the cracks in the earth huge bodies appeared that the local inhabitants were hesitant to move, although as a sample they sent to Rome a tooth of one of the bodies. It was not just a foot long but even greater than this measurement. The delegates showed it to Tiberius and asked him if he wished the hero to be brought to him.

Tiberius devised a shrewd plan such that, while not depriving himself of a knowledge of its size, he avoided the sacrilege of the robbing of the dead. He summoned a certain geometer, Pulcher by name, a man of some renown whom he respected for the man's skill, and bade him fashion a face in proportion to the size of the tooth. The geometer estimated how large the entire body as well as the face would be by means of the weight of the tooth, hastily made a construction, and brought it to the emperor. Tiberius, saying that the sight of this was sufficient for him, sent the tooth back to where it had come from.

An Exhibit of Bones

One should not disbelieve the foregoing narrative, since in Nitriae in Egypt bodies are exhibited that are no smaller than these and are not concealed in the earth but are unencumbered and plain to see. The bones do not lie mixed together in disorder but are arranged in such a manner that a person viewing them recognizes some as thigh bones, others as shin bones, and so on with the other limbs.

One should not disbelieve in these bones either, considering that in the beginning when nature was in her prime she reared everything near to gods, but just as time is running down, so also the sizes of creatures have been shrinking.

Rhodes

I have also heard reports of bones in Rhodes that are so huge that in comparison the human beings of the present day are greatly inferior in size.

The Coffin of Makroseiris

The same author says that there was a certain island near Athens that the Athenians wanted to fortify. As they were digging foundations for the walls they found a coffin that was a hundred cubits long and in which there lay a withered body matching the coffin in size. On the coffin was the following inscription:

I, Makroseiris, am buried on a small isle
After living a life of five thousand years.

Carthage

Eumachus says in his *Geographical Description* that when the Carthaginians were surrounding their territory with a trench they found in the course of their digging two withered bodies lying in coffins. One of them was twenty-four cubits in structure, the other twenty-three.

Bosporos

Theopompus of Sinope says in his work *On Earthquakes* that in the Cimmerian Bosporos there was a sudden earthquake, as a result of which one of several ridges in that region was torn open, discharging huge bones. The skeletal structure was found to be of twenty-four cubits. He says the local barbarian inhabitants cast the bones into the Maiotis Sea.

Monstrous Births

Multiple Features

A child was brought to Nero that had four heads and a proportionate number of limbs when the archon at Athens was Thrasyllus and the consuls in Rome were Publius Petronius Turpilianus and Caesennius Paetus.[3]

Multiple Features

Another child was born with a head growing out of its left shoulder.

Animal Child

An extraordinary omen occurred in Rome when the archon at Athens was Deinophilus and the consuls in Rome were Quintus Veranius and Gaius Pompeius Gallus.[4] A highly respected maidservant belonging to the wife of Raecius Taurus, a man of praetorian rank, brought forth a monkey.

Partly Animal Child

The wife of Cornelius Gallicanus gave birth near Rome to a child having the head of Anubis, when the archon at Athens was Demostratus and the consuls in Rome were Aulus Licinius Nerva Silianus and Marcus Vestinus Atticus.[5]

Animal Children

A woman from the town of Tridentum in Italy brought forth snakes that were curled up into a ball, when the consuls in Rome were Domitian Caesar for the ninth time and Petilius Rufus for the second time and there was no archon in Athens.[6]

Multiple Features

In Rome a certain woman brought forth a two-headed baby, which on the advice of the sacrificing priests was cast into the Tiber River. This happened when the archon at Athens was Hadrian, who later was emperor, and the consuls at Rome were the Emperor Trajan for the sixth time and Titus Sextius Africanus.[7]

Births from Males

A Homosexual
The doctor Dorotheus says in his *Reminiscences* that in Egyptian Alexandria a male homosexual gave birth, and that because of the marvel the newborn infant was embalmed and is still preserved.

A Slave
The same thing occurred in Germany in the Roman army, which was under the command of Titus Curtilius Mancias: a male slave of a soldier gave birth. This happened while Konon was archon in Athens and Quintus Volusius Saturninus and Publius Cornelius Scipio were consuls in Rome.[8]

Amazing Multiple Births

An Alexandrian Woman
Antigonus reports that in Alexandria a certain woman gave birth to twenty children in the course of four deliveries and that most of them were reared.

Another Alexandrian Woman
Another woman from the same city brought forth five children at one time, three of whom were male and two female, whom the Emperor Trajan ordered to be reared at his own expense. In the following year the same woman gave birth to another three.

Aigyptus
Hippostratus says in his book *On Minos* that Aigyptus begot fifty sons with one wife, Euryrrhoe, daughter of Neilus.

Danaus
Likewise Danaus had fifty daughters with a single wife, Europe, daughter of Neilus.

Abnormally Rapid Development

An Unnamed Male
Kraterus, the brother of King Antigonus, says he is aware of a person who in the space of seven years was a child, a youth, a man, and an old man, and then died, having married and begotten children.

Women in Pandaia

Megasthenes says that the women who dwell in Pandaia give birth when they are six years old.

Discoveries of Live Centaurs

Hippocentaurs

A hippocentaur was found in Saune, a city in Arabia, on a very high mountain that teems with a deadly drug. The drug bears the same name as the city, and among fatal substances it is extremely quick and effective.

The hippocentaur was captured alive by the king, who sent it to Egypt together with other gifts for the emperor. Its sustenance was meat. But it did not tolerate the change of air and died, so that the prefect of Egypt embalmed it and sent it to Rome.

At first it was exhibited in the palace. Its face was fiercer than a human face, its arms and fingers were hairy, and its ribs were connected with its front legs and its stomach. It had the firm hooves of a horse, and its mane was tawny, although as a result of the embalming its mane along with its skin was becoming dark. In size it did not match the usual representations, though it was not small either.

There were also said to have been other hippocentaurs in the city of Saune mentioned above. So far as concerns the one sent to Rome, anyone who is skeptical can examine it for himself, since as I said above it has been embalmed and is kept in the emperor's storehouse.

NOTES TO TRANSLATION

1. Homer, *Iliad* 9.558–560.
2. A cubit is approximately eighteen inches.
3. A.D. 61.
4. A.D. 49.
5. A.D. 65.
6. A.D. 83.
7. A.D. 112.
8. A.D. 56.

8

FABLES

In antiquity fables could be classified among the conversational genres of narrative, the kind of tale that might be recounted in the midst of a discussion. Greek authors represent it as being natural for persons in conversation occasionally to employ a fable to make a point more clearly or strikingly.

In a series of conversations described by Xenophon (*Memorabilia* 2.7), for example, Aristarchus informed Socrates that as a result of a political crisis a dozen or so female relations had recently moved into his house, and he was finding it difficult to support them in the present hard times. Socrates suggested that he could solve his financial problem and also make the women themselves happier if he should arrange for them to be engaged in productive work. Aristarchus accordingly provided them with wool to work with, and in fact they did become much more content, although now (as Aristarchus reports back to Socrates) they blamed him for being idle while they alone were working.

> Socrates said, "Then why don't you tell them the tale of the dog? For they say that back when animals could talk, a sheep said to her master, 'It's surprising that you give us sheep nothing beyond what we ourselves get from the land, though we supply you with wool and lambs and cheese, whereas you share your own food with your dog, who supplies you with nothing of the sort.' Now the dog heard this and said, 'Yes by Zeus he does, because it is I who keep you from being stolen by people or carried off by wolves. Without my protection you would not even be able to graze on your own for fear of being killed.' The sheep, they say, acknowledged that the dog should be honored above themselves. And so in your own case tell the women that you function as their watchdog and superintendent, and it is because of you that they live and work safely and happily, without external harm."

This incident is characteristic of ancient Greek fables and fable telling in a number of ways. Most important, perhaps, ancient authors regularly represent fables as being addressed by an adult to other adults. It is only recently in Western culture that the fable has become a genre of story primarily for children, for the simplicity and the fantasy of the fable appeal to children and the genre has mostly gone out of fashion among adults.

It is characteristic of the ancient use of fables in social situations that they play a subordinate role in a larger discourse of some sort, since fables basically serve the function of exemplifying a proposition metaphorically. "It was," as M. L. West puts it, "a technique of criticism and persuasion which by its indirectness might avoid giving offence, while at the same time making a powerful impression by its artistry."[1] But the indirectness of the fable is not only a gesture of courtesy; it is also a rhetorical device for slipping past the listener's defenses, defamiliarizing the issue at hand and encouraging the addressee to view the matter from a different perspective—that of the narrator.

Oral fables did not enjoy the status of stories meriting interest for their own sake, except perhaps among children and simple adults, since adult men generally held nonhistorical narratives, taken by themselves, to be unworthy of serious regard. Thus it would have been inconceivable for Socrates to have asked Aristarchus, "Did you hear the one about the dog and the sheep?" On the other hand, it was counterproductive for a fable to be too good a tale, for although it should be interesting enough to hold a listener's attention, it should not be so interesting as to continue to distract the listener from the issue at hand. In the present instance Socrates' tale is rhetorically apt for the context that he has in mind, but considered in isolation it is not a particularly engaging story.

Like most (but not all) other fables, Socrates' tale is fantastic rather than realistic in its content, in this case because it represents sheep and dogs as reasoning like humans and as possessing the faculty of human speech. The presentation of animals with a mix of animal and human traits has been termed *analogism*, signifying that the animals have been partially analogized to human beings, behaving in some ways like humans while retaining such features as the form and food habits of animals.[2] The quality of the fantastic, which lends fables much of their charm and facilites their rhetorical effectiveness, sets them apart from other kinds of exemplary stories.

Most fables are simple in form, normally involving one or two scenes and no more than two characters or groups of characters. So Socrates' narrative features a conversation among sheep, a master, and a dog on a single occasion, but the master is a mute character so that in effect the conversation is only between the sheep and the dog.[3]

Finally, a narrator often announces beforehand that he is about to relate a fable and concludes with an explanation of its relevance. When Socrates says that his tale is set during the time when animals could talk, he is saying in effect that it is a fable.[4] And when he concludes with "So also (you/I/etc.)" he employs the usual and familiar oral formula for introducing the application of the tale.

Although individual fables of this sort appear scattered throughout ancient Greek literature, reflecting oral usage, they did not constitute a form of literature until an author compiled a book of fables as such. So far as we know, this first happened toward the end of the fourth century B.C. when the politician, scholar, and Peripatetic philosopher Demetrius of Phalerum (ca. 350–280 B.C.) published a fable book entitled *Aisopeia*, one bookroll in length.[5] The work has not survived, so its precise nature is a matter of conjecture; but it was certainly a practical work, a sourcebook intended for the convenience of writers, speakers, and conversationalists, rather than a self-conscious work of belletristic literature. Demetrius was interested in rhetoric, for he wrote a work on the subject and published compilations of speeches of certain kinds as well as compilations of other materials. Indeed, it was in the spirit of the age to compile, for the Hellenistic period was rife with collections of inscriptions, decrees, proverbs, mythological narratives, epigrams, anecdotes, and doubtless jokebooks.[6]

A papyrus fragment (Rylands pap. 493) of an unidentified Greek fable book survives that may well belong to the lost book of Aesopic fables by Demetrius. It contains portions of a number of fables in prose, each one introduced by a heading that in the papyrus protrudes prominently to the left. For example:

Against those who treat others well but their friends poorly this tale is suitable.

A shepherd put aside his cloak, climbed an oak tree, and knocked down some acorns for his sheep. While fighting over the acorns his sheep destroyed his cloak. When he got down and saw what had happened he said: "You wretched sheep, you . . . wool for others . . ."

Here the text of this fable breaks off. Each fable in the book, so far as one can see, is prefaced with the same formula: "Against (such and such kind of person) this tale is suitable." This kind of line, called a *promythium*, or "foretale," obviously functions here as an indexer, allowing a reader to scan the contents without having to read the text of every fable. In other words, the collection is designed to be used primarily as a sourcebook from which the reader can draw an illustration for later use, rather than as an artistic work from which the reader should derive literary pleasure. So the fragment makes a good fit with the sort of work that it is supposed Demetrius wrote.

Launched now on a literary career, the ancient fable book developed different forms, some emphasizing the literary and others the practical. Beginning with the Latin poet Phaedrus in the first century A.D., some authors published collections of fables elaborated into little poems, developing the idea of the fable book as an artistic work to be enjoyed for its own sake, however low it might rank overall in the literary hierarchy. In later literature the best-known representative of this line is the famous fable book of the seventeenth-century French poet Jean de La Fontaine. Other fabulists stayed closer to the practical tradition presumably initiated by Demetrius and first represented for us by the Rylands papyrus.

In the ancient fable books the use of a promythium gives way in time to the employment of an *epimythium*, or "aftertale." This development produces the literary fable in the form that is most familiar to us: a brief exemplary tale followed by an explicit "moral."[7] The shift of position from fore to aft probably answers to a feeling that the proper place for a comment on a tale is at its conclusion, the position that was long established in oral fabulation, the position that does not anticlimactically reveal the point of the tale before its telling. Thus all fable books moved away from their original function as practical sourcebooks, the poetic branch emphasizing enjoyment, the prose branch emphasizing edification.

For the forms the epimythium can take, consider two fables from the prose fable book known as the *Collectio Augustana*.

> A hungry fox, spying some clusters of grapes hanging from a vine that had grown up a tree, wanted to get hold of them but could not. As it departed it said to itself: "They're sour."
>
> So also some persons, when they fail to reach a goal on account of their own weakness, blame circumstances.

> A fox whose tail had been cut off in a trap was so ashamed that it felt its life was unlivable. It realized that it must bring the other foxes into the same condition in order to conceal its own loss in the shared experience. And so it gathered all the foxes together and urged them to cut off their tails, saying that a tail not only was an ugly thing but also a heavy and superfluous attachment. One of the foxes present replied: "Well, if this matter were not to your advantage, you would not have given us this advice."
>
> This fable is fitting to use against those who give advice to their neighbors not because of goodwill but for their own advantage.[8]

The epimythia of these fables show the confluence of the oral and the literary traditions. The former ("So also some persons . . .") goes back ultimately to oral fable telling. Notice the similar diction in the narration of Socrates ("And so in your case . . ."). The latter epimythium ("This fable is fitting to use against . . .") derives from the indexing promythia of early fable books as we find them in the Rylands papyrus ("Against those who . . . this fable is suitable").

Whereas a fable recounted in an actual context pertains to the particular issue at hand, fables gathered into a book lack a particular context and can be equipped only with general applications. Accordingly, Socrates' fable addresses a problem that has arisen between Aristarchus and the women of his household and his statement of application is particular ("And so in your case . . ."), but the telling of the fable of the tailless fox arises from no immediate problem so that its application is necessarily generic ("This fable is fitting . . ."). Despite our labeling the epimythium the "moral" of the fable and the longstanding opinion among many adults that fables are appropriate—that is, edifying—reading for children, fables and their epimythia taken as a whole promote not so much an ideal ethical system as a kind of practical wisdom.[9]

The fable selection that follows is taken from an anonymous Greek fable book that dates to the second or third century A.D. Scholars refer to it as the *Collectio Augustana* (The Augustana Collection, from the fact that the principal manuscript was once preserved in Augsburg) or as *Recension I*. Composed in plain Greek prose it reflects the tradition of the practical sourcebook, while at the same time its lack of promythia suggests that its author conceived of his work as being more literary than a sourcebook but less so than a fable book in verse.

Since the ancients treated fable books as though they were authorless works in the public domain, unknown authors have added tales and removed them, modified their original sequence, and changed their wording in almost every ancient collection of fables. They have recast collections of prose fables as verse and paraphrased metrical collections in prose. Accordingly, the *Collectio Augustana* is one among a number of genetically related, anonymous collections of fables in Greek prose. In addition to *Recension I* there are compilations known to scholars as *Recension Ia*, *Recension II* (or *Collectio Vindobonesis*) and *Recension III* (or *Collectio Accursiana*). These collections are all younger in date than *Recension I* and derive from it. The original collection became a folkbook: its author was forgotten (and no ancient author mentions him), and the work itself, continuing to circulate for centuries and treated with considerable freedom, developed different editions.

The 231 fables of *Recension I* are arranged in a casually alphabetic order by the initial word of each fable, which is usually the name of a principal character. Because of this arrangement, fables featuring a particular animal tend to be grouped together; for example, the first three fables of the collection feature eagles. This system is also characteristic of the Sumerian rhetorical collections and may show their influence.[10] Since a fable was essentially a rhetorical device, any text from which a lesson could be drawn was potentially a fable. The ancient fable books therefore contain some narratives (jokes, urban legends, etiological tales, even supposed marvels of the natural world) that would not readily be labeled as fables were it not for the fact that they appear in a fable book.

The present excerpt consists of fables 10 to 31 of *Recension I* in the edition of Ben Perry.[11] Alphabetically we are in the As here, so that the fables mostly feature characters whose name in Greek begins with this letter: fox, fisherman, human being, and so on.[12] *Recension I* contains no promythia, only epimythia, although some fables have neither.

NOTES

1. West 1984: 107–108.

2. von Sydow 1948:134–144.

3. The structure of interaction follows Olrik's Law of Two to a Scene, according to which in oral stories no more than two characters in a scene are active; see Olrik 1992:43.

4. Aesop is represented as introducing some of his animal fables in this way in *The Aesop Romance* (chaps. 97, 99, 133): "When animals talked the same language as men . . ."

5. Diogenes Laertius, *Lives of the Philosophers* 5.80–81.

6. Perry 1940:406. We do not know if Demetrius invented the idea of the fable book or whether the idea was suggested to him by Oriental collections of rhetorical narratives, which date to the second millenium B.C. Mostly these are Sumerian fables and proverbs preserved in school texts from the Old Babylonian period. Among the evidence in favor of Oriental influence is the fact that Demetrius's teacher, Theophrastus, is said to have authored a book entitled *Akicharos*, that is, the Assyrian sage Ahikar, who like Aesop was a fount of tales and maxims.

7. For a discussion of promythia and epimythia in the ancient fable, see Perry 1940.

8. Perry 15 and 17 (that is, fables 15 and 17 in Perry 1952). Epimythia, by the way, are not always accurate. In the present case the fabulist says that the fox blames "circumstances," but in fact it does not; rather, finding its goal unattainable, it dishonestly depreciates the goal. On inaccurate epimythia, see Nøjgaard 1964–1967 1:370–374 and Hansen 1982.

9. On fables in children's literature, see Hunt 1995:12–15.

10. Nøjgaard 1964–1967 1:511–513.

11. Perry 1952.

12. A translation has never been made of the *Collectio Augustana* by itself as an ancient fable book, but its fables have been translated together with fables from other collections. The fables of the Augustana Collection constitute the first 231 fables in Daly 1961:93–189 (fables), 267–294 (morals).

LITERATURE

Adrados 1979–1987. Adrados and Reverdin 1984. Carnes 1985. Holbek 1962. Holzberg 1993b. Jedrkiewicz 1989. Nøjgaard 1964–1967. Perry 1940, 1952, 1965.

ANONYMOUS

Collectio Augustana

translated by William Hansen

Fox Who Saw a Lion

A fox that had never seen a lion encountered one by chance. The first time it saw one it was so agitated that it nearly died. The second time it lit upon one it was frightened but not so much as before. The third time it saw one it was so emboldened that it even went right up to it and engaged it in a conversation.

The tale illustrates how habituation softens even frightening things.

Fisherman Who Played the Flute

A fisherman who was an experienced flute player took his flutes and nets, went to the sea, and stood upon a projecting rock. At first he began to play, thinking that the fish would of their own accord come out toward the sweet sound, but after exerting himself for a long time to no effect, he lay aside his flutes, picked up his net, cast it on the water, and caught a lot of fish. As he tossed them from his net onto the shore and saw them quivering, he said: "You miserable fish, when I was playing my flutes you didn't dance, but now that I have stopped, you do."

Fox and Leopard

A fox and a leopard were having a dispute over their beauty. When the leopard kept bringing up the intricacy of its body, the fox replied: "How much more beautiful I am than you, since it is not my body but my mind that is intricate."

The tale illustrates how the world of thought is more beautiful than the world of the body.

Fishermen Catching a Stone

Some fishermen were drawing a dragnet. Since it was heavy they danced for joy, thinking they had a great catch. But after they had drawn it to shore and found that the net was full of stones and wood but few fish, they became very heavy-hearted, not so much angry at what had happened as at their having expected the contrary. But one of them, an old fellow, said: "Friends, let's stop this. Grief, it seems, is the sister of joy, and since we had so much pleasure beforehand, we had to have some grief as well."

So also when we see how easily things in life change, we should not always exult, but reckon that a fine day must necessarily be followed by a storm.

Fox and Ape Disputing about Nobility

A fox and an ape that were journeying together were disputing about the nobility of their families. As they each were going through every point in detail, they came upon some tombs, and the ape moaned upon seeing them. When the fox asked the reason for this, the ape showed it the monuments and said: "Well, why shouldn't I cry when I see the grave markers of my family's freedmen and slaves?" The fox responded: "You can lie all you want, for none of these are going to arise from the grave to refute you."

So also among human beings, liars are most given to boasting when there is no one around to refute them.

Fox and the Cluster of Grapes

A hungry fox, spying some clusters of grapes hanging from a vine that had grown up a tree, wanted to get hold of them but could not. As it departed it said to itself: "They're sour."

So also some persons, when they fail to reach a goal on account of their own weakness, blame circumstances.

Cat and Rooster

A cat that had caught a rooster wanted to feast upon it with the justification of a reasonable charge. And so it began making accusations, saying that the rooster's crowing during the night was irksome to human beings and did not permit them to get any sleep. When the rooster said that it did this to help them by rousing them to their accustomed work, the cat made a second charge: "Well, you are also profane by nature inasmuch as you mount your mother and your sisters." The rooster said that it also did this to help its masters, since by doing so it caused the hens to lay many eggs for them. Completely at a loss the cat said: "Do you think I'm not going to devour you just because you're always so good at finding excuses?"

The tale illustrates that an evil nature that chooses to do wrong behaves with undisguised evil if it cannot do so with a fine pretext.

Dock-Tailed Fox

A fox whose tail had been cut off in a trap was so ashamed that it felt its life was unbearable. It realized that it must bring the other foxes into the same condition in order to conceal its own loss by means of a shared experience. And so it gathered all the foxes together and urged them to cut off their tails, saying that a tail not only was an ugly thing but also a heavy and superfluous attachment. One of the foxes present replied: "Well, if this matter were not to your advantage, you would not have given us this advice."

This fable is fitting to use against those who give advice to their neighbors not because of goodwill but for their own advantage.

Fisherman and Sprat

A fisherman lowered his net and brought up a sprat, which beseeched him to release it for the present since it was small, and to catch it again later after it had increased in size and was more useful. But the fisherman said: "I would certainly be a great fool if I let go a gain in hand in order to chase after an uncertain hope."

The tale illustrates that a present gain, even if it is small, is preferable to one that is hoped for, even if it is great.

Fox and Bramble-Bush

A fox was climbing a fence and was about to slip so that it took hold of a bramble-bush, scratching its paw. Suffering terribly it accused the bramble-bush, saying that when the fox had turned to it for help, its treatment was worse than a fall from the fence would have been. The bramble-bush said in answer: "You did not use good sense in wanting to take hold of me, for it is I who am accustomed to take hold of everything."

So also with human beings, those who flee for refuge to persons for whom to injure is natural deceive only themselves.

Fox and Crocodile

A fox and a crocodile were disputing about the nobility of their families. As the crocodile was going in detail through the illustriousness of his ancestors and finally was saying that his forebears included gymnasiarchs,[1] the fox said in reply: "Well, even if you don't say so yourself, your hide implies that you are the product of considerable gymnastics."

So also for human liars, reality is the refutation.

Fishermen and Tunny-Fish

Some fishermen went out to fish and, having no success after a long time, caught nothing. As they sat on their ship in low spirits, a tunny-fish that was following along with a great sound leapt up and landed unawares in their hull. The men seized it and brought it to town, where they sold it.

So what art does not provide, luck often bestows.

Fox and Woodcutter

A fox was fleeing from hunters, and when it saw a woodcutter it begged him to hide it. The man advised it to go into his hut and hide itself there. Presently the hunters came and asked the woodcutter if he had seen a fox going past there, and the woodcutter said aloud that he had not seen one, while indicating by a gesture of his hand where the animal had hidden itself. The hunters, however, paid no attention to his gesture and trusted in his words. When the fox saw that they had left, it came out and proceeded to go its way without a word. After the woodcutter criticized the fox for uttering no acknowledgment though it had been saved by him, the fox said: "Well, I certainly would have thanked you if your actions had agreed with your words."

One might use this tale against those persons who openly proclaim their good services while in fact doing evil.

Roosters and Partridge

A certain man who kept roosters came upon a tame partridge for sale, bought it, and took it home to rear along with the roosters. Since, however, the other birds beat and pursued the partridge, it was heavy at heart, concluding that it was looked down upon as being a different kind of bird. But when it shortly observed that the roosters also fought one another, not parting till they had drawn blood, it said to itself: "Well, I'm no longer going to be upset when I'm beaten by them, for I see that they don't even spare one another."

The tale illustrates that sensible persons more easily bear the insults of their neighbors when they see that their neighbors do not even spare their own household.

Fox with a Swollen Belly

A hungry fox, spying some meat and loaves of bread that had been left in the hollow of an oak tree by some shepherds, went inside and ate them. Its belly became swollen, and since it was unable to get out, it moaned and groaned. Another fox was passing by and, hearing its moaning, went up to it and asked what the reason was. After it had learned what had happened, it said to the first fox: "Well, you'll have to wait there until you're the same size as you were when you entered, and then you'll easily get out."

The tale illustrates that time puts an end to difficulties.

Kingfisher

A kingfisher is a bird that is fond of solitude and passes all its time on the sea. It is said to build its nest in seaside promontories in order to guard itself against human hunters.

So when a kingfisher was about to lay its eggs, it went to a high place, and seeing a rocky ridge by the sea, it built its nest there. It happened when the kingfisher went out to feed that there was a violent wind so that the sea rose up in waves as high as the nest, which it swept away, destroying the nestlings. Upon its return the kingfisher recognized what had occurred, and said: "Wretched me, who guarded myself against the land, thinking it treacherous, and fled to this place, which has proved to be much less trustworthy."

So also of human beings, some persons guard themselves against their enemies but fall in with friends who are far harsher than their enemies.

Fisherman Striking the Water

A fisherman was fishing in a certain river. He stretched his net tight so as to span the stream from one side to the other, then tied a cord onto a stone and started striking the water with it so that the fish in their reckless flight might happen into his net. One of the persons who lived in the area, seeing him doing this, upbraided him for muddying the water and so not allowing them to drink clear water. But he replied: "But if I don't stir up the river like this, I'll have to die of starvation."

So also in cities, demagogues are always most active when they bring their states into discord.

Fox and the Mask

A fox went into a workshop of a molder and, examining closely each of the items therein, came upon a tragic mask. Raising it he said: "Such a head not to have any brains!"

Against a man who is magnificent of body but irrational of mind, this tale is fitting.

The Cheat

A poor man who was ill and in a sorry state prayed to the gods, promising to sacrifice a hecatomb if they saved him. Wishing to put the man to the test, they arranged for him to recover very quickly. He arose from his bed, and since he had no real cattle, he fashioned a hundred cattle out of dough and burned them, saying: "Gods, here's the fulfillment of my vow." Now the gods, wishing to delude him in return, sent him a dream in which they urged him to go to the seashore, where he would fetch a thousand Attic drachmas. Elated, the man took off running to the shore. Encountering some pirates, he was carried off and, when sold by them, fetched a thousand drachmas.[2]

The tale is suitable for use against a liar.

Charcoal-Maker and Fuller

When a charcoal-maker, who was working at a certain house, saw that a fuller had settled nearby, he went up to him and invited him to be his housemate, pointing out to him in detail how they would deal more closely with one another and would save money by sharing a single dwelling. But the fuller said in reply: "Well, for me at least such an arrangement would be completely impossible, for whatever I make bright, you will cover with soot."

The tale illustrates that dissimilarities cannot be reconciled.

Shipwrecked Man and Athena

A wealthy Athenian man was sailing with some other persons. After a violent storm arose and overturned the ship, all the other passengers started swimming, whereas the Athenian kept calling upon Athena, promising her countless gifts if she saved him. One of the other shipwrecked passengers, as he swam past, said to him: "Along with Athena's help, use your arms."

So also we ourselves, in addition to calling upon the gods for aid, must take our circumstances into consideration and act accordingly.

Middle-Aged Man and His Two Mistresses

A middle-aged man had two lovers, of whom one was young and the other old. Feeling ashamed at consorting with a man younger than herself, the woman who was advanced in age continually plucked out his black hairs whenever he was with her. The younger woman, concealing the fact that her lover was an old man, would pull out his gray hairs.

And so it happened that while his hair was being plucked by both of them he became bald.

So inconsistency in everything is harmful.

NOTES TO TRANSLATION

1. A kind of official in charge of athletic training.
2. The text plays on two different senses of the verb here rendered as "fetch."

9

JOKES

Jokes are comic tales that in their natural environment circulate among persons in live social interactions such as conversations; that is, they are a form of folklore. When someone gathers a number of independent jokes into a written collection, putting them into a particular arrangement and giving each one a fixed form, the result is a species of literature. Although it is commonly believed that the idea of compiling jokes in the form of a book arose first during the Renaissance,[1] written compilations of humor of various kinds are referred to in ancient sources, and one Greek jokebook has come down to us. It bears the title *Philogelos*, or *The Laughter-Lover*.

Nothing is known of its two authors, Hierocles and Philagrius, and its date of composition is also uncertain. A few of the jokes can be dated by their topicality to the third and fourth centuries A.D., which means that in its present form the collection as a whole cannot be earlier than this; but other jokes reflect earlier conditions, and most of the jokes are, as one might expect, undatable. So an old jokebook may have grown over time by the occasional addition of new jokes and the updating of older ones, or a late compiler may have drawn upon earlier jokebooks; the difference is hardly important. In any event *Philogelos* probably contains jokes of different vintages rather than being a sampling of jokes current among Greeks in, say, the fourth century A.D.

It was a common Greek notion that a participant in a dinner party who did not contribute to the food should contribute to the wit, that is, to the amusement of the guests (Athenaios 14.614c). Ancient literature frequently mentions the "buffoon" or "parasite" who is invited to a dinner party in order to amuse the other guests with his humor or who shows up uninvited hoping to trade his wit for a meal. At a gathering described by Xenophon (*Symposium* 1.11–16), for example, Philip the buffoon shows up uninvited and attempts—not very successfully—to amuse the rather intellectual guests with his simple wisecracks. In comedies such characters are sometimes represented as keeping jokebooks at home from which they can draw witticisms. So in Plautus's *Stichus* (400, 454–455) the parasite Gelasimus dashes home to consult his books in order to equip himself with jokes *(ridicula),* and in Plautus's *Persian* (392–395) the parasite Saturio boasts of possessing a whole chest full of books at home, vowing to extract 600 jokes as a dowry for his daughter. Since Roman comedies were based on Greek plays, now lost, of the fourth and third centuries B.C., jokebooks must have been in circulation in Greece by the fourth century B.C.

There was a tradition that in the fourth century B.C. a group of sixty Athenian wits met regularly in a temple of Herakles, presumably to exercise their humor. Athenians often quoted their witticisms, saying, "The Sixty said (such and such)." Their reputation was so great that Philip of Macedon sent them a talent of silver, asking them to write out their jokes and send them to him (Athenaios 614d–e). Whether they did so or not, such comically gifted persons are the sort who might have transformed their oral repertory into written jokebooks.

An indication that jokebooks were intended more as a means to a later end than as an immediate end in themselves is the manner in which written jokes are recounted. Consider, for example, the following joke (*Philogelos* 21):

> A numskull, wanting to go to sleep but not having a pillow, told his slave to set an earthen jar under his head. The slave said the jug was hard. The man told him to fill it with feathers.

The same joke is found in a modern compilation of Irish jokes:

> McCall and Linehan, two beggars, were making camp for the night.
> "Yerra, man, what do ya want with that length of drainpipe you're carryin'?" asked McCall.
> "I'm goin' to use it for a pillow," said Linehan.
> "That'd be as hard as hell."
> "Is it a fool you take me for? I'm goin' to stuff it with straw first."[2]

The Greek jokebook gives only the essence of the joke, which the reader can work up for retelling upon a future occasion. In contrast, the Irish jokebook presents the joke just as a narrator might actually tell it in live conversation, drawing it out and dramatizing it in direct speech. It lets the reader savor the joke, enjoying it as though the narrator were in the very room recounting it in person. The modern book attempts not to help the reader prepare for a social occasion but to serve as a substitute for live social interaction. The Irish joke is not an inherently funnier joke, since it is exactly the same comic idea, but it is told in a way that appeals to readers who are used to jokebooks as entertaining literature more than as sourcebooks, as a finished dish rather than a recipe.

Their brevity aside, the humorous narratives in *Philogelos* are the sort of thing that we ourselves would readily label as jokes if we should encounter them today. For the most part they are short, independent, comic tales recounted about unnamed characters and concluding with a punchline. Each narrative is little more than a setup for a final remark (or sometimes a final action), which usually is a silly comment made by a fool or a clever comment made by a wit. The humor of such tales resides in the punchline with which they conclude rather than in a situation that develops comically through the narrative as a whole. Jokes of the sort found in *Philogelos* therefore differ little from the kind of anecdote known as the apothegm—a quip allegedly made by a prominent person upon one or another occasion.[3] Indeed, the difference may be as slight as whether the characters are generic (joke) or named (anecdote). Here is *Philogelos* 148:

> When a talkative barber asked, "How shall I cut you?" a wit said: "In silence."

Compare this anecdote recounted of King Archelaos of Macedon:[4]

> When a garrulous barber asked him [King Archelaos of Macedon], "How shall I cut you?" he said: "In silence."

Some fragments have also survived of a Greek collection of what appears to be one-line comic insults, which one might regard as a kind of jokebook.[5] The insults are arranged thematically under headings, rather like fables under promythia. Thus in the section containing insults to be directed against redheads, we find:

> You don't have a face, but a setting sun.
> You don't have a face, but a fireplace.

Since compilations of humor might consist of punchline jokes, humorous anecdotes, situational tales, or insults, it must remain uncertain whether the references to jokebooks such as those that appear in Roman comedies refer precisely to jokebooks of the sort represented by *Philogelos* or to other sorts of witty compilation.

Most of the jokes in *Philogelos* feature fools, and in these most of the humor is based upon a false analogy. For example (*Philogelos* 1):

> A numskull ordered a lamp from a silversmith. When the smith asked how large a lamp he should make, the numskull answered: "Oh, big enough for around eight persons."

This would make sense if, as one commentator has observed, the buyer were ordering bread from a baker.[6]

Fools are denoted in a variety of ways, including being called by such terms as Abderites, Sidonians, and Cumaeans, that is, residents of the cities of Abdera, Sidon, and Cumae, whose entire citizenries were conventionally regarded in humorous tales as being numskulls, just as in many countries today tales about fools tend to cluster about a particular ethnic group or community—in English tradition the men of Gotham, in Germany the Schildburger, in Denmark the Molboer, in Greece the Chiotes. Other kinds of jokes in *Philogelos* feature misers, boasters, clever wags, grouches, cowards, lazy persons, envious persons, gluttons, drunkards, persons with bad breath, and misogynists.

In the telling of jokes in *Philogelos* the emphasis is upon content, for the style is quite ordinary, and no attempt is made to use the jokes as a vehicle for intellectual or philosophic statement or for special aesthetic effect. In other words, like most other jokebooks *Philogelos* reflects the popular aesthetic.

The selection that follows includes the first fifty-six (out of 265) jokes in Andreas Thierfelder's edition of *Philogelos*.[7]

NOTES

1. Wilson 1939:123: "And there is no harm in making the time-honored statement that the practice of collecting jests into a book began in Renaissance Italy with Poggio, if we do not forget that the jests which he and other early compilers assembled were traditional and dateless and may once have pleased a contemporary of Chaucer or Sir Dagonet." The ancient Greek jokebook is not mentioned at all by W. Carew Hazlitt in his history of jokebooks (Hazlitt 1890) and so must have been unknown to him. In fact, the history of jokebooks remains to be written.
2. Wilde 1983:9.
3. For these forms, see Hansen 1988.
4. Plutarch, *Moralia* 177a (Archel. 2).
5. Kassel 1956.
6. Thierfelder 1968:203.
7. For a complete rendering of *Philogelos* into English, see Baldwin 1983.

LITERATURE

Baldwin 1983, 1992. McCartney 1931. Rapp 1950–1951. Thierfelder 1968. Winkler 1985: 160–165.

HIEROCLES AND PHILAGRIUS

The Laughter-Lover

translated by William Hansen

A numskull ordered a lamp from a silversmith. When the smith asked how large a lamp he should make, the numskull answered: "Oh, big enough for around eight persons."

A numskull who wanted to swim nearly drowned. So he swore not to touch water again before he had learned how to swim.

A person went to a numskull doctor and said: "Doctor, whenever I get up from sleeping, I'm groggy for a half hour and only after that am I all right."
      The doctor: "Get up a half hour later."

A numskull had a horse for sale. A person asked him if it had had its first throw. When the numskull said that it had already had its second, the person said: "How do you know that?"
      He answered: "Because it has thrown me once and my father once."[1]

Meeting a numskull a man said: "Mister numskull, I saw you in a dream."
      He replied: "By the gods, I've been busy and didn't notice you."[2]

A numskull saw his family doctor coming and kept himself out of sight.
      When his companion asked him why he was doing so, he answered: "I haven't been sick for a long time, and I feel ashamed."

A numskull who had undergone an operation on his uvula was instructed by his doctor not to speak, and so he ordered his slave to return greetings on his behalf to persons who greeted him. Then he himself would say to each person: "Don't take it as arrogance if my slave greets you instead of I. My doctor has told me not to speak."

A numskull wanted to catch a mouse that was constantly nibbling on his books. So he bit into a piece of meat and sat down in a dark place.[3]

Wanting to train his donkey not to eat, a numskull stopped giving him any food. When the donkey died of starvation, the man said: "What a loss! Just when he had learned not to eat, he died."

A numskull who had a horse for sale was asked if it was easily frightened. He said: "Oh no, by the health of my father, it's not. Why, in the stall it stands all by itself."

A numskull wanted to see if he looked good when he slept. So he looked in a mirror with his eyes closed.

A numskull who was going on a trip was asked by a friend to buy him two slaves, each fifteen years old. "Certainly," he said, "and if I can't find you two fifteen-year-olds, I'll buy you one thirty-year-old."

Two patricidal numskulls were angry that their fathers were still alive. One said: "So, shall we each strangle our own father?"

"No, no," said the other, "we don't want to be called patricides. But if you want, you kill my father, and I'll kill yours."

A numskull bought a house. Then he would stick his head through the doorway and ask the passersby if the house seemed right for him.

A numskull dreamt that he had stepped on a nail. So he put a dressing on his foot.

When a companion of his asked about the dressing and learned the reason for it, he said: "People are right to call us idiots. Why ever do you go to bed without shoes on?"

For many days a numskull looked for a book of his without finding it. Then, as he happened to be eating some lettuce, he turned to a corner of the room and saw his book lying there.

Later he encountered a friend who was crying over the loss of some clothing. "Don't be upset," he said. "Just buy some lettuce, and while you're eating it turn toward the corner, and you'll find them."

A friend who was away from town wrote a numskull, asking him to buy some books for him.

The numskull neglected to do so, and when he encountered the friend upon his return, he said: "I never got the letter you sent me about the books."

A man encountered a numskull and said: "The slave you sold me died."

"By the gods," he said, "he didn't do anything like that when he was with me."

Seeing a lot of sparrows sitting in a tree, a numskull spread out his garment and shook the tree in order to collect the sparrows.

Two numskulls, acting out of respect, alternately escorted each other home after a dinner party and never got to bed.

A numskull, wanting to go to sleep but not having a pillow, told his slave to set an earthen jar under his head. The slave said the jug was hard. The man told him to fill it with feathers.

A numskull encountered a friend of his and said: "I heard that you had died."

He replied: "Well, you can see that I am alive."

And the numskull: "But the person who told me is much more trustworthy than you are."

A numskull went into a public bath just after it had opened up for the day. Finding no one else inside he said to his slave: "So far as I can tell, the public bath is not in operation."

A numskull who was having an argument with his father said to him: "You good-for-nothing, can't you see what kind of loss you have caused me? If you hadn't been born, I would have been my grandfather's heir."

While a numskull was voyaging, a powerful storm raged and his slaves were wailing.

"Don't cry," he said. "I have set all of you free in my will."

A numskull was trying to find the right spot to construct his tomb. When some persons said that a certain site was good, he said: "No, that area is unhealthy."

A numskull who was sick made an agreement with his doctor that if he should get well, he would pay the doctor. Presently his wife reprimanded him for drinking wine while he had a fever.

"Do you want me to get well," he said, "and have to pay the doctor his fee?"

A dog bit a numskull's thumb. The man said: "If he had gotten hold of my cloak, it would be ruined."[4]

There were twin brothers, and one of them died. When a numskull encountered the survivor, he asked, "Was it you who died, or your brother?"

A numskull was about to suffer shipwreck. So he requested some writing tablets in order that he might make out his will.

A numskull wanted to cross a river and embarked on the boat, riding his horse. When someone asked him why he did not dismount, he said: "Because I'm in a hurry."

A numskull was invited to dinner but did not eat anything. When one of the guests asked him why he was not eating, he replied: "I don't want to give the impression that I'm here only for the food."

The son of a numskull was playing ball, when the ball fell into a well. Peering down the well, the boy saw his own reflection and asked for his ball back. After he complained to his father that he had not gotten it back, the father peered down the well, saw his own reflection, and said: "Sir, give the boy back his ball!"

A numskull was visiting a sick friend and asked him how he was feeling. When the man didn't answer, the numskull grew angry and said: "Well, I hope that I get sick and don't answer you when you come by."

A numskull bought some stolen clothing. In order that they not be recognized as such, he smeared them with pitch.

A numskull was always estimating the value of the cloaks worn by the persons he encountered. His father heard about this from someone and rebuked his son.

"Father," he said, "you believe this slander, and you probably didn't hear it personally."

"On the contrary," he replied, "so and so told me."

"And you pay attention to him," the son said, "a man whose cloak isn't worth fifty drachmas?"

A numskull had a horse for sale. A man came along and was examining its teeth. The numskull said: "Why are you examining its teeth? I only wish it walked as well as it eats."

A numskull whose aged father was very ill asked his friends to bring garlands for the funeral procession. On the following day, however, the old man got better and the numskull's friends were irritated with him.

"I feel ashamed because of your wasted expense," he said. "So bring the garlands tomorrow and I'll conduct his funeral procession in whatever condition he is in."

Two numskulls were walking along together. When one of them saw a black bird, he said: "Brother, perhaps her mate has died."

A numskull lost his little son. When he saw that on account of his own importance many persons had come to the funeral, he said: "I'm ashamed to be burying so small a child in so large a company of persons."

A numskull was buying a house. He carried around a stone from it as a sample.

Two numskulls were traveling. One of them, needing to defecate, stayed behind. He found a message that the other had inscribed on a milestone: "Catch up with me. . . ."[5]

When a numskull heard from someone that his beard was coming, he went away to the gate to await it.

Another fool, after inquiring and learning about the situation, said: "People are justified in calling us idiots. How do you know that it's not coming through the other gate?"

A numskull was sleeping with his father. During the night he would stand up on the bed and eat some of the grapes that were hanging overhead.[6] His father hid a lamp under a pot and, when the son stood up, suddenly showed the light. The son started snoring as he stood upright, pretending to be asleep.

During the night a numskull got into bed with his grandmother. When his father beat him on account of this, he said: "You've been screwing my mother for a long time without any trouble from me, and now you're angry at finding me with your mother just once?"

An agent reported to a numskull that a river had overrun his property. "Then it's using force on us!" he cried out.[7]

A numskull went to the country after a long time and saw the farm animals going to pasture. When he heard them bleating in their usual way, he asked what was the reason for that. Making fun of him, the farm manager said: "They're greeting you."

"As I live and breathe," he said. "For my sake, then, give them some time off and don't lead them out to pasture for three days."

A numskull put on a new pair of sandals. Since they squeaked, he stopped and said: "Don't keep squeaking or you'll break your legs."[8]

A numskull saw the moon and asked his father if other towns also had such moons.

A numskull moneylender told a shipowner who owed him money to bring a coffin for himself and two children's coffins for his eight-year-olds, of the right size for their growing up.

Seeing a well on his farm, a numskull asked if the water was good. The workers said: "Yes, it is. In fact, your parents used to drink from it."

"How long were their necks," he asked, "since they were able to drink from so great a depth?"

A numskull fell into a cistern. He called out continually for help, and when no one responded, he said to himself: "I'm an idiot if I don't give everyone a flogging when I get out of here so that they'll at least respond and bring me a ladder."

A numskull was eating with his father. In front of them lay a large head of lettuce with many fine sideshoots. "Father, you eat the children," he said, "and we'll eat the mother."

A numskull was writing a letter to his father from Athens. Priding himself in his education, he added: "I only hope that when I come home I find you on trial for your life so that I can display for you my skill as an advocate."

A waggish numskull was unable to pay his expenses. So he sold off his books and wrote to his father, saying: "Congratulate me, father, for I am already supporting myself by my books."

A numskull, a bald man, and a barber were on a trip together, had to pass the night in a desolate spot, and agreed that each man in turn should stay awake for four hours and watch over their belongings.

The first watch fell to the barber. Deciding to play a trick on the numskull, he shaved off all of the numskull's hair. When his watch was over, he roused the numskull.

Stroking his head as people do when they wake up, the man found that he had no hair. "That worthless barber!" he said. "He woke up the bald guy instead of me."

NOTES TO TRANSLATION

1. The joke plays upon the ambiguity of the word *throwing* used in connection with horses. The inquirer wonders whether the animal has thrown its first set of teeth, whereas the numskull speaks about the horse's throwing a rider for the first time.

2. The numskull apologizes for not having returned the greeting that he presumes the other man gave him during the supposed encounter.

3. The numskull seems to assume the role of mouse-catching predator, corresponding to a cat in our day, but the joke remains unclear to me.

4. The numskull consoles himself that things could have been worse, but his values are topsy-turvey, since most persons would regard it as less desirable to suffer an injury to their body than to their clothing.

5. The text, and so also the joke, is incomplete, but essentially the same joke reappears later in the collection (*Phil.* 132):

A businessman from Sidon was traveling with another man, and because of a need to defecate he remained a little way behind. His traveling companion went on ahead after writing on the column of a milestone: "Hurry and catch up with me." When the first man read it, he inscribed beneath it: "No, you wait for me."

6. Bunches of grapes are probably hanging by strings from the ceiling, having been brought in for the winter; see Baldwin 1983:65, citing Pliny, *Natural History* 14.3.16.

7. The numskull speaks of the aggression of the river in legal terms that are appropriate for the aggression of a person; see Thierfelder 1968:215.

8. The point of this joke is obscure.

PART THREE

A Popular Handbook

10

FORTUNE-TELLING

The famed oracle of Apollo at Delphi was a place where a person might bring a question to Apollo and, through his priestess, get a response. Although stories about the oracle appear sporadically throughout ancient literature and the many alleged oracular responses can be thought of as a kind of literature, the great oracle itself was not a literary entity.

Many oracles did, however, consist of a fixed literary text and a device for sortition.[1] Dice oracles, for example, were found on the Greek mainland, the islands, Asia Minor, and as far east as India. The traveler Pausanias, writing in the second century A.D., describes one that he saw in a sanctuary of Herakles in Achaea.[2]

> As you descend from Boura toward the sea there is a river named the Boura and a small image of Herakles in a cave called the Herakles of Boura. You can get oracles there by means of knucklebones and a chart. The person consulting the god says a prayer in front of the statue and after praying takes four knucklebones (they are found in abundance next to Herakles) and casts them on the table. For every knucklebone throw there is inscribed on the chart for this purpose an explanation of the throw.

Knucklebones *(astragaloi),* employed as dice by the Greeks, had four sides marked 1, 3, 4, and 6. Cubical dice *(kyboi),* which had six sides, as well as other kinds of dice were also in use.

Although the dice oracle at Boura has not survived, fragments of the texts of many other Greek dice oracles dating from around the second century A.D. have been found at various sites. Most of these oracles were located in the sanctuaries of deities, but others stood beside public roads. Although they differ, they are all obviously variations of the same text. The oracle identifies itself in a couple of verses:

These oracles in five knucklebones come from Pythian Apollo,
Whose voice must always be heeded.

There then follows an oracular message for each possible throw of five
knucklebones, fifty-six messages in all. For example, a consultor who
cast a twenty-three would discover the following about his prospects:

16664   23   Athena
A one, three sixes, and the fifth a four.
Honor Pallas Athena, and everything you want
Will be yours, and your resolves will be achieved:
She will loosen fetters and rescue you in sickness.

The format is consistent throughout. The first line gives the five individual numbers of the throw (the bones were cast all at once, so sequence
was not a factor), their sum, and the divine name of the throw. The remaining lines are in verse, one line describing the throw verbally and the
others giving the oracle proper.

   The same kind of oracle is found in the form of a book, not in Greece
but in India. A user of the Sanskrit *Pasaka-kevali* (Dice Oracle), a poem
that goes back at least to the seventh century A.D., made three sequential
casts with a four-sided die. For each of the sixty-four possible combinations the poem offers an interpretation in several lines of verse which,
exactly as in the Greek texts, first describe the throw and then declare a
good or bad fortune.[3] Obviously it makes no essential difference whether
the text of the oracle was written on stone, as in Greece, or on paper, as
in India.

   Similar to the dice oracles are the so-called alphabet oracles, for
which Greek inscriptions on stone have been found in Asia Minor. The
texts feature twenty-four oracular messages, each consisting of a single
line. For example, representing the first three letters of the Greek alphabet (A, B, Γ), the first three oracles in one inscription are as follows:

You will achieve everything and manage well.
As your helper you will have the Pythian [= Apollo] along with Tyche
   [= Luck].
Sweet produce of the bee, but even more distress.

The device by which the consultor determined the proper oracle is unknown.

   A third kind of oracle with fixed responses was based on the poems
of Homer. A single example is preserved in a Greek papyrus of the third
or fourth century A.D.[4] The consultor cast a cubical die three times,
matched the numbers of his throws with the numbers in the papyrus, and
identified his oracle. For example, if he cast a four, a six, and another

four, he would get the following oracle taken from Homer's *Iliad* (2.200):

464 Wretch, sit still and listen to the words of others.

The idea underlying all these oracles was a productive one, since oracles of this sort were widespread and found in different forms and formats. Two elements run through them all: a fixed list of oracular messages and a device for sortition, usually a form of dice. Since the user did not pose a specific interrogation, the messages necessarily are general in nature, like the fortunes in Chinese fortune cookies.

Building probably upon the structure of these oracles, an unknown person invented a more complex kind of oracle book by adding a fixed list of questions. The consultor now selected a question before employing a means of sortition for reaching the response. Since the oracles were responses to specific questions, they were less general than those described earlier.

The oldest surviving example of this kind of oracle is the so-called *Oracles of Astrampsychus (Sortes Astrampsychi)*, a Greek work that came into being around the second century A.D.[5] It is not known who composed it or where it was composed; nor has the original work survived. But we possess two descendants of it, known to scholars as the first and second editions. The first edition, which arose from a botched attempt to restore a damaged copy of the work, preserves for the most part the phraseology of the archetype, whereas the second edition is more faithful to the structure of the archetype while altering its wording considerably. I focus on the second edition, which is translated here (the first edition does not survive complete). The second edition did not itself remain a static text but frequently underwent change, most markedly as Christians transformed it to a Christian document.

The oracle is made up of an introduction, a list of ninety-two questions numbered 12–103, a table of correspondences, and 1,030 responsed divided into decades, or groups of ten. The introduction takes the form of a letter allegedly written by Astrampsychus of Egypt to King Ptolemy in which the former declares that he is sending the book to the latter. The book, he declares, is the work of Pythagoras and was used by Alexander the Great, who owed to it his success as ruler of the world. But the instructions for its use (at least in their current form) ignore this representation of the book as an oracle for one's personal use and always assume that the user of the book and the owner of the book will be two different persons.

The roster of prominent names is too good to be true, of course, and the epistle is a fraud. Its author represents Astrampsychus as commending the work because Astrampsychus was a renowned sage and magician, and he makes Ptolemy the recipient because as a king he is an important person and because as an Egyptian—even a Greek Egyptian—he can be assumed to be a connoisseur of magic. If a magical book is good enough for the king of Egypt, it ought to be good enough for anyone else.[6] Pythagoras, famed for his mystical doctrines, is made to be its author, and Alexander of Macedon is made to offer an indirect testimonial because he was the most successful man of action known to the Greek world. Although the letter is addressed to a king, the instructions are really intended for an oracle-monger, a professional soothsayer who sold glimpses of the future.

The book was used in the following way. A customer selected one of the ninety-two questions from the list (the introductions in some manuscripts speak of the questions, table, and responses being contained in separate bookrolls). The vendor then told the questioner to pick a number between 1 and 10, assuring him that god would put the number in his mouth. Let us suppose that he chose 91 ("Have I been poisoned?") and god placed the number 3 in his mind. The vendor added these two numbers together (91 + 3 = 94) and located the sum (94) in the table of correspondences. The number next to it (in this case, 29) indicated the particular decade of answers in which the response should be sought. Locating decade number 29 in the bookroll of responses, the oracle-monger now looked down the list of responses until he reached the number that the questioner had originally picked at random (in this case, 3). Response number 3 in decade number 29 read: "You have not been poisoned. Do not be distressed."

The ninety-two questions deal with topics of a personal nature—romance, money, travel, health, and job—focusing generally upon themes of fortune-telling that remain familiar to us today. Many questions imply a male questioner, and none requires a female. Among them a wide range of concerns is attested: slave ("Am I going to be sold?") and free ("Will the fugitive escape my detection?"), public ("Will I be a senator?"), and private ("Will I be caught presently as an adulterer?"), lay ("Will I sell my cargo?") and cleric ("Will I become a bishop?").[7]

For each of the ninety-two questions, there are ten possible answers. For example, a questioner who asked question 70 ("Am I going to marry my girlfriend?") might learn, depending upon the random number he chose,

> You'll marry your girlfriend presently.
> You won't marry your girlfriend just now. She has become a prostitute.
> You won't be able to marry your girlfriend.
> You'll marry your girlfriend. You'll be without care.

And so on, with a balance between positive and negative responses.

In creating his work the author composed ninety-two questions and ten answers to each question, grouping the answers into ninety-two decades. Although it was possible to compose an oracle book of this sort in a straightforward manner, the designer chose not to do so, and on the contrary went to considerable pains to render the structure of his book as opaque as possible, doubtless in order to baffle the customer and increase the mystery attaching to the process. He staggered the ten answers to each question such that the first answer appeared as number 1 in its decade, the second answer appeared as number 2 in the following decade, and so on, until the ten answers to each question were distributed over ten different decades. But even that was not enough, for he then created eleven decades of dummy responses, increasing the number of decades thereby from 92 to 103. The extra 110 answers look as real as the others, but it is impossible for a questioner ever actually to reach them. Since he placed the mute decades at the beginning, he was obliged to number his 92 questions 12–103 (rather than 1–92) in order that no one might ever reach decades 1–11. Nor did even this satisfy him, for the author now shuffled all 103 decades, randomizing the sequence in which they appeared in the book. Finally, he added a table of correspondences, which while appearing mysterious was a key to the decades in their preshuffled state, although this fact was not apparent to the user. The overall result was a book that was easy to use but difficult to fathom, and this must have been his intent.[8]

The work quickly became a folkbook. Its true author was unknown or forgotten, its popularity continued, and the text was reworked in smaller and larger ways in the passage of time. An interesting change was the transformation of the work from a pagan to a Christian oracle. The introductory epistle acquired a Christian continuation, including a prayer to Almighty God that the questioner and soothsayer were instructed to utter together before the consultation, a list of days on which one ought and ought not to consult the oracle (the approved days were Tuesday, Thursday, Saturday, and Sunday), and a list of approved hours for consultation. Some questions, especially those of an erotic nature, were transformed into queries of specifically Christian interest, and the corresponding answers were adjusted accordingly. For example, question 66, which had read "Will I be reconciled with my girlfriend?" became in the first edition "Will I become a bishop?" and in the second edition "Will I become a cleric?"[9] And to the table of correspondences in some manuscripts there was added after each correspondence the instruction "Ask (a particular biblical figure)," such as "Ask Noah" or "Ask Gabriel"; and the names of different biblical figures (replacing, it seems, the names of pagan deities) were placed at the head of the decades of answers, as though the responses in the decades were provided by the figures.

The kind of oracle book represented by the *Sortes Astrampsychi* has proved to be extraordinarily productive, for many versions have been in circulation in many lands. The earliest derivative to survive in Latin, the so-called *Sortes Sangallenses,* was probably composed in southern Gaul in the fourth century A.D.[10] Versions from the Middle Ages, the Renaissance, and later centuries up to the present day are found in Arabic, Persian, Hebrew, Latin, Provençale, French, Italian, Spanish, Romanian, Polish, German, English, and Modern Greek. They differ in magnitude, means of sortition, degree of obfuscation, prescribed ritual, artistic elaboration, and tone (some are serious, others whimsical).[11] For example, *El Mofarandel de los oráculos de Apolo,* a sophisticated sixteenth-century version in Spanish, features elaborate imagery and rhymed responses. A Modern Greek production, *The Great Pythia,* contains eighty questions, which are divided into queries for men (e.g., "Is my beloved faithful to me?"), queries for women (e.g., "Should I believe the oaths of my beloved?"), and common queries ("e.g., "Will I get an inheritance?"), as well as a list of days on which it is forbidden to consult the oracle. In contrast *Napoleon's Book of Fate,* published in England, is a relatively small and simple work of sixteen questions; nevertheless, according to its introduction it was found in an Egyptian tomb and became a treasured possession of Napoleon.[12]

Translators Randall Stewart and Kenneth Morrell render the second edition of the *Oracles of Astrampsychus* into English, omitting the most obvious Christian accretions to the non-Christian original. Their translation is the first into English.

NOTES

1. On the Greek dice oracles and alphabet oracles, see Heinevetter 1912, Ormerod 1912, and Weniger 1917.
2. Pausanias 7.25.10; see further Frazer 1898 4:172–174.
3. Bolte 1903:284–286.
4. For the text see Preisendanz 1973 2:VII 1–167. Following the oracle there is a table of days of the month, indicating which days one may consult the oracle and which days one may not, and, if so, whether to consult in the morning, midday, or afternoon, or anytime.
5. Stewart 1995.
6. Diogenes Laertius (1.2) includes Astrampsychus in a list of Persian magi, of whom the first is Zoroaster. He is credited with a work in Greek on dream interpretation (see no. 2642 in Berkowitz and Squitier 1986) and appears as the author of a Greek magical text (Preisendanz 1973 2:45–50).
7. For the implied world of the *Sortes Astrampsychi,* see Hoogendijk and Clarysse 1981:68–75.
8. On the composition of the work, see Browne 1970.
9. Stewart 1995:139; Stewart (in press).
10. For the *Sortes Sangallenses* (Oracles of St. Gall, named from the monas-

tery in which the manuscript was found), see Winnefeld 1887, Dold 1948, Meister 1951.

11. For a historical survey of oracle books, see Bolte 1903 and 1925.

12. See respectively Quoquim 1986, Anonymous 1984: 87–135, Anonymous 1994:250–268.

LITERATURE

Björck 1939. Bolte 1903, 1925. Browne 1970, 1983. Hoogendijk and Clarysse 1981. Skeat 1954. Stewart 1985, 1995, in press. Tannery 1896.

ANONYMOUS

The Oracles of Astrampsychus

translated by Randall Stewart and Kenneth Morrell

Notes accompanying the translation are by the translators

Introduction

From Astrampsychus the Egyptian to King Ptolemy concerning the foretelling of different questions.

Knowing that nothing that is good and that is useful for human life ought to escape your notice since you are quite inquisitive and zealous about such things, I have gone to great trouble and sent you another book. Culling from the innermost sanctuaries those things which seem to have escaped your notice, I now make them clear so that nothing that is pertinent may remain unknown to you. This book, an invention of Pythagoras the philosopher, is (as you will find when you work through it) a system of prognostication through numbers.

Written at the beginning is a list of the individual questions by means of which the one who comes to you makes his inquiry. Alongside these questions are numbers beginning with 12 and continuing on according to the natural order of counting. Take the number next to the query lying before you, that is, the one selected by the questioner, remember it, and tell the questioner to take by lot and to name for you a number between one and ten, whichever he wants and god gives him at the moment he opens his mouth. Take this number and add it to the number of the question. Moving along, you will find a page which has numbers in black* beginning with 13 and continuing in numeric order, and next to them other numbers in red, not in consecutive order from one, but randomly ordered in accordance with the answer to the question. When you have searched out, in the presence of the questioner, the red number, the one next to the black number, which is the sum of the number of the question and the number that the questioner named, you will find it in the catalogue of decades that are displayed. And, as you examine this decade, look at the numbers arranged in a row at the beginning of the lines and look at the answer next to the number the questioner gave you as his lot. Read this answer.

For example, suppose someone wants to know "Will I advance in office?" next to which is the number 16, and suppose the questioner gave you the number 5 as his lot. Add these numbers together and you will get 21. Search out, in the presence of the questioner, this figure among the numbers in black on the page of numbers and you will find next to it the number 8 in red. Search out, in his presence, the eighth decade and you will find that the answer next to the number 5, the number of his lot, is "You'll advance after a time as you desire."

Again, in the case of the same question—number 16—if the questioner gives as his lot the number 10 (since he is not permitted to obtain any higher number as his lot), you have the number 26 as the sum of both figures. Look at this number among the black numbers on the page and you will find next to it the figure 18 in red. When you search out the eighteenth decade you will find in it that the answer next to the number 10, the number of his lot, is "You'll advance to your good and be distinguished."

Employ this same reasoning and method if another number is obtained as the lot.

Before you, King Alexander of Macedon ruled the world by using this method of deciding matters. And you also will have unwavering renown among all people if you use it.

Farewell.

Questions

12 Will I sail safely?
13 Is it a time to consult the oracle?
14 Will I serve in the army?

15 Will I have a share in the business?
16 Will I advance in office?
17 Will I go out of town?

---

*In the translation, the originally black numbers are printed in bold type and the originally red numbers in ordinary type. —W.H.

18 Is it to my advantage to enter into an agreement?
19 Will I be successful?
20 Will I purchase what is offered?
21 Will I marry and will it be to my advantage?
22 Can I be harmed in the business affair?
23 Will I move from this place?
24 Is my wife having a baby?
25 Will I be able to borrow money?
26 Will I pay back what I owe?
27 Will the traveler return?
28 Will I soon give an accounting?
29 Am I safe from prosecution?
30 Will I rear the baby?
31 Will I be harmed in the business affair?
32 Will I be freed from servitude?
33 Will I inherit from my father?
34 Will I inherit from my mother?
35 Will I be an official in this matter?
36 Will I find the fugitive?
37 Will I have a good end?
38 Will I inherit from a friend?
39 Will I be an agoranomos?[1]
40 Will I find what I have lost?
41 Will I be a teacher?
42 Will I survive the sickness?
43 Will I open a workshop?
44 Will I have a long life?
45 Will I obtain the petition?
46 Will I come to terms with my masters?

47 Will I beget children?
48 Will I inherit from my parents?
49 Will I get the dowry?
50 Will I retain possession of my property?
51 Will I argue my case?
52 Will I inherit from my wife?
53 Will I be safe if informed against?
54 Will the one who is sick survive?
55 Will I get the woman I desire?
56 Will I be released from detention?
57 Will I sell my cargo?
58 If I lend money will I not lose it?
59 Is my wife going to miscarry?
60 Will I be an oikonomos?[2]
61 Will I take a lease and will it benefit me?
62 Will I have an inheritance from someone?
63 Will I defeat my opponent in the trial?
64 Am I going to see a death?
65 Will I be a general?
66 Will I be made a cleric?
67 Will I get the call to office?
68 Will I have hope of trust?
69 Will I win if I put down a deposit for an appeal?
70 Am I going to marry my girlfriend?
71 Will I get my deposit back?·
72 Will I get provisions?
73 Will I remain where I'm going?
74 Am I going to be sold?

---

1. An official or clerk in the marketplace.
2. A minor municipal administrator, a middle-manager, so to speak.

75 Will I get some benefit from my friend?

76 Is it granted to me to have dealings with another?

77 Will I be restored to my place?

78 Will I get an escort?

79 Will I get the money?

80 Is the traveler alive?

81 Will I profit from the undertaking?

82 Are my belongings going to be sold at auction?

83 Will I find a way to sell?

84 Will I buy the thing I have in mind?

85 Will I be prosperous?

86 Will I be banished?

87 Will I be an ambassador?

88 Will I be a senator?

89 Will the fugitive escape my detection?

90 Will I be estranged from my wife?

91 Have I been poisoned?

92 Will I get a bequest?

93 Will I finish what I undertake?

94 Will I be able to see my homeland?

95 Will I become a decemvir?[3]

96 Will I get free from my lot?

97 Will my wife stay with me?

98 Will I remain an elder?

99 Will I buy land or a house?

100 Will I be caught as an adulterer presently?

101 Will I become a bishop?

102 Will I be estranged from my girlfriend?

103 Will the one who is detained be set free?

Table of Correspondences

13 = 20	28 = 37	43 = 70	58 = 94
14 = 101	29 = 56	44 = 99	59 = 86
15 = 44	30 = 102	45 = 62	60 = 61
16 = 98	31 = 38	46 = 31	61 = 75
17 = 19	32 = 34	47 = 33	62 = 52
18 = 93	33 = 3	48 = 5	63 = 6
19 = 79	34 = 68	49 = 45	64 = 42
20 = 35	35 = 76	50 = 100	65 = 78
21 = 8	36 = 50	51 = 41	66 = 48
22 = 46	37 = 53	52 = 39	67 = 59
23 = 24	38 = 4	53 = 11	68 = 7
24 = 27	39 = 96	54 = 74	69 = 1
25 = 71	40 = 40	55 = 10	70 = 95
26 = 18	41 = 21	56 = 49	71 = 90
27 = 15	42 = 23	57 = 83	72 = 17

3. A minor magistrate in a village or town.

73 = 22	84 = 87	95 = 25	106 = 36
74 = 80	85 = 26	96 = 89	107 = 63
75 = 60	86 = 66	97 = 77	108 = 82
76 = 84	87 = 67	98 = 54	109 = 88
77 = 43	88 = 9 .	99 = 65	110 = 91
78 = 14	89 = 72	100 = 73	111 = 92
79 = 55	90 = 13	101 = 32	112 = 97
80 = 30	91 = 81	102 = 16	113 = 103
81 = 64	92 = 12	103 = 2	114 = 47
82 = 58	93 = 57	104 = 51	115 = 69
83 = 85	94 = 29	105 = 28	

Decades of Answers

1

1 You won't have hope of trust.   68
2 You won't get the call to office just now.   67
3 You'll be made a cleric, but late.   66
4 You'll be a general, you'll thrive, and you'll be distinguished.   65
5 You're going to see a death and to rejoice presently.   64
6 You'll have satisfaction. You'll win. Do battle.   63
7 You'll have an inheritance with another trial.   62
8 If you take a lease, you'll suffer a great loss.   61
9 You'll be an oikonomos and you'll be envied by someone.   60
10 She'll miscarry with peril, but she'll be safe.   59

2

1 You'll be reconciled with your wife and with your girlfriend.   102
2 It's not your fate to be a bishop. Don't hope for it.   101
3 It's your lot—and a putrid one—to be an adulterer.   100
4 You'll buy the land or house that you want.   99
5 You'll remain an elder until death.   98
6 Your wife won't stay with you. Marry someone else.   97
7 You'll get free from your lot if you want to.   96
8 You'll become a decemvir soon.   95
9 You'll be able to see your homeland in time.   94
10 You won't finish what you're considering. Don't expect to.   93

3

1 You won't be freed just yet.   32
2 You'll be harmed, but not excessively. Don't be upset.   31
3 With effort the baby will survive.   30

4   You won't be safe from charges just yet. Be concerned.   29
5   You'll soon give an accounting.   28
6   The traveler will return in good health.   27
7   You'll soon pay what you owe and you'll be happy.   26
8   You won't be able to borrow money just yet.   25
9   She'll have a baby and be in peril up to the point of death.   24
10   You won't soon move from your place. Don't fear.   23

4

1   You won't have a good end.   37
2   You won't find the fugitive now.   36
3   You'll be an official and succeed.   35
4   You'll inherit from your mother.   34
5   You'll inherit from your father.   33
6   You won't be freed just yet. Don't expect it.   32
7   You'll be harmed up to the point of words.   31
8   The baby will grow up.   30
9   You won't be safe from the accusation.   29
10   You'll give an accounting, but not for a while.   28

5

1   You won't beget children now. It's not to your advantage.   47
2   You won't come to terms with your masters now.   46
3   Submit the petition. You'll be successful.   45
4   You'll have a long life—and a good one.   44
5   You'll open a workshop to your benefit.   43
6   You'll survive your sickness, but it will take a while.   42
7   You'll be a teacher in a foreign country and become rich.   41
8   You won't find what you have lost now.   40
9   You'll be an agoranomos, but not just yet.   39
10   You won't inherit from your friend; you'll be forsaken.   38

6

1   You won't have an inheritance.   62
2   You'll take a lease and profit greatly.   61
3   You'll serve well as an oikonomos and be distinguished.   60
4   She'll prevail in her future pregnancy.   59
5   Don't make the loan because you'll lose the money.   58
6   You won't sell your cargo right away.   57
7   You'll be freed from detention now.   56
8   You'll get the woman you want and then have second
     thoughts.   55
9   The sick person will be in danger.   54
10   Through your friends you'll be safe from the allegation.   53

7

1	You'll get the call to office.	67
2	You won't be made a cleric.	66
3	You'll be a general and be in peril.	65
4	You're going to see a death now.	64
5	You'll win soon. Do battle rejoicing.	63
6	You'll have an inheritance, but not all of it.	62
7	You won't take a lease just now, since it won't benefit you.	61
8	You'll be an oikonomos soon and you'll be distinguished.	60
9	Your wife won't miscarry. Don't worry.	59
10	If you lend the money, make the loan once you have collateral.	58

8

1	You won't purchase what is offered.	20
2	You'll succeed at last, when you have grown a little older.	19
3	Having come to an agreement, you'll profit greatly.	18
4	Don't travel out of town. It's not to your advantage.	17
5	You'll advance after a time as you desire.	16
6	You'll have a share and fail.	15
7	If you serve in the army, you'll regret it.	14
8	You don't have the hour for inquiring.	13
9	If you sail soon, you'll be in danger.	12
10	The one who is detained will be set free in time.	103

9

1	You have not erred. Become an ambassador.	87
2	You won't be banished, but you'll be maltreated to some extent.	86
3	You'll never be prosperous.	85
4	You'll buy the thing you have in mind and sell it after you've used it.	84
5	If you sell just now, you'll suffer.	83
6	Your belongings won't be sold at auction. Don't be afraid.	82
7	You'll profit from the undertaking a little.	81
8	The traveler isn't alive. He was poisoned.	80
9	You'll get the money with much trouble.	79
10	You'll get an escort presently.	78

10

1	He will recover from the sickness soon.	54
2	You won't be safe from the allegation. Circumvent it.	53
3	You'll inherit from your wife, because she'll die first.	52
4	Don't argue your case right now. You'll lose.	51

5 Not all of your property will remain in your possession.   50
6 You'll get the dowry after a time.   49
7 You'll inherit from your parents, but not as the sole heir.   48
8 You'll beget children, rear them, and bury them.   47
9 With effort you'll come to terms with your masters.   46
10 You'll submit your petition and benefit.   45

11

1 You won't inherit from your wife.   52
2 Argue your case right now. You'll win.   51
3 All of your property will remain in your possession.   50
4 You won't obtain the dowry right away.   49
5 In a short time, you'll inherit from your parents.   48
6 You'll be blessed with children, but you'll be distressed by
    them.   47
7 You won't come to terms with your masters now.   46
8 You won't be successful with your petition right away.   45
9 You'll have an average lifespan. Don't be upset. Pray instead.   44
10 You'll open a workshop with a struggle.   43

12

1 You have been poisoned. Treat yourself.   91
2 You won't be estranged from your wife until you die.   90
3 The fugitive is escaping your detection now.   89
4 You'll be a senator, but not just yet.   88
5 You won't be an ambassador by yourself. Don't hope for it.   87
6 You won't be banished. Don't be afraid.   86
7 You won't be completely prosperous.   85
8 You won't buy the thing you have in mind just yet.   84
9 You'll sell to your detriment.   83
10 Your belongings won't be sold at auction. Don't be afraid.   82

13

1 The fugitive won't escape your detection.   89
2 You'll become a senator by means of a gift.   88
3 You'll be an ambassador by yourself and you'll profit.   87
4 You'll be banished for a time and you'll profit.   86
5 You won't be prosperous.   85
6 You won't buy it just yet. Get it out of your mind.   84
7 You won't find a way to sell just now.   83
8 Your belongings won't be sold at auction.   82
9 You'll profit from the undertaking.   81
10 The traveler is alive and healthy.   80

14

1	You won't be restored to your place.	77
2	It's not granted to you to have dealings with another.	76
3	You'll benefit from your friend's business.	75
4	You'll be sold, but not just yet.	74
5	You won't remain where you are going.	73
6	You'll get provisions, but not just now.	72
7	You'll get your deposit back.	71
8	If you marry your girlfriend, you'll suffer.	70
9	Put down a deposit. You'll win.	69
10	You won't have hope of trust.	68

15

1	You won't pay back what you owe.	26
2	You'll borrow money with collateral.	25
3	Your wife will have a baby and it will survive.	24
4	You'll move from your place for the worse.	23
5	You'll be harmed, but only a little.	22
6	You'll marry, but then you'll dissolve the marriage.	21
7	You'll purchase what is offered and you'll suffer.	20
8	You'll be successful finally. Don't worry.	19
9	You'll come quickly to an agreement and profit.	18
10	You'll go out of town suddenly and it will be for your good.	17

16

1	It's not your lot to be a bishop.	101
2	You'll be caught in adultery soon.	100
3	You'll buy the field or house that you want.	99
4	You'll remain an elder until old age.	98
5	Your wife won't stay with you. She's committing adultery.	97
6	You'll get free from your lot with a fight.	96
7	You'll become a decemvir soon.	95
8	You'll be able to see your homeland to your advantage.	94
9	You'll finish quickly what you undertake.	93
10	You won't get a bequest. You've been discredited.	92

17

1	You won't get your deposit back.	71
2	You won't marry your girlfriend now. She's become a prostitute.	70
3	Don't put down a deposit. You'll be defeated.	69
4	You'll have excellent hope of trust.	68
5	You'll get the call to office.	67
6	You'll be made a cleric.	66

7	You won't be a general. It will be to your benefit.	65
8	You're going to see a death that is advantageous.	64
9	You'll win. Do battle to the end.	63
10	You'll have an inheritance soon.	62

18

1	You won't be able to borrow money.	25
2	Your wife will give birth to a fine baby and do well.	24
3	You won't move from your place just yet.	23
4	You won't be harmed. Don't be distressed.	22
5	You'll marry and, though you desired the marriage, you'll dissolve it.	21
6	You'll quickly purchase what is offered.	20
7	You'll be successful as a result of your own efforts.	19
8	You won't come to an agreement with anyone yet.	18
9	You won't go out of town now. Wait.	17
10	You'll advance to your good and be distinguished.	16

19

1	You won't advance just now.	16
2	You'll share in the business well and benefit.	15
3	You'll serve in the army with suffering and you'll regret it.	14
4	Don't inquire. The day is adverse.	13
5	You'll sail after being delayed.	12
6	The one who is detained will be freed from his confinement.	103
7	You'll be reconciled with your wife by force.	102
8	You'll become a bishop and be profited.	101
9	You'll be caught in adultery. Take heed.	100
10	You won't buy the property now.	99

20

1	You won't sail well.	12
2	The one who is detained will be set free.	103
3	You'll be reconciled with your wife in a way you don't expect.	102
4	You'll become a bishop in a way you don't expect.	101
5	You'll be caught in adultery soon.	100
6	You won't buy land now.	99
7	Your girlfriend won't remain with you. She's getting married.	98
8	Your wife will stay with you until old age.	97
9	You'll get free from your girlfriend.	96
10	You'll become a decemvir in a way you don't know.	95

21

1	You won't find what is lost.	40
2	You won't be an agoranomos just yet. Wait.	39
3	You'll inherit from your friend with a trial.	38
4	You won't have a good end. It's up to you to inquire further.	37
5	You won't find the fugitive now, but after a time.	36
6	You'll be an official, and you'll be esteemed and honored.	35
7	You'll inherit half of your mother's estate.	34
8	You won't inherit from your father, because you'll die first.	33
9	You won't be freed now, but after a time.	32
10	You'll be harmed, but not just yet.	31

22

1	You'll get provisions.	72
2	You won't get your deposit back.	71
3	You won't be able to marry your girlfriend.	70
4	Put down a deposit. You'll win.	69
5	You'll have excellent hope of trust.	68
6	You'll get the call to office.	67
7	You'll be made a cleric, but not for a while.	66
8	You'll be a general, you'll thrive, and you'll be distinguished.	65
9	You're going to see two deaths that are unprofitable.	64
10	You won't win for a while. Don't think about it.	63

23

1	You won't be able to be a teacher.	41
2	You won't soon find what is lost.	40
3	You'll soon be an agoranomos.	39
4	You won't inherit from your friend. Don't hope for it.	38
5	You'll have a good end.	37
6	You won't find the fugitive. He has sailed away.	36
7	It's your lot to be an official.	35
8	You won't inherit from your mother. She'll bury you.	34
9	You'll inherit a third of your father's estate.	33
10	You won't be freed. Be silent.	32

24

1	You'll be harmed greatly.	22
2	You'll marry and then be sorry because you'll have gained nothing.	21
3	You'll purchase what is offered if you desire.	20
4	You'll succeed, having inherited from others.	19
5	You'll come to an agreement and benefit greatly.	18
6	You'll go out of town and have second thoughts.	17

7   You'll advance as a result of the unexpected.   16
8   It's not to your advantage to have a share. You'll suffer losses.   15
9   You'll serve in the army and you'll advance quickly.   14
10 Wait today and inquire tomorrow.   13

25

1   You won't be able to see your homeland.   94
2   You won't finish what you undertake.   93
3   You'll get a bequest, but a small one.   92
4   You haven't been poisoned, but you have been bewitched.   91
5   You'll be estranged from your wife, but you'll be derided.   90
6   The fugitive will escape your detection for a little while.   89
7   You'll be a senator and a bankrupt fraud.   88
8   You'll be an ambassador and you'll prosper, if you press for it.   87
9   You won't be banished. Don't be afraid at all.   86
10 You'll be prosperous and distinguished.   85

26

1   You'll buy the thing you have in mind.   84
2   You won't find a way to sell and make a profit just now.   83
3   Your belongings won't be sold at auction. Relax.   82
4   You'll profit a little from the undertaking.   81
5   The traveler is alive. Don't be distressed. He's coming.   80
6   You'll get the money after a while.   79
7   You won't get an escort just now.   78
8   You'll be restored to your place.   77
9   Don't have dealings with another just now. You'll be harmed.   76
10 You won't get any benefit from your friend.   75

27

1   You won't move from your place.   23
2   You won't be harmed. Don't be distressed. Pray instead.   22
3   You'll suddenly marry a woman whom you know and want.   21
4   You'll purchase with effort what is offered.   20
5   You'll succeed as a consequence of your own efforts.   19
6   You'll soon come to an agreement and profit greatly.   18
7   You won't go out of town for a while.   17
8   You'll advance suddenly when you don't realize it.   16
9   Don't share in the business. It's not to your advantage.   15
10 You'll serve, but not just yet.   14

28

1   You'll sail well.   12
2   The one who is detained will be set free with effort.   103

3	You'll be reconciled with your girlfriend and you'll be sorry.	102
4	You'll become a bishop after you have worked a great deal.	101
5	You won't be caught as an adulterer. Don't be distressed.	100
6	You'll buy land and a house.	99
7	You won't remain an elder.	98
8	Your wife will stay with you if you wish.	97
9	You won't get free from your lot until you die.	96
10	You'll become a decemvir.	95

29

1	You'll finish what you undertake.	93
2	You won't get a complete bequest.	92
3	You haven't been poisoned. Don't be distressed.	91
4	You won't be reconciled with your wife.	90
5	The fugitive won't escape your detection.	89
6	You'll be a senator, but not just yet.	88
7	You'll be an ambassador, but not by yourself.	87
8	You won't be banished. Don't be distressed.	86
9	You'll become prosperous suddenly.	85
10	You'll buy the thing you have in mind, if you want to.	84

30

1	You won't get the money just yet.	79
2	You'll get an escort with much effort.	78
3	You'll be restored to your place.	77
4	You won't be able to have dealings with another.	76
5	You won't benefit at all from your friend.	75
6	You won't be sold just yet, but it won't benefit you.	74
7	You won't remain where you are going.	73
8	You won't get provisions.	72
9	You won't get your deposit back.	71
10	You'll marry your girlfriend and you'll suffer.	70

31

1	You'll submit your petition in vain.	45
2	You won't have a long life.	44
3	You'll eventually open a workshop.	43
4	You'll survive your illness, if you take heed.	42
5	You'll become a teacher suddenly.	41
6	You won't find what is lost.	40
7	You'll be an agoranomos and you'll benefit.	39
8	You won't inherit from your friend. Don't expect it.	38
9	You'll have a good end.	37
10	You'll soon find the fugitive.	36

32

1	You won't be caught in adultery.	100
2	You won't buy land or a house.	99
3	You won't remain an elder.	98
4	Your first wife won't stay with you.	97
5	You'll get free from your lot.	96
6	You won't become a decemvir just yet.	95
7	You won't be able to see your homeland just now.	94
8	You won't finish what you undertake.	93
9	You won't get a bequest. Don't expect it.	92
10	You've been poisoned. Treat yourself.	91

33

1	You won't come to terms with your masters.	46
2	Don't submit your petition just yet.	45
3	You'll have a long life and suffer pains in your feet.	44
4	You won't open a workshop just yet.	43
5	You'll survive your illness, for you've been called back.	42
6	You won't be a teacher in your homeland.	41
7	You won't find what is lost.	40
8	Know well; you won't soon be an agoranomos.	39
9	You won't inherit from your friend. You'll scoff.	38
10	You won't have a good end. You'll ask for more.	37

34

1	You'll be harmed terribly.	31
2	You'll rear the baby.	30
3	You'll be safe from the accusation.	29
4	You'll give an accounting. Don't be distressed.	28
5	The traveler won't return. He has married.	27
6	You won't pay back what you owe.	26
7	You'll borrow money and immediately spend it.	25
8	She'll have a baby girl with peril.	24
9	You'll move from your place. Get packed.	23
10	You won't be harmed. Don't be distressed.	22

35

1	You won't be successful.	19
2	You'll suddenly come to an agreement and you'll profit.	18
3	You won't go out of town for a while.	17
4	You'll advance quickly to a good place.	16
5	Don't share in the business. It's not to your advantage.	15
6	If you serve, you'll be sorry.	14
7	Now is not the time. Give up just now.	13

8	Don't sail just yet. You'll be shipwrecked.	12
9	The one who is detained will be set free soon.	103
10	You won't be reconciled with your wife.	102

36

1	You won't get any benefit from your friend.	75
2	Don't sail. I'm warning you.	12
3	The one who is detained will be set free.	103
4	You won't be estranged from your girlfriend.	102
5	You won't become a bishop. Don't expect it.	101
6	You won't be caught as an adulterer for the time being.	100
7	You'll buy the property and it won't stay with you.	99
8	You'll remain an elder.	98
9	Your wife won't stay with you.	97
10	You won't get free from your lot.	96

37

1	The traveler won't return.	27
2	You'll now pay back what you owe.	26
3	You'll borrow money and suffer. It won't last.	25
4	She'll give birth to a boy with peril.	24
5	You won't move from your place for a while.	23
6	You won't be harmed. Don't be distressed.	22
7	You'll marry a woman from your daily acquaintance.	21
8	You'll purchase with effort what is offered.	20
9	You'll succeed in everything.	19
10	You'll come to an agreement and devote your time to the business.	18

38

1	The baby will survive for the good.	30
2	You won't be safe from the accusation. You've been prejudged.	29
3	You'll soon give an accounting for the good.	28
4	The traveler won't return just yet. Don't expect him.	27
5	You'll now pay back what you owe and you'll rejoice.	26
6	No one will lend money to you just now. Wait.	25
7	She'll have a baby girl who won't live long.	24
8	You'll soon move from your place for the better.	23
9	You'll suffer a loss at first, but in the end you'll have a profit.	22
10	You'll be harmed in your first marriage. Persevere.	21

39

1	Argue your case.	51
2	Your property will remain in your possession.	50

3	You won't obtain the dowry unless you sue.	49
4	You alone will inherit from your parents.	48
5	You'll soon beget the children and be distressed by them.	47
6	You won't come to terms with your masters now.	46
7	You'll soon submit your petition.	45
8	You'll have a long life and wealth. You'll ask for more.	44
9	You won't open a workshop now. Wait.	43
10	You'll recover from your illness quickly. Just be cheerful.	42

40

1	You won't be an agoranomos.	39
2	You won't inherit from your friend. Why do you hope?	38
3	You'll have a good end, but it will be short.	37
4	You won't find the fugitive now.	36
5	You have the favorable lot of an official.	35
6	You'll inherit from your mother now.	34
7	You'll never inherit from your father.	33
8	You'll be freed with a good bequest.	32
9	You won't be harmed. Don't be distressed at all.	31
10	The baby will survive and grow quickly.	30

41

1	Your property won't remain in your possession.	50
2	You won't obtain the dowry. Don't sue.	49
3	You won't inherit from your parents. You'll die first.	48
4	You won't beget children with her. Don't expect it.	47
5	You'll come to terms with your masters after a while.	46
6	You won't submit your petition soon. It will be to your advantage.	45
7	After a time you'll succeed and grow old.	44
8	You'll open a workshop and be rich.	43
9	You won't recover from your illness.	42
10	You won't be a teacher. Do something else.	41

42

1	You won't win. Keep silent.	63
2	You'll have an inheritance when you are not hoping for it.	62
3	You won't take a lease just now. Wait. Don't rush.	61
4	You'll be an oikonomos and many people will bring charges against you.	60
5	Your wife won't miscarry. Be happy.	59
6	Don't lend the money. You'll recover it slowly.	58
7	You'll sell your cargo and profit.	57
8	You won't be released from detention. Persevere.	56

9 You'll get the woman you desire and be rich. 55
10 The sick person will be ill for some time, but he will regain
his health. 54

43

1 It won't be granted to you to have deaings with another. 76
2 You'll benefit a little from your friend. 75
3 You'll be sold and you'll be sorry when you don't profit at
all. 74
4 Where you are going you won't remain, because it won't
benefit you. 73
5 You'll get provisions in part. 72
6 You won't get your deposit back. 71
7 It won't benefit you to marry your girlfriend. 70
8 Don't put down a deposit. You'll be defeated. 69
9 You'll have very excellent hope of trust. 68
10 You won't get the call to office now. 67

44

1 It isn't granted to you to serve in the army. 14
2 Inquire and hear the truth. 13
3 You'll sail soon and you'll suffer bad weather. 12
4 The one who is detained will be set free presently. 103
5 You'll be reconciled with your wife and you'll be sorry. 102
6 You'll become a bishop when you have grown old. 101
7 You'll be caught in adultery and you'll be punished. 100
8 You won't buy the property. Don't expect it. 99
9 Your girlfriend won't remain with you. She desires someone
else. 98
10 Your wife will stay with you until old age. 97

45

1 You'll inherit from your parents. 48
2 You'll be the father of a boy and a girl and you'll rejoice. 47
3 You'll come to terms with your masters and benefit. 46
4 You'll submit your petition in vain. 45
5 You won't have a long life. Put your affairs in order. 44
6 You won't open a workshop. It's not granted to you. 43
7 You'll recover from your illness, but it will take some time. 42
8 You'll become a teacher and succeed in the business. 41
9 You'll find what is lost now. Give it some thought. 40
10 You won't be an agoranomos. You'll be hindered. 39

46

1	You won't marry just now.	21
2	You won't purchase what is offered.	20
3	You'll succeed as a consequence of your own labors.	19
4	You won't come to an agreement. Don't do it.	18
5	You'll go out of town suddenly and benefit greatly.	17
6	You'll advance when you're not expecting it.	16
7	You'll have a share in the business, you'll suffer, and you'll be sorry.	15
8	You'll serve in the army and advance quickly.	14
9	Ask with faith and hear the truth.	13
10	You'll sail well after being delayed.	12

47

1	You'll be safe from the accusation by means of a weighty appeal.	29
2	You'll give an accouanting after a while.	28
3	The traveler will return soon in good spirits.	27
4	You'll pay back in part what you owe. Don't be distressed.	26
5	You'll borrow money with collateral and, at the right time, tear it up.	25
6	She'll have an unprofitable baby. Don't be distressed.	24
7	You'll move from your place. Get ready. Be happy.	23
8	You can be harmed. Be afraid and look out for yourself.	22
9	You'll marry and, filled with regret, you'll blame yourself.	21
10	You won't purchase what is offered, dear friend.	20

48

1	You'll never be a general.	65
2	You're not going to see a death now. Don't be distressed.	64
3	You'll win. Do battle to the death.	63
4	You'll have an inheritance and you'll die soon.	62
5	You'll take a lease and profit greatly.	61
6	You'll be an oikonomos, you'll be charged, and you'll be begrudged.	60
7	She won't miscarry. Don't be afraid; pray instead.	59
8	You'll lend the money and gratefully recover it.	58
9	You'll sell your cargo without a problem.	57
10	You'll be released from detention. Be cheerful.	56

49

1	You'll get the woman you want.	55
2	The sick person will recover with considerable effort.	54
3	You won't be safe from the allegation. Circumvent it.	53

4	You'll inherit from your wife, but you won't be the sole heir.	52
5	Don't argue your case just yet. You'll lose.	51
6	Your property will remain in your possession.	50
7	You won't get the dowry.	49
8	You alone will inherit from your parents.	48
9	You'll beget the children and find great happiness in them.	47
10	You won't come to terms with your masters just yet.	46

50

1	You won't be able to be an official now.	35
2	You'll inherit half of your mother's estate.	34
3	You won't inherit from your father. Don't hope for it.	33
4	You won't be freed just yet, but after a time.	32
5	You won't be harmed. Don't be distressed, but persevere.	31
6	The baby will survive with toil.	30
7	You'll be safe from the accusation through a good friend.	29
8	You'll soon give an accounting for the good.	28
9	The traveler will return in good health.	27
10	You won't pay back what you owe just yet. Wait.	26

51

1	The one who is detained won't be set free.	103
2	You'll be estranged from your girlfriend presently.	102
3	You'll become a bishop soon and you'll be sorry.	101
4	You'll be caught as an adulterer and you won't suffer at all.	100
5	You'll buy the property you desire.	99
6	You'll remain an elder until old age.	98
7	Your wife won't stay with you, since she's committing adultery.	97
8	You'll get free from your lot. See to it.	96
9	You'll become a decemvir in a hurry.	95
10	You won't see your homeland. Count on it.	94

52

1	If you take a lease just now, you'll suffer a loss.	61
2	Very soon you'll serve well as an oikonomos.	60
3	She'll miscarry and be in danger. Take heed.	59
4	You'll lend the money; eventually you'll recover it with a fight.	58
5	You'll sell your cargo quickly and be pleased.	57
6	You'll be released from detention quickly.	56
7	You'll get the woman you desire to your ill.	55
8	The sick person will recover with risk.	54

9 You'll be safe from the allegation by means of a weighty appeal.   53
10 You won't inherit from your wife. Don't hope for it.   52

53

1 You won't find the fugitive.   36
2 You'll be an official and succeed and be distinguished.   35
3 You alone will inherit from your mother.   34
4 You won't inherit from your father. You'll die first.   33
5 You'll be freed with an appeal once you've paid money.   32
6 You'll be harmed terribly, but don't worry.   31
7 The baby won't live. It will die soon.   30
8 You won't be safe from the accusation. Make preparations.   29
9 You'll soon give an accounting and you'll benefit.   28
10 The traveler won't return because he's busy.   27

54

1 Your wife won't stay with you.   97
2 You won't be able to get free from your lot.   96
3 You won't become a decemvir. Don't hope for it.   95
4 You'll see your homeland very soon.   94
5 You won't finish what you undertake.   93
6 You'll get a bequest to your great detriment.   92
7 You have not been poisoned, but you have been bewitched.   91
8 You won't be estranged from your wife. Persevere.   90
9 The fugitive will escape your detection for a little while.   89
10 You won't be a senator for a while. Wait.   88

55

1 You won't get an escort.   78
2 You'll be restored to your place.   77
3 You'll have dealings with another and you'll profit from the works of others.   76
4 You'll get a great benefit from your friend.   75
5 You won't be sold. It won't benefit you. Stand fast.   74
6 You'll stay where you're going for a short season.   73
7 You'll get the provisions after a while.   72
8 You'll get your deposit back without peril.   71
9 You won't marry your girlfriend. Don't ramble.   70
10 If you put down a deposit, you'll be worsted.   69

56

1 You'll give an accounting.   28
2 The traveler won't return just yet.   27

3   You'll now pay back what you owe, if you wish. 26
4   You won't be able to borrow money just yet. Wait. 25
5   She'll give birth with great peril. 24
6   You'll move from your place for the better. 23
7   You can be harmed a little, but don't be distressed. 22
8   You won't marry just yet. Wait. It will be to your advantage. 21
9   You'll purchase what is offered and rejoice. 20
10 You'll soon succeed for the better. 19

57

1   You won't get a bequest. Don't expect it. 92
2   You've been poisoned. Treat yourself. 91
3   You'll be reconciled with your wife and you'll be sorry. 90
4   The fugitive will escape your detection for a season. 89
5   You won't be a senator just yet. Don't think about it. 88
6   You won't be an ambassador by yourself since it won't benefit you. 87
7   You won't be banished. Don't be afraid. Be cheerful. 86
8   You'll be prosperous and pleasing. 85
9   You'll buy the thing you have in mind and you'll be sorry. 84
10 You won't find a way to sell just now. Wait. 83

58

1   You'll profit a little from the undertaking. 81
2   The traveler is alive and will return after a time. 80
3   You'll get the money after a time. 79
4   You won't get an escort just now. 78
5   You'll be restored to your place. 77
6   If you have dealings with another, you'll be harmed. 76
7   You'll benefit from your friend. 75
8   You won't be sold to your benefit. 74
9   You'll remain where you are going if you hurry. 73
10 You'll get provisions—and in a good way. 72

59

1   You won't be made a cleric. 66
2   You won't be a gereral just now. Don't hope for it. 65
3   You're not going to see a death. 64
4   You won't win completely. Don't hope for it. 63
5   You'll have an inheritance, but you won't be the sole heir. 62
6   You'll take a lease and be greatly enriched. 61
7   You won't be an oikonomos just now. It's not granted to you. 60
8   She won't miscarry. Don't be afraid. 59

9   Don't lend the money. Don't be trusting lest you have regrets.   58
10 You'll sell your cargo without a problem.   57

60

1   You'll be sold, but not just yet.   74
2   You'll remain where you're going for a short while.   73
3   You'll get provisions now—and good ones.   72
4   You'll get your deposit back.   71
5   You'll marry your girlfriend, but not now.   70
6   Put down a deposit. You'll win and you'll profit.   69
7   You won't have hope of trust at all.   68
8   You'll get the call to office quickly.   67
9   You'll be made a cleric after a while.   66
10 You won't ever be a general. Don't hope for it.   65

61

1   She'll miscarry and she'll be in danger.   59
2   You'll lend as much money as you wish once you have collateral.   58
3   You'll sell your cargo eventually. Don't despair.   57
4   You won't be released from detention. Wait.   56
5   You won't get the woman you desire.   55
6   The sick person will recover after being ill for a long time.   54
7   You'll be safe from the allegation through your friends.   53
8   You won't inherit from your wife.   52
9   State your case soon. You'll win. Fight it out.   51
10 Your property won't remain in your possession for very long.   50

62

1   You won't have a long life.   44
2   You won't open a workshop just yet.   43
3   You won't recover from your sickness. Settle your affairs.   42
4   You won't be a teacher. Do something else.   41
5   You won't find what is lost now.   40
6   You won't be an agoranomos just yet. Don't hope for it.   39
7   You won't inherit from your friend now.   38
8   You won't have a good end. Help yourself.   37
9   You won't find the fugitive now.   36
10 You won't be able to be an official just yet, but after a time.   35

63

1   You'll serve in the army to your detriment.   14
2   You'll work with toil and much exertion.   13
3   You'll sail well now and you'll have great enjoyment.   12

4	The one who is detained won't be set free just now.	103
5	You'll be reconciled with your wife to your benefit.	102
6	It's not your fate to be a bishop. Don't hope for it.	101
7	You're not an adulterer, but your wife loves another man.	100
8	You won't buy land or a house just now.	99
9	You won't remain an elder. You'll have very bad luck.	98
10	Your wife won't stay with you.	97

64

1	The traveler is not safe.	80
2	Concerning the money, send away quickly.	79
3	You won't get an escort in the way you want.	78
4	You won't be restored to your place.	77
5	You'll benefit, if you have dealings with another.	76
6	You won't have a benefit in your friend.	75
7	Where you'll be purchased, you'll have regrets.	74
8	You'll remain where you're going and you'll fare well.	73
9	You'll come to terms in the matter of the provisions.	72
10	You won't get your deposit back.	71

65

1	You won't remain an elder.	98
2	Your wife won't stay with you until old age.	97
3	You won't get free from your lot until you die.	96
4	You'll become a decemvir very quickly.	95
5	You won't be able to see your homeland.	94
6	You'll finish quickly what you undertake.	93
7	You'll get a bequest, but a little one.	92
8	You've been poisoned. Treat yourself.	91
9	You'll never be estranged from your wife.	90
10	The fugitive will escape your detection for a little while.	89

66

1	You'll be prosperous.	85
2	You won't buy what you have in mind, since it won't be to your benefit.	84
3	You'll sell and you'll profit a great deal.	83
4	Your belongings will be sold at auction and you'll acquire others.	82
5	You'll profit from the undertaking a little.	81
6	The traveler is alive and will return in good health.	80
7	You'll get part of the money.	79
8	You won't get an escort just now.	78

9   You won't be restored to your place.   77
10 If you have dealings with another, you'll be harmed.   76

67

1   You'll be banished for a little while.   86
2   You won't be completely prosperous.   85
3   You'll buy what you have in mind and you'll be happy with
    it.   84
4   You'll find a way to sell—late, but well.   83
5   Your belongings won't be sold at auction. Don't be afraid.   82
6   You'll profit from the undertaking a great deal.   81
7   The traveler is not alive. He won't return.   80
8   You'll get the money presently.   79
9   You won't get an escort now.   78
10 You won't be restored to your place.   77

68

1   You won't inherit from your father.   33
2   You won't be freed just yet. Don't expect it.   32
3   You won't be harmed. Don't be afraid, but rather be happy.   31
4   The baby will survive with toil.   30
5   You'll be safe from the accusation by means of an appeal.   29
6   You'll give an accounting freely.   28
7   The traveler, having been delayed, will return. Be happy.   27
8   You won't pay back what you owe just yet, but after a while.   26
9   You'll eventually borrow money from the person you desire.   25
10 She'll have a baby that is unprofitable.   24

69

1   You'll sail now.   12
2   The one who is detained will be set free now.   103
3   You'll be reconciled with your wife after a time.   102
4   It's not your lot to be a bishop. Don't hope for it.   101
5   You won't be caught as an adulterer.   100
6   You'll buy land or a house.   99
7   Your wife will remain with you since she has self-control.   98
8   Your wife won't stay with you. She has a boyfriend.   97
9   You'll get free from your girlfriend, because you'll be jealous
    of her.   96
10 You won't ever become a decemvir.   95

70

1   You'll recover from your illness.   42
2   You won't be a teacher. Do something else.   41

3	You'll find what is lost quickly and be happy.	40
4	You'll be an agoranomos and benefit greatly.	39
5	You'll inherit half of your friend's estate.	38
6	You'll have a good end. Just pray.	37
7	You'll find the fugitive soon.	36
8	You'll be an official, you'll succeed, and you'll be honored.	35
9	You won't inherit from your mother. That's reserved for someone else.	34
10	You alone will inherit from your father.	33

71

1	She'll have a baby with peril.	24
2	You'll suddenly move from your place for the better.	23
3	You'll be harmed in this affair, but in the other you'll benefit.	22
4	You can marry to your benefit, if you hurry.	21
5	You won't purchase what is offered. You don't have the means.	20
6	You'll succeed at last and be master of the household.	19
7	You'll come to an agreement and profit through others.	18
8	You'll go out of town suddenly and profit.	17
9	You won't advance just yet. Don't expect it.	16
10	If you share in the business, you'll suffer greatly.	15

72

1	You won't be a senator.	88
2	You won't be an ambassador by yourself since it won't benefit you.	87
3	You won't be banished. Don't be afraid.	86
4	You won't be prosperous at all.	85
5	You'll buy the thing you have in mind and you'll be sorry.	84
6	You'll find a way to sell after a while.	83
7	Your belongings will be sold at auction. Take heed.	82
8	You'll profit from the undertaking. Work at it.	81
9	The traveler is returning with a good friend.	80
10	You won't get all of the money.	79

73

1	You won't buy land or a house.	99
2	You'll remain an elder until old age.	98
3	Your wife won't stay with you. She's committing adultery.	97
4	You'll get free from your lot in your old age.	96
5	You'll become a decemvir suddenly.	95
6	You'll be able to see your homeland, but late.	94
7	You'll finish quickly what you undertake.	93

8	You'll get a bequest, but a little one.	92
9	You haven't been poisoned. Why are you being irrational?	91
10	You won't be estranged from your wife. Relax.	90

74

1	You won't be safe from the allegation.	53
2	You alone will inherit from your wife.	52
3	Argue your case. You'll win. Fight it out.	51
4	Your property will not remain in your possession until old age.	50
5	You won't get the dowry. You'll find nothing.	49
6	You won't inherit from your parents. You're hated.	48
7	You won't beget children soon. Don't expect it to happen.	47
8	You'll come to terms with your masters and be treated with affection.	46
9	Submit your petition. You'll obtain whatever you need.	45
10	You'll have a long life—and a very good one.	44

75

1	You won't be an oikonomos.	60
2	She'll miscarry and be in danger up to the point of death.	59
3	If you lend money, you'll recover it slowly.	58
4	You won't sell your cargo quickly.	57
5	You'll be released from detention right away.	56
6	You'll get the woman you desire to your ill.	55
7	The sick person will recover with great effort.	54
8	You'll be safe from the allegation quickly.	53
9	You won't inherit from your wife as sole heir.	52
10	Argue your case. You'll win. Fight it out.	51

76

1	You'll inherit from your mother.	34
2	You won't inherit from your father. Don't hope for it.	33
3	You'll be freed, but not just yet.	32
4	You won't be harmed now, but after a time.	31
5	Don't rear the baby. I counsel you.	30
6	You'll be in peril with regard to the accusation.	29
7	You'll give an accounting with insolence.	28
8	The traveler won't return. He's busy.	27
9	You'll now pay back what you owe as a result of your efforts.	26
10	You won't be able to borrow money just yet. Someone doesn't trust you.	25

77

1	Your lot won't stay with you.	96
2	You'll become a decemvir in a way you don't know.	95
3	You'll be able to see your homeland suddenly.	94
4	You'll finish what you undertake and you'll be distinguished.	93
5	You won't get a bequest. Don't hope for it.	92
6	You haven't been poisoned. Don't be afraid; pray instead.	91
7	You'll be estranged from your wife to your benefit.	90
8	The fugitive won't escape your detection; you'll stumble onto him.	89
9	You'll be a senator, but not just yet.	88
10	You'll be an ambassador by yourself and you'll be very distinguished.	87

78

1	You're going to see a death that you don't want.	64
2	You won't win just now. Be patient; it will benefit you.	63
3	You won't have an inheritance just now. Be silent. You won't profit at all.	62
4	You'll take a lease and profit as much as you desire.	61
5	You'll be an oikonomos presently. No one is hindering you.	60
6	She won't miscarry. Don't be afraid at all.	59
7	Lend the money with collateral and you won't lose it.	58
8	You won't sell your cargo quickly. Don't hurry.	57
9	You'll be released from detention contrary to expectations.	56
10	You won't get the woman you desire. It's to your advantage.	55

79

1	It's not to your advantage to enter an agreement.	18
2	You'll go out of town suddenly and for some time.	17
3	You won't advance just yet. You're hindered by others.	16
4	You'll share well in the business and be grateful.	15
5	You'll serve in the army and advance quickly.	14
6	Inquire in the sixth hour and you'll hear the truth.	13
7	You'll sail well after being delayed.	12
8	The one who is detained will be set free with effort.	103
9	You'll be reconciled with your wife very soon.	102
10	You'll become a bishop after a long while.	101

80

1	You'll remain where you're going.	73
2	You won't get provisions just now. Don't expect it.	72
3	You'll get your entire deposit back.	71
4	You'll marry your girlfriend. You'll be without care.	70

5	Put down a deposit because you'll win.	69
6	You'll have hope of trust and very excellent hope.	68
7	You'll get the call to office very quickly.	67
8	You won't be reinstated as a cleric. Do something else.	66
9	You won't be a general just now. Don't expect it.	65
10	You're going to see a death that is hurtful.	64

81

1	You'll be estranged from your wife.	90
2	The fugitive won't escape your detection; you'll stumble onto him.	89
3	You'll become a senator after a while and you'll suffer a loss.	88
4	You'll be an ambassador by yourself and it won't benefit you.	87
5	You won't be banished. Don't be afraid. Persevere.	86
6	You'll be prosperous and you'll acquire many good things.	85
7	You'll buy the thing you have in mind and then sell it.	84
8	You won't be able to sell in the way you want.	83
9	Your belongings will be sold at auction presently. Be concerned.	82
10	You won't profit from the undertaking.	81

82

1	Don't share in the business. It's not to your advantage.	15
2	You'll serve in the army, but not to your advantage.	14
3	You'll work, laboring for the good, and you'll take pleasure.	13
4	You'll sail unexpectedly and well.	12
5	The one who is detained won't be set free.	103
6	You won't be estranged from your girlfriend for many reasons.	102
7	You'll become a bishop after you've taken great pains.	101
8	You won't be caught in adultery. Don't be afraid.	100
9	You'll buy land with your toil.	99
10	You won't remain an elder.	98

83

1	You won't be released from detention.	56
2	You'll get the woman you desire and you'll be her guardian.	55
3	He'll recover quickly from the illness, if you're attentive.	54
4	You won't be safe from the allegation although you have had great influence.	53
5	You won't inherit from your wife. It's granted to someone else.	52
6	If you present your case, you'll win. Fight it out.	51
7	A little of your property will remain in your possession.	50

8	You'll get the dowry and waste it.	49
9	You won't inherit from your parents. It's granted to someone else.	48
10	You won't beget children just yet. Wait.	47

84

1	You won't have a benefit in your friend.	75
2	You'll be purchased and it will go well for you with those to whom you're sold.	74
3	You won't remain where you're going, since you won't be the first.	73
4	You won't get provisions just now.	72
5	You'll get your deposit back.	71
6	You'll marry your girlfriend and she won't stay with you.	70
7	If you put down a deposit, you'll lose it since you'll be defeated.	69
8	You'll have excellent hope of trust.	68
9	You'll get the call to office for which you yearn.	67
10	You'll be made a cleric after a while. Don't be fainthearted.	66

85

1	Your belongings will be sold at auction.	82
2	You'll profit from the undertaking a little.	81
3	The traveler is alive and will return.	80
4	You'll get part of the money.	79
5	You'll get an escort.	78
6	You'll be restored to your place very soon.	77
7	You'll have dealings with another and profit a great deal.	76
8	You won't have any benefit from your friend.	75
9	You'll be sold and you'll be set free.	74
10	You'll remain where you're going.	73

86

1	Don't lend anything.	58
2	You'll sell your cargo quickly.	57
3	You won't be released from detention just yet.	56
4	You'll get the woman you desire.	55
5	The sick person will be ill for a long time, but he'll regain his health.	54
6	You'll be safe from the allegation, if you're attentive.	53
7	You'll inherit from your wife, but not as the sole heir.	52
8	You'll win the case, if you work to the end.	51
9	Not all of your property will remain in your possession.	50
10	You'll get the dowry after you've fought many battles.	49

87

1 You won't find a way to sell your goods.   83
2 Your belongings won't be sold at auction. Don't worry.   82
3 You won't profit from the undertaking.   81
4 The traveler isn't alive. Don't expect him.   80
5 You'll get a small part of the money.   79
6 You won't get an escort just now. Count on it.   78
7 You'll be restored to your place with joy.   77
8 If you have dealings with another, you'll be harmed a great deal.   76
9 You'll have a great benefit from your friend.   75
10 You won't be sold, but you'll be set free with a bequest.   74

88

1 You'll advance well.   16
2 Don't share in the business. It's not to your advantage.   15
3 You'll serve in the army and advance quickly.   14
4 You'll work, envied by the crowd.   13
5 At length the marriage will be finalized out of necessity.   12
6 The one who is detained will be set free.   103
7 You'll be estranged from your girlfriend because of jealousy.   102
8 You'll become a bishop, but not just yet. Wait.   101
9 You won't be caught as an adulterer just now. Take heed.   100
10 You won't buy land or a house.   99

89

1 You'll become a decemvir.   95
2 You'll be able to see your homeland and to rejoice.   94
3 You'll finish what you undertake.   93
4 You'll get a large bequest, if you take heed.   92
5 You've indeed been poisoned. Treat yourself.   91
6 You won't be estranged from your wife in a good way.   90
7 The fugitive will escape your detection up to a point.   89
8 You'll be a senator and you'll profit so as to become wealthy.   88
9 You'll be an ambassador and you'll profit in the matter.   87
10 You'll be banished and you'll be treated humanely in the matter.   86

90

1 You'll marry your girlfriend presently.   70
2 Put down a deposit because you'll win. Be cheerful.   69
3 You won't have hope of trust at all.   68
4 You'll get the call to office for which you've prayed.   67
5 You'll be made a cleric and you'll become a pest.   66

6	You'll be a general and thrive until the end.	65
7	You're going to see a death at home very soon, but persevere.	64
8	You won't win. Don't do battle at all.	63
9	You'll have an inheritance and suffer a great financial loss.	62
10	If you take a lease, you'll suffer a great loss.	61

91

1	You'll be able to go out of town presently.	17
2	You won't advance now. Stop imagining.	16
3	Don't share in the business. It's not to your advantage. You'll suffer losses.	15
4	You'll serve in the army and suffer greatly.	14
5	If you work, you'll derive great benefit and you'll profit.	13
6	You'll sail with danger, but be brave.	12
7	The one who is detained will be set free in time.	103
8	You'll make up with your girlfriend and you'll be harmed.	102
9	You'll become a bishop after a while.	101
10	You won't be caught as an adulterer. Don't be distressed.	100

92

1	Enter an agreement. You'll benefit.	18
2	If you go out of town, you'll suffer.	17
3	You'll advance just as you have prayed.	16
4	It's not to your advantage to share in the business.	15
5	You won't serve in the army. Don't expect to.	14
6	Inquire with fear and you'll hear the truth.	13
7	You'll sail, but not just yet.	12
8	The one who is detained will be in danger and will die.	103
9	Your girlfriend won't become estranged, since she's being fed.	102
10	You won't be able to be a bishop. Don't expect it.	101

93

1	You won't go out of town now.	17
2	You'll advance suddenly when you don't realize it.	16
3	You'll share in the business to your detriment.	15
4	You won't serve in the army just yet. Why are you in a hurry?	14
5	If you're inquiring in good faith, inquire.	13
6	You'll sail after being delayed, and it will be to your advantage.	12
7	The one who is detained will be set free.	103
8	You'll be reconciled with your wife and you'll be sorry.	102
9	You'll become a bishop after a while.	101
10	You won't be caught as an adulterer now, but you will be later.	100

94

1	You won't sell your cargo just yet.	57
2	You'll be released from detention.	56
3	You won't get the woman you desire.	55
4	He'll recover quickly from his illness.	54
5	You won't be safe from the allegation. Be careful.	53
6	You'll inherit from your wife.	52
7	Argue your case. You'll win in accordance with the truth.	51
8	Your property will remain in your possession.	50
9	You'll get the dowry in part.	49
10	You won't inherit from your parents. You'll die first.	48

95

1	Put down a deposit. You'll win.	69
2	You'll have hope of trust.	68
3	You'll get the call to office.	67
4	You'll be made a cleric after a time.	66
5	It won't benefit you to be a general.	65
6	You're not going to see a death just now.	64
7	You won't win. Keep silent.	63
8	You'll have an inheritance, but not as sole heir.	62
9	If you take a lease, you'll suffer a loss.	61
10	You'll be a trusted oikonomos and you'll be distinguished.	60

96

1	You won't inherit from your friend.	38
2	You won't have a good end. Help yourself.	37
3	You'll find the fugitive immediately and you won't be vexed.	36
4	You won't be an official now. Why are you expecting it?	35
5	You'll inherit from your mother, but not as sole heir.	34
6	You won't be the only heir of your father.	33
7	You'll be freed after some time, but don't be distressed.	32
8	You won't be harmed. Don't be distressed, but take heart.	31
9	The baby will die, not live.	30
10	You'll be safe from the accusation after a little while.	29

97

1	You'll succeed happily.	19
2	You won't enter an agreement. Wait for the time being.	18
3	You won't go out of town soon, because you're hindered.	17
4	You'll advance and you'll be successful in a hurry.	16
5	You'll share in the business, but it won't benefit you, since you'll suffer a loss.	15
6	You'll serve in the army now and benefit greatly.	14

7 Consult with a pure conscience.   13
8 You'll sail after being delayed.   12
9 The one who is detained will be set free from his confinement.   103
10 You'll be estranged from your girlfriend. She's acting
    foolishly. It will benefit you.   102

98

1 You'll share in the business and suffer.   15
2 You won't serve in the army now. Wait.   14
3 It's not time for consultation.   13
4 You won't sail now, because you're not ready.   12
5 The one who is detained won't be set free.   103
6 You won't be estranged from your girlfriend.   102
7 You'll become a bishop, if you have love.   101
8 You'll be found to be an adulterer, but you'll come through
    safely.   100
9 You'll buy property or a house as a result of your own efforts.   99
10 You'll remain an elder until death.   98

99

1 You won't open a workshop.   43
2 You won't recover from your sickness. You'll die.   42
3 You'll become a teacher suddenly and you'll be distinguished.   41
4 You'll find what is lost, but it will take some time.   40
5 You'll be an agoranomos, but not just yet. Why are you so
    eager?   39
6 You won't inherit from your friend.   38
7 You won't have a good end, but a painful one.   37
8 You won't find the fugitive.   36
9 You won't be an official now in the matters you desire. Don't
    expect it.   35
10 You won't inherit from your mother. Don't hope for it.   34

100

1 You won't get the dowry.   49
2 You won't inherit from your parents. You'll die first.   48
3 You'll beget children, but not just yet. Wait.   47
4 You won't come to terms with your masters. It's not to your
    advantage.   46
5 You'll obtain your petition for what you need.   45
6 You won't have a long life.   44
7 You'll open a workshop with short notice.   43
8 You'll recover from your sickness. Don't be distressed.   42
9 You'll be a teacher with great honor.   41

10   You'll never find what is lost.   40

101

1   Consult only once in the third hour.   13
2   You'll sail, but you'll be delayed in the undertaking.   12
3   You'll serve in the army and be very sorry.   14
4   You'll share in the business and suffer many losses.   15
5   You won't be able to advance just yet. You're being hindered.   16
6   You'll go out of town, where you desire, for your good.   17
7   You'll succeed as a consequence of many fine efforts.   18
8   Don't enter the agreement, because you'll suffer greatly.   19
9   You'll purchase what is offered.   20
10   You won't marry just yet. Wait.   21

102

1   You'll soon be safe from the accusation.   29
2   You'll soon give an accounting to your benefit.   28
3   The traveler won't return. He's hindered.   27
4   You won't pay back just yet what you owe.   26
5   You'll borrow money and you won't suffer a loss. You'll
     profit.   25
6   You'll father a baby, but the baby will be unprofitable.   24
7   You won't move from your place. Don't be distressed.   23
8   You can be harmed a little. Don't be distressed.   22
9   You'll marry and you'll be distressed, because you'll be filled
     with regret.   21
10   You won't purchase what is offered. You won't be able to.   20

103

1   You won't be made a cleric.   66
2   You won't become a bishop. Don't wait for it.   101
3   You'll be found to be an adulterer after much time.   100
4   You won't buy land or a house.   99
5   You won't remain an elder. Despise yourself.   98
6   Your wife will stay with you, because she has self-control.   97
7   You'll get free from your lot in a hurry.   96
8   You'll become a decemvir and be distinguished.   95
9   You won't set eyes on your homeland.   94
10   (text missing)   103

PART FOUR

Popular Literature in Public Places

II

POPULAR LITERATURE
ON STONE

The practice of marking a burial site semantically is an old one in Greece as elsewhere. Homer recounts that when Odysseus encounters his recently deceased but as yet unburied companion in the death realm, Elpenor begs him to

Bury me along with all my equipment
And pile up a tomb for me on the shore of the gray sea,
A tomb for an unfortunate man, for persons still to be born to learn from.
Do this for me, and plant on it the oar
With which I used to row beside my companions when I was alive.[1]

In the nonliterate world of Odysseus and Elpenor the presence of a mound communicates that here lies a man important enough to merit a tomb, and the oar signifies that he was a mariner. In the *Iliad* Hector imagines how a man he hopes to overcome will be buried in a mound beside the sea,

And then persons born afterward will say,
As they sail by in a many-oared ship on the wine-dark sea:
"This is the tomb of a man who died long ago,
A courageous man whom once shining Hector slew."[2]

It is not clear how the passing mariners will know that the tomb marks the burial site of a man slain by Hector,[3] but perhaps we are to assume that the story of the tomb will be familiar locally so that the landmark will naturally call this information to mind each time it is seen.

Sepulchral inscriptions appear in Greece from the seventh century B.C. onward, after which time the literate are able to read whatever message the bereaved choose to inscribe on a monument. Since stone is a durable material, thousands of such epitaphs have survived, most of them in prose and quite brief, simply a name or a little more:

Aphrodisia, farewell.[4]

The earliest verse epitaphs tend to be brief and dignified, as in this single, not very poetic hexameter line:

I am the gravestone of Xenwares, son of Meixis, upon his tomb.[5]

This inscription, in which the monument itself is made to speak, reminds us that genuine epitaphs differ from most other poetry in that they always appear in a material context—and, if they are *in situ,* in a spatial one as well. A number of epitaphs feature a dialogue between the monument and the reader. One begins:

"Gravestone, who set you up so stately to look upon?"
"The mother of Timocrates, that she might have a consolation for herself."[6]

Sometimes the message can be fully appreciated only when one understands the nature of the monument of which it forms a part, as when the epitaph features a sphinx or other creature that addresses the reader.

Although Greek epitaphs, like ours, are mostly anonymous, some were signed so that their authors are known. Indeed, some were composed by well-known poets. In the Hellenistic period and later it was fashionable for poets to compose sepulchral epigrams that were purely literary and not intended for monuments at all, and some poets produced both epigraphic and pseudepigraphic epitaphs.[7] It is not always easy or even possible to distinguish between genuine epitaphs taken from actual stone markers that no longer exist and purely literary epitaphs that mimic the conventions of genuine epitaphs. For example, this anonymous epigram is preserved only in a collection of poems, the *Palatine Anthology:*[8]

I lie here, Dionysius, sixty years old,
From Tarsus, never married. I wish my father had not either.

Is the poem a genuine epitaph copied from a monument, or is it a purely literary artifact?

Graves and their messages were located outside the boundaries of towns, usually alongside roads, where we find memorials for persons of every social standing: statesman and prostitute, rich and poor, free and slave. The more frequented the road, the more desirable the site.[9] Epitaphs often address the passerby, and townsfolk and visitors must sometimes have strolled among the tombs, studying the monuments and reading the inscriptions. *The Aesop Romance* represents Aesop and Xan-

thus taking a walk together one day and coming eventually to the out-
skirts of the city, where they enjoy discussing the epitaphs they come
upon (chap. 78). The intent of the composers certainly was to capture
the interest of readers, doing honor to the deceased by propagating their
memory.

Who composed these poems? Probably the persons commissioning
the monument discussed the inscription with the maker of the monument
and came to a decision. In the case of simple poems there would have
been little to talk about, but in the case of more elaborate messages the
bereaved and the experienced professional may have talked the matter
over at some length. Because of the widespread use of formulas in the
epitaphs, some scholars have speculated that ancient stonecutters possessed pattern books, collections of sample epitaphs that customers might
peruse while devising one themselves.[10] Although none has survived from
antiquity, such compilations, if they did exist, were perhaps more likely
to be personal notebooks kept by individual professionals than to be
published books, so that there would have been little incentive to preserve them.

The existence of handbooks might explain how it is possible for very
similar epitaphs to be found in different regions and at different times.
For example, the following lines appear in a verse epitaph in Phrygia in
the third century A.D:

> It is not dying that distresses me, since this is measured out to all,
> But before my prime of life and before my parents.[11]

Essentially the same verses appear six or seven centuries earlier on a grave
on the island of Rhodes:

> It is not dying that is grievous, which is appointed for all,
> But before my prime of life and before my parents.[12]

But compare the variations in these lines that occur in a Christian epitaph
in Phrygia.

> It is not dying that is grievous—this is appointed for all—
> But Plouteus snatched me from my wedded wife, Demetriane.[13]

The first verse in each of these epitaphs is a close variation on a manifestly traditional sentiment for which the diction is also conventional.
The second verse in each case contains the idea of predeceasing someone,
although the survivors vary between parents and spouse. One might possibly explain the near identity of the first and second epitaphs by the
supposition that the composers drew upon pattern books, but one could
not easily explain the third epitaph in this way, for whereas the underly-

ing idea of the second verse in it is more or less the same, the surface realization is quite different and the diction entirely dissimilar. Rather, this mix is more like that which one encounters in an oral tradition than in a book-based tradition.

There is a suggestive analogy in the phenomenon of letters to the dead, which in the present day is the obituary form that perhaps is most comparable to the developed epitaphs of former times. Customary in some regions of the United States, letters to the dead are memorials in prose or verse composed by the bereaved, addressed usually to a deceased person, and published in a local newspaper, often on the anniversary of a death or birth. This poem was addressed to a deceased woman:

> So many times I've needed you
> A million time I've cried.
> If love could have saved you,
> You never would have died.
> It broke my heart to lose you,
> But you did not go alone.
> For part of me went with you
> The night God called you home.[14]

As in ancient epitaphs, many themes and phrases recur from poem to poem. In the case of letters to the dead we happen to know something of the use of pattern books. The office of the local newspaper in Bloomington, Indiana, in which letters to the dead appear frequently, possesses two booklets consisting of earlier published samples that it puts at the disposal of customers who wish to consult them while composing their own letters. Interestingly, only around 20 percent of the customers actually do so. The rest presumably draw ideas from their memory of letters they have read in the past and from examples that appear in current issues of the newspaper.[15] The situation may not have been much different in antiquity. There may have been ancient pattern books, and if so, some persons would have consulted them when faced with the task of composing an epitaph, but others, perhaps most persons, might have drawn for inspiration upon their memory of epitaphs read or discussed in the past and upon epitaphs that were accessible in the local cemetery.

So at least it happens in a literary representation of the composition of a verse epitaph. In Book Three of *An Ephesian Tale* Xenophon of Ephesus tells of the lovers Hippothoos and Hyperanthes whose ship overturns in a storm. The younger of the two, Hyperanthes, drowns, but Hippothoos manages to get the body ashore, buries it, and erects a stone marker over the grave, inscribing on it an epitaph that he improvises:

> Hippothoos fashioned this tomb for famed Hyperanthes,
> A grave not worthy of the death of a sacred citizen,

A renowned flower, whom a deity snatched from the land to the deep,
On the sea, when a great gale had blown.[16]

Hippothoos devises an encomiastic epitaph in verse, but he does so using familiar structures and commonplace ideas of the tradition.[17] The verse is dactylic hexameter, the meter of Greek epic poetry, and contains epic echoes, as epitaphs in hexameters often do. Moreover, the idea that death is due to supernatural agency, a deity having snatched the person away, is found frequently, for many epitaphs recount how Hades, the Moirai (Fates), Tyche (Fortune), or simply a *daimon* (deity), as here, has taken the victim away. Recall the Phrygian epitaph excerpted above:

For it is not dying that is grievous—this is appointed for all—
But Plouteus snatched me from my wedded wife, Demetriane.

An epitaph from Smyrna begins this way:

Though you had not completed your twentieth year,
Untimely fate, everlasting death, snatched you.[18]

The image of a youthful victim as a flower also appears elsewhere.

Though a maiden, I Leonto am dead, like a young flower.[19]

So begins the epitaph of a girl who died at the age of fifteen, just as she was to be married. In the epitaph for Hyperanthes the metaphor of the flower also plays upon his name, a compound containing the root of the word "flower" as one of its elements. Finally a mention of death at sea is found in a number of poignant epitaphs. For example:

Far from my homeland of Bithynia I lost my life,
Trusting in a baneful voyage and my own ship.
I lie in Scheria by the shore of the windy sea,
Looking in the end at the sea that was baneful to me.[20]

The Greek tradition of verse epitaphs was adopted by the Romans, among whom poetic epitaphs begin appearing in the third century B.C.[21] Developed epitaphs in verse blossomed again in the Middle Ages only to die down again in the course of the nineteenth century when a reaction set in against gravestones with long and laudatory epitaphs.[22] Via the Romans the tradition influenced later epitaphs in prose and verse. The epitaph of William Shakespeare, for example, shows commonplaces of the ancient Greek and Latin epitaph, the direct address to the passerby and the threat against anyone who disturbs the grave.[23]

Good friend for Iesus sake forbeare,
To digg the dust encloased heare:
Bleste be ye man [tha]t spares thes stones,
And curst be he [tha]t moves my bones.

As in antiquity, modern collectors have published compilations of striking and memorable epitaphs, and inspired by the genre, poets have composed purely literary examples, including parodies. And as in ancient times the loss of many tombstones often makes it impossible to check published epitaphs against the original monuments, real or alleged.

Chosen from monuments erected in the first several centuries A.D., the sepulchral poems that follow are contemporary with the other literature in this anthology. They illustrate some of the creativity as well as formulism of Greek gravestone poetry.

NOTES

1. *Odyssey* 11.74–78.
2. *Iliad* 7.81–91.
3. For a discussion see Raubitschek 1968.
4. Athens, first century B.C. Woodhead 1967:50, no. 16, from *IG* II² 10920.
5. Corcyra, ca. 600 B.C. Friedländer 1948:9–10, no. 1 (a photograph of the inscribed column faces the title page); Peek 1955:21, no. 52. Gravestone poetry employs a variety of meters, including dactylic hexameters and elegiac distichs.
6. Athens, 2nd century A.D. Peek 1955:552, no. 1836.
7. On Alexandrian epigrams see Fraser 1972 1:553–617.
8. *AP* 7.309 = Peek 1955:98, no. 399.
9. Humphreys 1993:91–92.
10. See Lattimore 1962:18–20, Griessmair 1966:27, Drew-Bear 1979:315–316, Courtney 1995:15. I have come upon little information about epitaph manuals in modern times, but according to Shushan (1990:ix–x) they were available for customers to pore over in the offices of nineteenth-century stonecutters, and H. H. Armstrong, writing in 1910, mentions them as being in use in his day (quoted by Lattimore 1962:19).
11. Phrygia, 3rd century A.D. Drew-Bear 1979:308–309.
12. Phrygia, 1st–2nd century A.D. Drew-Bear 1979:309–310 = Peek 1955:499, no. 1668.
13. Drew-Bear 1979:310. Plouteus = Hades, the lord of death.
14. Robinson 1993:100. The item appeared in the *Herald-Times* (Bloomington, Indiana) in 1990.
15. See Dégh 1994:169–170. On the genre see Robinson 1993, Dégh 1994:153–193.
16. *Eph.* 3.2.13.
17. Ruiz-Montero (1994:1129–1130) points out the conventional features of the epitaph, citing Lattimore 1962:147–149, 192, 199–201.
18. Lattimore 1962:150.

19. Larisa, 2nd–3rd century A.D. Peek 1955:275, no. 988. See further Lattimore 1962:195.

20. Corcyra, Roman period. Lattimore 1962:200.

21. For a sampling of Latin epitaphs with English translation, see Courtney 1995.

22. Shushan 1990:vii–xiii.

23. See Friedländer 1948:1, Strubbe 1991:33, Rees 1993:199–201.

LITERATURE

Drew-Bear 1979. Friedländer 1948. Griessmair 1966. Lattimore 1962 [1942]. Peek 1955. Raubitschek 1968.

DIFFERENT AUTHORS, MOSTLY ANONYMOUS

Gravestone Verse

translated by William Hansen

A Traditional Couplet:
"IT IS NOT DYING THAT IS GRIEVOUS"

It is not dying that is grievous, since Moira has spun this destiny,
But before my prime of life and before my parents.
Cyzicus[1]

Alexander (erected this) for his own son Iannas as a memorial.

It is not dying that is grievous, since this is destined for all,
But before my prime of life and before my parents.
Having seen no wedding, no wedding song, no bridal bed,
I lie, an object of love for many, in the future for even more.
Phrygia, 1st–2nd century A.D.[2]

It is not dying that is grievous, since it is destined for all,
But before my prime of life and before my parents.
Lydia[3]

It is not dying that is grievous—this is appointed for all—
But Plouteus snatched me from my wedded wife, Demetriane.

Phrygia[4]

It is not dying that has caused the pain, since Moira has spun this destiny,
But before reaching the prime of life and the measure of youth.
Swift death has snatched my child Tatas,
Wherefore his good father Zoticus and Domna who bore him
Have erected for their perished son this memorial eternal.

Phrygia, 2nd–3rd century A.D.[5]

It is not dying that is painful, since Moira has spun this destiny,
But before my prime of life and before my parents.

Smyrna, 2nd–3rd century A.D.?[6]

It is not dying that is grievous, since Moira has spun this destiny,
But before my prime of life and before my mother.

Euboea, early Roman period?[7]

For Aurelius Eutychides, as a memorial.

Kerellaios the chief soothsayer says:
What is evil is not dying, since Moira has spun this destiny,
But before one's prime of life and before one's parents.

Lykia, 2nd–3rd century A.D.[8]

It is not dying that is painful, since Moira has spun this destiny,
But before my prime of life and before my parents.

Mitylene[9]

It is not dying that is painful, stranger, since Moira has spun this destiny,
But before my prime of life and before my parents.

Bithynia[10]

Good . . . , farewell.
It is not dying that is grievous, since Moira has spun this destiny,
But before one's prime of life and before one's parents.

Erythrae[11]

It is not dying that distresses me, since this is measured out to all,
But before my prime of life and before my parents.
Having seen no wedding, no wedding song, no bridal bed,
I died eighteen years old, and my parents

Honored me with this tomb for the sake of everlasting memory.
    For Demosthenes, fond of hunting.
                                    Phrygia, 3rd century A.D.[12]

Miscellaneous Epitaphs

Of Nyse, orderly and industrious, this is the tomb.
                                    Smyrna, 1st–2nd century A.D.?[13]

Do not insult this holy tomb, passerby,
Lest Agesilas and Persephone, daughter of Demeter,
Be bitterly wroth with you. Rather, as you go by,
Say to Aratius: "May the earth lie lightly upon you."
                                    Crete, 1st century A.D.[14]

Lysimachus made this tomb for a beloved one who died untimely.
Antiochis, take courage. The end is the same for all.
                                    Syria, 1st century A.D.[15]

Parthenis lies here, ageless and immortal.
                                    Rome, 2nd–3rd century A.D.[16]

If anyone applies to this gravestone a malicious hand,
May he leave the rays of light and the light of the sun.
                                    Phrygia, 2nd–3rd century A.D.[17]

Here is the tomb of swift-fated, mindful Crispinus
For whom no stock of children will later appear.
A destructive Ker overcame them both before him.
So his wedded wife Sozomene inscribed his gravestone
For mortals still to be born to learn from.
                                    Berrhoea, 2nd–3rd century A.D.[18]

Barbarianus, child of Pontianus, lies here,
Whom once Amastris reared but, when a youth, a deity snatched away.
                                    Rome, 1st–2nd century A.D.[19]

To the immaculate and holy ones. This is the tomb of a prudent mind.
If you wish to know her name and origin, stranger,
She is charming Syracosia, child of Herodes.
                                    Syracuse, 2nd–3rd century A.D.[20]

I Herais lie here, stranger, five times seven (years old),
And I urge you, my husband,
Not to keep weeping. For the thread of the Moirai calls everyone.

Amorgus, 2nd–3rd century A.D.[21]

"Having seen no wedding nor wedding song, no bridal bed,
Placed beneath a tombstone I lie beside the road."
"Farewell, Florus." "And farewell also to you, stranger, whoever you
    may be."

Carnuntum, 1st century A.D.[22]

To the gods beneath the earth.
Here I lie, Moschianus of Smyrna, having died,
A comic actor, and this my tomb makes clear.
Wayfarers, Marcianus buried and tended to me.
He did not abandon my corpse nor, when I was still among the living,
Did he neglect me. I reached life's end and fulfilled my lot.

Rome, 2nd century A.D.[23]

You who pass by on the path, if perchance you notice this tomb,
I beg you not to laugh that it is the grave of a dog.
I was wept for, and the dust was mounded up by the hands of my master,
Who also inscribed this message on my gravestone.

Rome, 2nd–3rd century A.D.[24]

I, most excellent Spoude, lie here, twenty-one years old.

Amorgus, 3rd century A.D. or
later[25]

In the vigorous prime of my youth cruel Moira slew me,
Though I had already reached the famed chambers of the Paphian.
My mournful parents were worn down with unholy grief,
Being unable to leave another child for their house.
If you wish to know of my life, passerby,
By trade I was a stonecutter, Midias by name.
I have departed to the gods and am among the immortals,
For those whom the gods love all die young.

Mysia, 2nd–3rd century A.D.[26]

"Who lies here?" "Passerby, wait, listen.
A worthy man, honored, sincere, an affable comrade,
Displaying his craft and honesty among all persons,
Giving pain to no one, nor pained by his children.
Paratus is the name he was called among all persons.

He was punished by no long illness but went to his fate
With an easy death because of his piety."
Berytus, late Imperial period[27]

Zoelus, most excellent of charioteers, lies here.
Rome, 2nd–3rd century A.D.[28]

"Stop beside this dear tomb, passerby." "Who bids me?"
"I do, the guardian lion." "The one made of stone?"
"Yes." "How is it that you can talk?" "By the voice
Of the buried man's spirit." "Who is this man
So honored by the immortal gods that he can thus
Fashion a human voice with stone?"
"He is Heras of Memphis, friend, a glorious hero,
Strong, eminent in many ways, mighty,
Known to natives of the land and to men afar off
For his good cheer, for his splendor,
Swift-fated, whom the city lamented, whom his companions buried.
For he was indeed the flower of his garlanded homeland."
"I swear, spirit, I weep after hearing what
This beast says." "Don't shed tears, stranger."
"May your famed name continue forever." "And a deity will guard you
and Fortune will preserve your entire livelihood."
Egypt, 1st–2nd century A.D.[29]

Here lies a man who labored much,
In farming experienced and in voting wise.
Bithynia, 1st–2nd century A.D.[30]

Behold, friend, the sacred beauty of Asclepiodote,
Both of her immortal soul and of her body, for nature
Granted her unmixed beauty in both. And if Moira
Has snatched her away, she has not conquered her. For though she has
    died, she did not die alone.
Nor has she forsaken her husband, though she has left him, but now even
    more
From heaven she sees him and is gladdened and protects him.
Athens, 3rd–4th century A.D.[31]

"Marble gravemarker, whose tomb are you?" "The tomb of a swift
    horse."
"And what is his name?" "Euthydicus." "What renown does he have?"
    "For bearing away the prize."

"How many times was he crowned in the race?" "Many." "Who drove
    him?"
"Coeranus." "An honor greater than that of the demigods!"
                              Rome, 2nd century A.D.?[32]

     "Lucius Licinius, farewell."
"And may you too fare well, passerby, because you said
This holy greeting to me on account of your piety."
                              Mysia, 2nd century A.D.[33]

Do not move this stone from the earth, you rogue,
Lest, when you die, wretch, dogs drag you around unburied.
                              Athens, 3rd–4th century?[34]

. . . . of a prosperous homeland,
Called Callistonice among mortals.
But since Moira has spun for me a destiny of leaving life
And of obtaining this piece of earth as my meager lot,
Do not allow a body to be placed
Next to my body. There is in the sky
A single defender of the dead, father Zeus.
So now if any of my enemies arrogantly laughs at me,
Daughter of Isagorus,
May Zeus strike his hateful body with a thunderbolt,
Laughing at him as once he laughed at me.
                         Sparta, 3rd century A.D. or later[35]

Daphnis wrought this monument for kindly Aste,
Having loved her when she lived, longing for her now that she has
    perished.
                              Naples, 1st century A.D.[36]

If anyone mistreats this monument,
May he experience the misfortune of untimely deaths
And be execrable to all the gods.
                         Phrygia, 2nd–3rd century A.D.?[37]

"Farewell, Diomedes Symbritius." "Farewell, everyone."
                              Crete, Roman period[38]

NOTES TO TRANSLATION

1. Drew-Bear 1979:312. Moira = Fate. On the theme "It's not dying that grieves me," see Peek 1955:497–499, Griessmair 1966:24–28, Drew-Bear 1979. This lament for a premature death, especially favored in Asia Minor, appears with variations on Greek gravestones over a period of six centuries. The two verses sometimes constitute the entire epitaph and sometimes appear as part of a longer message.

2. Drew-Bear 1979:309–310; Peek 1955:499, no. 1668; Lattimore 1962:184–185. Words in parentheses are supplied for the sake of clarity.

3. Drew-Bear 1979:312.

4. These lines appear within a long Christian epitaph; see Drew-Bear 1979:310. Plouteus = Hades, lord of the dead.

5. Peek 1955:499, no. 1669; Drew-Bear 1979:311.

6. Peek 1955:498, no. 1666; Drew-Bear 1979:313.

7. Drew-Bear 1979:314.

8. Peek 1955:498, no. 1665; Griessmair 1966:24–26; Drew-Bear 1979:311–312.

9. Peek 1955:498, no. 1667; Drew-Bear 1979:313.

10. Drew-Bear 1979:312.

11. Kaibel 1878:114, no. 300; Drew-Bear 1979:313.

12. Drew-Bear 1979:308–309.

13. Peek 1955:28, no. 88

14. Peek 1955:410, no. 1370. Disrespect for a grave could take a variety of forms, from placing a body in a tomb that belonged to someone else to robbing a grave of its valuables. For epitaphs containing warnings and curses, see further Lattimore 1962:106–118, Gager 1992:178, Strubbe 1991 and 1994, and, for an interesting study of an apotropaic device employed in modern graffiti, Grider 1975.

15. Peek 1955:50, no. 183.

16. Peek 1955:90, no. 357.

17. Peek 1955:411, no. 1376. Above the curse in verse stands a prose inscription giving the names of the dedicator and of the deceased.

18. Peek 1955:33, no. 107. A Ker is a spirit of doom or fate.

19. Peek 1955:91, no. 362.

20. Peek 1955:29, no. 93.

21. Peek 1955:93, no. 372.

22. Peek 1955:557, no. 1853; Drew-Bear 1979:314. Above the Greek epigram, an epitaph in Latin prose explains that Florus, a slave, died at age twenty-six and that the tombstone was erected by his master.

23. Peek 1955:108, no. 438; Parca 1995:50–55. The line "A comic actor, and this my tomb makes clear" presumably refers to a relief of a comic mask, now lost, on the tomb.

24. Peek 1955:408, no. 1365.

25. Peek 1955:90, no. 360.

26. Peek 1955:265, no. 961. The Paphian = Aphrodite. The second verse seems to say that he had wed. The consolatory thought "Those whom the gods love die young," which was devised or at least popularized by the poet Menander, appears in at least five Greek epitaphs, but unlike some other themes, the means of expressing it did not become standardized and formulaic; see Lattimore 1962:259–260, Griessmair 1966:101–102. A similar consolation recurs in mod-

ern letters to the dead: "God picks the best to go first / And leaves the rest to mourn" (Dégh 1994:164).

27. Peek 1955:553, no. 1840.

28. Peek 1955:90, no. 358.

29. Peek 1955:554, no. 1843.

30. Peek 1955:91, no. 364.

31. Peek 1955:380, no. 1282; Lattimore 1962:302. A Christian epitaph.

32. Peek 1955:555, no. 1844.

33. Peek 1955:558, no. 1855. The Greek imperative χαῖρε, used upon encountering someone ("Greetings!") as well as at departure ("Farewell"), literally signifies "Rejoice!"

34. Peek 1955:410, no. 1373.

35. Peek 1955:411–412, no. 1374.

36. Peek 1955:50, no. 182.

37. Peek 1955:1377; see further Strubbe 1991:41–42. The epitaph threatens the abuser with experiencing multiple untimely deaths in his family.

38. Peek 1955:557, no. 1852.

WORKS CITED

Aarne, Antti, and Stith Thompson. 1961. *The Types of the Folktale: A Classifi-cation and Bibliography*. FF Communications No. 184. Helsinki: Academia Scientiarum Fennica.

Abrahams, Roger D. 1985. *Afro-American Folktales*. New York: Pantheon.

Adrados, Francisco R. 1979. The "Life of Aesop" and the Origins of the Novel in Antiquity. *Quaderni Urbinati di Cultura Classica* 30, NS 1:93–112.

———. 1979–1987. *Historia de la fábula greco-latina*. 3 vols. Madrid: Editorial de la Universidad Complutense.

———, and Olivier Reverdin, eds. 1984. *La Fable: Huit exposés suivis de discus-sions*. Entretiens sur L'Antiquité Classique 30. Geneva: Fondation Hardt.

Anderson, Graham. 1996. Popular and Sophisticated in the Ancient Novel. In Schmeling 1996:107–113.

Anonymous. 1984. Νέος Προφητικός· Ὀνειροκρίτης μετὰ Πυθίας· Ἀθῆναι: Ἀστήρ.

Anonymous. 1994. *The Complete Book of Fortune: How to Reveal the Secrets of the Past, the Present and the Future*. London: Bracken.

ANRW = Aufstieg und Niedergang der römischen Welt.

Artemidorus. 1975. *The Interpretation of Dreams: The Oneirocritica of Artemi-dorus*. Trans. Robert White. Noyes Classical Studies. Park Ridge: Noyes Press.

Ashton, John. 1882. *Chapbooks of the Eighteenth Century*. London: Chatto & Windus.

Baldwin, Barry. 1983. *The Philogelos or Laughter-Lover*. Translated with Intro-duction and Commentary. London Studies in Classical Philology, 10. Amster-dam: J. C. Gieben.

———. 1992. Jokes Old and New. *The Classical Outlook* 69:77–81.

Bayer, Dorothee. 1971. *Der triviale Familien- und Liebesroman im 20. Jahrhund-ert*. 2nd ed. Tübingen: Tübinger Vereinigung für Volkskunde E. V. Tübingen Schloss.

Bell, Michael J. 1989. The Study of Popular Culture. In *Handbook of American Popular Culture*, ed. M. Thomas Inge. Westport, Conn.: Greenwood Press. Pp. 1459–1484.

Berkowitz, Luci, and Karl A. Squitier. 1986. *Canon of Greek Authors and Works*. 2nd ed. New York: Oxford University Press.

Betz, Hans Dieter, ed. 1992. *The Greek Magical Papyri in Translation, Including the Demotic Spells*. 2nd ed. Vol. 1. Chicago: University of Chicago Press.

Bird, S. Elizabeth. 1992. *For Enquiring Minds: A Cultural Study of Supermarket Tabloids*. Knoxville: University of Tennessee Press.

Björck, Gudmund. 1939. Heidnische und christliche Orakel mit fertigen Antwor-ten. *Symbolae Osloenses* 19:86–98.

Blanck, Horst. 1992. *Das Buch in der Antike*. Munich: C. H. Beck.

Bolte, Johannes. 1903. Zur Geschichte der Losbücher. In *Georg Wickrams Werke*, ed. Johannes Bolte. Bibliotek des Litterarischen Vereins in Stuttgart, 230. Tübingen: Gedruckt für den Litterarischen Verein in Stuttgart. 4:276–348. Addenda in 241 (1906) 349–350.

————. 1925. Zur Geschichte der Punktier- und Losbücher. *Jahrbuch für historische Volkskunde* 1:184–214.

Bourdieu, Pierre. 1984. *Distinction: A Social Critique of the Judgement of Taste.* Trans. Richard Nice. Cambridge, Mass.: Harvard University Press.

Bovon, François, et al., eds. 1981. *Les Actes Apocryphes des Apôtres: Christianisme et Monde Païen.* Publications de la Faculté de Théologie de l'Université de Genève, 4. Geneva: Labor et Fides.

Bowie, Ewen. 1996. The Ancient Readers of the Greek Novels. In Schmeling 1996:87–106.

Browne, Gerald M. 1970. The Composition of the Sortes Astrampsychi. *Bulletin: Institute of Classical Studies* 17:95–100.

————, ed. 1983. *Sortes Astrampsychi I: Ecdosis Prior.* Leipzig: BSB B. G. Teubner Verlagsgesellschaft.

Burke, Peter. 1994. *Popular Culture in Early Modern Europe.* Rev. reprint. Hants: Scholars Press.

Burrus, Virginia. 1987. *Chastity as Autonomy: Women in the Stories of Apocryphal Acts.* Lewiston, Maine: Edwin Mellen Press.

Bødker, Laurits. 1965. *Folk Literature (Germanic).* International Dictionary of Regional European Ethnology and Folklore, vol. 2. Copenhagen: Rosenkilde and Bagger.

Carlé, Birte. 1980. *Thekla: En kvindeskikkelse i tidlig kristen fortællekunst.* Copenhagen: Delta.

Carnes, Pack. 1985. *Fable Scholarship: An Annotated Bibliography.* New York: Garland.

Castelli, Elizabeth. 1991. "I Will Make Mary Male": Pieties of the Body and Gender Transformation of Christian Women in Late Antiquity. In *Body Guards: The Cultural Politics of Gender Ambiguity,* ed. Julia Epstein and Kristina Straub. New York: Routledge. Pp. 29–49.

Chappell, Warren. 1970. *A Short History of the Printed Word.* New York: Knopf.

Classen, Albrecht. 1995. *The German Volksbuch: A Critical History of a Late-Medieval Genre.* Studies in German Language and Literature, 15. Lewiston, Maine: Edwin Mellen Press.

Conybeare, F. C., J. Rendel Harris, and Agnes Smith Lewis. 1913. *The Story of Ahikar, from the Aramaic, Syriac, Arabic, Armenian, Ethiopic, Old Turkish, Greek and Slavonic Versions.* 2nd ed. Cambridge: Cambridge University Press.

Courtney, Edward. 1995. *Musa Lapidaria: A Selection of Latin Verse Inscriptions.* American Classical Studies, 36. Atlanta: Scholars Press.

Dagron, Gilbert. 1978. *Vie et miracles de Sainte Thècle: Texte grec, traduction et commentaire.* Subsidia Hagiographica, 62. Brussels: Société des Bollandistes.

Daly, Lloyd W., trans. and ed. 1961. *Aesop without Morals: The Famous Fables, and a Life of Aesop.* New York: Thomas Yoseloff.

————, and Walter Suchier. 1939. *Altercatio Hadriani Augusti et Epicteti Philosophi.* Illinois Studies in Language and Literature 24, nos. 1–2. Urbana: University of Illinois Press.

Davies, Stevan L. 1980. *The Revolt of the Widows: The Social World of the Apocryphal Acts.* Carbondale: Southern Illinois University Press.

Davis, Natalie Zemon. 1975. *Society and Culture in Early Modern France: Eight Essays.* Stanford: Stanford University Press.

Day, Joseph W. 1989. Rituals in Stone: Early Greek Grave Epigrams and Monuments. *Journal of Hellenic Studies* 109:16–28.

Dégh, Linda. 1994. *American Folklore and the Mass Media*. Bloomington: Indiana University Press.

Diels, Hermann A. 1907–1908. *Beiträge zur Zuckungsliteratur des Okzidents und Orients, I–II*. Abhandlungen der Preußischen Akademie der Wissenschaften, philosophish-historische Klasse.

Dold, Alban. 1948. *Die Orakelsprüche im St. Galler Palimpsestcodex 908 (die sogenannten 'Sortes Sangallenses') auf Grund neuer Lesung und mit erweitertem Text nach Materien geordnet herausgegeben*. Österreichische Akademie der Wissenschaften, phil.-hist. Klasse, 225.4. Vienna: Rudolf M. Rohrer.

Dorson, Richard M. 1967. *American Negro Folktales*. Greenwich, Conn.: Fawcett.

Drew-Bear, Thomas. 1979. A Metrical Epitaph from Phrygia. In *Arktouros: Hellenic Studies presented to Bernard M. W. Knox on the Occasion of His 65th Birthday*. Berlin: Walter de Gruyter. Pp. 308–316.

Easterling, P. E., and B. M. W. Knox, eds. 1985. *The Cambridge History of Classical Literature*. Vol. 1. Cambridge: Cambridge University Press.

Escarpit, Robert. 1964. Y a-t-il des degrés dans la littérature? In *Littérature savante et littérature populaire: Bardes, conteurs, écrivains*. Société Française de Littérature Comparée: Actes du Sixième Congrès National, Rennes, 1963. Paris: Didier. Pp. 1–10.

Falk, Kathryn. 1990. *How to Write a Romance and Get It Published*. Rev. ed. New York: Signet.

Frank, Eva. 1941. Phlegon. In *Paulys Real-Encyclopädie der classischen Altertumswissenschaft* 20:261–264.

Fraser, P. M. 1972. *Ptolemaic Alexandria*. 3 vols. Oxford: Clarendon Press.

Frazer, J. G. 1898. *Pausanias's Description of Greece*. Vol. 4. London: Macmillan.

Friedländer, Paul, with the collaboration of Herbert B. Hoffleit. 1948. *Epigrammata: Greek Inscriptions in Verse from the Beginnings to the Persian Wars*. Berkeley: University of California Press.

Gager, John G., ed. 1992. *Curse Tablets and Binding Spells from the Ancient World*. New York: Oxford University Press.

Gardner, Alan H., ed. 1935. *Hieratic Papyri in the British Museum*, Third Series: Chester Beatty Gift, Vol. 1: Text. London: British Museum.

Gentili, Bruno (and discussants). 1968. Epigramma ed elegia. In *L'Épigramme grecque: Sept exposés suivis de discussions*. Entretiens sur l'Antiquité Classique, 14. Geneva: Fondation Hardt. Pp. 39–90.

Giannini, Alessandro. 1963. Studi sulla paradossografia greca I. Da Omero a Callimaco: motivi e forme del meraviglioso. *Istituto Lombardo (Rend. Lett.)* 97: 247–266.

———. 1964. Studi sulla paradossografia greca II. Da Callimaco all'età imperiale: la letteratura paradossografica. *Acme* 17:99–140.

Giannini, Alexander, ed. 1965. *Paradoxographorum Graecorum Reliquiae*. Milan: Istituto Editoriale Italiano.

Ginzburg, Carlo. 1980. *The Cheese and the Worms: The Cosmos of a Sixteenth-Century Miller*. Trans. John and Anne Tedeschi. Baltimore: Johns Hopkins University Press.

Glassie, Henry. 1989. *The Spirit of Folk Art*. New York: Abrams.

Grider, Silvia Ann. 1975. Con Safos: Mexican-Americans, Names and Graffiti. *Journal of American Folklore* 88:132-142.

Griessmair, Ewald. 1966. *Das Motiv der Mors immatura in den griechischen metrischen Grabinschriften*. Commentationes Aenipontanae, 17. Innsbruck: Universitätsverlag Wagner.

Gunderson, Lloyd L. 1980. *Alexander's Letter to Aristotle about India.* Beiträge zur Klassischen Philologie, 110. Meisenheim am Glan: Anton Hain.

Hägg, Tomas. 1971. *Narrative Technique in Ancient Greek Romances: Studies of Chariton, Xenophon Ephesius, and Achilles Tatius.* Acta Instituti Atheniensis Regni Sueciae, 8. Stockholm: Almqvist & Wiksells Boktryckeri.

———. 1983. *The Novel in Antiquity.* Berkeley: University of California Press.

Haight, Elizabeth Hazelton. 1945. *More Essays on Greek Romances.* New York: Longmans, Green.

———, trans. and ed. 1955. *Pseudo-Callisthenes: The Life of Alexander of Macedon.* New York: Longmans, Green.

Hansen, William. 1982. The Applied Message in Storytelling. In *Folklorica: Festschrift for Felix Oinas,* ed. Egle Victoria Žygas and Peter Voorheis. Indiana University Uralic and Altaic Series, 141, Bloomington. Pp. 99–109.

———. 1983. *Saxo Grammaticus and the Life of Hamlet: A Translation, History, and Commentary.* Lincoln: University of Nebraska Press.

———. 1988. Folklore. In *Civilization of the Ancient Mediterranean: Greece and Rome,* ed. Michael Grant and Rachel Kitzinger. New York: Scribner. 2:1121–1130.

———. 1996. *Phlegon of Tralles' Book of Marvels.* Exeter Studies in History. Exeter: University of Exeter Press.

———. 1997a. Homer and the Folktale. In *A New Companion to Homer,* ed. Ian Morris and Barry Powell. Leiden: E. J. Brill. Pp. 442–462.

———. 1997b. Idealization as a Process in Ancient Greek Story-Formation. *Symbolae Osloenses* 72:118–123.

Harris, William V. 1989. *Ancient Literacy.* Cambridge, Mass.: Harvard University Press.

Hazlitt, W. Carew. 1890. *Studies in Jocular Literature: A Popular Subject More Closely Considered.* London: E. Stock.

Heinevetter, Franz. 1912. *Würfel- und Buchstabenorakel in Griechenland und Kleinasien.* Dissertation, Breslau.

Holbek, Bengt. 1962. *Æsops Levned og Fabler.* 2 vols. Copenhagen: J. H. Schultz Forlag.

Holzberg, Niklas. 1992. Unter Mitarbeit von Andreas Beschorner und Stefan Merkle. *Der Äsop-Roman: Motivgeschichte und Erzählstruktur.* Classica Monacensia, 6. Tübingen: Gunter Narr.

———. 1993a. A Lesser Known "Picaresque" Novel of Greek Origin: The *Aesop Romance* and Its Influence. *Groningen Colloquia on the Novel* 5:1–16.

———. 1993b. *Die antike Fabel: Eine Einführung.* Darmstadt: Wissenschaftliche Buchgesellschaft.

———, ed. 1994. *Der griechische Briefroman: Gattungstypologie und Textanalyse.* Classica Monacensia, 8. Tübingen: Gunter Narr.

———. 1995. *The Ancient Novel: An Introduction.* Trans. Christine Jackson-Holzberg. London: Routledge.

———. 1996. Fable: Aesop. Life of Aesop. In Schmeling 1996:633–639.

Hoogendijk, Francisca A. J., and Willy Clarysse. 1981. De Sortes van Astrampsychus: Een orakelboek uit de Oudheid bewerkt voor het Middelbaar Onderwijs. *Kleio* 11:53–99.

Humphreys, S. C. 1993. *The Family, Women and Death: Comparative Studies.* 2nd ed. Ann Arbor: University of Michigan Press.

Hunt, Peter, ed. 1995. *Children's Literature: An Illustrated History.* Oxford: Oxford University Press.

Jedrkiewicz, Stefano. 1989. *Sapere e paradosso nell'Antichità: Esopo e la favola.* Rome: Edizioni dell'Ateneo.

Junod, Eric. 1981. Acts apocryphes et hérésie: Le Jugement de Photius. In Bovon et al. 1981: 11–24.

Kaibel, Georgius. 1878. *Epigrammata Graeca ex Lapidibus Conlecta*. Berlin: G. Reimer.

Kassel, Rudolf. 1956. Reste eines hellenistischen Spassmacherbuches auf einem Heidelberger Papyrus? *Rheinisches Museum für Philologie* 99:242–245.

Keller, John E., and L. Clark Keating. 1993. *Aesop's Fables, with a Life of Aesop.* Translated from the Spanish with an introduction. Lexington: University Press of Kentucky.

Kenyon, Frederic G. 1951. *Books and Readers in Ancient Greece and Rome.* 2nd ed. Oxford: Clarendon Press.

Knox, B. M. W., and P. E. Easterling. 1985. Books and Readers in the Greek World. In Easterling and Knox 1:1–41.

Koester, Helmut. 1995. *History, Culture, and Religion of the Hellenistic Age.* 2nd ed. New York: Walter de Gruyter.

Köhler, Ines, and Rudolf Schenda. 1975. Alexander der Grosse. In *Enzyklopädie des Märchens* 1:272–291.

Konstan, David. 1994. Xenophon of Ephesus: Eros and Narrative in the Novel. In Morgan and Stoneman 1994:49–63.

Krappe, Alexander. 1927. The Origin of the Secundus Biography. *Balor with the Evil Eye: Studies in Celtic and French Literature.* New York: Institute des Études Françaises, Columbia University. Pp. 181–190.

Kratz, Dennis M., trans. 1991. *The Romances of Alexander.* Garland Library of Medieval Literature, 64. New York: Garland.

Kytzler, Bernhard. 1996. Xenophon of Ephesus. In Schmeling 1996:336–360.

La Penna, Antonio. 1962. Il Romanzo di Esopo. *Athenaeum* N.S. 40:264–314.

Lattimore, Richmond. 1962 [1942]. *Themes in Greek and Latin Epitaphs.* Urbana: University of Illinois Press.

LiDonnici, Lynn R. 1995. *The Epidaurian Miracle Inscriptions: Text, Translation and Commentary.* Atlanta: Scholars Press.

Lindenberger, J. M. 1985. Ahiqar. In *The Old Testament Pseudepigrapha,* ed. James H. Charlesworth. New York: Doubleday. 2:479–507.

McCartney, Eugene S. 1931. Ancient Wit and Humor. In *Classical Studies in Honor of John C. Rolfe,* ed. George Depue Hadzsits. Philadelphia: University of Pennsylvania Press. Pp. 191–211.

MacDonald, Dennis Ronald. 1983. *The Legend and the Apostle: The Battle for Paul in Story and Canon.* Philadelphia: Westminster Press.

———. 1986. The Forgotten Novels of the Early Church. *Semeia* 38:1–6.

Malherbe, Abraham J. 1988. *Ancient Epistolary Theorists.* SBL Sources for Biblical Study, 19. Atlanta: Scholars Press.

Mason, Hugh J. 1994. Greek and Latin Versions of the Ass-Story. In *ANRW* 2 34.2:1665–1707.

Megas, Georgios A., ed. 1970. *Folktales of Greece.* Trans. Helen Colaclides. Chicago: University of Chicago Press.

Meister, Richard. 1951. *Die Orakelsprüche im St. Galler Palimpsestcodex 908 (die sogenannten 'Sortes Sangallenses'): Erläuterungen.* Österreichische Akademie der Wissenschaften, phil.-hist. Klasse, Sitzungsberichte, 225.5. Vienna: Rudolf M. Rohrer.

Merkelbach, Reinhold. 1954. *Die Quellen des griechischen Alexanderromans.* Zetemata 9. Munich: C. H. Beck.

Miles, Margaret R. 1989. *Carnal Knowing: Female Nakedness and Religious Meaning in the Christian West.* Boston: Beacon Press.

Modleski, Tania. 1982. *Loving with a Vengeance: Mass-Produced Fantasies for Women.* Hamden, Conn.: Archon.

Montague, Holly W. 1994. From *Interlude in Arcady* to *Daphnis and Chloe: Two Thousand Years of Erotic Fantasy.* In Tatum 1994:391–401.

Morgan, J. R., and Richard Stoneman, eds. 1994. *Greek Fiction: The Greek Novel in Context.* London: Routledge.

Müller, Carl Werner. 1985. Die Archilochoslegende. *Rheinisches Museum für Philologie* 128:99–151.

———. 1992. Die Legende von der Erwählung des Dichters Archilochos. *Fabula* 33:102–107.

Neuburg, Victor E. 1977. *Popular Literature: A History and Guide: from the Beginning of Printing to the Year 1897.* Harmondsworth: Penguin.

Nisard, Charles. 1864. *Histoire des livres populaires ou de la littérature du colportage depuis l'origine de l'imprimerie jusqu'a l'établissement de la commission d'examen des livres du colportage—30 novembre 1852.* 2nd ed. 2 vols. Paris: E. Dentu.

Nøjgaard, Morten. 1964–1967. *La Fable antique.* 2 vols. Copenhagen: Nyt Nordisk Forlag, Arnold Busck.

Nye, Russel. 1971. *The Unembarrassed Muse: The Popular Arts in America.* New York: Dial Press.

Nyerup, Rasmus. 1816. *Almindelig Morskabslæsning i Danmark og Norge igjennem Aarhundreder.* Copenhagen: Brødrene Thiele.

Olrik, Axel. 1992. *Principles for Oral Narrative Research.* Trans. Kirsten Wolf and Jody Jensen. Bloomington: Indiana University Press.

Oppenheim, A. Leo. 1956. *The Interpretation of Dreams in the Ancient Near East, with a Translation of an Assyrian Dream-Book.* Transactions of the American Philosophical Society 46, part 3. Philadelphia: American Philosophical Society.

Ormerod, H. A. 1912. A New Astragalos-Inscription from Pamphylia. *Journal of Hellenic Studies* 32:270–276.

O'Sullivan, James M. 1995. *Xenophon of Ephesus: His Compositional Technique and the Birth of the Novel.* Berlin: de Gruyter.

Papathomopoulos, Manoles, ed. 1990. Ὁ βίος τοῦ Αἰσώπου: ἡ παραλλαγὴ G. Κριτικὴ ἔκδοση μὲ Εἰσαγωγὴ καὶ Μετάφραση. Ἰωάννινα: Γ. Τσολής.

Parca, Maryline. 1995. *The Franchetti Collection in Rome: Inscriptions and Sculptural Fragments.* Opuscula Epigraphica 6. Rome: Edizioni Quasar.

Paré, Ambroise. 1982. *On Monsters and Marvels.* Trans. Janis L. Pallister. Chicago: University of Chicago Press.

Parker, Holt. 1992. Love's Body Anatomized: The Ancient Erotic Handbooks and the Rhetoric of Sexuality. In *Pornography and Representation in Greece and Rome,* ed. Amy Richlin. New York: Oxford University Press. Pp. 90–111.

Paulli, R. 1936. Bidrag til de danske folkebøgers historie. In *Danske Folkebøger fra 16. og 17. Aarhundrede,* ed. J. P. Jacobsen, Jørgen Olrik, R. Paulli. Copenhagen: Gyldendalske Boghandel-Nordiske Forlag. 13:171–291.

Peek, Werner, ed. 1955. *Griechische Vers-Inschriften.* I: Grab-Epigramme. Berlin: Akademie-Verlag.

Perry, Ben Edwin. 1920. *The* Metamorphoses *Ascribed to Lucius of Patrae: Its Content, Nature, and Authorship.* Dissertation, Princeton University, 1919. Lancaster: New Era.

———. 1981 [1936]. *Studies in the Text History of the Life and Fables of Aesop.* Reprint. Chico, Calif.: Scholars Press.

————. 1940. The Origin of the Epimythium. *Transactions of the American Philological Association* 71:391–419.

————. 1952. *Aesopica: A Series of Texts Relating to Aesop or Ascribed to Him or Closely Connected with the Literary Tradition that Bears his Name.* Urbana: University of Illinois Press.

————. 1959. The Origin of the Book of Sindbad. *Fabula* 3:1–94.

————. 1964. *Secundus the Silent Philosopher: The Greek Life of Secundus, Critically Edited and Restored So Far as Possible Together with Translations of the Greek and Oriental Versions, the Latin and Oriental Texts, and a Study of the Tradition.* Philological Monographs Published by the American Philological Association, 22.

————. 1965. *Babrius and Phaedrus.* Cambridge, Mass.: Harvard University Press.

————. 1967. *The Ancient Romances: A Literary-Historical Account of Their Origins.* Sather Classical Lectures, 37. Berkeley: University of California Press.

Pervo, Richard I. 1987. *Profit with Delight: The Literary Genre of the Acts of the Apostles.* Philadelphia: Fortress Press.

————. 1994. Early Christian Fiction. In Morgan and Stoneman 1994:239–254.

————. 1996. The Ancient Novel Becomes Christian. In Schmeling 1996:685–711.

Petropoulos, J. C. B. 1995. Transvestite Virgin with a Cause: The Acta Pauli et Theclae and Late Antique Proto-"Feminism." In *Greece & Gender*, ed. Brit Berggreen and Nanno Marinatos. Papers from the Norwegian Institute at Athens. Bergen. 2:125–139.

Preisendanz, Karl, ed. and trans. 1973. *Papyri Graecae Magicae: Die griechischen Zauberpapyri.* 2nd ed. 2 vols. Stuttgart: B. B. Teubner.

Preston, Cathy Lynn, and Michael J. Preston, eds. 1995. *The Other Print Tradition: Essays on Chapbooks, Broadsides, and Related Ephemera.* New York: Garland.

Propp, V. 1968. *Morphology of the Folktale.* Trans. Laurence Scott. 2nd ed. Austin: University of Texas Press.

Quoquim, Maestro. 1986. *Mofarandel de los oráculos de Apolo.* Ed. Margarita Peña. Puebla: Universidad Autónoma de Puebla.

Radway, Janice. 1987. *Reading the Romance: Women, Patriarchy, and Popular Literature.* London: Verso.

Rapp, Albert. 1950–1951. A Greek "Joe Miller." *Classical Journal* 46:286–290, 318.

Raubitschek, Anton E. (and discussants). 1968. Das Denkmal-Epigramm. In *L'Épigramme grecque: Sept exposés suivis de discussions.* Entretiens sur l'Antiquité Classique, 14. Geneva: Fondation Hardt. Pp. 1–36.

Reardon, B. P., ed. 1989. *Collected Ancient Greek Novels.* Berkeley: University of California Press.

Rees, Nigel. 1993. *Epitaphs: A Dictionary of Grave Epigrams and Memorial Eloquence.* New York: Carroll & Graf.

(Ripley, Robert.) 1946. *Ripley's Believe It or Not!* Garden City, N.Y.: Garden City.

Robinson, Jennifer Meta. 1993. If Love Could Have Saved You: Newspaper Obituary Poems. *Midwestern Folklore* 19:99–112.

Rordorf, Willy. 1986. Tradition and Composition in the *Acts of Thecla:* The State of the Question. *Semeia* 38:43–52.

Rosenmeyer, Patricia. 1994. The Epistolary Novel. In Morgan and Stoneman 1994:146–165.

Ruiz-Montero, C. 1994. Xenophon von Ephesus: Ein Überblick. *ANRW* 2 34.2:1087–1138.

Schenda, Rudolf. 1970. *Volk ohne Buch: Studien zur Sozialgeschichte der populären Lesestoffe 1770–1910.* Frankfurt am Main: Vittorio Klostermann.

Schmeling, Gareth L. 1980. *Xenophon of Ephesus.* Twayne World Authors Series, 613. Boston: Twayne.

———, ed. 1996. *The Novel in the Ancient World.* Leiden: E. J. Brill.

Schneemelcher, Wilhelm, ed. English translation ed. R. McL. Wilson. 1992. *New Testament Apocrypha.* Rev. ed. of collection initiated by Edgar Hennecke. 2 vols. Cambridge: James Clarke; Louisville: Westminster/John Knox Press.

Schubart, Wilhelm. 1921. *Das Buch bei den Griechen und Römern.* Berlin: de Gruyter.

Scobie, Alexander. 1983. *Apuleius and Folklore: Toward a History of ML3045, AaTh567, 449A.* London: Folklore Society.

Shushan, E. R. 1990. *Grave Matters.* New York: Ballantine.

Skeat, T. C. 1954. An Early Mediaeval "Book of Fate": The Sortes XII Patriarcharum, with a Note on "Books of Fate" in General. *Mediaeval and Renaissance Studies* 3:41–54.

Steinberg, S. H. 1961. *Five Hundred Years of Printing.* 2nd ed. Harmondsworth: Penguin.

Stephens, Susan A. 1988. Book Production. In *Civilization of the Ancient Mediterranean: Greece and Rome,* ed. Michael Grant and Rachel Kitzinger. New York: Scribner. 1:421–436.

———. 1994. Who Read Ancient Novels? In Tatum 1994:405–418.

———, and John J. Winkler, eds. 1995. *Ancient Greek Novels: The Fragments.* Princeton: Princeton University Press.

Stewart, Randall. 1985. The Oracular εἰ. *Greek, Roman, and Byzantine Studies* 26:67–73.

———. 1995. The Textual Transmission of the *Sortes Astrampsychi. Illinois Classical Studies* 20:135–147.

———, ed. In press. *Sortes Astrampsychi.* Vol. II: Ecdosis altera. Leipzig: B. G. Teubner.

Stirewalt, M. Luther, Jr. 1993. *Studies in Ancient Greek Epistolography.* Atlanta: Scholars Press.

Stoneman, Richard. 1991. *The Greek Alexander Romance.* Harmondsworth: Penguin.

———. 1994a. The *Alexander Romance:* From History to Fiction. In Morgan and Stoneman 1994:117–129.

———. 1994b. Romantic Ethnography: Central Asia and India in the Alexander Romance. *Ancient World* 25:93–107.

———. 1995. Naked Philosophers: The Brahmans in the Alexander Historians and the Alexander Romance. *Journal of Hellenic Studies* 115:99–114.

———. 1996. The Metamorphoses of the *Alexander Romance.* In Schmeling 1996:601–612.

Storey, John. 1993. *An Introductory Guide to Cultural Theory and Popular Culture.* Athens: University of Georgia Press.

Strubbe, J. H. M. 1991. Cursed Be He That Moves My Bones. In *Magika Hiera: Ancient Greek Magic and Religion,* ed. Christopher A. Faraone and Dirk Obbink. Oxford: Oxford University Press. Pp. 33–59.

———. 1994. Curses against Violations of the Grave in Jewish Epitaphs from Asia Minor. In *Studies in Early Jewish Epigraphy,* ed. Jan Willem van Henten and Pieter Willem van der Horst. Leiden: E. J. Brill. Pp. 70–128.

Sydow, C. W. v. 1948. *Selected Papers on Folklore: Anniversary Volume*. Copenhagen: Rosenkilde and Bagger.

Tannery, Paul. 1896. Astrampsychos. *Revue des études grecques* 11:96–106.

Tatum, James, ed. 1994. *The Search for the Ancient Novel*. Baltimore: Johns Hopkins University Press.

Thiel, Helmut van. 1971–1972. *Der Eselroman*. 2 vols. Zetemata, 54.1–2. Munich: C. H. Beck.

———, ed. 1974. *Leben und Taten Alexanders von Makedonien nach der Handschrift L*. Darmstadt: Wissenschaftliche Buchgesellschaft.

Thierfelder, Andreas, ed. 1968. *Philogelos: Der Lachfreund von Hierokles und Philagrios*. Griechisch-deutsch mit Einleitung und Kommentar. Munich: Heimeran.

Thompson, Stith. 1953. The Star Husband Tale. *Studia Septentrionalia* 4:93–163. Reprinted in *The Study of Folklore*, ed. Alan Dundes. Englewood Cliffs, N.J.: Prentice-Hall, 1965. Pp. 414–459.

Tissot, Yves. 1981. Encratisme et Actes Apocryphes. In Bovon 1981:109–119.

Waegeman, Maryse. 1987. *Amulet and Alphabet: Magical Amulets in the First Book of Cyranides*. Amsterdam: J. C. Gieben.

Weinreich, Otto. 1911. *Der Trug des Nektanebos: Wandlungen eines Novellenstoffs*. Leipzig: B. G. Teubner.

Weniger, Ludwig. 1917. Losorakel bei Griechen und Römern. *Sokrates* NF 5:305–318.

West, M. L., ed. and comm. 1978. *Hesiod: Works and Days*. Oxford: Clarendon Press.

——— (and discussants). 1984. The Ascription of Fables to Aesop in Archaic and Classical Greece. In Adrados and Reverdin 1984:105–136.

Wilde, Larry. 1983. *The Last Official Irish Joke Book*. New York: Bantam.

Wilson, F. P. 1939. The English Jestbooks of the Sixteenth and Early Seventeenth Centuries. *Huntington Library Quarterly* 2:121–158.

Winkler, John J. 1985. *Auctor & Actor: A Narratological Reading of Apuleius's The Golden Ass*. Berkeley: University of California Press.

Winnefeld, Hermannus, ed. 1887. *Sortes Sangallenses*. Bonnae: Typis Caroli Georgi Vniv. Typogr.

Wolohojian, Albert Mugrdich, trans. 1969. *The Romance of Alexander the Great by Pseudo-Callisthenes*. Translated from the Armenian Version. New York: Columbia University Press.

Woodhead, A. G. 1967. *The Study of Greek Inscriptions*. Cambridge: Cambridge University Press.

Wroth, Lawrence C., ed. 1938. *A History of the Printed Book*. New York: Limited Editions Club.

Zeitz, Heinrich. 1936. Der Aesoproman und seine Geschichte: Eine Untersuchung im Anschluß an die neugefundenen Papyri. *Aegyptus* 16:225–256.

Ziegler, Konrat. 1949. Paradoxographoi. In *Paulys Realencyclopaedie der classischen Altertumswissenschaft* 36:1137–1166.

William Hansen is Professor of Classical Studies and of Folklore at Indiana University. He has published widely on early Greek epic, Greek mythology, and folklore. His books include *Saxo Grammaticus and the Life of Hamlet* (a study of the Hamlet legend) and *Phlegon of Tralles' Book of Marvels* (a study of popular literature).